RUNNING THROUGH MY MIND

RUNNING THROUGH MY MIND

Confessions of an Every Day Runner

Scott Ludwig

iUniverse, Inc.

New York Lincoln Shanghai

Running through My Mind

Confessions of an Every Day Runner

iUniverse books may be ordered through booksellers or by contacting:

iUniverse
2021 Pine Lake Road, Suite 100
Lincoln, NE 68512
www.iuniverse.com
1-800-Authors (1-800-288-4677)

Because of the dynamic nature of the Internet, any Web addresses or links contained in this book may have changed since publication and may no longer be valid.

The views expressed in this work are solely those of the author and do not necessarily reflect the views of the publisher, and the publisher hereby disclaims any responsibility for them.

ISBN: 978-0-595-46523-1 (pbk)
ISBN: 978-0-595-70322-7 (cloth)
ISBN: 978-0-595-90822-6 (ebk)

Printed in the United States of America

To everyone who has what it takes to cross the finish line.

CONTENTS

Prologue

I moved to Atlanta, Georgia in the summer of 1979 with barely a year of calling myself a 'runner' under my belt. Most weekends would find me at a local race–usually a 5K or a 10K–and I would be mesmerized by the many runners who would speak of their past trials and tribulations participating in the greatest sport in the world.

Granted, the faster runners impressed me, but my true fascination was with the older and dare I say wiser runners I would refer to as the 'grizzled veterans.' They spoke of races that were of distances greater than a marathon–distances that one day would become very well known to me.

My life as a runner, 28 years and counting, has led me on a path I'm quite sure those 'grizzled veterans' followed in their respective lives as runners. At first there was the simple wonder of running, and the many physical and psychological benefits it offered. Then there was the transition into racing shorter distances, and the years of achieving 'personal bests' on a relatively fresh set of legs. Eventually, the racing evolved into the longer distance and magic of the marathon. Ultimately, once the accumulated mileage and pounding began to take its toll on a (no longer fresh) set of legs, a transition into the even longer distances and mystique of the ultramarathon.

Naturally, along the way my running allowed me to meet some incredible athletes, many of whom you will be introduced to in the following pages. To me they are all superheroes, and once you read about them I trust you will feel the same way.

For years, I've looked for a book about running that would offer me the motivation and inspiration for those rare occasions when I needed a boost to get me out the front door … a book that would inspire me to take that extra step or go that extra mile … a book that would encourage me to attempt to accomplish things I never thought possible … a book that would remind me of why I love running, and what amazing things can be accomplished with a little dedication, determination and perseverance … a book that would show me how I *can*, not why I *can't*.

I imagine you've been looking for that book as well. Unfortunately, I was never able to find it.

However, I'm hoping ***this* is the book _you_ were looking for.**

Now, as 2007 is drawing to a close, I have been running each and every single day for almost twenty-nine years. I still enjoy the physical and psychological benefits of the sport, but no longer find myself achieving 'personal bests' as 110,000 miles and 52 years of life on this earth have caught up with me. I find that I am now one of those runners who inspired me so many years ago: a grizzled veteran.

I hope you find this book both motivating and inspiring, and are able to gain a little knowledge and enjoy a little humor along the way.

By the way, many of the grizzled veterans I met in the summer of 1979 are still out there doing what they've always done: running like there's no tomorrow.

Author advisory: Long-distance running is a strenuous physical activity. Consult a physician before attempting anything you are about to read in this book. In fact, it might be advisable to consult a psychologist before you begin reading this book.

Just to be safe.

Foreword

It has never really dawned on me how loony my dad and his friends (Team Dark-side*) really are. My dad's book *Running through my Mind* is an interesting book that is composed of stories and tips on running as well as stories written by people that I have grown up around for most of my life. The book is much more com-pelling than the 'ordinary' running book, as it offers the reader inspiration, enter-tainment, and knowledge, while still throwing in a keen sense of humor.

There has never been a moment when I have stopped to think about all of the amazing accomplishments and adventures of Team Darkside. The funny thing is all of these events that the average person might consider impossible or insane are completely normal for the Darkside Running Club. As I began reading the book an acquaintance of mine was questioning me about what I was looking at and why one would ever want to read a book about running. 'What a stupid idea,' he said. Agreeing with him that your typical book on running is boring, I discussed the topics of the book with him and told him that if he wanted to read it, he would most likely find it interesting and learn about events that he would never even think exists (because of the complications and complexities of some of them). Two parts that I pointed out for him to read were my dad's attempts (one failure and one success) at running across the state of Georgia, as well as the sec-tion about the 2003 Badwater Ultramarathon. After reading about my dad suc-cessfully running across Georgia in 1992–and for some crazy reason his decision to hobble for his three mile runs for the next couple days while wearing a leg brace–my friend's face was in a state of utter shock as he asked 'Dude ... what's wrong with that man?' I glanced at him with a gigantic smile and said 'That's my dad for you!' Needless to say, after learning about Badwater, my buddy just shook his head in disbelief, and I figured I would keep him in the dark about my dad's now 28-year streak of running every day.

As I stated earlier, I have never taken a minute to thing about why Team Darkside chooses to work so profusely in everything and where in the world they find the motivation to do the things they do. After growing up around (and being supported by) Scott Ludwig, I have learned not to whine about the little things because I have witnessed him put himself through some of the most tortuous things possible. I have watched him over the years, and not once has he thought about quitting anything. He probably has the most hideous feet I have ever seen, having year-round black toenails (on the few still attached to his toes). There have been times when he was unable to walk up or down the stairs of our house on Saturday night after a particularly hard race. But of course, he still manages to wake up at 4:00 a.m. on Sunday morning for a 20-mile stroll with Al, Paula, Susan, Eric and the rest of the gang. Sometimes, I just want to slap him around and talk some sense into the man until I remember that it is a lost cause. I believe that my mom shares some of those same feelings that I do when it comes to my dad's obsession.

For all of you sports fanatics out there, I am certain that you have sat down and watched a game on television and listened to the announcers break down the statistics to the infinite degree. I know that my dad and I have, and we always ask questions like why and how? Well, dad, it seems your brain is capable of answering those same questions when it comes to the sport of running. Throughout the book, my dad presents quite a variety of statistics for all 28 years of his involvement in the sport. The data ranges from the amount of miles he has run per year all the way to breaking down PR's (personal records, or personal 'bests') in races and the percentage of time necessary to take off his PR's to being in contention with the world record holders. It seems to me that you have a little too much time on your hands!! Or maybe your obsession has reached a certain level to where you are incapable of restraining it.

I know that many of you are aware of Team Darkside's completion of the Badwater Ultramarathon in Death Valley, California. Although there is no chance that I would ever let my dad put himself through it again (as if I could stop him), it was quite an amazing experience for me. Before our adventure in Death Valley, I seriously doubted the fact that it was possible for the temperature to be as blistering hot as it was as it approached the 130-degree mark. As Dean Karnazes said about

Badwater, "it's as close to Hell as I ever want to be." It is difficult to believe that a human being is actually able to complete an event that provides so much pain and agony from start to finish. I personally ran about 10 miles throughout the race with my dad, and I thought I was going to die from heat stroke. Taking into consideration all of these facts, I supposed that this is the most perfect competition my dad could ever choose to take part in.

Overall, throughout the years of my life, my dad has supported me with much knowledge about dedication and passion without ever realizing it. In my teenage years I had a strong love for all sports, but unfortunately that interest started to fade in my sophomore year of high school. I would give anything to be able to go back to my past and talk myself into continuing with sports because I had so much potential.

My dad recently reminded me that I still owe it to him to one day run the Boston Marathon. Although it may be a long shot, all of you are witnesses that I am vouching this will occur one day. I really just hope that some day soon I can discover a hobby, or perhaps a career that I love and have as much dedication for as the things that my dad pursues.

Josh Ludwig

Team Darkside is a reference to the Darkside Running Club, started by Al Barker and my dad. Whenever a member competes in races anywhere in the country, the 'Darkside Distance Team' banner is proudly waving somewhere along the course.

CHAPTER ONE
RUNNING OUT THE DOOR
(How it all began)

When I first began running, I was so fascinated and enamored with the sport I decided almost immediately that I wanted to write a book about my adventures. In fact, in time I'm not so sure that some of the races I found myself running or things I found myself doing weren't simply so I could have something extraordinary to write about. Whatever the case, I began writing some of the material that would eventually find its way inside the covers of this book in the early 1980's when I was heavily influenced by the writing style of legendary Southern humorist Lewis Grizzard. Grizzard was very passionate about his writing, and he managed to inject a touch of humor in virtually everything he wrote. He also had a knack for compassion and understanding, and was able to ignite a spark in his readers regardless of the subject he was writing about. I read his column in the *Atlanta Journal-Constitution* religiously, bought and read every one of his books, and my mom even managed to get his autograph for me in one of them as a birthday present—one that I'll cherish forever.

Although his writing style was short and sweet, he had an uncanny ability to stir every possible human emotion through his words. I would like to think that his inspiration can be found in the pages you are about to read. I have trusted my sense of humor, my passion for the sport of running, and the inspiration of Lewis

Grizzard to get me to the last page of this book, my literary finish line. Most of the articles you'll find to be short and sweet, and I trust a wide array of your emotions will be stirred along the way.

Grizzard passed away before he reached the age of 50, but he left a legacy that will not be forgotten. At least not in my book.

In this chapter:

- In the Beginning …—My early days in organized team sports indicated I needed to find my niche doing something I could do alone.

- Dancing Through My First Marathon–My first experience at an endurance event served as a prelude of things to come.

- Who's Responsible?–Reflecting back on how I was indoctrinated into the sport of running (but don't expect any earth shattering revelations; after all, his happened almost three decades ago).

In the Beginning …

I was born in Norfolk, Virginia on December 10, 1954. For almost the first half of my life (at this point), I fluctuated from one sport to another, looking for my niche.

My dad was a career Navy man, so my family moved every three years when I was growing up. My parents were avid bowlers, and they had me bowling as far back as I can recall. As a 12-year old, I would consistently hold one of the highest averages (around 150) in the youth bowling leagues. Once I reached my teen years, my average hovered in the 170's. Ultimately, I gave up the sport entirely after my sophomore year in college, at 'the pinnacle of my bowling career' (more on this later).

My first attempt at organized sports was playing Little League baseball in Quonset Point, Rhode Island. As a 9-year-old, playing a sport I wasn't particularly good at in front of people (even if they *were* mostly parents) was frightening. My coach would usually put me in the safest place possible—right field—and pray nothing would be hit my way. Fortunately for him, most of the time he got what he prayed for. Unfortunately, he had to let me *bat* several times a game. My first time in the batter's box, I struck out on three straight pitches. If I remember correctly, I think only *one* of them didn't bounce in front of home plate before I swung at it, and it was so far outside the strike zone I had to take two steps *forward* to get *close* to the ball. At season's end I was selected for the all-star team—*only* because I was the only player on our team old enough to be eligible. They put me at third base (for the first time in my life), and unfortunately this time the coach wasn't so lucky. PLENTY of balls were hit my way, most of them eventually finding their way out to the left fielder.

After mastering baseball, I moved on to football. As a chunky, overweight 13-year-old pushing the Pearl Harbor (Hawaii) Youth Football League weight limit of 135 pounds, I found myself in the sauna the day before our games so I'd make 'game weight' and be eligible to play. That happened only once. No, not making game weight—actually playing in a game! My team, the Commodores, was in the process of destroying a team by an eventual final score of 56-0. Once it was obvious we were going to have no problem winning the game, the coach put me in to play middle linebacker. I'm pretty sure the score at the time was, oh, 56-0. While I didn't make any solo tackles or intercept any passes, I did manage to jump on the pile a couple of times after a tackle was made without being penalized for a late hit. That day I played the first, last, and only game of organized football in my life.

Now that I had two sports under my belt (*three* if you count bowling), I finally found one I enjoyed—basketball! Without boasting, I had the best jump shot in my high school. *I* knew it, my *best friend* knew it, and *all the guys who played at the high school gym on Tuesday and Thursday nights* knew it (many of them being on the high school team). The only one who didn't seem to know it was the high school basketball team *coach!* During team tryouts, each player had to take 20 free throws at the end of practice. I guess the coach failed to notice that over the five days of practice, one of the players only missed *one* of his free throws ALL WEEK LONG! I couldn't believe it when the team was announced, and I wasn't on it. However, my best friend, who was about 5 inches taller than me and knew I had the best jump shot in high school (I know he knew it because he saw enough of them sail over his head when I would beat him like a drum playing one-on-one!), *made* the team. O.K., what's next?

How about *golf?* I had been playing golf since I was 12 years old. In fact, I won the Oahu (Hawaii) Junior Golf Association 'B' Division Championship in 1967 by shooting an 18-hole score of 87! I tried out for the Fletcher High School

(Neptune Beach, Florida) golf team as a freshman, and by my sophomore year I was playing the #1 position and eventually earned All-City (Jacksonville) honors with my 37 average (for 9 holes). During my senior year, however, my golf coach (in all honesty, the 'golf coach' was whichever assistant football coach wanted to play some free golf in the springtime) and I disagreed over a very vital issue—the length of my hair! I had just started dating Cindy (my future wife) in January of my senior year, and there was no way I was cutting my hair in *March*, because I just knew if I did Cindy would dump me. I quit the team, as did the #2 and #4 players on the team to show their support. Unfortunately, this did not matter one iota to the coach, who went on to lead our team to one of the worst golf seasons in the history of our school.

When I enrolled as a freshman at the University of Florida, I tried out for the golf team as a 'walk on.' After playing 7 rounds of golf in an impressive (well, at the very least *I* was impressed!) 10 over par, I was shown the same door my high school basketball coach had shown me several years ago. Apparently, he wasn't as impressed with my scores as I was.

As a sophomore, I tried out for the University of Florida bowling team, mainly because it meant I would be able to bowl 30 games for free. Would you believe I actually *made* the team!? I averaged 188, and bowled my (still) all-time high 3-game series of 670 in the process. Making the university bowling team meant that I got to bowl as many games as I wanted throughout the year absolutely free. It also meant I could bowl in matches against other college teams; however, if we did in fact bowl against other college teams, no one ever told me. Not once I was notified of any matches. And yes, I *know* I was on the team because every time I showed up to bowl I said I was on the team and the person behind the desk would say 'Oh, yeah, here it is—Ludwig. No charge.' It would have been nice to have bowled in a match at least once.

As you'll discover in this book, I found my true love in sports when I was in graduate school at the University of Florida. Thinking back to when I was in 10th grade, I should have realized *then* I had potential as a runner. Part of our 'final exam' in P.E. was the 600-yard run. I finished in 3rd place out of my entire 10th grade class, being beaten only by two runners on the cross-country team. Both of them vomited after they finished running the 600 yards. Not me—I was officially 'the fastest 600-yard runner in 10th grade who didn't throw up afterwards.' I built on that title to become the runner that I am today.

One of the things I like most about running is that success or failure is determined by *you and you alone.* Don't get me wrong: team sports such as football and basketball are terrific, but the success or failure of the team is based on *everyone's* efforts. In running, you have no one to blame (in failure) or thank (in victory) other than yourself. THAT'S what makes running so unique and special, and THAT is why I still enjoy the sport as much today as I did when I started running 28 years ago.

Besides, I never did recover from the trauma of playing third base …

<u>Dancing Through My First Marathon</u>

During my sophomore year at the University of Florida, I pledged a fraternity. Why? Let's just say that most of the fraternity brothers worked at the on-campus bar, the Rathskellar. On my limited budget, it was convenient to be able to drink beer for free—er—at a slightly reduced cost.

This happened also to be (my future wife) Cindy's first year as a Gator, as she had attended the University of North Florida her freshman year. Cindy lived on campus in a dormitory with her roommate Wanda.

In the spring of 1975, the Rathskellar was hosting a 28-hour dance marathon for charity. The rules were simple:

- Couples only.
- Couples had to dance ('move your feet') the entire 28 hours.
- Couples got a 10 minute break each hour.

Even though I was not yet a runner, I knew I had a lot of endurance. I did enough "all nighters" my sophomore year (as I needed to make up for my poor academic showing during my freshman year) to know dancing for 28 hours would be a piece of cake. Cindy, however, thought otherwise. She knew I could do it, and she also knew that if she were my partner and we failed to go the distance, I would be really upset with her.

She was 100 percent correct. That's why she volunteered Wanda, her roommate.

Unfortunately, Wanda's boyfriend Wayne was opposed to the idea. Fortunately, Wanda was incredibly strong willed (and even more feisty), and she agreed to be my partner.

The dance marathon was to begin at 8:00 p.m. Friday night. Wanda, Cindy, Wayne and I showed up at the 'Rat' for our 'pre-marathon dinner' at 7:00. You must understand that as a shy 20-year old, I needed a little 'motivation' to get out on the dance floor. I used my last hour wisely (or so I thought) by drinking the better part of two pitchers of beer. By 8:00 I was more than ready to dance. By 8:15 I had to pee so bad I thought I would pass out—and my first (bathroom) break wouldn't be until 8:50. I spent 35 minutes keeping both feet moving while holding my thighs tightly pressed together. Try it sometime–it's not easy.

The disc jockey started off by playing lots of Motown and disco songs. Thirty minutes into the evening, one of my fraternity brothers (who had an uncanny resemblance to 'D-Day' from <u>Animal House</u>) took control of the turntable and put on 'Black Dog' by Led Zeppelin. At first all the couples on the dance floor cheered—until we collectively realized it was *not* a song to dance to. Eventually sanity was restored, and the remaining 27 hours were filled with music you could dance to. (Note: I believe this was the beginning of my fondness for disco music. No, I'm not kidding–I *love* Donna Summer and the Village People).

At our first break at 8:50 I headed straight for the men's room. I was there so long that I barely made it back to the dance floor by 9:00 to resume dancing. Within the next hour, my beer buzz had worn off. Around 10:30 pm that evening I danced for the first time without any effects from 'liquid encouragement.' After a few hours, I began to feel comfortable with what I was doing.

Wanda and I had a few rough spots during the marathon. When Cindy went back to the dorm to go to sleep … when Wayne (finally) gave in and went back to his car for a short nap … when the sun came up Saturday morning (my usual bedtime following an all-nighter) … when Wayne did his best to persuade Wanda to quit (fortunately, Wanda–like Cindy–knew I would be really be upset if she didn't go the distance). But we persevered and we made it.

Much to our chagrin, four other couples 'made it' as well. But to be totally honest, Wanda and I were the only ones still abiding by the rules. The other couples were basically leaning on one another when midnight rolled around signifying the end of the contest.

All five couples were declared winners, but we all know which couple really made it to the finish line. In time, I would discover that standing on my feet for 28 straight hours would become something near and dear to me with one minor difference: I would be doing just a little bit more than simply standing in one place.

Who's Responsible?

It's odd, because I'm not really sure. I simply can't remember.

Once I ballooned to 194 pounds during graduate school, it should have been me. But it wasn't.

On one hand, Cindy started her own running program. She encouraged me to read Kenneth Cooper's book that introduced aerobic points and to join her in her afternoon jog around our married housing complex.

On the other hand, my graduate school faculty advisor, Thomas Jefferson Saine III, repeatedly asked me to join him in one of the two aerobic sports he participated in, running or racquetball.

I remember during the summer of 1978 I began running the 4/10 mile loop around my married housing complex five times in the afternoon (two miles!), never straying too far from my front door 'in case of emergency and/or fallout.'

I remember during the summer of 1978 I ran three miles in Piedmont Park in Atlanta with Tom (although I would alternate running and sitting out the one mile loops he was running).

I remember during the summer of 1978 I had a 38 inch waist.

I remember by the end of 1978 I weighed 150 pounds and had a 33 inch waist.

I remember in the spring of 1979 I ran my first marathon, with Tom joining me for the eight final (*and triumphant!*) miles. I remember Cindy being there to wish me well as I began my adventure and there to greet me three hours and forty-four minutes later as I crossed the finish line.

28 years later, I remember the 105,495 miles and 676 races I've run, the multitudes of people I've met in my travels, and most every pair of running shoes I've ever owned. But just who is responsible for getting me running? I simply can't remember.

CHAPTER TWO
RUNNING EVERY DAY

One thing that has stuck with me through my entire running career is 'the streak.' A streak is defined by running a distance of one continuous mile or more every day under your own power. For the sake of my streak, I've always considered three miles as a daily minimum.

In this chapter:

- The Streak (circa 1991)–This article was my official introduction to the members of the Peachtree City (Georgia) Running Club. Is it any wonder my membership only lasted five years?

- The Streak (update 12/31/06)–Not much has changed in the past 15 years. Well, actually my mileage is a tad bit higher.

- Dumb Things to Keep the Streak Alive–I've done some strange and unusual (OK, 'dumb') things to keep it going over the years.

- End the Streak? NEVER!–Although the thought to end the streak has crossed my mind a few times, don't expect it to happen anytime soon.

- Meet the U.S.R.S.A. (United States Running Geek ... er, Streak Association)-Folks, some of these runners are downright amazing.

- Mileage over the Years–A chart showing–by year–total mileage, average miles per day and total number of races

The STREAK

November 29, 1978 ... the day before 'the streak' began. I was a 23-year old graduate student (and newlywed) attending the University of Florida. Today as I write this on April 6 1991–4,511 days (and two sons) later, the streak lives on. Every day for the last 12 years I have laced up running shoes to battle the elements (pretty much every conceivable element) to keep the streak alive.

A running streak is defined as running a minimum of one mile a day–EVERY day. Once a daily run is skipped, the streak is over. The real question behind running a streak is 'why?' I'm not sure I'm capable of answering that one.

However, my streak has had its share of highs and lows:

- I have run 35,630 miles, an average of 7.9 miles per day, with a daily low of 3 miles and a daily high of 84 miles (part of a 24-hour endurance run).

- I've run in all types of weather, including temperatures ranging from 111 degrees to minus 59 degrees (once the wind chill was factored in). The latter remains the only run I have had to return home before my run was over to change clothes; I didn't have enough insulation for my ... well, let's just say it's a good thing I already had two sons.

- I've run in 12 states, one foreign country (the former Yugoslavia), and 'on' two oceans (on the jogging deck of two cruise ships, 16 laps to the mile).

- I've been chased by dogs too numerous to count, but have only been caught/bitten once (*that* I remember!).

- I've run in 289 road races, amassing enough T-shirts to make the Salvation Army my friend for life.

- I've lost 46 pounds since the day the streak began, and I know that should the streak end, the pounds will return instantly. This I am sure of.

- 'Guestimating' that to run an average mile for me over the course of the streak took 7-½ minutes, I have run the equivalent of 186 straight days, 24 hours a day, to amass my mileage.

I've tried to avoid answering the questions 'why' on several occasions by (intentionally) bringing my streak to an end–three times I made it my New Year's resolution to take a day off, five times I wanted to reward myself after a marathon with a day off, 11 times I wanted to take the day off before a marathon to rest, and once I thought I *really* could use a break (after my 84 mile day). However, none of these (feeble) attempts were successful.

Deep down inside, I believe I am focused on England's Ron Hill who, as far as I know, has the longest active streak at 23+ years. Sure, his streak is 11 years longer than mine. But then again, he *is* 11 years older than me, and should we *both* live to be the same age–who knows?

The STREAK
(updated 12/31/06)

Earlier you read an entry entitled 'The Streak' which was written almost fifteen years ago. What follows is an update.

Let me begin by reminding you a running streak is defined as running a minimum of one mile every day. For those who fit into this category, I'm sure each of them has their reason(s), although I would be hard-pressed to tell you what they are. Everything one reads in running literature suggests that it's best to take days off to allow your muscles to heal and your body to rest.

Now that I've surpassed the 28-year anniversary of my running streak, I have a personal understanding of 'why' it pertains to me. Simply put, I want to be the best. I realize my streak is more than ten years behind the longest active streak (held by Mark Covert of Lancaster, California). To be exact, 3,791 days behind (factoring in leap years). Then, of course, there's the small matter of the 34 runners with streaks shorter than Mark's but longer than mine. But realizing patience is a virtue, I figure I've got time on my side.

Here's an update on some of the odds and ends I mentioned in my earlier entry:

- I have run 105,495 miles, an average of 10.22 miles per day, with a daily low of 3 miles and a daily high of 84 miles.
- I've run in all types of weather, including temperatures ranging from 133 degrees to minus 59 degrees (when the wind chill was factored in).

- I've run in 20 states, two foreign countries (again, the former Yugoslavia as well as Germany), and 'on' two oceans.

- I've been chased by dogs too numerous to count, and *still* have only been caught/bitten once.

- I've run in 676 races, amassing enough T-shirts that even my own friends and family no longer want them. Nor the Salvation Army.

- I've lost 50 pounds since the day the streak began, and I *still* know that should the streak end, the pounds will return instantly.

- 'Guestimating' that to run an average mile for me over the course of the streak took 8 minutes (I factored in the 'slow down due to advancing age' factor since my earlier calculation), I have run the equivalent of 586 straight days, 24 hours a day, to accumulate my mileage.

By the way, Ron Hill's streak is over. Mine is more alive than ever. Stay tuned.

Dumb Things to Keep the Streak Alive

Now that my streak has reached the 28 year mark and I've been 'promoted' to the 'Dominators' category (according to the United States Running Streak Association), I was requested to list the dumbest things I've done to keep the streak alive. Since this list has the potential of being a book in and of itself, I've decided to limit it to the ten things that came to mind the quickest. They are (in no particular order):

1. In the early days of my running career, I was an 'afternoon' runner. However, when Cindy was close to delivering our first child I started running in the morning, figuring I'd have my work cut out in the afternoons as 'Mr. Mom.' My first day of switching to pre-dawn runs was the day Cindy's doctor called, coincidentally, right after I finished my run and advised her that there was a complication with her pregnancy and she needed to come in *that day* for a C-section delivery (November 16, 1982 for you historians). For the next 20+ years, my weekday ritual involved a 2:00 a.m. 'pre-alarm, a 2:40 wake-up alarm, and a 3:30 a.m. run. Obviously, my new bedtime rolled back to 9:00 p.m. (9:30 when I stayed up 'late'). Waking up before the chickens for 20+ years sounds pretty dumb, now that I think about it.

2. The first time I attempted my 280-mile run across Georgia (October of 1982), I ended it prematurely (after 159 miles) due to knee problems and severe blisters on the bottoms of both feet. However, I continued my streak, trying to run by landing 'softly' so my knees wouldn't buckle and biting my tongue to override the pain from running on two feet missing several layers of skin on the bottom.

3. The second time I attempted—and completed, this time—my 280-mile run across Georgia (October of 1992), a (I'll be nice and call him a) doctor thought I had a stress fracture on my left shin. He advised me to wear an air cast and take some time off from running. For the next three days I took my air cast off each afternoon and hobbled three miles. On the fourth day, I ran a totally pain-free seven miles—as I remember it to this day, it remains one of the best runs of my life.

4. In the early '80's, I experienced severe pain in my left knee. I actually went to a (again, being nice) doctor who stuck me with cortisone with what had to be the biggest needle I've ever seen. He advised me to take some time off from running. I immediately went to the track and ran three miles. I figured if the cortisone was doing its job, I'd be fine. It didn't, and I wasn't.

5. Occasionally my job required me to be at work early (as if my normal 6:30 a.m. start wasn't early enough). These 'early' days would require me to do my 90-minute run at midnight, which allowed me 30 minutes to get ready and 45 minutes to drive to work—putting me behind my desk before 3:00 a.m.

6. In the early '80's, back when I could drink more than two beers and not regret it the next morning, I had a few too many at the annual office Christmas party. The next day I got out of bed—*finally*—at 4:00 p.m. for a less-than-brisk seven mile run. As I recall, it was the longest seven miles I've ever run, and if there was ever a citation issued for R.U.I. ('running under the influence'), this would have been the one.

7. Before I converted to early morning runs, one day my job required me to stay at work beyond midnight, which meant my streak was in jeopardy. My assignment was to monitor some questionable nighttime occurrences, so I was asked to stay in a stationary position outside our building next to a trash dumpster and 'observe.' Just after the sun went

down, I ran 'laps' around the trash dumpster for 90 minutes in my work clothes. I did remove my tie, however.

8. Cindy and I went on a cruise on the SS Norway just after we were married. Several days required us to be on the ocean all day long, so I had to do my daily runs on the 'jogging deck,' which required me to run back-and-forth along one side of the ship more times than I care to remember. I don't think I've made that many total U-turns in my entire running career as I did that week on the SS Norway.

9. After completing the 135 miles of Badwater in 2003, four of my crew members (my son Josh slept in) and I ran three miles together to keep the streak alive. Less than 12 hours after crossing the finish line on Mount Whitney.

10. After completing the JFK 50 Mile Run (which tore me up, as I am not by nature a 'trail runner'), I woke up early the following morning (to catch an early flight) and literally *hobbled* three miles. I was in so much pain I had to gingerly 'step' on and off the curbs. Three miles in a blazing 33 minutes. After my flight back to Atlanta, I drove home, unpacked … and ran three more miles. In yet another blazing 33 minutes.

A couple 'honorable mentions' should be given to a few multi-day runs that required me to run from one day to the next (which had me running on either side of midnight, thus satisfying *two* 'streak' days):

- Four 24-hour runs (1988–101 miles, 2002–129 miles, 2004-111 miles, and 2005-114 miles).

- Two 100-mile run (2003 and 2006)

- Badwater's 135 miles (2003).

Actually, 'honorable mention' probably doesn't do them justice. They probably deserve the same accolades as the ten items listed above.

You remember. 'Dumb.'

End the Streak? *NEVER!*

The thought *has* crossed my mind, however—to end the streak, I mean. There was the time we went skiing in Yugoslavia and I was accused of being a spy while running up and down the mountain—past the same military installation numerous times. Then there was the time I was forced to run lap after lap after lap for a mere *mile* aboard the S.S. Norway. Both of these gave me serious pause to consider ending the streak. Then there was my *intentional* attempt at ending my streak in Birdsboro, Pennsylvania, only to venture out in a snowstorm late one January night to keep the streak alive.

Looking back over my running logs, it appears the origin of the streak was in 1979, when one of my resolutions was to 'run every day.' Unlike two of my running partners, Al Barker and Prince Whatley, who were able to determine the length of the streak they wished to achieve and had the good sense to *end* their respective streaks on the appropriate day (Al after running every day for an entire year took January 1st of the following year off, and Prince ran for 100 consecutive days and quit on day #101), I never showed that much resolve.

I've had some days when it's been particularly tough keeping the streak going. Several days come to mind:

- The afternoon (back when I ran *after* I got home from work) when there was a seemingly endless hailstorm (in which the hail was literally the size of golf balls).

- The many times I was asked to go to 'Happy Hour' immediately after work (only to refuse by saying I had to go home and run. No, I never had the reputation of being a 'party animal' with my coworkers).

- Several New Year's Days—*REST*—what a better way to start the year!

- The Saturday I woke up—at 4:00 p.m. in the afternoon—with the worst hangover in history *(OK, so occasionally I was a party animal)*.

- The morning I woke up (literally) too dizzy to get out of bed (no, this time it *wasn't* a hangover!).

- After my successful run across Georgia and was told by a doctor that I may have a stress fracture and was forced to wear an air cast on my leg.

Except for the last instance (which happened in 1992), the others all occurred in the early 1980's. So, *yes*, the thought to end my streak *has* crossed my mind. But *no*, it hasn't lately.

To be honest, I doubt that it will ever again.

Meet the U.S.R.S.A.

(United States Running Geek ... er, Streak Association)

In 1994, George Hancock of Windber, Pennsylvania searched the country for any and all runners who had an active running streak. A streak (by definition) is covering a distance of one or more miles per day under one's own power. By the end of the year, George had a list compiled and I was proud to have the 9th long-est streak (at that time) in the United States.

Twelve years later, my streak is still alive. And twelve years later, I am proud to say I've moved all the way up to ... 36th (*36th*)?

George's work evolved into the formation of the USRSA in 2001. If you were a known 'streak runner,' you had the distinct privilege of being able to join for a meager annual fee of $20.

As I was appreciative of George's hard work at compiling the original list of streak runners, I felt obligated to join. So I did, and was officially assigned membership #19 (first come, first served). Membership entitles me to a quarterly newsletter *(The Streak Registry)* as well as 'votes' on important issues such as '*should less than a mile per day count towards a streak*' (I voted no) and '*should total mileage be rec-ognized in the newsletter*' (I voted yes).

I mentioned I joined pretty much out of my gratitude for George's research and efforts. Otherwise, I wouldn't have thought twice about joining an organization which I perceived to be essentially a society of geeks (I don't know what this says about me personally, so don't ask).

However, once I began reading the profiles of some of the members, I have a little different attitude about being in the USRSA. In fact, I think I'll refer to them as *our* members.

Following are some of my 'teammates' and their credentials (note: the date they began their perspective streaks is included in parentheses):

- **Mark Covert** (7/23/68): 4:09 mile; 2:21 marathon; 7th in 1972 Olympic Marathon trials. The longest active streak by any runner in the United States.

- **Don Slusser** (1/3/72): 4:23 mile; 2:17 marathon; 31st in 1980 Olympic Marathon trials; streak retired after 27 years (since then he began a new one).

- **Jon Sutherland** (5/26/69): 4:10 mile; 28:51 10K; 46:22 15K; 161,000 lifetime miles (average of *13 miles each day!*).

- **Steve DeBoer** (7/20/70): 2:42 marathon; 103,000 lifetime miles; 1,000,000 lifetime *pushups*.

- **Jim Pearson** (2/16/70): 2:22 marathon; 5:12 50-miler; 7:07 100K; ran in 1972 and 1976 Olympic Marathon Trials.

- **Ken Young** (7/6/70): 4:08 40-miler (US Track Record); 14:14 100-miler; 2:35 marathon.

- **John Strumsky** (5/23/83): has run *twice a day* since 5/31/92.

- **Margaret Blackstock** (9/9/79): longest active streak by a female.

- **Homer Hastings** (9/8/84): has run 24 consecutive Mount Rushmore Marathons (2:32 best); 4:41 mile; 31:57 10K; 47:44 15K.

- **David Hamilton** (8/14/72): 31:42 10K; 2:32 marathon; 3:26 50K

- **Craig Davidson** (11/5/78): 5:37 50-miler; 143,000 lifetime miles; an average of *16.8 miles each day.*

- **Ronald Kmiec** (11/28/75): 6:49 50-miler; 8:54 100K

- **John Watts** (10/4/80): 2:29 marathon

- **John Roemer IV** (11/1/78): 4:17 mile (his girlfriend, Eleanor Simonsick, has a faster time!).

- **Robert Kraft** (1/1/75): runs the same eight mile stretch on Miami Beach every day (4:00 PM in the winter and 5:00 PM in the summer. Look him up!)

Other Notable Performances

- **Most races completed:** Ralph McKinney–1,553 (Mark Courtney–1,406).
- **Overall miles ran:** Jon Sutherland–161,650 (Don Slusser–160,425)
- **Most miles ran in one year:** Don Slusser–6,263 (Jon Sutherland–6,206).
- **Most miles ran in one month:** Jon Sutherland–860 (Don Slusser–637).

Where do I stand on all this? Believe it or not, I made a few of the 'Top Ten' lists:

- My 56:22 **15K** ranks me at #5
- My 3:44 **50K** ranks me at #2
- My 585 **total races** ranks me at #5
- My 129 miles in **24 hours** ranks me at #1
- My 7:28 **50-miler** ranks me at #3
- My 105,495 **lifetime miles** ranks me at #8
- My 5,402 **miles in one year** ranks me at #4
- My 538 **miles in one month** ranks me at #5
- My 266 **miles in one week** ranks me at #1

Considering the company I'm keeping, I'm proud to be 'ranked.' Not bad for a geek.

Mileage over the Years

(Average Miles/Day and Total Races)

This chart is a condensed version of my running logs. You are probably wondering what happened in 1994 that shifted my focus on the sport. You'll find out soon enough.

Year	Total Mileage	Average Miles per Day	Number of Races
Oct–Dec 1978	441	5.25	5

1979	2154	5.90	23
1980	1787	4.99	26
1981	2578	7.06	26
1982	2765	7.58	26
1983	2821	7.73	27
1984	3074	8.40	23
1985	3285	9.00	31
1986	3812	10.44	34
1987	3082	8.44	24
1988	2954	8.07	20
1989	3089	8.46	15
1990	3034	8.31	13
1991	3036	8.32	19
1992	3078	8.41	10
1993	2822	7.73	10
1994	4649	12.74	30
1995	4744	13.00	33
1996	4404	12.03	38
1997	4628	12.68	30
1998	5402	14.80	30
1999	4630	12.69	26
2000	4644	12.69	29
2001	4777	13.09	24
2002	4586	12.56	22
2003	5037	13.80	22

2004	4758	13.00	19
2005	4637	12.71	21
2006	4787	13.12	20
28 Year Total	**105,495**	**10.22**	**676**

Chapter Three
Running Around in Circles
(Experimenting with speed)

When I got my one and only triple—my best hit ever—playing little league baseball in Rhode Island, I stood proudly on third base only to hear someone in the bleachers yell: 'If you weren't so slow, you would have had a home run.' Those words echoed in my head for many years to come. In time, I would have my fair share of 'home runs'—just not of the baseball variety. I discovered I wasn't so slow after all.

This chapter is for you, dad.

Early in my career, I had a slight propensity to run fast. I say 'slight' because I never had any interest in doing speed work. If my speed didn't come naturally, I could certainly live without it.

Besides, I'm a firm believer in the old adage 'speed kills.'

In this chapter:

- Counter-Clockwise Fever–At one point I found myself on a track, and the speed work actually worked! That didn't keep me from hating it.

- TEN-HUT; about PACE–I wanted proof that I run as hard as world-class runners, and I found it. Read this, then get out your calculator and surprise yourself!

- World Records Mean Nothing to Me … or DO They?–A close examination of the current world records in the sport of running could possibly help you determine your true (distance) calling.

- PEACHTREE–There's only one race I've managed to run for twenty-eight consecutive years.

- Like a Fine Wine–Examining some of my personal bests to determine whether or not I was improving with age.

- Slowing Down at an Annual Rate of One Percent—Once I reached the age of 40, I discovered that my fastest times were behind me.

- Tapering–I never was a proponent of tapering, although I have given it a try. Statistics prove I was right, to a degree.

- The How and Why Book of RECOVERY–I was never a proponent of allowing time for recovery either. Again, I was right … to an even greater degree.

- Evolution of my Personal Bests–A chart showing the chronological history of my best times in four major distances: the mile, 5K, 10K and the marathon.

Counter-Clockwise Fever

I hate running on a track. I've *always* hated running on a track.

I take that back: I **detest** running on a track.

But you'll probably start seeing me at the track quite often in the future.

But I still hate it; always have, always will. No, detest is the right word.

I think one track workout a week will be enough. The Thursday night track meets this summer have started to pay dividends. I lowered my former mile best (set at age 28) by five seconds (now age 36). The speed work helped me to *finally* (after eight tries) break 30 minutes (29:47!) at this year's Maggie Valley Moonlight 8K.

Maybe two track workouts a week would be better. Yeah, that will work. Maybe I can eventually break a five-minute mile. Who knows: a 29:30 Maggie Valley could even by in my future. Or a 36:00 Peachtree. Or … wait, what am I thinking?! I hate running on a track. Always have, always will.

I wonder what track workouts will do for my marathon times? Perhaps a 2:44 at Boston, or a 2:47 at hilly Charlotte? Maybe three nights a week at the track is what I need! When are the Olympic trials?….

Good Lord, Scott–get a grip on yourself. You hate running on a track. What are you thinking? That's it! Settle down. Get your thoughts together. Your game is distance, not speed. 70 miles a week is your salvation, not 70 second intervals.

There, there. Feel better now? A nice, easy 15 miler should just about cure your cloudy thinking. Here, let me help you get ready. Shorts … singlet … socks … spikes. *Spikes?!? Wait, come back!!!! God, I've lost him* …

But I know deep down inside he hates running on a track. No, he *detests* running on a track. Remind him of that when you see him there, will you?

Ten-*HUT*; about *PACE*

As I was watching a replay of this year's Peachtree Road Race on television, one thought is foremost in my mind: the leaders don't run *nearly* as hard as I feel like *I'm* running! I've felt this way for years, and with the assistance of my trusty calculator, I'm going to prove I'm right. Here goes …

Why Scott runs harder than a world class runner

Step 1:
My average stride length is (generously) five feet and a world class runner's (WCR) is (conservatively) eight feet.

Step 2:
My average 10K time is (generously) 38:30 (a total of 2,310 seconds) and a WCR's is 28:30 (1,710 seconds).

Step 3:
As a 10K race is 32,790 feet in length, I require 6,558 paces to cover the distance while a WCR requires 4,099 paces.

Step 4:
My feet are moving at a rate of 2.84 paces per second while a WCR is moving at 2.40 paces per second.

Step 5:
My legs are working 18 percent harder than those of a WCR.

See my point? Sure, some of you are saying 'it takes more physical effort to achieve a longer stride' or 'world class runners have slower paces per second as they are staying in the air longer between steps.' I'm not arguing any of these points. I'm just saying it sure *feels* like I'm working harder than the elite runners appear to be.

For the sake of argument, let's say I'm right. I *am* working harder (and conversely, the WCR is not working as hard):

Lesson 1: If a WCR (with a stride of 8 feet) moved at my pace (2.84 paces per second), a 10K race would be covered in 24:03, easily a world record.

Lesson 2: If I (with my 5 foot stride) ran at a WCR's pace (2.40 per second), my 10K time would balloon to 45:45.

You can draw your own conclusions at this point. Are WCR's overrated? Are you underrated? Is Scott, in his own way, a world class runner? You decide: you now have the information to make an intelligent, logical decision.

And while we're on the subject of pace, maybe we should campaign for new divisions for awards at road races. These work for me:

- Puddle jumpers–strides of 5 feet or less
- Middle of the road–over 5 feet but less than 8 feet
- Grand Canyon striders–8 feet and over

See you at the awards ceremony!

World Records Mean Nothing to Me ... or DO They?

Unless you're a world class runner, world records at various distances don't mean a whole lot to you unless you're like me and take the time to calculate that if I took my fastest 400 meters and ran it 105 times in a row–without stopping–I would be competitive at the Boston Marathon. Since the odds are against that happening, I just simply sit back in amazement at the speed at which some human beings–both men and women–are able to run in distances from the mile to the marathon.

However, I've begun looking at world records in a different light. Before I explain how, I will list the present world records for both men and women at common road race distances (including the mile):

Distance	Men	Women
Mile	3:44	4:15
5K	13:12	15:05
8K	22:04	24:48
10K	27:24	30:39
15K	42:13	46:57
10 miles	45:38	51:39
Half Marathon	59:47	1:07:58
Marathon	2:06:50	2:21:06

One way I look at world records is by determining how much slower my personal bests are (expressed as a percent slower) than the world record (keep in mind that world records for different distances are held by *different* runners, while all of my P.R.'s are held by *me*! (i.e. I have no 'specialty distance'). For example my P.R. is closest in the 5K, a mere 30.3 percent slower than the world record, while my P.R. in the mile would be considered my 'worst' distance, as I am 41.3 percent slower than the world record. I consider the marathon my best distance, but my P.R. is 33.0 percent off the world record. According to these results, I should concentrate on the 5K more, although personally, I hate the distance (i.e. too short, too fast, and it *hurts*). I recommend you look at the world records in this light to see if there is a distance that 'stands out' to you.

Another way to look at world records is to focus on your 'closest' event; in my case, the 5K. As I mentioned, I am 30.3 percent off the world record at that distance. If I could focus on the marathon with a goal of 30.3 percent slower than the world record, it appears logical that—in time—I would be able to run a 2:45:16, which is 3:25 faster than my current P.R. I don't know if that will ever happen, but it certainly provides me a target to shoot for.

For some runners, the percentage their P.R.'s are over the world record may either increase or decrease as the distance increases, which may indicate if they are better suited for shorter or longer events. In my case, this doesn't appear to be applicable, but it may be for you. I do know that by virtue of my 'differential' between the world record in the mile and my P.R. that I definitely don't have fast twitch muscles (or is it slow twitch; I always get these confused) in my legs.

Note: These world records 'date' me, as they were valid at the time this article was originally written—1988. To update the records and my corresponding PR's was much too depressing for me to even consider. Sigh ...

<u>PEACHTREE</u>

If you claim to be a runner and live in or anywhere near Atlanta, you will inevitably be asked if you are running or have ever run (depending on the time of year) the Peachtree Road Race. For years I would measure my entire worth as a runner by how fast I ran the 6.2 miles down Peachtree Street on the 4th of July. After all, the top finishers are listed in the *Atlanta Journal-Constitution* without fail on July 5th every year, and all my friends and fellow runners always look for my time to either see how I did or see if I won (my non-running friends never seem to understand why someone who runs so many miles can never win such a short race).

In 1979, my first year running Peachtree, I ran a blazing 42:03. I say 'blazing' because I worked in a company of over 2,000 employees and I was the only one who ran the race, and since the employees didn't have anyone to compare me to, I was considered to be a *fast* runner. Since that time, I have run the race every year and have seen it grow in size from 7,000 runners to its present limit of 55,000. Amazingly, the Atlanta Track Club has done a fine job in coordinating the logistics of the race—no small feat considering how narrow Peachtree Street is when you try to sandwich that many runners in between hundreds of thousands of spectators watching the event while enjoying an early-morning cocktail on a national holiday.

I had a good run of Peachtree performances in the decade of the '90's, including a personal best of 36:56 in 1996 when the temperature at the start of the race was an unseasonably cool 63 degrees. I managed to earn a coveted 'Nike Top 1,000' award (a coffee mug) for eleven straight years (1993 to 2003) until I broke my string in 2004 after running 45:44 only seven days after my first experience in the Western States Endurance Run. As for Nike, I lost all respect for the company in 2003 when I went to pick up my award (at a Nike-only store over 50 miles from my house) only to find that they were all gone. I asked how that could be if there were 1,000 awards for the top 1,000 finishers, and was told that Nike only supplies as many awards as they believe will be picked up (figuring that out-of-town runners won't stick around to pick up the award). In other words Nike—a zillion dollar company—wouldn't 'go out on a limb' and shell out enough money to ensure a coffee mug for all one thousand of us. I haven't run in a pair of Nikes since, and I don't intend to in the future.

Forgive me for digressing, but that really bothered me, and obviously still does. But getting back to the Peachtree Road race, it is one other streak I have going (2006 marked my 28th consecutive stroll through Atlanta on America's birthday). No longer do I measure my entire worth as a runner by my performance; in fact, a private joke I have with my friends is that I am only trying to beat my age in minutes at this stage of the game (for example, a 50-minute time at age 51 would be considered a victory).

One thing I know is that I will continue to run the race (and as such keep my 'other' streak alive) as it is a celebration of many of the things I value: running, camaraderie, fitness, freedom and national pride. God bless America.

1989 Peachtree Road Race

Like a Fine Wine ...

I thought it might be interesting to examine the various race distances I've run to see which one I've improved upon the most. I looked at my performances in eight distances (from the mile to the marathon) by comparing the first time I raced the distance with my PR at the same distance. Additionally, I compared my age at the time of both. Then, I determined how much faster (percent faster) my PR was than the first time I raced each distance. The following table shows this data:

Distance	First Race	Age	PR	Age	% Faster
1 Mile	5:57	24	5:10	41	13.2
5K	21:07	24	17:12	33	18.5
5 Miles	36:32	23	29:27	32	20.6

10K	48:53	23	36:14	39	25.9
15K	1:09:55	24	56:23	31	19.9
10 Miles	1:15:12	24	1:01:50	42	18.9
13.1 Miles	1:31:45	26	1:22:33	31	10.0
26.2 Miles	3:44:11	24	2:48:41	33	24.8

What conclusions can I draw from this information? It's hard to say; for example, my half-marathon (13.1 miles) showed the least improvement (10.0 percent). This is due in part to the fact that I just don't race that many half marathons because (a) there aren't that many and (b) most are held in conjunction with a full marathon, and (with two exceptions at Atlanta that I still regret) I ordinarily opt to do the full. But if I absolutely had to make a couple inferences from this information:

- My greatest improvement was at the 10K distance (25.9 percent). This may be in part because I've run more 10K races than any other distance, and the 36:14 may be attributed slightly to the 'shotgun effect' (fire a shotgun at a flock of ducks and you're bound to hit one of them). If you run the distance enough, sooner or later you're going to fire on all cylinders and run a great race.

- The 24.8 percent improvement in the marathon reflects a reduction of almost a full hour from my initial attempt at that distance. It's interesting that I ran my marathon PR in the vicinity of 'prime marathoning age' (rumored to be in the early to mid-30's).

- Although an improvement of only 13.3 percent was realized in the mile, my PR was accomplished at the age of 41, the beginning of 'lose 1 percent of your speed each year' period.

- None of my PR's were set in my 20's; however two were set in my 40's.

- Six of the eight PR's listed were set in my early 30's while the other two were set as I entered into the masters' division (age 40 and over).

One last thing I noticed: I haven't set a PR in any of these distances in ten years. My best bet? Find a new distance. Or stick with ultras.

I believe I'll go for the latter. After all, I *do* want to be like a fine wine and improve with age.

Slowing Down at an Annual Rate of One Percent

Once a runner turns age 40, their race times slow down at a rate of 1 percent per year. Myth or reality? Let's find out by looking at the nine Peachtree Road Race times I've run since I turned 40:

YEAR	AGE	TIME	% CHANGE (from previous year)
1995	40	38:17	—
1996	41	36:56	+3.5%
1997	42	38:23	-3.9%
1998	43	38:57	-1.5%
1999	44	38:37	+0.9%
2000	45	39:06	-1.3%
2001	46	38:46	+0.9%
2002	47	40:03	-3.3%
2003	48	40:16	-0.5%
			-5.2% change over 8 years

*Note: '+' indicates *faster;* '-' indicates *slower.*

For this analysis, we must assume that (a) I actually *raced* Peachtree each year and (b) I approached the race each year the same (with respect to mileage, training, health, etc.). For the sake of argument, these assumptions would be correct.

For the '1 percent' rule to be accurate, I would have had to run a 41:27 in 2003 (1 percent slower each year once turning 40, the year I ran 38:17). As I ran a 40:16, we have exhibit (a) to show the rule to be a myth.

Additionally, there was no single year where my performance slowed down 1 percent. In fact, the closest to a change of 1 percent in any years were two years that I ran 0.9 percent *faster* than the previous year. This is exhibit (b) showing the rule to be a myth.

Three years reflect changes of over 3 percent (one year being faster, two years being slower) from one year to the next, well outside the boundaries of the 1 percent rule. We now have exhibit (c) showing the rule to be a myth.

As there is *no* statistical evidence to support the 1 percent rule, we have to assume it to be more fact than fiction.

Let's hope so, at least. Or else I'll be running Peachtree in 46:43 when I'm 60.

Addendum: The author ran the 2004 in Peachtree—one week after the first DNF of his life (Western States Endurance Run)—in 45:44.

Tapering

One of the great debates in running is whether or not to taper before a big race. Having been a streak runner since 1978, tapering has always been a foreign concept to me. Factoring in (a) I don't have the proper genes and/or muscle twitch to be fast and (b) an extreme dislike for (and aversion to) speed work, there's never been a whole lot of reason *for* me to taper. That doesn't stop me from thinking that most runners run quicker race times than me because (a) of genetics or (b) their legs are more rested (as they run fewer miles, don't 'streak,' actually taper, etc.) than mine. Therefore, who beats me in any given race never really bothered me.

That's not to say that I haven't tapered before. There have been a couple marathons in which I reduced my mileage the week prior to the actual event, culminating in a 3-mile 'jog' the day before the marathon. Some 'tapers' have been successful; most haven't.

However, I did research my mileage the week and the day before my five fastest times at three distances—5K, 10K and marathon. (Note: refer to charts on next page) Additionally, I examined the three 50K's that I—for whatever reason—managed to finish in first place. Here's what I found:

5K

An average of 76 miles in the week preceding my five fastest 5K races, my theory being if you're averaging $\underline{X}$ miles a day, 3.1 miles—no matter how hard you run them—can't be too tough (of course, my theory is most likely *wrong!*).

Date	Time	Mileage Week Before	Mileage Day Before
May 88	17:12	65	6
May 95	17:24	87	8
Aug 87	17:41	67	8
Sep 96	17:45	74	4
Sep 99	17:46	85	10
Average	**17:34**	76	7

10K

An average of 86 miles in the week preceding my five fastest 10K races. Interesting that the 5th fastest time followed a 120-mile week and a 26-mile day before the race. Taper my ass.

Date	Time	Mileage Week Before	Mileage Day Before
Mar 94	36:14	88	9
Nov 85	36:17	84	9
May85	36:42	56	7
Mar 95	36:45	84	8
Sep 94	36:54	120	26
Average	**36:34**	86	12

Marathon

An average of only 60 miles in the week preceding these marathons, and only 5 miles the day before. Actually, this is pretty close to a taper. It's interesting that my marathon times are actually faster than the 'predictor charts' indicate for someone with 5K and 10K times comparable to mine. Maybe this 'tapering' works after all.

Date	Time	Mileage Week Before	Mileage Day Before
Jan 88	2:48:41	47	4
Oct 94	2:48:45	83	5
Oct 99	2:53:15	60	5
Apr 87	2:53:18	46	3
Jan 86	2:53:29	54	5
Average	**2:51:30**	**58**	**4**

50K

Remember what I just said about tapering working after all? Forget it. The *more miles* I ran the day and the week before these 50K's, the *faster* my time. In fact, when I ran my fastest 50K, I felt strong enough to run another 4-6 miles at the same pace I ran the first 31 miles.

Date	Time	Mileage Week Before	Mileage Day Before
Dec 98	3:44:58	114	11
Jan 95	3:48:23	106	8
May 03	4:10:00	83	7
Average	**3:54:27**	**101**	**9**

Like I said earlier: taper my ass. And no, I didn't write this just to get a lifetime pass from doing speed work. But I'll certainly use it as such.

The How and Why Book of RECOVERY

You already know my thoughts on tapering. For those of you who may have forgotten, allow me to summarize:

Bulls#&$!!!

The following will now challenge the age-old principle that a runner needs 'one day of recovery for every mile of a race' (for example, six days of recovery following a 10K race). I charted 50 marathons and 10 ultramarathons between February 1998 and July 2003, followed by the number of miles I ran the *day after* the event as well as the *week after* the event.

The charts make it readily apparent that I give as much credence to the principles of recovery after a race as I do the principles of tapering before a race. Granted, not all these races were all-out efforts. However, some of them *were,* like the Tallahassee 50K on 12/12/98, and it certainly didn't take me 31 days to 'recover.' In fact, the week after that event was the 2nd-highest mileage week of the 60 weeks listed on the chart, exceeded only by the following week (after the 12/19/98 Jacksonville Marathon).

Looking over the chart brings out a few interesting points:

- Marathons held on Saturday are usually followed by my traditional long run on Sunday (Museum of Aviation, Chickamauga, and Macon).

- Out-of-town marathons are usually followed by low mileage due to next-day early-morning airline reservations (Boston, Shamrock, and St. George).

- Sunday marathons are usually followed by a shorter run on Mondays (Callaway Gardens, Mercedes).

- The Atlanta Marathon, always held on Thanksgiving, is usually followed by a shorter run on Friday (a workday for me).

- Ultramarathons that incapacitate me—like the JFK 50-Miler, the 24-Hour Run, and Badwater—are usually followed by a (very) short (albeit very *painful*) run.

- Weekly average miles following a marathon (91.8) reflect my average weekly mileage for the past ten years (91 miles). In other words, I don't 'break stride' following a marathon.

Granted, I've been very fortunate in my running career with respect to injuries and/or illness that may negatively impact my mileage. But remember, recovery is recommended to allow your body to do just that—*recover*—from strenuous activity. However, I guess what I'm trying to say is:

> *If you condition your body to adapt to high mileage, the principles of tapering and recovery do not necessarily apply.*

I would be remiss if I failed to mention that in my late 20's and early 30's, I was consistently running 18-minute 5K's and 37-minutes 10K's. Hugh Toro—my running 'archrival' at the time—constantly asked me if I had 'broke seventeen minutes' yet for a 5K. I would tell him that when I broke *eighteen* I was thrilled. He would always have the last word by saying I could be breaking seventeen minutes—*easily*—if I would only cut back on my miles. Easy for a guy with the right muscle twitch to say.

Maybe I should have found a 5K after Badwater and tested his theory. Actually, my recovery after Badwater was probably my most challenging. I had fairly severe blisters on the balls of both feet, and it was painful to *walk* on them (let alone run … actually, it was *easier*—or at least less painful—to run, now that I think about it). For the nine days immediately following Badwater, my daily mileage was as follows:

3–3–3–10–6–7–8–9–10

The first '10' was on a Sunday, and it bothered me that I wasn't in condition to do my normal 'Sunday 20.' However, when my friend and running partner Paula May informed me that she was still 'crew chief' until the end of the week (of Badwater) and 'I'm *telling* you to only do ten,' I felt a little better. The good news is that on the 10th day after Badwater, I managed 33 miles (20 with Kelly in the morning, and 13 with Gary—who was in the midst of an 8-hour run in Roswell—in the afternoon). Then the next day I was able to resume my 'Sunday 20' with Al and *Eric.

Since the 'legend' of this run will take on a life of its own over time, let me give you the facts before Eric tells anyone his version:

I was recovering not only from Badwater but my 33 miles the previous day, and Al was still not properly re-hydrated from Badwater. Eric, on the other hand, had one of his better days and left Al and I around the 18-mile mark. In fact, Eric was already driving home when Al and I finished. So when Eric tells you he 'ran Scott and Al into the ground,' take it with a (very large) grain of salt. Even if he did run Al and I into the ground. Just make sure to ask him how much he ran on Saturday ...

The only other recovery as painful as this was following my 280-mile 'Run Across Georgia' in 1992. After spending seven days running from Columbus to Savannah, I was fairly certain I had a shin splint in my left leg. In fact, after limping three miles the Sunday after I completed the crossing, I saw a doctor the following Monday. He informed me that I 'probably' did indeed have a shin splint (although he couldn't be sure), and he put my left leg (from the knee down) in a plastic cast. He told me not to run, and to see him again in two weeks. Those that know me know I won't miss a day running unless I (a) lose a limb and/or (b) am totally unconscious/comatose for an entire day (from midnight to midnight). Therefore, for the next three days when I got home from work I removed the cast and hobbled my requisite three miles (yes, they were painful). However, on that *fourth* day (five days after the completion of my run across the state), a miracle happened: I ran TOTALLY pain-free and ran the best and most memorable seven-miler of my life (those of you who are able to resume running following an injury that prohibits you from it know the feeling)! In fact, I can still remember cresting a hill around the 5-mile mark and doing my 'Rocky on the steps of the Philadelphia Library' dance.

What's really interesting is that five days is what I have found to be the normal (full!) recovery time for me following a hard effort in a marathon (i.e. run the marathon on Saturday, and by Thursday 'all systems are go'). Coincidence? Foreshadowing? Who knows, but the 'five-day formula' for recovery seems to work. For me, at least.

Maybe the five-day recovery from my run across Georgia made a lasting impression on my subconscious. This makes total sense: after all, I've always preached that 'mind over matter' is the best kind of treatment for what ails you.

As for the 'one day per mile' rule of thumb for recovery, allow me to summarize:
Bulls#&$!!!

Post Marathon/Ultra Marathon Mileage

Date	Marathon	# Miles Day After	# Miles Week After
2/7/1998	Tybee Island	16	85
2/28/1998	Museum of Aviation	22	83
3/21/1998	Shamrock	9	95
4/20/1998	Boston	13	95
7/11/1998	Grandfather Mountain	22	98
10/11/1998	Steamtown	14	110
11/7/1998	Chickamauga	26	111
11/8/1998	Vulcan	15	117
11/26/1998	Atlanta	15	118
12/19/1998	Jacksonville	15	121
	1998 Totals	167 (16.7 avg)	1033 (103.3 avg)
2/7/1999	Callaway Gardens	10	89
2/3/1999	Tybee Island	19	83
3/20/1999	Shamrock	10	81
4/19/1999	Boston	9	97
10/2/1999	St. George	7	73
11/7/1999	Vulcan	19	105
11/14/1999	Chickamauga	15	88

11/25/1999	Atlanta	10	86
	1999 Totals	**99 (12.4 avg)**	**702 (87.8 avg)**
1/22/2000	Museum of Aviation	22	85
2/5/2000	Tybee Island	26	85
2/6/2000	Callaway Gardens	10	80
3/18/2000	Shamrock	8	85
4/17/2000	Boston	11	89
10/7/2000	St. George	7	74
11/11/2000	Chickamauga	22	98
11/23/2000	Atlanta	10	79
12/9/2000	Rocket City	22	92
	2000 Totals	**138 (15.3 avg)**	**767 (85.2 avg)**
1/20/2001	Museum of Aviation	21	96
2/3/2001	Tybee Island	26	97
2/4/2001	Callaway Gardens	10	92
3/17/2001	Shamrock	8	95
4/16/2001	Boston	8	84
10/20/2001	Baltimore	21	86
11/10/2001	Chickamauga	16	87
11/22/2001	Atlanta	12	97
12/15/2001	Jacksonville	21	116
	2001 Totals	**143 (15.9 avg)**	**850 (94.4 avg)**

1/19/2002	Museum of Aviation	14	74
2/2/2002	Tybee Island	26	84
2/3/2002	Callaway Gardens	10	84
2/10/2002	Mercedes	10	82
3/16/2002	Shamrock	9	77
3/23/2002	Macon	21	89
4/15/2002	Boston	8	75
10/20/2002	Bay Bridge	15	94
11/28/2002	Atlanta	10	88
	2002 Totals	**123 (13.7 avg)**	**747 (83.0 avg)**
1/11/2003	Museum of Aviation	20	87
2/1/2003	Tybee Island	26	97
2/16/2003	Tallahassee	20	100
3/29/2003	Macon	20	91
4/21/2003	Boston	8	114
	2003 Totals	**94 (18.8 avg)**	**489 (97.8 avg)**
	Grand Totals	**764 (15.3 avg)**	**4,588 (91.8 avg)**

Date	Ultramarathon	# Miles Day After	# Miles Week After
12/12/1998	Tallahassee 50K	23	120
1/9/2000	Atlanta FatAss 50K	9	82
11/4/2000	JFK 50 Miler	6	79
12/8/2001	Tallahassee 50K	21	96

9/14/2002	USATF 24 Hour Run	3	59
11/10/2002	Peachtree City 50K	10	87
5/3/2003	Strolling Jim 40 Miler	20	87
5/17/2003	Posey's 50K	20	93
6/7/2003	Pennar 40 Miler	20	97
7/22/2003	Badwater 135	3	40
	Grand Totals	**135 (13.5 avg)**	**840 (84.0 avg)**

Evolution of my Personal Bests in the Mile, 5K, 10K and Marathon

Mile

Date	Time	Age
Feb 1979	5:57	24
Mar 1979	5:55	24
May 1979	5:54	24
May 1979	5:49	24
Sep 1979	5:43	24
Oct 1979	5:37	24
Apr 1981	5:34	26
Apr 1983	5:24	28
Jun 1991	5:22	36
Jun 1991	5:20	36
Jul 1991	5:19	36
Jul 1991	5:17	36
Apr 1994	5:16	39

| May 1996 | 5:10 | 41 |

5K

Date	Time	Age
Feb 1979	21:07	24
Mar 1979	20:20	24
Apr 1979	19:43	24
Apr 1980	19:33	25
Oct 1980	19:01	25
Oct 1981	18:39	26
Oct 1982	8:25	27
May 1983	18:08	28
May 1985	17:49	30
Aug 1987	17:41	32
May 1988	17:12	33

10K

Date	Time	Age
Nov 1978	48:53	23
Dec 1978	47:19	23
Apr 1979	41:35	24
Jul 1979	41:31	24
Aug 1979	39:38	24
Oct 1980	39:31	25
Mar 1981	38:49	26

Sep 1981	38:43	26
Mar 1983	38:23	28
Mar 1983	38:14	28
May 1983	37:36	28
Oct 1984	37:04	29
Apr 1985	36:56	30
May 1985	36:42	30
Nov 1985	36:17	30
Mar 1994	36:14	39

Marathon

Date	Time	Age
Mar 1979	3:44:11	24
Nov 1979	3:33:41	24
Jan 1981	3:25:20	26
Nov 1981	3:13:00	26
Jan 1984	3:00:22	29
Jan 1986	2:53:29	31
Apr 1987	2:53:18	32
Jan 1988	2:48:41	33

Personal Bests in Various Other Distances

Distance	Date	Time	Age
4 Miles	Oct 1979	23:55	34
5 Miles	May 1987	29:27	32

7 Miles	Apr 1987	43:49	32
8 Miles	Feb 1988	50:27	33
15K	Mar 1986	56:23	31
10 Miles	Jan 1997	61:50	42
20K	Feb 1983	79:45	28
13.1 Miles	Mar 1986	82:33	31
25K	Oct 1986	1:46:32	31
30K	Nov 1991	2:00:50	36
50K	Dec 1998	3:44:58	44
50 Miles	Dec 2003	7:26:58	49
100 Miles	Sep 2003	18:23:18	48
24 Hours	Sep 2002	129 Miles	47

CHAPTER FOUR
RUNNING THROUGH THE WALL

An affinity for marathons

I became enamored with the thought of running a marathon in 1972, and I still don't know why it took me seven years until I was ready to give it a try. But once I lined up for my first marathon, hit the wall for the first time and somehow managed to find my way to the finish line, I was hooked.

In this chapter:

- Searching for Shorter—The 1972 Olympic Marathon proved to be the 'right stuff' to put my marathon aspirations in order.

- All in My Head, Part I—Negative thoughts managed to keep me from excelling in my first true love—golf.

- All in My Head, Part II—Certainly my second true love, running, wouldn't subject me to negative thoughts about my abilities and performances. Or would it?

- My Chronological History of the Atlanta Marathon—Three things I'll never do: (1) jump out of an airplane; (2) eat a cockroach; (3) break three hours in the Atlanta Marathon.

- Wishing Upon a Star—I've been fortunate to have found more success in running than I could ever have imagined. You can too, if you have a dream and follow it.

- The One I'll Always Remember—Every runner has one race they'll never forget. For me, the 1994 Vulcan Marathon is that race.

- Marathon Man (by Bob Dalton)—I gained a little regional exposure in an article that originally appeared in the *Georgia Runner*.

- Boston—I've been fortunate enough to participate in this prestigious event eleven times. Each one is special in its own unique way.

- My 28 Mile Warm-up—I reached a milestone at the 2003 Boston Marathon—100 lifetime marathons. To make it that much more memorable, I ran it twice.

- 100* and Counting—100 lifetime marathons is the first milestone I managed to reach in my running career. Here are some of the highlights.

- Boston Swan Song—The 2004 Boston Marathon was brutal; just brutal. My 11th trip to Hopkinton may well be my last.

- The Olympics Come to Atlanta—Find out how the world's finest marathoners did on my home turf (Hint: one or two managed to break three hours).

- You Have GOT to be Sh#**ing Me—Stuff like this is impossible to make up.

- A Sprint Down Memory Lane—Gainesville, Florida offered its first marathon in over two decades, and it was good to return to the scene of the original crime (my first marathon).

- Running Through the (Berlin) Wall—Business took me to Germany, so I figured 'why not take advantage of this opportunity?'

- Twenty-eight Years of Marathons—A composite listing of the marathons I've been lucky enough to run (and finish!) in my running career.

Searching for Shorter

The first time I was ever exposed to the idea of running a distance of 26.2 miles was in 1972. It was the day Frank Shorter won a gold medal for the marathon in the Olympic Games on national television. I remember the feature on Shorter shown just before the race in which he revealed his pre-race meal: two pans of lasagna, 42 pancakes (heavy syrup), and three loaves of bread. He called it 'carbo-loading.' I called it 'heaven.' What ever it was called, it worked and it brought Shorter the fame and wealth he rightfully deserved for running 26 consecutive miles at a five minute pace. I remember thinking, 'if it worked for Frank, it'll work for me.' After all, I could run 600 yards faster than anyone in my 10th grade class in high school (without throwing up) and 600 yards was a pretty long way!

Well, six years later (mental preparation takes time) I decided it was time to seek my own fame and fortune through running. Besides, being fifty pounds overweight, running sounded like a good way to lose weight. I started by running around my apartment complex (roughly 600 yards) five or six times a day in basketball shoes. I figured if I passed out on my 'course,' someone would recognize me and drag me to my doorstep. Besides, if I got tired or thirsty, it wasn't very far to walk across the courtyard to my apartment and the ice cold beer inside. The five or six laps became five or six miles and I eventually lost five or six inches off my waistline (true fact!). I ran my first competitive (?) event in November of 1978, and was instantly hooked on racing. I was a runner; graceful, quick and lean—just how I remembered Frank on that summer day in 1972. I was ready for the ultimate running challenge—the marathon!

I decided to make the Florida Relays Marathon (March of 1979) my first ultimate running challenge. With seven months of running behind me and a long run of 13 miles, I felt ready. (NOTE: the aforementioned 13 mile run was the result of a bet—which I won, and later celebrated by spending the next two days on the toilet).

The morning of the marathon arrived. Since the race didn't start until 7:30 am, I woke up at 5:00 am to eat my pre-race meal. I 'carbo-loaded' on seven delicious glazed doughnuts and two cups of black coffee (I hate coffee, but I read that coffee would increase my performance by 5 percent). I felt confident and ready. One of my college professors, Tom Saine, who I thank (I think) for helping me get my start in running, said he would meet me at the eighteen mile mark and run the rest of the marathon with me. We decided to meet at 10:00 am, which we felt would be the approximate time I would reach that point.

My wife and nephew Chris drove me to the race, and I did my stretching along with 350 other runners in front of the small group of well wishers sitting in the stands outside the track. I asked the University of Florida's track coach, Roy Benson, for some marathon advice. I'll never forget it: '*Don't run marathons.*' Thanks for the encouragement, Coach. As 7:30 approached, I took my position in the middle of the pack of runners, about 50 yards behind the starting line. The starter fired his gun and we were off—circling the track one time before we would leave the confines of the University of Florida and cover 26 miles of relentless, cruel asphalt throughout the city of Gainesville. The well-wishers cheered, and I felt strong.

The pace was smooth and even at first. My first mile was an easy 7:14. The second was 7:21 followed by a 7:19. I was flying! I met up with a veteran of three marathons at the five-mile mark and we ran together for a while. We told each other that we looked strong. I felt like this race was going to be a breeze! It looked like the former 10th grade-600 yard-without-throwing-up champ was going to cruise! At the halfway point, my time was 1:41—way ahead of schedule. I left the veteran in my tracks at this point. I mentally decided I would be ready to take on Frank sooner than I had expected. I felt stronger, and the rest of the race was downhill! Easy street. Just coast in and relax.

I met up with my professor slightly ahead of schedule, just before 9:45 a.m. Naturally, he seemed surprised to see me (he wasn't aware of my high school credentials). He asked me how I as doing and I replied confidently 'no problem.' At precisely that moment I learned about THE WALL. I had read and heard about it before; no energy, mind wanders, no desire to continue, extreme thirst—and those are the good things about it. I was finding about it first hand … and fast! Yes, at mile 18 I became quite (and instantly) familiar with 'the wall.' I drank 4 cups of water, but didn't feel particularly tired. I JUST DIDN'T WANT TO RUN ANYMORE. The thought of putting one foot in from of the other was literally making me sick. A female runner caught up with me, and we ran together for a short while. We told each other that we looked strong. I think she was lying; I know I was.

I was thirsty and craving apples (odd, as I never really cared for apples…. until then!). My professor, realizing my physical and mental condition, tried to get my mind off running by asking me sports trivia questions (my specialty). He asked me the name of the Cleveland Browns' quarterback … the #1 pitcher on the Baltimore Orioles … the number of yards O.J. Simpson ran in his record-breaking year … the Lakers' longest winning streak. I drew a total blank on everything. I could only think about apples, water and how good it would feel to stop running. I would have given anything to quit, but I knew Frank would never let me live it down.

I managed to walk, run, shuffle and drag myself the final six miles. As I entered the track for the final quarter mile of the marathon, the adrenaline began to flow. I couldn't begin to tell you where it came from…. perhaps a belated second wind. I sprinted along the final straightaway, feeling graceful, quick and lean once again. Catch me if you can, Frank. I crossed the finish line in a semi-respectable time of 3:44. As my wife, nephew and professor approached me to offer their congratulations, all I could say was 'Brian Sipe, Jim Palmer, 2003, 33 and please, PLEASE, get me an apple!' Running 26+ miles does strange things to your mind. I decided it would be a cold day in Hell before I ever did that again.

*The cold day in hell came sooner than expected: at the Brunswick (Georgia) Marathon on May 10, 1979—I ran a 3:58 in 90 degree heat, barely surviving an attack of heat exhaustion.

EPILOGUE: Alas, the Florida Relays Marathon exists no more. Apparently, Coach Benson got his way after all.

All in My Head–Part I

Everyone has heard the cliché that '(fill in any sport) is 10 percent physical and 90 percent mental.' Regardless of which sport you used to complete the previous sentence, the success you will encounter in that sport is primarily dictated by the battle going on between your ears; the battle that determines which side of the fine line dividing triumph and failure you will be on.

Before I began running at the age 23, I spent eleven years on the fairways of any and every golf course I could get my spikes on. I played the number one spot on my high school golf team, won several junior tournaments, lowered my handicap to a '1' when I was 16 years old, and even had a hole-in-one (April 8, 1972). But not once in those eleven years did I feel like I had conquered the mental aspect of the game. Instead of concentrating on the positive (taking the offensive), I seemed to focus on the negative; specifically, what could go wrong and how I could avoid it (taking the defensive). And, as any golfer will attest, there are so many things that can go wrong and only one way for it to go right. For example, a 'right' shot would be hitting a driver 250 yards down the middle of the fairway. Now, let's look at the negative thoughts which have run through my mind as I stood over many a tee shot in my life:

- What if the ball goes ____? (fill in the blank with a direction other than straight)

- If I hit the ball too short (long), it's in the _____! (fill in a body of water)

- If I hit this ball too high in this wind, it's liable to end up in ____! (fill in the neighboring county)

You get the idea. And those disturbing thoughts were for an *elementary* golf shot! You would not believe the fear in my mind of *difficult* shots (behind trees, out of sand traps, in tall rough). I desperately needed a sport which I could succeed in mentally as well as physically, so I turned to running. Not that my 38-inch waistline and who-knows-how-much body fat didn't have anything to do with my decision, but I felt that if I could physically run then the mental aspect of the sport would be a cinch. What could go wrong? What would there be to fear? How could I fail at something so elementary? There couldn't possibly be anything *negative* that could creep into my head.

Could there?

All in My Head—Part II

Remember, running is 10 percent physical and 90 percent mental

My major running goal in 1991 was to run the Atlanta Marathon in under three hours (I had run it seven times previously without ever breaking that mark). My previous best in Atlanta was a 3:07 several years prior when I was in my running prime (at least in terms of my age). For some inexplicable reason, I've just never run well on Thanksgiving Day (the traditional day for the Atlanta Marathon).

But this year was going to be different. I had never trained harder for a marathon ... seven months of Sunday long runs of 13 to 21 miles, weekly track workouts done religiously for the first time in my life, a base of over 60 miles a week for the entire year, and to top it off, my weight was the lowest it had been since I was 13 years old (over 20 years ago). Physically, I thought I was in the best shape of my life.

Notice I said 'physically.' So 10 percent of me was ready. What about the other 90 percent? One would think that with the training I had done that the psychological pieces would simply fall into place. One would think that my body was totally acclimated to pain and therefore a sub-three hour marathon would be automatic. One would think that my Thanksgiving goal would be a simple and logical extension of my training. One would think that the least of my problems would be ... *thinking!*

Successful running is dependent on a victory of mind over matter. As you follow my race day thoughts, judge for yourself which of the two—mind or matter—was victorious:

- 4:15 a.m.   (Note: race time is 7:30 a.m.). I just know I didn't get enough sleep last night. Eleven hard months of training and I throw it all away because I didn't get to bed early enough last night. Next year I'll just tape 'Night Court' on the VCR.

- 5:20 a.m.   I can't believe I ate toast for breakfast. I know I'll be paying for that in stomach cramps once the race gets underway. Speaking of eating, I wonder if I've eaten enough pasta this week? Or bananas?

- 6:20 a.m.   It sure is hot on this bus taking me to the starting line. I bet when I get off the bus and step out in the 35 degree weather I'll catch pneumonia within the hour. And sitting in these cramped seats is putting my legs to sleep. I'll bet they will feel like lead once the race begins.

- 7:00 a.m.   Thirty minutes to race time. Should I warm up or stay on the bus until race time? How soon should I put Vaseline on my feet? Should I drink anything else? If I do, how soon will it be before nature calls again? Is it too early to stretch? I bet that toast is going to tear my stomach up any second now. Should I keep my singlet over my long-sleeved shirt? What about gloves? Should I get in line at the porta-john now just to be safe? Am I *really* ready for this race? I should have eaten one more banana yesterday ... just to be safe. And another plate of spaghetti last night wouldn't have hurt. Just look at that line at the porta-john ... I'll never get through it before race time. And now I'm *positive* I need to use it!

- 7:30 a.m.   What did I decide yesterday that my race strategy would be? Come on, Scott ... *think!* Now I remember: a 6:45 pace for the first 10 miles, and then pick it up slightly.

- Mile 1   A 6:19 for the first mile! Too fast! I've got to back off now, or I just know I'll pay for it later on.

- Mile 5   Just slightly under a 6:45 pace so far. It feels like I'm out for a Sunday stroll. My training is paying off. Everything is going great. I just wish I had answered nature's call one last time before the race started.

- Mile 7   I'm still maintaining a 6:45 pace, and it *still* feels like a Sunday stroll. Maybe I'm taking it *too* easy. No, no—don't rush. I've still got over 19 miles to go. Besides, I'm going to pick up the pace in three miles anyway.

- Mile 8   Oh, no ... a 7:05 mile! I'm spending too much time thinking about pace and not enough time concentrating on running it. Now I need to run two 6:35's to get back on pace. That shouldn't be too tough—it feels like I've got plenty left.

- Mile 10   Those two 6:35's *killed* me! Maybe I've overextended myself. I can't believe picking up the pace a mere ten seconds per mile could do this to me. I feel like I've just run intervals on the track. I better wait to pick up the pace later—maybe in three miles or so.

- Mile 13   I've reached the half-marathon split in 1:28:30 and I still feel fairly fresh. I guess it's time to pick up the pace a bit. Better yet, I'll see what I have at 15 miles before I decide. It's no time to act too hastily.

- Mile 15   Still on a 6:45 pace without much trouble. But I've still got over 11 miles left. Maybe I'll wait to hit 18 miles before I pick it up.

- Mile 18   Still on pace. Just to be safe I won't pick up the pace until mile 20. That way I'll only have the equivalent of a 10K race left. That shouldn't be too difficult.

- Mile 20   I feel like I just got hit by a bus! What happened? Two miles ago I was feeling like a 2:55 marathon was within reach. Now I feel like it may take me 2:55 to finish the remaining six miles of this damn race! I knew I should have gotten to bed earlier last night!

- Mile 21   A 7:22 mile, and that's the *good* news. I think I feel a blister forming on the bottom of my right foot. Actually, I *know* I feel a blister forming …

- Mile 22   My body has utilized every last bit of pasta it consumed this week. My energy level gauge is on empty. I have no idea what I ran (was it really 'running'?) that last mile in. I'm not sure I even care.

- Mile 23   Am I still running? I know I'm moving forward because I saw the 23 mile marker. I was right about that extra banana, too—I've got the worst stomach cramp I can remember. If I can just keep moving forward for three more miles …

- Mile 24   The only thing keeping me going is the hope that I can still reach my objective of a sub-three hour marathon. I think I can cover (notice I didn't say 'run') these last 2.2 miles in about 16:30 to make it.

- Mile 25   To hell with the sub-three! Right now my *only* priority is to *get this thing over with!* One thing keeps me plodding forward: the cheers of the modest crowd lining the final mile of the course as it winds through Piedmont Park. (Note: Yes, it occurred to me that the faces in the crowd might be amused by the pained expressions on my face and the deathly stature of my body. The secret is to not make eye contact with them; that way, their sounds can be interpreted as 'cheering' as opposed to 'heckling.')

- Mile 26   The digital clock reads 2:59:00 as I hit the 26 mile mark! That leaves me only 59 seconds to run the last 2/10's of a mile. My mind is beyond the point of calculating pace, but I know that I couldn't cover the last 2/10's on a *bicycle* in 59 seconds!

- The Finish Line   As I cross beneath the digital clock, it reads 3:00:20. I feel no disappointment, only relief. Even though I failed to achieve my primary goal, I did run my fastest Atlanta Marathon ever. And it's over … finally. (I've always compared running a marathon to hitting yourself over the head with a hammer—it feels so good when you stop.)

Well, what do you think? Was the mind enjoying the spoils of victory? I think not! I'll bet you never realized how prominent a role the mind plays in the success (or failure) of a runner. Think about it.

Or better yet, don't.

My Chronological History of the Atlanta Marathon

My goal of breaking three hours at the Atlanta Marathon on Thanksgiving is—in my mind—ancient history. Seeing my 24 (sometimes feeble) attempts over the years in black and white drives the point home even further:

YEAR	TIME	COMMENT
1981	3:13:00	
1982	3:38:14	
1983	3:13:35	Bruce Cowart paced me on a bicycle
1984	3:01:36	Cold and windy—perfect!
1985	3:05:04	
1986	3:33:50	Paced Ed Rush
1987	3:25:13	Paced Ed Rush
1988	3:08:22	
1989	1:51:53	Only ran the half-marathon (*wimp!*)
1990	1:27:56	Ditto (*ditto!*)
1991	3:00:20	Rats. After all that speed work, too.
1992	3:05:21	

1993	3:30:24	Paced Valerie Reynolds (to a Boston qualifier!)
1994	3:03:27	Valerie paced me on a bicycle
1995	3:38:25	Ran with Valerie
1996	3:06:39	Ran with Richard Penland
1997	3:31:11	Ran with Valerie
1998	3:03:52	Ran with Richard
1999	3:49:45	Ran with Al Barker
2000	3:24:42	Ran with Valerie, Al and Kelly Murzynsky
2001	3:23:03	Ran with Al
2002	3:16:39	Ran with Al and Prince Whatley (Negative splits—1:38:43 for the first half)
2003	3:36:43	Ran with Al and Prince (we did an 8.8 mile warm-up, so our total mileage for the day was 35–to celebrate Prince's 35th birthday)
2004	3:33:44	Ran with Al and Prince
2005	3:53:05	Ran with Eric, Susan Lance and Paula (I celebrated my 100,000th lifetime mile as I crossed the finish line)
2006	3:48:06	Ran with Susan

There you have it: 0-for-24! Will I keep plugging away? Ancient history, remember ...

<u>Wishing Upon a Star</u>

If there is anyone in this world who needs to set a personal goal to stay motivated, it's a runner. Whether the goal is to run faster, run farther, or simply to lose weight, it's difficult to stay focused without setting one's sights on that elusive 'light at the end of the tunnel,' that hard-to-reach 'brass ring,' that evasive 'wish upon a star.' However, that's not to say that goal-orientation is limited to runners.

Take me for example. My life has been one long series of goal-orientations, starting when I was a 'beefy' 13-year old Boy Scout. Although camping, hiking and building fires did nothing to stimulate my interest (I know you're asking why I even *bothered* being a Boy Scout), I did, however, want to become an Eagle Scout. That was my 'brass ring,' the 'star I wished upon every night.' I would have earned this–the highest honor in Scouting–except for one small detail: I simply could not earn the required Lifesaving merit badge. I had a difficult enough time earning the required Swimming merit badge, and now I was supposed to earn yet another aquatic badge that required me to swim while dragging someone with me? I had a better chance of starting a fire with two rocks and some dry wood. Heck, I had a better chance of starting a fire with just two rocks. I finished my Boy Scout career as a Life Scout, one elusive merit badge shy of becoming an Eagle Scout.

In 9th grade, I desperately wanted to play junior varsity basketball. I spent (conservatively) 30 hours a week the summer following 8th grade in anticipation and preparation of the upcoming fall team tryouts. I even convinced my parents that a new pair of $30 Adidas basketball shoes would help guarantee me making the team (at age 15, I was certain spending $30 on a single pair of shoes meant they would last a lifetime). Well, the time for team tryouts arrived and I worked my tail off for an entire week. When the announcement of who made the team was made, I was happy to hear that my best friend (who I could beat one-on-one 100 times in a row–I know this for a fact because I did it over the summer) made the team. At this point I was holding my breath, waiting until the coach would announce that I, too, had made the team. Imagine my shock/surprise/amazement/disappointment (pick one; better yet, pick *all four*) when he read the last name on the list and it *still* wasn't Ludwig. I guess my friend's height (5 inches taller than mine) earned him a spot on the team. Coach said I could play on the 'taxi squad' and 'IF' a spot opened on the regular team and 'IF' I was busting my butt, I 'MIGHT' get to play on the Junior Varsity team. Right …

Let's move on. Having taken up golf as a 12-year-old, I always wished for a hole-in-one. As a 17-year-old who managed to work his handicap down to a '1' (I played a lot of golf that year–probably around 5,400 holes or 300 18-hole rounds), the odds were in my favor. On April 8, 1972, my wish came true. Mayport Naval Station Golf Course (near Jacksonville, FL), hole #5, 174 yards, par three with a 3-iron. A low right-to-left shot hitting on the front of the green, taking three bounces and rolling into the cup. And it couldn't have come at a better time–a four-man best-ball tournament. I was on cloud nine for exactly one year, because on April 8, 1973, my dad–a 24 handicapper who had never broken 90 in his life–matched my performance of a year earlier by acing the 12th hole on the very same golf course. Right in front of me! Reflecting back on the two goals that I failed to achieve (Eagle Scout and J.V. basketball team), I realized this goal (a hole-in-one) was the only one of the three that required a large dose of *luck*. I still had not achieved a major goal that could be attained only through pure effort, dedication and hard work.

Then at age 23 I became a runner. Initially, I set my sights on several unrealistic goals, like running the marathon in the Pan-Am Games for a small third world country. Once reality set in, my ultimate goal in running was narrowed down to one: competing in the historic Boston Marathon. Nothing was more important to me as a runner. Nothing.

When I first started running, I read everything I could get my hands on about Boston. I read about the tradition, the history, and the honor of running the 26.2 miles from Hopkinton to Boston in April. I desperately wanted to be a part of it. Initially, to qualify for Boston, one had to run a marathon in 2:50 or less, which to me was the equivalent of earning the Lifesaving merit badge.

Several years later, I read the best news I'd ever heard: *Boston was raising the qualifying time to three hours!* I had a chance, as I had run a personal best marathon a couple of years earlier in 2:53. All I had to do was repeat that performance. To do that, I returned to the 'scene of the crime,' the Jacksonville Marathon in January of 1987. I wasn't in particularly great shape, but I had my sights focused on breaking three hours. Come hell or high water, I was going to make it. And I did, running 2:56 despite experiencing gigantic blisters on the bottoms of both feet and one of the worst cases of hypothermia ever seen in the state of Florida. Boston, look out; a frustrated ex-Boy Scout and ex-basketball player was on his way!

April 20, 1987. Boston, Massachusetts. 55 degrees. Light mist falling. Light headwind. I ran the 26.2 miles from Hopkinton to Boston in 2:53:18 and it was all over much too soon. The feeling of accomplishment *just running* on these hallowed roads was overwhelming. There were fans cheering along the entire length of the course. It was my personal mission not to disappoint any of them. And I didn't. One other person I didn't disappoint was me. For once, I had set a goal I desperately wanted–one I felt was the ultimate achievement for a runner of my abilities … that had to be *earned*–and I made it.

When I crossed the finish line, the feeling of accomplishment was overwhelming. It's hard to describe, but suffice it to say that I have only felt that way two other times in my life: (1) when the minister proclaimed that Cindy and I were 'husband and wife,' and (2) the first time I held my oldest son Justin in my arms after his premature birth. You may know the feeling from an experience in your life: a large knot forms in your throat and you're incapable of talking as your sense of personal pride has pushed aside your ability to speak.

I'll never forget how proud I felt when a Boston Marathon volunteer draped a medal around my neck for completing the 91st running of the B.A.A. Boston Marathon. Never. Life can be wonderful when your wish upon a star comes true.

1988 Jacksonville Marathon–Moments before a Personal Best

<u>The One I'll Always Remember</u>

Runners, as a rule, remember their marathons. There is always something about each and every one of them that leaves a unique, indelible impression in a runner's mind. Naturally, some of the impressions are clearer and more vivid than others. For me, the memory of November 6, 1994 will always be crystal clear.

My son Josh (age nine) and I drove to Birmingham the afternoon of Saturday, November 5 as I was going to run the Vulcan Marathon the next morning. I had gotten approval from the Race Director for Josh to 'pace' me on his bicycle as long as we didn't interfere with other competitors in the race. Josh assured me that he was in shape to peddle 26 miles (even after I told him it would take over three hours!), so we were all set for a unique father-and-son activity.

After we checked into the hotel in Birmingham Saturday night, Josh and I went looking for the expo. Unfortunately we missed the expo by 30 minutes, so we decided to return to the room for some much-needed sleep before our 'big day.' Before we actually went to sleep, Josh mirrored everything I did. I drank a bottle of Gatorade; Josh drank a bottle of Gatorade. I ate a Powerbar; Josh ate a Powerbar. I drank some water; Josh drank some water. I went to the bathroom; Josh went to the bathroom. You get the idea.

The next morning, Josh and I were up three hours before race time (my norm). Again, Josh followed my exact (pre-race) routine: he even tied and retied his shoelaces several times like I invariably do before every race. A small passenger van carried us to the starting line. Josh and I managed to squeeze ourselves (and his tiny bicycle) into the back luggage compartment of the van for the (thankfully!) short ride. We arrived at the starting line a mere ten minutes before the start of the race. I hurriedly picked up my race number and lined up behind all the runners (maybe 300 in all) near the starting line. Once the 'start' command was given, Josh and I held back until all the runners had ventured out onto the course. When everyone was a good 300 yards past the starting line, we began *our* marathon.

The race went by quickly; *too quickly*, in fact. Josh was a fantastic 'pacer,' as he rode his bicycle in a steady, unobtrusive manner the entire time. He was sure that I didn't miss any of the sights either. After all, it isn't everyday we got to go to Birmingham! For the longest time, Josh kept a verbal tally of how many runners we passed (*'that's 34, dad'*). Listening to Josh talk, he almost had me convinced that it was *him* who was competing. Twice I stopped to answer nature's call, and Josh got *really* impatient ('Dad, we're getting *passed!*'). Josh peddled furiously with his tiny legs, successfully negotiating the course, although there were two lengthy uphill stretches in the final ten miles where he needed a slight 'push.'

As we crossed the finish line, Josh asked if he would get a finisher's medal. I explained to the volunteer what Josh had done, and she wanted to give him a medal, but an official was within earshot and quickly nixed the idea. I told Josh that he had earned *my* medal; after all, I couldn't have done it without him. We went back to the hotel for a quick shower (we were in a hurry, as Josh had soccer practice back home later that afternoon), and as we were about to get into the van to leave, Josh asked if I had won an award. I told him there wasn't a chance of that, but he insisted I at least ask. I found the Race Director, asked if I'd won an award, and wouldn't you know I finished 2nd in my age group! Prior to that day, I had *never* won an award in a marathon. As I was in a hurry to leave, the R.D. went ahead and gave me my trophy. I walked over to Josh to show him what 'we' had won, and he was ecstatic. "Gee, dad, we won a medal *and* a trophy!'

When we got home, Josh couldn't wait to show our awards to everyone—mom, brother, neighbors, family dog. Once everyone got a glimpse of them, Josh proceeded upstairs to clean off a spot on the bookcase, where he placed the trophy and draped the medal over it. To this day, *OUR* awards have stayed in place exactly as Josh placed them back in 1994. So has the memory of that marathon weekend.

Marathon Man
By Bob Dalton

(Originally appeared in the *Georgia Runner*, May 1998)

Editor's Comment: Bob Dalton 'introduced' me to the running population. If he had only waited six or seven more years, he might have called me 'Ultra Marathon Man' and beaten Dean Karnazes to the punch.

If anyone deserved the above title, it is certainly Scott Ludwig. This 43-year-old University of Florida graduate recently completed his 50th marathon this past Thanksgiving Day in Atlanta. In fact, he has run the Atlanta Marathon 15 times in addition to six in Jacksonville and four in Boston. Boston is his favorite but says 'Others I would recommend are Chicago, Chickamauga, St. George (in Utah), the Vulcan, and Silicon Valley.' He should know. He's done them all—and then some.

His most memorable was his first Boston in 1987. 'I ran a 2:53 and at that time it was my PR (personal record). You never forget your first Boston—there's nothing like it for an amateur runner.' His least favorite is the New York City Marathon ('they treat you like a number, not a runner') and the most difficult would be Grandfather Mountain ('almost all uphill'). Another memorable marathon for Scott was the 1994 Vulcan Marathon. 'My (then) nine year old son, Josh, paced me on his bicycle the whole way. I came in second in my age group that day, and Josh proudly displays 'our' trophy on the bookcase in the den.' His best marathon time, 2:48, was run in Jacksonville in 1988. His PR's for shorter races are equally impressive: 17:12 for the 5K in 1986 in Sawgrass, Florida and 36:14 for the 10K in 1995 at the Piedmont Classic. His forte is and will remain marathons, however. He'll tell you, 'the longer the race, the better I do.'

When asked how he got into the sport, Scott says, 'I started running in 1978, as my two professors in graduate school were runners and they got me interested. That, plus the fact I gained almost 30 pounds the first year after I got married.' You would never know looking at him today that he was once overweight. Now he says, 'The more I run, the more I get to eat.' The only dietary concession he makes is avoiding food he doesn't like. This includes chocolate (!), coconut, liver, and raisins.

Scott averages 90 miles per week, including a 20-miler on Sundays with 10-14 the other six days. He normally gets these runs in at 4:00 in the morning due to his work schedule. Amazingly, he says he 'hopes to cut back to 75 miles per week next year.'

Scott also has another record going–that of running every day consecutively, or, as it's known in the parlance of those who practice it, running a 'streak.' Scott says, 'I have run every day since November 30, 1978, so I recently completed my 19th year. During that time, I've run almost 62,000 miles, so I've averaged almost nine miles a day during that time. I consider three miles a minimum requirement to constitute a run, although I understand most runners count one mile as a run.'

Scott admits there were a couple of times when he was ready to give it up. 'January of 1981, I decided to end my streak while vacationing in Pennsylvania, but I ran three miles at 11:30 p.m. in three feet of snow to keep it going. Also, I partied really hard one Friday night in 1984 and I didn't wake up until 4:00 p.m. Saturday. I managed to fight through seven miles, however.'

Scott is quick to add, however, 'I would not recommend starting a streak to anyone. However, I must point out that at some point in time it simply becomes as simple as brushing your teeth. I'm thinking this was somewhere around the 14 year mark for me.' Last time he checked, Scott's streak record was 9th in the nation.

When asked about his goals, Scott replies, 'Short term, I would like to win a 'major' ultramarathon. I realize this is setting a high goal, but I figure I may as well try to focus on what I do best.' Long term goals are just as ambitious. 'I have decided on three goals: 100,000 miles, 1,000 races, and 100 marathons. I would like to concentrate more on ultras in the near future. I've run four of them so far, including 101 miles in a 24 hour endurance race.' His biggest ultra win was the

Atlanta Fat Ass 50K in 1995, less than one month after he became a Masters runner. He won it in a time of three hours and 48 minutes.

One goal already realized was Scott's attempt to run across the state. 'I attempted to run across Georgia from Columbus to Savannah along Highway 280–a distance of 280 miles–in the fall of 1982. I made it through the morning of the fourth day after covering 159 miles, but had to quit as my knees were killing me' (due to running toward traffic the entire time on the crown of the road). Not one to give up easily, Scott continued to train and run and made another attempt ten years later in the fall of 1992. This time he made it, covering the entire distance in just over six days. It also helped that his company, J. C. Penney, sponsored him, as it was a fund raiser for the United Way. He was able to raise approximately $10,000 during the effort.

One other goal closer to home that Scott wants to do is work with his sons, Justin and Josh, on their running abilities. Who knows? If they start their streak now, they might eventually surpass their old man–or make that 'Marathon Man.'

<u>BOSTON</u>

It's no secret that the Boston Marathon is my favorite running event. When I first started running and thought that me qualifying for Boston was a pipe dream, I would always write 'Boston—not this year' in my running journal on Patriot's Day. I was eventually able to realize my dream of lining up on the starting line in Hopkinton when (a) Boston's qualifying standards were relaxed and (b) I got faster.

Now that I reached a Boston 'milestone' by running my 10th Boston Marathon (and 100th marathon overall) in 2003, I'll recap my 10 runs from Hopkinton to Boston:

1987

My first Boston, and my most memorable. Not only was it my first run on those hallowed roads, but I managed a P.R. (2:53:18, half-marathon split in 1:25:41) as well. My official place of finish was 980th. I stayed with two friends who lived in Connecticut, and their support throughout the race was amazing. So was our post-race pizza-and-beer fest.

1994

I was content to 'rest on my laurels' after my first Boston (how do you improve upon a P.R. in your first Boston Marathon?), but Al Barker and Valerie Reynolds were quite 'persuasive' in their quest for me to make a return engagement. I'm glad they were, as it's become a part of my annual calendar that I have found I miss when I do without (as I discovered in 1997). I ran 3:04:18 (half-marathon split in 1:29:11), good for 1,655th place. I noticed the Atlanta Track Club (ATC) Masters Team placed 60th (I was a member of the team, but not on the official 'Boston roster'), and also noticed my time was faster than all three members of the team. One other interesting fact about the race: Al was in front of me for most of the race, and when I caught up to him around mile 20 an official race photograph was taken—with Al and I both in the frame. An omen? Most definitely.

1994 Boston Marathon—Side by side with Al

1995

I competed as a member of the ATC Masters Team and ran a respectable 2:59:36 (half-marathon split in 1:24:49). I finished in 1,015[th], and our team placed 11th.

1996

The 100th Anniversary of the Boston Marathon, with over 36,000 runners! I ran 2:59:57 (half-marathon split in 1:24:29), good for 2,245[th] place (and our ATC team finished 28th).

Celebrating the 100th anniversary of the Boston Marathon

1998

I paced my friend Valerie Reynolds, taking photographs all along the route (particularly at Wellesley College!). 'We' ran 3:21:22 (half-marathon split in 1:41:01), good for 3,458[th] place.

1999

My son Josh accompanied me to Boston, and he had a great time (and by extension, so did *I*). He got a lot of autographs at the runner's expo, and enjoyed participating in the pre-and post-race pasta parties. I ran 2:58:53 (half-marathon split in 1:27:41), good for 722nd place (my highest Boston finish). The ATC Masters Team I was on (the 'B' Team) placed 14th, while the 'A' Team finished 5th. It gave me some personal satisfaction to know my time was faster than one of the three runners on the 'A' Team.

The night of the race my Mom called me at my hotel in Boston to tell me that my Grandmother ('Nana') had passed away … yesterday. She didn't want me to run Boston with a heavy heart, she explained. I ran Boston that day in a pair of shoes (my personal racing favorite, the Adidas Adios) that I bought with money Nana gave me *specifically* to buy a pair of running shoes. I have thought of Nana every year since as I stand among the finest marathoners in the world at the starting line of the world's greatest marathon on Patriot's Day. I'm quite sure I always will.

2000

I ran a less-than-inspiring 3:04:18 (half-marathon split in an encouraging 1:27:09), good for 1,688th place. I was nursing a pull in my right hamstring, and the pain caught up with me in the hills of Newton. My ATC team (again, Team *'B')* finished in 43rd, although my time was faster than *two* of the three runners on the 'A' Team—which finished 21st.

2001

Another uninspiring performance (3:05:54) following an encouraging half-marathon split (1:28:11). I finished 1,291st, and wondered how I could move up almost 400 places over last year with a time over a minute slower.

2002

A *very* uninspiring performance (3:10:56) after yet *another* encouraging half-marathon split (1:29:32). I finished 2,306th—more in line with my drop off from the previous year.

2003

My 100th lifetime marathon! I had been targeting this race for over two years for this milestone in my running career. To make it 'special,' I ran the race from finish line to the start for a 'warm-up,' and then ran the race itself. I ran 3:56:15 (half-marathon split of 1:48:49—not too encouraging), good for 9,703[rd] place. (Note: I ran the 'backwards route' in a respectable 3:30). However, all these numbers are meaningless. The only thing that mattered was that *I ran my 100th marathon in the greatest marathon in the world!*

I consider running different marathons in April: London … Big Sur. And then I think about how I felt on Patriot's Day in 1997, not being a part of my absolute favorite running celebration.

You know where to find me on Patriot's Day.

My 28 Mile Warm-up

I decided to do this at some point in 2001 when I mentioned that the 2003 Boston Marathon would in all likelihood be my 100th lifetime marathon. Al Barker innocently suggested I run the course twice, by running from Boston (at the finish line) to Hopkinton (the starting line) and then the actual marathon to commemorate the occasion. As those who know me would expect, I said I would. At that time, Al said he would do it with me.

Al suggested we make it known that we were doing a 'Boston Out-and-Back' so that we would get media coverage, PR, or whatever else we were due. I explained to a BAA official in February what our intentions were, primarily to make sure we would be *allowed* to run the course in reverse prior to the noon start of the actual marathon. I was told it was acceptable, as long as we were off the course by 11:00 a.m. The next thing I know Don Makson from WCVB Channel 5 in Boston (an ABC affiliate) sends me an E-mail asking for specifics of our upcoming adventure. Once I did, he said he'd get with me the week before the marathon to go over the details of their 'coverage' of the event.

Sometime in March, Al hit me with some bad news: he wasn't going to do the out-and-back with me. He didn't think his back would hold up for 52+ miles. Of course, since I already stated I was going to do it, *DARKSIDE* regulations dictated that I *had* to do it (besides, if I remember correctly, this was one of the rules *I* suggested). The week before the marathon, Don Makson called and advised me to find Heather Unruh in Hopkinton Commons for a *live* interview at 10:20 a.m. I decided I would start my journey at 6:00 a.m., as I wanted to run the first 26.2 miles in four hours.

Race morning, I left a little early: 5:45 to be exact. I wanted to allow myself a little extra time in case I got off course (I took a map with me). As I expected, Al had second thoughts about *not* joining me the instant I left our hotel room. He expressed regret about backing out, but offered to take my change of clothes to the starting line for me.

I couldn't believe how the course looked without the spectators and other runners … *DIFFERENT!* So different, in fact, I had to look at the map several times. Each time I looked at the map, I was reminded of one small detail I overlooked: it was impossible for me to *read* it without my glasses … which I didn't have with me. Not to worry: I could just ask someone for directions. Certainly all Bostonians know the route, right? Wrong! Of the 20 people I asked if I was on the proper course, only 10 knew. Naturally, some of those that 'knew' really didn't. In time, I could tell the difference between a definitive 'yes' and an 'I'll never see this nut job again so I'm *telling* him yes to *get rid of him* yes.'

Fortunately, I only ran 15 minutes off course, losing the route somewhere near Beacon Street. Once I was sufficiently lost, I retraced my steps until I got back on course. Thinking back, I don't know how I got lost, but I think it was because I started following the Marathon banners on the street poles and once I felt confident I *couldn't* get lost, I ran out of banners … and got lost.

Once I returned to the course, I began following the porta-johns and/or the ESPN towers. This worked out a lot better, as these two objects were a lot larger than the fine print on my map. The run to the start was pretty uneventful, except for these few 'highlights:'

- 5 or 6 people along the course yelled 'hey, I heard about you on TV/the radio.' No one, however, asked for my autograph or wanted to take my picture.

- One man in a car at a stop light offered me a ride to the start, even though he was going in the opposite direction.

- Too many people to remember were kind enough to tell me I was 'running the wrong way.'

- I passed one other runner doing what I was doing but his 'out' distance (of *his* out-and-back) was only 12 miles. He was basically walking, taking photographs, and training for the Western States 100.

- Wellesley College is amazingly quiet at 8:00 a.m. Are there *really* students living there?

- Water is hard to find along the course prior to noon. In fact, I found that in some gas stations, when you ask for 'water' the attendant will give you a key to the bathroom.

- My unofficial time for the actual 26.2 miles (excluding the 'extra' 15 minutes) was 3 hours 30 minutes … the time I was hoping to run in the actual marathon.

I arrived at the starting line around 9:30, almost an hour early for my 10:20 interview. I stretched out on the road for almost 30 minutes (still thirsty!) before I began looking for the Channel 5 tent. Once I found the tent and met Heather, she took me to their hospitality tent where I drank cranberry juice (I couldn't find any water). She then conducted a 'practice' interview (to be honest, it was better than the live one), which included the following exchanges:

Heather: Boston today will be your 100th lifetime marathon. So the run OUT here this morning was your 99th, right?
Scott: No, I only count official marathons in my total.
Heather: What do you call the run out here then?
Scott: A 28-mile warm-up.
Heather: So where's Al?
Scott: He's physically exhausted after winning his age group three weeks ago at a marathon in Macon.
Heather: (Looking at my singlet) What is the DARKSIDE Running Club?
Scott: A group of people I run with who consider what I'm doing today normal.
Heather: Are all runners as good-looking as you?
Scott: Don't count on it, sister.

OK, so actually only her first two questions were real; the final three I imagined. But I *did* have those answers ready anyway … just in case she asked!

After the interview I made my way to the 'Athlete's Village' to meet up with Al, Paula and Keith Wright (who I was going to run with in the actual marathon). I was eager to put on a fresh, clean running outfit (including a BRAND NEW *DARKSIDE* racing singlet) only to find that *someone* had accidentally spilled a bottle of Gatorade *inside* my bag, saturating my entire change of clothing. Fortunately, it was cool in the morning so I didn't perspire much and didn't really need a fresh outfit, so wearing the same outfit again wasn't too big an inconvenience (but don't tell Al … guilt is *good!*).

The marathon itself? Pretty uneventful. I waited for Keith at the two-mile mark and ran with him for eight miles. At that point we lost contact, which I used to my advantage. For the last sixteen miles, every time I needed a walk break, I looked back over my shoulder and called out Keith's name … as if I was actually *looking* for him.

One last thing: comedian Will Ferrell passed me around the 25 mile mark, and I didn't have the legs to stay with him. Not to worry: he didn't actually *qualify* for Boston; he was invited because he's a celebrity (according to *some* people). Since he wasn't an official runner, he wasn't really there (another *DARKSIDE* rule!).

<u>100 * and Counting</u>
(Not birthdays … marathons!)*

Although now that I think about it, my body has been *feeling* like its 100 years old lately. Completing 100 Marathons is a goal I set for myself about two years ago. Ten years ago I would have never thought it possible, but after I crossed over to the DARKSIDE, I knew it was only a matter of time.

Looking back over my running logs, I have found some interesting statistics and some worthwhile information to pass along. Here it is, in no particular order:

<u>*Total Number of Marathons*</u>
100

<u>*Total Time Spent Running 100 Marathons*</u>
13.6 Days (or 326 Hours)

Average Time/Marathon
3:15:30

Total Marathons Under 3 Hours
15
(the most surprising statistic I found ... especially now that a 3 hour marathon is
virtually unattainable)

Total Marathons between 3 hours and 3:01
4
(if it weren't for 'nature stops', I could have had 19 marathons under 3 hours)

Number of Marathons I Paced Someone
36
(including Kelly Murzynsky*, Al Barker, Paula May, Valerie Reynolds, Ed Rush,
Jerry Shoemaker, Thomas Jones, Earl Tyler, Sue Bozgoz, Eric Huguelet, Paul
Anderson, Gary Griffin, Fred Johnson*, Nancy Stewart, Sandy Geisel, Prince
Whatley, Keith Wright, Richard Penland*, and Paul Wilson)—* actually, I'm
not sure who was pacing who!

Most Marathons by Month
November–31
(February–17, January–13)

Most Marathons in One Year
10 (1998)

Fewest Marathons in One Year
0 (1980)

Number of Decades Running a Marathon
4 (70's through 00's)

Most Marathons by State
Georgia (46)
(Florida–11, Massachusetts–10)

Number of States Running a Marathon
16
(Georgia, Massachusetts, Florida, North Carolina, South Carolina, New York,

Minnesota, Utah, Alabama, Nevada, Virginia, Maryland, Pennsylvania, Washington DC, California, Illinois)

Fastest Marathon
Jacksonville, 1988 (2:48:41)
(38 degrees, steady rain, excessive winds, hypothermia for a full hour after the race … in other words, a PERFECT day!)
St. George 1994–2:48:45; St George 1999–2:53:15

Slowest Marathon
Brunswick 1979 (4:03:00)
Although my official race time was 3:58. I always trust my watch, however, as I know when 'it' crosses the starting line.
Chesapeake Bay Bridge 2002–3:57:52; Boston 2003–3:56:15

Most Memorable
Vulcan 1994–Josh paced me on his bike; I won my first marathon award.
Jacksonville 1987–the first time I qualified for Boston
Boston 1987–My first Boston Marathon (and at that time, my PR)

Favorite
Boston (as if there was any doubt)
Honorable mention: Atlanta, Tybee Island, Vulcan (RIP)

Least Favorite
Brunswick (no aid, no traffic control, 90 degree heat, and to top it all off, a loss of consciousness after the race)
This race was mercifully canceled after the 1979 event
Honorable mention: Huntsville, Baltimore, Bay Bridge, Mercedes, Las Vegas and New York City

Most Scenic Course
St. George
Honorable Mention: Steamtown

Least Scenic Course
Brunswick
Run out and back on two-lane highway
Honorable Mention: Las Vegas–one way run on two-lane highway

Most Over-hyped
Marine Corps
Honorable Mention; New York City

Most Underrated
Atlanta
Honorable mention; Tybee Island

Number of Back-to-Back Marathon Pairs
4
Chickamauga/Vulcan–November 7&8, 1998
Tybee Island/Callaway Gardens–February 5&6, 2000
Tybee Island/Callaway Gardens–February 3&4, 2001
Tybee Island/Callaway Gardens–February 2&3, 2002

Only Month I've Never Run a Marathon
August

Hopefully you found something to help you, to motivate you, or to entertain you (maybe all three!). As for me, it was fun 'reliving' some of these marathons. Even after 100 marathons over the course of 24 years, I can still recall most of them as if I ran them yesterday.

Maybe 'tomorrow' I can review my second 100.

Boston Swan Song (2004)

Up until this year, I had run in ten Boston Marathons. My first, 1n 1987, was like a dream–finally making it to Hopkinton ... passing Wellesley College ... running a (then) P.R. of 2:53. After that, I ran every Boston Marathon since 1994 (skipping 1997–a mistake), always referring to Patriot's Day as 'Christmas in April.' I couldn't imagine doing anything else on the third Monday in April. This was the top of the mountain, and I was proud (and yes, ecstatic) to be there. I didn't think I would ever lose that feeling.

I was wrong.

Boston has provided some wonderful memories in my running career. My afore-mentioned first Boston, after an eight year quest to get there ... running the

100th anniversary of the marathon in 1996 with 36,000 other 'guests' ... being a part of a top ten masters team in 1998 ... running the course from finish to start and then start to finish in 2003 ... making the turn on Boylston Street in front of my 13 year old son Josh on my way to a 2:58 in 1999. I've made the journey to Boston to celebrate the first Boston Marathon for many of my closest training partners: Valerie Reynolds, Brenda Davis, Paula May, Trish Vlastnik, Kelly Murzynzky, Keith Wright, Eric Huguelet, and Prince Whatley to name a few.

For some reason, Boston didn't feel the same to me this year. I felt that way Sunday afternoon (the day before the marathon) when our group had to take two subway rides followed by one shuttle ride to get to the expo to pick up our race numbers (for the past several years it was only a short three block walk from our hotel). Of course, to return we had to take one shuttle ride and two subway rides back to the hotel, later followed by two subway rides to the pasta dinner and yet two *more* subway rides back to the hotel. I was already disappointed the entry fee had increased from $75 last year to $95 this year (has your *salary* ever increased 27 percent in one year?), and thinking back to the 45 minute wait at the airport luggage carousel only magnified my feelings. I never thought I would NOT want to be a part of the Boston Marathon.

I thought wrong.

I was certain I would wake up race morning and my attitude would change. However, I began my morning by waking up with my first ever case of vertigo. Every time I moved my head, the room would keep moving in that direction ... even after my head was still. Then, when I finally had enough balance to get out of bed, I noticed the battery in my chronograph had died during the night. However, once I put on my running attire and shoes I knew things would be brighter when we all headed to the bus that would take us to the starting line in Hopkinton.

I was wrong. Again.

We waited two hours and fifteen minutes for the bus. Standing in the shade of the tall buildings in Boston, freezing our collective asses off. Starving ... thirsty ... joints stiffening. But wait, a volunteer tells us that seven school buses are on the way. We see the buses turn down our street ... only to see them drive by as they're ALREADY FULL OF CHILDREN! Yeah, they were *school buses* all right!

Then the volunteer tells us the buses have been delayed by the parade in Boston commemorating Patriot's Day. Nice planning, Boston Athletic Association! Paula used her cell phone to call City Hall to tell them there were 500 maratho-ners stranded at Boston Commons, almost certain to miss the starting gun at noon. City Hall hung up on her. Twice. Around 10:30 (90 minutes before the start and still awaiting a 60 minute ride to Hopkinton) a bus finally arrived to pick us up. Things were looking up.

Or not.

Following a 'rushing the stage at an out-of-hand rock concert' boarding of the bus (no fatalities to report–that's the good news), we were greeted on the bus by the alluring smell of ... *vomit* (that's the bad news)! Yes, we were on the 'vomit bus.' I failed to mention earlier that Paula had used a severely 'soiled' porta-john at Boston Commons, and as she was 'tidying up the area' inside–with her shorts around her ankles–she was 'greeted' by another runner as she had forgotten to lock the door behind her. So the smell of vomit was nothing to her. But for the rest of us ... *open the freakin' windows!*

As we arrived in Hopkinton–a mere 30 minutes before the starting gun and fac-ing a 20 minute walk to the starting line–we realized we hadn't eaten anything all day, as we were all looking forward to a bagel or two at the Athlete's Village prior to the start of the race. Of course, by the time we arrived, they were fresh out of bagels. I felt I could 'rely on the kindness of strangers' and find something to eat along the course.

Wrong again.

At least there would be some cold water and sports drink along the course to combat the soon-to-be 86 degree heat that we would be facing.

Wrong again. At least the temperature didn't reach the *record* high ... of 87 degrees.

The drinks were 'room temperature' at best. Let me be the first to say that warm fluids do NOT refresh you when you're running 26 miles in 80+ degree heat.

How did I run, you ask? 'Run' being the operative word, let's just say that I 'ran' the first half of the race in 1:45 followed by a whole lot of walking the second half (in fact, for the first time ever, I received a race photo proof of me walking. Thanks, a lot Marathon Foto ... and while I'm thinking about it, *kiss my ass*). It might have been my imagination, but I think the girls at Wellesley were quieter than normal this year.

Wellesley allows a runner a chance to 'stop and smell the roses' so to speak. This year I saw a coed holding a sign that said *'Kiss me, I'm a Georgia Peach.'* Since I was in dire need of a break anyway at the time ...

Once I crossed the finish line, it took me another hour to get back to my room. I was in such bad shape my *shins* cramped up (can they even *do* that?)! I made it a few blocks, and had to sit on the sidewalk and figure out where I was, 'cuz I was seeing buildings I'd never seen in all my (now) eleven trips to Boston. After asking for directions (twice, as I immediately forgot after the first time I asked), I made it to a subway station and used the restroom (I'm pretty sure I was in the *men's* room). I made it to the hotel lobby, got on the elevator and pushed '17.' There were other people on the elevator, and after five or six stops, I was close to creating a bus-like odor myself, so when the elevator stopped on the 16th floor, I literally *dove* out of the elevator, as I feared I was going to vomit. I didn't, but I sat on the 16th floor for 20 minutes before I had the capacity to catch another elevator to the next floor. When I did, I made it to the *door* of my room, and lay down–flat on my back–in front of the door as I couldn't stand up long enough to open it. A young couple ran down the hallway at one point, as they thought I had suffered a heart attack. The hotel doctor was paying a house call to the room next to mine and asked if I was O.K. I said yes. I lied.

I finally got on my knees (my head was spinning ... again) and opened the door and literally crawled to my bed. I lay there for almost an hour before Al returned to the room. All I can say is Al made *me* look <u>*good!!*</u> Eventually I took a shower, although midway through I had to lie in the tub as I was spinning so fast I could no longer stand up. Besides, I was close (once again) to creating a bus-like odor.

At dinner that night (yes, I made it to dinner at our usual post-Boston restaurant, the California Pizza Kitchen), our group had a lot of interesting things to say. Some of the highlights being:

- *I can't believe the difference between qualifying times and race times.*—Todd Davison

- *Today was a day that required walking the up hills. And by 'up hills', I mean the flats too.*—Al Barker

- *This one will be remembered as the Boston Death March.*–Paula May

- *I ran this marathon slower than I did last ... and last year, I ran 28 miles before I even ran the marathon.*—that one was mine

- *Years from now, people will look back on this race and we'll be remembered as heroes.*—Prince Whatley

As I think about it, I think time will prove Prince to be right.

But then, I've been wrong before.

The Olympics Come to Atlanta

Since the 24-Hour Endurance Run didn't look like it had a shot at becoming an Olympic event, I figured the closest I would ever get to the Olympics would be watching them on television. I was wrong, of course, when the 1996 Olympic Games were awarded to the city of ... 'Aht-lahn-tah' ... as the famous announcement heard around the world had pronounced the name of our fair city.

As you can probably guess, that meant I was going to be there–in person–when my favorite Olympic event, the marathon, was held. I was very familiar with the course they would be running, as it also doubled as the Atlanta Marathon on Thanksgiving Day. The course was difficult, primarily due to the number of hills along the course. In fact, at the part of the marathon widely recognized as 'the wall,' the runners would be asked to run up the infamous (Piedmont Hospital) 'cardiac hill' on world-famous Peachtree Street. It would be interesting to see how the finest marathoners in the world, both male and female, would handle this same course in the worst possible months to run a marathon, July and August, respectively.

The women ran first, on Sunday, July 28th to be exact. My personal favorite, Uta Pippig failed to finish ... as did 20 other women. In fact, over 23 percent of the women didn't complete the 26.2 miles. Fatuma Roba of Ethiopia won the gold medal in a time of 2:26:05. The top U.S. woman was Ann Marie Lauck, who finished in 10th place with a fine 2:31:30. I first met Ann Marie at a four-mile race in Atlanta several years earlier that she won, finishing over three minutes ahead of me.

The men ran the following Sunday, on August 4th. The men apparently learned something from the women, as only 13 men (slightly over 10 percent) failed to finish. Josiah Thugwane of the Republic of South Africa won the gold medal in a time of 2:12:36. In a really close finish for the three medals, only eight seconds separated the top three runners. The top U.S. man was Keith Brantley, who finished 28th in a time of 2:18:17. Keith, by the way, is a fellow University of Florida graduate. In fact, several years ago at the Barnesville Buggy Days 10K, I wore a University of Florida singlet, and while I was warming up, someone mistook me for Keith. Of course, once the race began this mistake was quickly corrected. But, I digress.

Should you ever see a replay of either of the two 1996 Olympic Marathons, pay particular attention as the leaders approach the 17-mile mark (near Phipps Plaza on Peachtree Street.). If you look really close, you will be able to spot yours truly cheering on the participants. Of course, if you'd just like to borrow my copy on video, you can watch it in slow motion and freeze frame at the appropriate time. By the way, I ran the Atlanta Marathon in 3:06:29 that year. That time was faster than five of the Olympic marathon women and one of the men. If I were a citizen of Afghanistan, 'I coulda been a contendah!'

You Have GOT to be Sh#**ing Me

Normally, my biggest inconvenience while running is having to make 'pit stops' to take care of Nature's Call ... the *first* one.

However, in the fall of 1999, I had three experiences with Nature Call number *two* that I wouldn't wish on my worst enemy. Actually, I *would* wish them on my worst enemy (stupid figure of speech!).

On October 9th I was driving to north Atlanta to run the Reagan Marathon. I had run the St. George Marathon the week before in 2:53 and was in fairly good shape (my usual recovery after a marathon takes five days, so a full week of recovery was 'gravy') and thought I had a good chance at the master's title. On my way, I had to answer call #2 so desperately that I stopped one exit short of the exit for the race to 'take care of business' at a gas station. When I returned to my van, it wouldn't start, and it was making noises more peculiar than the ones my stomach had been making for the past ten minutes. I couldn't decide between calling a taxi to take me to the race or calling a tow truck to pick up the van. As I feared that if I selected the former I wouldn't have a van when I returned (I was in a bad section of town), I selected the latter. Three hours later I was at the dealer where I purchased the van ... 23 miles from home! As it was now raining, I got a plastic bag from the service manager for my wallet, checkbook, clothing, etc and took off for home ... on foot. Hills, rain, wind, five pounds of 'baggage' in my hand ... I finally made it home yet *another* three hours later. Now that the day was pretty much wasted, I opened a beer and called a friend who ran the marathon to see how it turned out. Adding insult to injury, I learned that the male winner only ran a 3:08 ... and won three hundred dollars! And the masters winner ran a 3:15 and won $150. As it turned out, the net 'loss' for the day was: $25 entry fee + $300 I think I coulda won + $77 van repair = $402. Pretty expensive for a nature call. And that's without adding the expense of the seven or eight beers I needed to 'soften the blow' of the day's tragic events.

Experience number two found me in Birmingham, Alabama on November 5th for the Vulcan Marathon. My wife Cindy made the trip west with me, and we stayed in a local hotel the night before the race. While Cindy made a trip to the hotel lobby, I used the restroom to answer Nature's Call once again. When I finished, I discovered that the doorknob turned–and turned, and turned–but failed to open the door. I was trapped inside for almost an hour, missing my beloved Florida Gators beating the dickens out of an overwhelmed and undermanned Vanderbilt football team on television in the next room. Cindy finally returned to let me out (at halftime, no less), laughing at my expense. It was poetic justice when she did the same thing several hours later (locking herself in the very same restroom). Although this experience was not as dramatic as the first one, neither one compared to the next one, which can best be described as traumatic.

I was in Chesapeake, Virginia with my parents over the Christmas holidays. Cindy, the boys and I were leaving December 26th (a Sunday) to return to Atlanta, and we wanted to get an early start (as it was almost an 11 hour drive home). I wanted to get my run in before we left, so I took off at 4:00 a.m. for a 12-miler. Picture 25 degrees with a 30 mile-per-hour wind in the early morning darkness the day after Christmas. And a *Sunday* at that. Not a living soul to be found anywhere. As I reached the absolute farthest point away from my parent's house, I urgently needed to find a restroom to take care of (yet again) call #2. Now, it's about 4:45 a.m. on the Sunday after Christmas, and *nothing* is open. Unbelievably, I came across a gas station with (a) the men's room *unlocked*, (b) an ample supply of toilet paper, and (c) a sink with running water *and soap*! And the restroom was actually clean! Happy Holidays, right? WRONG!! Once I took care of business, guess what wouldn't open?! The damn door! I was trapped! I instantly knew how a mouse caught in a mousetrap feels, except I couldn't escape by chewing off my tail. I did everything I could to escape. I banged on the door while screaming at the top of my lungs (I think the howling wind was louder than my screaming–besides, there wasn't anyone to hear me). I tried to crawl through the vent which I thought might lead to the inside of the gas station where I might find a telephone (I didn't have anything to unscrew the bolts in the vent, although I did tear apart a trash can so I could use a piece of the metal as a 'screwdriver'). After I was a good 30 minutes into a major panic attack, I desperately kicked the door handle 'karate style.' And guess what? It *worked!* Happy Holidays–I was FREE! Scared sh#@less, maybe, but free! I just knew I was going to be locked inside until Monday morning when the gas station opened for business, because no one in my family knew my running route (go ahead and feel free to learn from my mistake) and would have no earthly clue where to look for me.

Up until this point, some of my friends knew of the first experience in October, all of my friends knew of the second experience in November (thanks, Cindy), and only my inner circle of friends knew of the third experience in December. Until now.

A Sprint Down Memory Lane

Although the date for this event coincides with that of many other marathons in the southeast (Tallahassee, Pensacola, Myrtle Beach among others), I would highly recommend the Five Point of Life Marathon in Gainesville, Florida. 2006 was the inaugural year for this event; I'm sure many more will follow.

My wife Cindy—like me, a University of Florida alumnus—took the opportunity to return to 'Sin City' (as Gainesville was known during our days of campus life) to enjoy the sights and sounds of the home of our beloved orange and blue— one of the finest places on the planet.

As we drove through Gainesville the day before the event, I pointed out the gas station where—in 1977—gas skyrocketed to 77 cents a gallon … the movie theater where we saw 'Halloween' for the first time … the diner where we bought our very first 'Gator Tail,' one of the best-tasting sandwiches you'll find anywhere. Cindy asked me how I remembered so many minute details, seeing as it was almost 30 years ago since we lived there. I told her that being a Navy brat (and having to move every three years), my time at the University of Florida was the longest I had ever lived anywhere in my life up until that point.

Fellow marathon participants Al Barker and Susan Lance joined us for dinner the night before the race. I took the opportunity to teach them a few things about Gainesville: the legend of campus' Century Tower ('A brick falls from the tower for every virgin that graduates from the University of Florida'), the sandpit volleyball courts at the married housing complex where Cindy and I lived in graduate school that were built after our fellow residents and us trampled our courtyard playing volleyball *every night* after class, and that the Carraba's where we were having dinner was built on virtually the exact same spot where the trailer I lived in during my senior year was located. I also pointed out the ABC Liquor Store/ Bar across the street, where Cindy and I spent hours working on our disco moves to Donna Summer songs in between Billy Joel ballads.

Coincidentally, the starting line for the marathon was located less than a quarter mile from the married housing complex we lived in during graduate school. The course took in many of the (both formerly and currently) famous landmarks in Gainesville, including:

- The spot where the original Athletic Attic—now a distant memory—was located (where I bought my very first pair of running shoes in 1978).

- The famous Leonardo's Pizza at Millhopper Square.

- The historic section of Gainesville, including the (also now a distant memory) Great Southern Music Hall, which used to feature the then-unknown comedic talent of one Steve Martin and music of local favorite Tom Petty.

- Second Avenue, home of In-and-Out Burger *(drive-through only!)* and my very own Phi Kappa Tau fraternity (located right next to Alpha Tau Omega, whose yard served as our fraternity's own personal 'outdoor urinal').

- The College of Education, where I spent the better part of two years as an undergraduate.

- Century Tower—it was not surprising to find all of the bricks in place.

- The Arts and Sciences Building, where I spent the better part of my fifteen months in graduate school.

- Ben Hill Griffin Stadium, in which we actually ran a lap inside the breezeways. My 'stadium mile' was a brisk 7:20—which was faster than *any* trip to the bathroom I've ever made during a Florida Gator football game.

- Fraternity Row (thank goodness we ran *down* the hill).

- Lake Alice, home of the meanest, strongest, fastest reptile on earth—the alligator!

- The world-famous and widely-recognized Shands Teaching Hospital.

- Williston Road (a long stretch of three or four miles in which I spotted six runners spread out in front of me, and made it my personal mission to pass each and every one of them—which I did … man, I *love* running in Gainesville!).

- Archer Road and 34th Street (the intersection where my trailer park used to be).

- The finish line on Hull Road which, coincidentally, served as part of the course for the first race I ever ran—the 5-mile Leonardo's Lap (yes, *that* Leonardo) in 1978.

What did I like about the event? The weather was cooperative (cool and overcast), I felt mentally strong the entire race *(Gainesville gives off good running vibes),* the finisher medals were fantastic (an alligator wrapped around a star, the five points of the star signifying the five points of life), and the delicious, hot and plentiful post-race pizza.

The glitches for a first-time marathon of this magnitude were minor, and I'm sure will be worked out prior to next year's event (marathoners having to run *through* the half-marathoners, who started about ¼ mile in front of the marathoners; several mile markers were missing; one mile marker was misplaced—like I said, nothing major). Will I be back next year? Do you really have to ask?

Running Through the (Berlin) Wall

One of the nice things about my new job with Porsche Logistics is that I am required to make an annual business trip to Ludwigsburg, Germany to meet with my counterparts 'across the ocean' to discuss various issues, resolve problems, and drink more than my fair share of German beer. One of the nice things about my *boss* is that he listens to my ideas about when the trip should be scheduled.

As I had never run a marathon in a foreign country, I suggested to him that it might be nice if our 2006 trip would coincide with the Berlin Marathon. His answer: 'Would you prefer to run it before or after the business portion of the trip?'

I immediately downloaded an application form, included my VISA number on it (the application was 90 euros, or I as found out when I received my VISA statement, a little over $119—and that didn't include a race T-shirt), and put it all in the mail. I had one question about the application, however: it asked for my fastest marathon time. Since my fastest marathon was run in 1987 (a time which I ran again in 1994), I was certain they would somehow realize I was past my prime.

Once the business portion of my trip was over, my wife and I (this was Cindy's first trip to Germany) headed northeast towards Berlin. Getting *to* Berlin was the easy part (in spite of all the construction on the Autobahn). Getting *through* Berlin was another story.

The expo was at a convention center on the west side of Berlin, while our hotel was on the east side. The plan was to get to the hotel by 2:00 p.m. Saturday (the race was at 9:00 a.m. on Sunday) and take a train to the expo to pick up my race packet. When we got to Berlin, we missed our exit and ended up–believe it or not–right next to the convention center. After spending 30 minutes finding a parking space, we made it inside the convention center. I was required to stand in lines to (a) find my bib number, (b) receive my bib number, (c) get my chip–which I was required to rent for 31 Euros, of which 25 would be refunded when I returned my chip after the race, (d) ensure my chip was activated, and (e) purchase a race T-shirt (which I declined, although I'm not sure why I had to stand in line to do it). I shopped for a little while–just enough to realize shoes and clothing cost a lot more than they do in the United States.

Now it was time to get to the hotel and get some rest. It was only 4:00 p.m., so I figured I would get a good night's sleep as the hotel was only five or six miles away. Unfortunately for us the marathon sponsors also offered a rollerblade race Saturday afternoon. As we headed east towards our hotel, we found road after road after road closed by the local authorities due to the roller-bladers, although we never caught a glimpse of any actual competitors.

We checked in a little after 7:00 P.M. (if you did the math, you realize it took us over three hours to drive six miles). Actually, with all the roads being closed and after being redirected by the local police an infinite number of times, we probably drove close to 50 miles. Regardless, it was time to get some sleep–after a German beer or two, of course.

Race morning arrived, and Cindy and I took the train to the start of the race–back over in West Berlin. We followed a runner from England and his mother, as it appeared they knew what they were doing (i.e. which train to board, and more importantly, where to get off). The runner–who was running his first marathon–had hopes of breaking four hours. Cindy ended up spending the morning with his mother, as she had several vantage points lined up to see her son compete. Cindy figured since she had all the logistics figured out, she would take advantage of her offer to tag along. I told Cindy that whatever marker they were at, multiply it by five and that's approximately how far into the race I would be (in minutes). For example, at the 15 kilometer mark (remember European marathons are measured in kilometers, not miles), my time would be around 75 minutes (15X5), as I figured I would lock into a pace of eight minutes per mile (or approximately five minutes per kilometer). This was exciting: in all of my previous marathons, I had never run a five minute pace! (I know what you're thinking–so don't even think about raining on my parade!)

I left for my position behind the starting line at 8:00. By 8:30, wearing my over-sized racing bib with the number 4785 (when I received my bib number, I figured I was well back in the pack), I found my assigned starting group–right behind the seeded runners! I came to find out that we were seeded according to our fastest marathon time, which in my case was about 42 minutes faster than I planned on running. It seems our time groups were indicated on our bibs by a small letter on the side; in my case a 'B." It was odd–runners with two digit, three digit and four digit bib numbers were in my time group.

Besides being odd, it was also downright frightening. I honestly thought there was a good possibility I might be trampled, as I had no business being up there with runners capable of running marathons well under three hours. Not only that, almost 40,000 runners were lined up behind me. I thought that perhaps the marathon application was actually requesting projected marathon times (not fastest marathon time), although the meaning was lost in translation from German to English.

Amidst a race soundtrack featuring the theme from the X-Files and an armada of Adidas balloons launched into the air at precisely 9:00 A.M., the race was underway.

I maintained my 'five minute pace' throughout the race, although in all honestly I was a shade quick the first ten miles and a shade (or two) slower the last six. Running a marathon measured in kilometers takes some adjusting–it's mentally tough to know you have markers in the teens, the twenties, the thirties and into the forties before you see the finish line. Then again, they click off a little better than a third faster than they do on a course measured in miles. It's hard to say which is mentally easier based on my sample of one marathon, but personally I would have to go with the old standby–miles.

The course was well-supported by the people of Berlin. With the exception of the glamorous start and the picturesque finish through the Brandenburg Gate (one of the few remaining sections of the Berlin Wall), you would think you were in any other major city in the world. Besides all the signage through the city being in German, the local sports drink tasting like liquid aspirin, and one of the latter aid stations serving hot tea, the only thing that stood out in my mind was the music I heard along the course. There were 15 or so musical performers along the course, and if I didn't know better, I would swear that a large truck carrying 1970's American sheet music exploded in the middle of Berlin. Ever hear a punk rock version of Sunny (*Sunny, once so true, I love youuuuuuuu*)? I did. Three times. Then the standard version two more times on the radio as we drove back to Frankfurt to fly home.

I crossed the finish line in 3:31:52, and if I wasn't deceived by the finish (I thought we were finished as we ran through the Brandenburg Gate–I came to find out we had another quarter mile or so after that), I might have hit that magical 5:00 pace. My pace ended up being 5:02 (OK, OK–that's per kilometer), and I can't explain how Cindy missed me at the three check points she was at along the course. Most likely she had trouble multiplying without a calculator....

My official finish was 4,550[th], so I figured I was passed by approximately 4,400 runners at some point in the race. But I was just glad my fear of being trampled was never realized. Once I received my finisher's medal, I proceeded to turn in my chip. I was directed to the chip refund booth, and right next to that was a booth selling finisher's T-shirts for–a mere 19 euros. I declined (19 Euros can buy a case of fine German beer!).

I was pretty dehydrated, and was really tired of drinking the German 'sparkling' water and I certainly wanted no part of the German sports drink. So I found a booth giving out what I wanted most–German beer. I proceeded to the meeting place Cindy and I agreed on. No Cindy. I proceeded to the backup meeting place we agreed on. For two hours, no Cindy. I was worried that something bad happened. After all, I've seen a lot of movies about couples going to foreign countries and one gets ... well, you know the story. As I was feeling a bit weary, I lied down on the sidewalk fully content to take a nap until Cindy showed up.

After a half hour or so, I heard the familiar siren of a German police car (you've seen those movies as well, right?) and just prayed it wasn't coming to check on me. Apparently, I wasn't praying hard enough. Neither of the two policemen could speak a bit of English, but my finisher's medal was enough to prove to them that I wasn't some derelict passed out on the sidewalk. Soon afterwards Cindy showed up (apparently she had the same problem traversing the sidewalks on foot that we had the previous afternoon trying to get to our hotel room in the car). However, we managed to find a way to ease our frustrations ... our aggravations ... our pains ...

We discovered a biergarten in the train station.

Once we got to Frankfurt for our flight home, I discovered they were having *their* marathon in five weeks. Danke schein–NOT!!!

Twenty Eight Years of Marathons

(So many marathons ... so little time)

- Florida Relays (Gainesville, Florida)—1979
- Brunswick Hospital (Brunswick, Georgia)—1979
- Callaway Gardens (Pine Mountain, Georgia)—1970, 1999–2002, 2004-2006
- Savannah (Savannah, Georgia)—1981
- Atlanta (Atlanta, Georgia)—1981-1988, 1991-2006
- Charlotte Observer (Charlotte, North Carolina)—1982
- Jacksonville (Jacksonville, Florida)—1984, 1986–1990, 1998, 2001
- Boston (Boston, Massachusetts)—1987, 1994-1996, 1998-2004
- New York (New York City, New York)—1990
- Tallahassee (Tallahassee, Florida)—1994, 2003
- Grandma's (Duluth, Minnesota)—1994
- St. George (St. George, Utah)—1994, 1995, 1999, 2000, 2003, 2004
- Vulcan (Birmingham, Alabama)—1994-1996, 1998, 1999
- Las Vegas International (Las Vegas, Nevada)—1995
- Shamrock Sportsfest (Virginia Beach, Virginia)—1995, 1997-2002, 2006
- Marine Corps (Washington, D.C.)—1995, 1996
- Carolina (Columbia, South Carolina)—1996
- Grandfather Mountain (Boone, North Carolina)—1996-1998
- Tybee Island (Tybee Island, Georgia)—1997-2006
- Silicon Valley (San Jose, California)—1997
- Chickamauga Battlefield (Chickamauga, Georgia)–1997-2001, 2003, 2006
- Museum of Aviation (Warner Robbins, Georgia)—1997, 2000-2003, 2006

- Steamtown (Scranton, Pennsylvania)—1998
- Rocket City (Huntsville, Alabama)—2000
- Baltimore (Baltimore, Maryland)—2001
- Mercedes (Birmingham, Alabama)—2002, 2005, 2006
- Macon Cherry Blossom (Macon, Georgia)—2002, 2003, 2005
- Bay-bridge (Chesapeake, Virginia)—2002
- Blue Angel (Pensacola, Florida)—2004
- First Light (Mobile, Alabama)—2004
- Twisted Ankle (Summerville, Georgia)—2005
- Greenville (Greenville, South Carolina)—2005
- Five Points of Life (Gainesville, Florida)–2006
- Berlin (Berlin, Germany)–2006

The one true thrill I never tire of is crossing the finish line of a marathon and having the medal draped around my neck. Every time I do, it feels like the first time. And it still manages to take my breath away.

2004 Tybee Island Marathon—with Susan, Al and Paula

Chapter Five
Running with the Cows

Writing on a Runner's High

The first time I ran the Tallahassee Marathon, there were so few runners that the only 'company' I had most of the race were the cows in the pastures lining most of the course. This inspired the following trilogy of articles that appeared in the newsletter of the Darkside Running Club.

The cover of the second issue featured a photograph of me running in the 1994 Tallahassee Marathon with runner #650—a *cow*—behind me. I wrote in the issue that 'a cow had never beaten me in a footrace,' and in later issues boasted that I had 'never been beaten by a bovine in a marathon' and implied that I never *would* be.

The cow ('Heathcliff') took exception to this, and made his sole purpose in life to see that this 'streak' would come to (in his words) a 'sudden, screeching halt.'

A trilogy of articles (the first two by Heathcliff the Cow and the third one by me) followed in subsequent issues of the newsletter, capturing the imaginations of the club members. The entire trilogy which—just to be clear, is pure *fiction*—is presented in these pages.

Additionally, several other run-in's with the animal world are included, which will dispel the myth of the 'loneliness of the long-distance runner.'

In this chapter:

- An Open Letter to Scott Ludwig—Heathcliff announces his intentions of bringing my streak (of beating bovines in marathons) to a halt.

- (Yet another) Open Letter to Scott Ludwig—Heathcliff legally changes his name (in an obvious attempt to intimidate me). Adding fuel to the fire, he reviews the intense training regimen he is going through in preparation for the 2003 Tallahassee marathon—where he intends to put an end to my streak.

- Battle in Tallahassee—After almost a year of trading barbs, it was time for Heathcliff and I to put our cards on the table. In our wildest dreams, we could have never imagined it would end this way.

- Stampede!—After living with the presence of Heathcliff for years, this was bound to happen.

- Close Encounters of the Third (and Fourth-Legged) Kind—It was fate that I would run into a few of Heathcliff's close and personal friends at some point.

An Open Letter to Scott Ludwig

From Heathcliff the Cow

Dear Scott Ludwig:

First, allow me to introduce myself. My name is Heathcliff, and I am a close personal friend of Gary Griffin, the Race Director of the Tallahassee Marathon. Gary showed me the issue of your DARKSIDE newsletter with the cow on the cover. I understand you are proud of the fact that you've 'never been beaten by a cow in a marathon.' Well, pal, that's gonna change.

A little bit about myself: I'm in the modeling business, so running is not necessarily my 'specialty.' I am proud to include Chick-Fil-A® on my resume, as I am their model for all of their major advertising campaigns. You've probably seen me (as well as some friends of mine) in billboards along most major highways.

My career has been taking off lately. Recently I posed for the cover of the coffee table book *Cow.* Perhaps you've seen it in your local Barnes and Noble.

I am particularly proud of my latest gig. I have been selected as the new model for Gateway® Computers. They noticed me during one of my interval sessions at the Florida State University track, and they were so impressed with me that they featured me in their latest 'hurry up and get your Gateway' campaign. Let me tell you—I'm in much better shape than the cow you outran in the 1994 Tallahassee Marathon.

I bet you're wondering why I've been doing interval workouts. Let's just say I expect to see you at the *next* Tallahassee Marathon (scheduled for February 16, 2003). Your 'unbeaten by a bovine' streak will come to a sudden, screeching halt. Count on it.

Regards,

Heathcliff the Cow

(Yet Another) Open Letter to Scott Ludwig
By Khalid Cownnouchi

Dear Scott Ludwig:

So much has happened since I wrote you last. I don't know where to begin. How's this for starters:

I have legally changed my name to Khalid Cownnouchi (*1). 'Heathcliff' just wasn't indicative of the speed and talent I've acquired these past six months. You may have seen my name in some of the south's race results this fall: I have quite an impressive unbeaten streak in my age group (*2).

'Where is he getting this amazing speed?' you may be asking yourself. Well, for one thing, I've been working with a dietician who has altered my diet so that all four of my stomachs (*3) complement one another. For example, one stomach focuses on my complex carbohydrates, another on my protein and calcium supplies, etc.

Secondly, I've been doing intervals twice a week on a pasture just south of Tallahassee with one of the fastest fillies in the south, Pippig (*4). Man, those horses from Europe can flat out fly!

Third, an exercise physiologist has been working with me on my leg turnover and hoof strike (*5). Previously I was putting an unnecessary amount of pressure on the backs of my hooves. The good doctor has worked with me so that I land on the front of my hooves, which allows me a stronger push, resulting in a quicker leg turnover. My four legs (*6) have never been more in synch with one another and another and another and another (*7).

Finally, I've been doing my long runs religiously. 80 furlongs (*8) every Sunday! My endurance has never been better.

Scott, I've got to be honest: I've turned into a machine! If I were you, I'd be afraid … very afraid. See you in February.

Regards,
Khalid Cownnouchi

Author's comments: Forgive me for my bovine sense of humor. If you had a hard time following my attempts at humor, an explanation (indicated in my letter with an * and a number) of all the humorous references follows:

1. Khalid Cownnouchi is a play on the name of Khalid KHAnnouchi, the world record holder in the marathon.

2. As Khalid is less than three years old, his age group in most races would be '14 and under,' meaning he is competing with mere children.

3. Cows have four stomachs. However, it would be virtually impossible to isolate which foods go to which stomach. Plus, it's just funny that cows have four stomachs and humans only have one (except for Marlon Brando, who must have about—oh, FIVE!).

4. 'Pippig' is a play on the name of Germany's 'Uta Pippig,' three-time women's winner of the Boston Marathon. Also, 'filly' is a female horse (and Uta Pippig is a female human!).

5. A human has feet, therefore has a 'foot strike.' 'Hoof strike' just sounded kinda funny. I'm still in stitches over that one.

6. Humans have only two legs. Can you imagine how clumsy we all would be with four?

7. I repeated 'another' for each of Khalid's four legs. I don't know about you, but I'm rolling on the floor right about now.

8. Most of us measure our runs in miles, but domestic farm animals measure distance in furlongs. Of course, then you have the Europeans, who run kilometers. Remember when we were going to convert to the metric system? Good thing we didn't–I couldn't ever get a handle on the whole concept. And Lord knows how much a liter of milk is …

<u>Battle in Tallahassee</u>

I'll be the first to admit: the past twelve months have been tough on me. I have never felt more pressure to run well than I did at the 2003 Tallahassee Marathon. Flashback to 12 months ago: the cover of the second issue of the DARKSIDE newsletter that shows me beating a cow in the 1994 Tallahassee Marathon. As I found out the day before this year's Tallahassee Marathon, that wasn't just *any* cow: it was Hepzibah Heifer, the great-grandfather of Heathcliff Heifer, known of late as Khalid Cownnouchi, the finest distance-running cow in the world. I realized that for the past year not only was Cownnouchi out to defend the honor of the cow population by defeating me in Tallahassee; he was out to defend the honor of his *family!* To *me,* our competition was going to be 'friendly.' But to Cownnouchi, it was much more than that—it was *personal!*

It was apparent from the start this bit on information got under my skin. For the first time in my life, I *forgot* my running shoes for the trip to Tallahassee. I was forced to run the marathon in shoes belonging to Al Barker (who accompanied me to Tallahassee to witness the event), a ten-year-old pair of Saucony's he wears when he lifts weights. The good news is they *almost* fit. The bad news is my little toes ended up looking like ground beef after the race.

As if the forgotten shoes weren't enough, on racing morning Al and I woke up to one of the loudest and brightest thunder and lightning storms imaginable. We drove to the Florida State University track (where the race was to start and finish) in a torrential downpour, only to find out the marathon had been (at best) postponed. The Race Director, Gary Griffin (correctly) decided that the conditions were unsafe, and there was no relief from the weather in the foreseeable future. However, there was a small contingent of runners—myself and Cownnouchi being the most vocal—that wanted to 'run' the marathon regardless. The lead (and now *only*) cyclist, Dana Stetson, volunteered to do his part (a necessary ingredient, as this was a brand new course), so for my four-legged adversary and I, *the race was on.* The Race Director then gave his 'seal of approval' that the marathon would indeed *BE* a marathon, even with a now-abbreviated field and the ominous threats of nature lurking overhead. I'm guessing there were 15 of us who ventured out in ankle-deep water at 8:00 a.m., intent on completing the event *in spite of* Mother Nature. It would have brought tears to my eyes—if it weren't for the intent stare of the dreaded Cownnouchi.

I was amazed at the amenities that were available to Cownnouchi. Not only did he sport race number 'B-1' (being the top-seeded bovine), he also had his own elite aid stations (including Power Cuds, salt licks, and *three* assorted varieties of grass—seriously, does any cow really need three types of grass to choose from?), and all the mile markers included 'furlong' markers (FYI—a marathon is 207.75 furlongs) for his benefit. And since the aid station volunteers had been sent home due to the adverse conditions, the only 'support' on the course was *cattle!* I even noticed 93-year-old Mac Donald at the turnaround (Mac owns the farm on which Cownnouchi lives and trains. E-I-E-I-O).

A runner from North Carolina took the early lead—a lead he held for the first 23 miles. That's when Fred Johnson, Cownnouchi and I made our move. Up until then, we were content to draft off one another a couple minutes behind the leader, running in a tight pack. I could tell by looking in Cownnouchi's big brown eyes that he felt confident: it was readily apparent that while I had been seriously 'pounding the pavement' for the past 12 months, he had been equally serious about 'pounding the pastures.' But now it was 'crunch time,' or as Fred so aptly put it once we passed the North Carolina runner: *'Game on!'*

Fred made the first move to the front, then Cownnouchi, and then at the 24-mile-mark it was *my* turn. As I pulled 10, then 20, and finally 50 yards ahead,

I was feeling stronger and stronger. I surged at a turn, intent on increasing my lead, when out of the corner of my eye I saw the most horrifying thing I've ever witnessed: *Cownnouchi was struck by a bolt of lightning!* Immediately he collapsed to the ground. Fred and I flagged down one of Tallahassee's finest who in turn called for an ambulance. Help was on the way. But was it going to be too late? The policeman successfully gave Cownnouchi mouth-to-snout resuscitation, which kept him alive long enough for the paramedics to transport him to the hospital. After the ordeal, Fred and I decided we would finish the marathon together: no clear-cut winner, but a 'shared' victory in honor of our fallen competitor.

You may be wondering what happened to Cownnouchi after the fateful lightning strike. I'm happy to say that the emergency room staff was able to get Cownnouchi to stand on his own four legs again later that afternoon. At about the exact same time, Al and I were having lunch at a local Burger King enjoying—what else?—*a Whopper.*

Eaten in honor of my worthy adversary, of course.

STAMPEDE!

Running with the Cows

It has become a tradition with me to run long on Memorial Day, usually a little 23-mile route that runs from Peachtree City to Brooks to Senoia and then back to Peachtree City. In 2005 Susan Lance and I added another eight miles and included the small town of Haralson in the route, extending it to a convenient 31 miles through three counties—Fayette, Spaulding and Coweta. Danielle Goodgion joined us as we set out at 6:30 a.m. on a warm Monday morning and headed towards Brooks.

About six miles into our route—along the Highway 85 Connector—we noticed two police cars with blue lights flashing in the distance. Next we noticed several cars backed up in the opposite direction behind the police cars. Finally, we noticed a small black cloud cresting a hill moving directly towards us.

Before we had a chance to determine what the black cloud was, a woman appeared at the top of the same hill and began shouting at us to 'turn them around.' We then examined the small black cloud and determined it to be a small stampede of black cows (maybe 20 in all) rushing towards us along the side of the road. The three of us did our best cattle-rustling impression and to our amazement we managed to turn them around—just as the woman had requested. We stayed with the herd for almost a half-mile at which point they were directed back into their fenced-in pasture by a man working in concert with the woman.

Yee-haw! Mission accomplished. Any one of the three of us would have given anything to have this adventure captured on film. We wondered how many other runners were ever involved in rustling up a herd of stampeding cows in the middle of a run—perhaps this was a first. Whatever the case, it will always be one of those indelible moments that will be impossible to erase from our memories— poetic justice on Memorial Day, I imagine.

Heathcliff would have been proud of us.

Close Encounters of the Third (and Fourth-Legged) Kind

Every runner—at one time or another—has a close call with our furry four-legged friends. You'll be hard pressed to find a runner who has not been barked at, snapped at, or bitten by a German Sheppard or a Doberman pinscher or, God forbid, a poodle. These occasions are cause for alarm for any runner, because no matter how big or small the dog, they still have very sharp teeth and, when applied firmly to human skin they can cause very severe damage.

I've been very fortunate in this respect. In all my years of running, I've been bitten exactly once: on the right elbow in Atlantic Beach, Florida in 1979 by a Shepard. Of course, I've been barked at and snapped at more times than I can remember. But a trick I learned a long time ago—bend over as if to pick up a rock—usually causes man's best friend to make a hasty retreat with its tail firmly tucked between its legs.

However, I've had plenty of close calls with *other* four-legged creatures. One morning around 4:00 a.m., a raccoon dashed out of the woods and got tangled between my legs as I was running. I don't know who was more frightened, me or the raccoon, as we both ran off in opposite directions with our respective tails between our respective hind quarters. I was lucky, as I've heard raccoons have pretty sharp teeth, too.

Then another morning, also around 4:00 a.m., I heard the faint footsteps of *two* four-legged creatures following me in the dark. I would stop every minute or so, and the footsteps would stop. I would begin running again, and the footsteps would resume. Finally, after I began to break out in a mild sweat (from fear, not exertion), I stopped beneath a streetlight so that I could at least see who ... or *what* my pursuers were. As they slowly left the darkness and entered into the light, I could begin to see the figures of ... of ... two basset hound puppies with their tongues hanging out of their mouths and dragging the ground as they continued their dogged *(sorry)* pursuit of yours truly!

But the most frightened I have ever been was the morning a white possum jumped off the sidewalk and literally ran between my legs as I was running. It startled me so much that I literally 'screamed like a girl.' After the scream, I stopped to regain my composure/heartbeat/breath and realized how lucky I am that as long as I continue to run at 4:00 a.m. the chances are remote that anyone will ever be around to hear the mighty runner 'scream like a girl.' And up until now, that was a secret shared only by the possum and I.

Not all moments are as life-threatening as those mentioned thus far. I've run across families of deer (clip and save: if one deer crosses in front of you, the chances are good that more will follow. One time I counted 14 deer cross in front of me single file), raced cows (in the 2003 Tallahassee Marathon. I won.), and raced horses (many times. The horse always wins).

And this tale *(again, sorry)* wouldn't be complete if I didn't mention my always-there running companion, my black lab Magic, who has gotten up with me for many years to go for our early morning run. For Magic, the morning run is the highlight of her day. For me, too.

CHAPTER SIX
RUNNING WITH THE PACK
My Supporting Cast

I have been very fortunate to have a family that supports me and my running. My wife Cindy and our two sons, Justin and Josh, have always encouraged me to take that extra step (or two). While I was taking those extra steps, I managed to meet many sensational people who I now have the privilege of calling 'friend.' Many of them shared some amazing and incredible adventures with me, and I can honestly say it wouldn't have been the same without them.

Two things I know to be true:
1. You can't be a successful runner without the support of your family.
2. Assuming you have #1, you can be a much more successful runner with the support of your friends.

In this chapter:

- Cindy—The only person in my life who has been with me every step of the way is a lady I've shared my life with for over 33 years. I'm already looking forward to the next 33.

- Going the Distance—I managed to get my good friend Bruce interested in running, and before you knew it he became quite competitive. An unfortunate accident put a premature end to his running career, but not his desire to get to the finish line.

- Through the Eyes of a Child—Running one beautiful spring morning with my youngest son Josh opened my eyes to understand what I really love about the sport of running.

- (Re)Birth of a Runner—It took a seven-year-old's focus and determination to give my running career a 'second wind.'

- Passion—My older son Justin never had any desire to be a runner. But that didn't prevent us from having one very important thing in common.

- Melissa: A Story of a Champion—One summer evening I met a very young lady whose will and determination left an indelible impression on one (much) older man.

- Your Pace or Mine—Reflecting on my most memorable pacing experiences.

- Once Around the Block (by Valerie Reynolds)–Valerie has a special place in her heart for the Boston Marathon.

- Thanks, Pacemaster (by Kelly Murzynsky)—I've always enjoyed pacing other runners in races. Even runners that made me work extra hard.

- A Record to be Reckoned With (by Fred Johnson)—Military duty has allowed Fred to run all over the world. But that's not all he's 'done' all over the world.

- Looking Over My Shoulder (by Paula May)—My good friend, training partner and Badwater crew chief discusses the people who helped make her the (very talented) runner she is today.

- Baby Steps (by Stephanie Sudduth)—My good friend and next door neighbor Stephanie lost her younger son Alex to leukemia. But she never lost her spirit: through her efforts, Alex's memory lives on.

- Farewell to a Friend—Paul Allen was my good friend in both high school and college. He was a very special person, and it's a crime that I didn't stay in touch with him over the years. Very special people should live longer than 46 years.

Cindy

It seems appropriate to begin by acknowledging someone who has been there for me every step of the way, my wife Cindy. We met as seniors in high school, dated through college, and got married just before we began graduate school together. Thinking back to our first date over 30 years ago, it seems odd that a girl who could have had her choice of any boy in school would select someone who attracted her attention for the first time by shooting spitballs in her hair at a high school basketball game.

When I first started running, Cindy ran as well. In fact, she has a couple of 5K's and 10K's to her credit. But her love for the sport didn't last, and before long I was running on my own. Of course, she was always there to lend her support in so many ways.

Early in my running career, Cindy would attend races with me. She was there to see me start and finish my first marathon in 1979. However, Cindy was not there to see me finish my 100th marathon this year at Boston. In fact, I've run Boston 11 times and Cindy has never gone with me; she wants to take a 'Boston Marathon' vacation once the boys are on their own. I can't wait to take her for a walk—or perhaps a *run*—along the Charles River, one of my favorite places to run.

Cindy has been the ultimate supporter in all my (sometimes ridiculous) running endeavors:

- She's put up with my (pre) 3:00 a.m. alarms every weekday for the past 25 years (although at this point she is able to block them out entirely).

- She's put up with my 9:30 p.m. bedtime on weeknights to accommodate my early-morning running for these same 25 years. In fact, on most workdays I manage to wake up, drink coffee, take the dog for a walk, run 10+ miles, shave, shower, dress, eat breakfast, and leave for work—*before* Cindy's alarm rings.

- Before making any weekend plans, she always remembers to first ask me if I have a race.

- She realizes that any family trips and/or vacations she suggests need to have a race nearby in order for me to agree to go willingly.

- She's allowed me to go on countless weekend trips to out-of-town races: Utah, Virginia, South Carolina, Minnesota, Illinois, Ohio, Pennsylvania, Alabama, Florida, Nevada, Maryland, Tennessee, and California, to name a few (again, she'll go along 'once the boys are on their own').

- She planned two vacations for us to California to visit the best man at our wedding, and allowed me to 'squeeze in' a race on both occasions: the San Francisco Bay-to-Breakers and the (inaugural) Silicon Valley Marathon.

- On our most extravagant vacations (a ski trip to Yugoslavia, a cruise on the SS Norway, several trips to the Bahamas and Mexico, an anniversary trip to Maui), she allowed me time every day for my run.

- Occasionally after a long drive, she'll let me jump out of the car to 'run the rest of the way,' knowing I feel a need for a few extra miles.

- When I'm injured and/or ill, she'll always plead with me to 'do the minimum—three miles … *please.*' Once in a blue moon I'll comply. Make that every *other* blue moon. OK, *never!*

- She always remembers to prepare a large pasta meal before races of marathon distance or greater.

- She supported me in a van for the first two days of my initial attempt to run across Georgia—even though she was only two weeks away from delivering our first son.

- She, along with our two boys, drove to Savannah after a soccer game to see me complete my second (and successful) attempt to run across Georgia.

- She's rubbed my back and legs, popped the blisters on my feet, and rubbed ointment on my body too many times to count.

- On our 25 year wedding anniversary trip to Maui, she didn't mind me participating in a track meet on a Friday night—our *only* Friday night on the island!

I've noticed recently that Cindy has also begun to *think* like a runner. When someone asked her if she was going to go to Badwater with me, she answered 'It wouldn't be a good idea for Scott to see me, because I know I'll be upset and that wouldn't be good for *him.*'

Now you know why I love her.

Cindy

Going the Distance

As runners, all of us have a tendency to set goals for ourselves. They may range from the modest (running a seven minute mile, earning a Peachtree t-shirt) to the demanding (winning a local road race, qualifying for the Olympic trials). Whatever goals we set for ourselves as runners, we have an inclination to take one very important thing for granted: the simple fact that we are physically able to go the distance.

For many I am referring to taking two or three consecutive steps without assistance would be a uniquely challenging goal in itself. Seven minute miles and Peachtree T-Shirts are the farthest thing from their minds. Being able to fix themselves a glass of ice water or making their bed suffices for their personal Olympics.

The many I am referring to are those affiliated with physical and/or mental handicaps, limitations or disabilities which limit them from enjoying the full, healthy lifestyle that most of us are able to lead. For those, every single day of their lives is a challenge so severe, so demanding, and so very real that it is virtually impossible for us to imagine. Every 24 hours of their lives is an ordeal and challenge that most of us will never realize or understand. Their goal each and every day of their lives is to make it through another day; to go the distance.

Bruce is a friend of mine who I have known for 27 years. I was the best man at his wedding, and every final weekend in August, Bruce and I and our wives used to head for Maggie Valley (North Carolina) to run the annual Moonlight 8K Road Race. Every year Bruce and I set the same individual goals; mine to break 30 minutes, and Bruce's to make it to the finish line. Let me explain:

Twenty-seven years ago I introduced Bruce to running. He was already 26 years old, but he managed to lower his 10K time to 42:00 in two short years. He set many challenging goals for himself and he trained hard to achieve them. Then, something happened one Thursday morning in February 1982 which changed not only his running goals but his whole life as well.

As Bruce was driving to work on that fateful day, a van driven by an intoxicated teenager veered off into the oncoming lane of a blind curve and struck Bruce's little Mazda head on. The Mazda flipped over several times with Bruce trapped inside. A rescue team, with an assist from the Jaws of Life, managed to free Bruce from the demolished vehicle. Bruce's injuries were numerous and severe. He spent many weeks in the hospital for surgery and therapy. Through the efforts of many specialists, Bruce made a miraculous recovery. Everything was almost as good as new with one small exception; his left ankle had been completely shattered at the moment of impact, and the best the doctors could do was to fuse the remains of it together to provide his left leg some semblance of support. To this day Bruce has no flexibility in his left ankle. He walks with a noticeable limp, and the pain is obvious in his face when he attempts to push off with his left foot.

However, despite all the pain and frustration, Bruce continued to run. He doesn't have the fluid, seven-minute stride he had prior to the accident. At best, he is able to run a tiring ten-minute mile with a stride that reveals Bruce's limitations with every other step. He tells me often how much he wishes he had the full use and flexibility of his left ankle once again, and how much it hurts knowing this will never be. He occasionally runs 10K races, and always reminds me of his two goals; breaking 60 minutes and not finishing last. But I know well enough to know his true, unspoken goal: to go the distance.

I relate Bruce's story in an attempt to allow all of us to put things in their proper perspective. Running a seven-minute mile, earning a Peachtree t-shirt, of winning a local road race are all accomplishments we can be proud of, to be sure. But the one thing we must always remember to do is put everything we've got into achieving our number one goal in life which is to go the distance.

And be thankful that we have the determination and perseverance to do it.

Through the Eyes of a Child

I have kept precise statistical records of every run I have made since January 1, 1979. My annual runner's logs have daily entries of distance, time, weather, splits and place of finish (for races), and any other relevant miscellaneous information (who I ran with, physical ailments, etc.). At my fingertips I have such specific information as total miles per week, month and year; races I ran sorted both chronologically and by distance; total number of days with 10 or more miles … in other words, enough information to choke the memory of a small computer.

I think I learned the true value of my attention to detail when my five year old son Josh 'paced' me on his 20-inch two-wheeler one beautiful springtime Saturday morning. As I timed our run/ride with my chronograph (so I could base my mileage on our pace/total time ran), we traveled over countless paths, roads, and fields throughout Peachtree City. The workout resembled a fartlek session, as I would be forced to sprint as Josh flew down the hills or when he would hurry to see something which excited him (like a dead snake in the road). Then, we would come to a (literal) standstill when we discovered a playground or when he found anything that fascinated him (a chipmunk, a lake, horses, a large fallen tree). I couldn't get over the excitement in his eyes as he made one 'discovery' after another. To Josh, this was much more than an ordinary bike ride: this was an honest-to-goodness adventure!

Towards the end of our journey, Josh looked at me while his tiny legs were pumping away on his two-wheeler and he asked me why I kept looking at my watch.

At that exact moment it became perfectly clear to me. I don't know, Josh ... I really don't know.

✳   ✳   ✳   ✳

Father's Note: I originally wrote the following article in 1992, right after my youngest son Josh's 7th birthday. Josh was the most athletically gifted child I'd ever seen. At age four, the first time he played soccer he scored a goal a mere three minutes into the game. His first year of T-ball at age six he was routinely hitting the baseball over the fence in center field. One time he hit the ball so hard it hit the top of the metal fence in center field and bounced all the way back to home plate. In his first basketball game at age seven he scored 30 points, including a basket he made after being knocked to the floor and shooting with his rear end firmly planted on the court. When Josh was eleven I came home from work one day to find him bouncing (I believe he called it dribbling) a soccer ball on his knee. I heard him counting '748 ... 749 ... 750.' I think he lost his 'dribble' just shy of '900.' At age twelve Josh would put on his baseball glove and ask me to throw him ground balls, encouraging me to make the baseball take the worst hop imaginable. Rarely would he fail to field the baseball—even on the worst hops imaginable.

As a distance runner, Josh showed even more potential. When he was ten years old, he ran the tough Stone Mountain 10-miler. I happened to run with Josh that day, and I was amazed how even a pace he ran—even though the course requires running two severe uphill sections during both five-mile loops around the mountain. Josh's time that day was 76:36, almost nine minutes faster than the boy's 10-mile state record for ages 10-11. However, as the course had never been certified, it was not recognized as such. As the Atlanta Track Club has held this event there for many years, I'm fairly certain the course is a legitimate 10 miles. Even today his time remains faster than the current state record.

When Josh turned 15, his interest in his two primary sports—running and basketball—began to wane. I'm hoping when Josh reads this, he will remember the Josh I remember from not so long ago.

(Re) Birth of a Runner

I have always taken a lot of pride in my endurance as a runner. I have never been particularly fast, but I have always been able to run long distances without giving in to fatigue, pain, or inclement weather. Do you know whose picture you see when you look up the work 'endurance' in the dictionary? Neither do I, but I do know the description is closer to defining my running than words like 'fast,' 'quick' … you get the idea.

However, I have met my match when it comes to endurance, and he didn't come from Kenya, or any of the other countries that seem to breed endurance runners. He didn't even come from another state. Or another city, for that matter. Heck, he didn't even come from another household.

My match sleeps at the other end of my very own home. He has appeared in the form of a 4'3" six-year-old barely weighing 60 pounds who apparently doesn't know the meaning of the word 'quit.' Or maybe, like his father, he just doesn't know *when* to quit. His name is Josh.

Josh began running six months ago to get ready for the Peachtree Junior, a 3K race held every May in Piedmont Park for children between the ages of 7 and 12. (OK, I know Josh isn't seven yet, but since a birth certificate isn't required …) He trained diligently for six weeks, occasionally running as long as three miles in preparation for the 'big day.' On race day, he ran a steady, even nine-minute pace and was told as he crossed the finish line by a race official that he was the first 'seven-year-old' to finish. I heard what he told Josh, and I couldn't wait to hear the excitement in his voice when he would repeat this information to me. Josh picked up his race T-shirt and hurried over to me with an anxious look on his face and simply asked 'daddy, am I going to be on time for my T-ball game?' So much for the race.

Josh has stuck with running over the past six months, usually running six or seven miles a week. He ran in six track meets over the summer and always wanted to run in *every* event: 50 yard dash, 100 meter dash, 400 meter dash, 800 meter run, the mile, the two-mile, the three-mile … and a relay if a team was short handed at the end of the evening. All those events in one night, and not once did I see him stop or walk. Like I said earlier, I have met my match. I never thought he would be wearing a size 4½ running shoe.

Over the summer, I paced Josh in three 5K road races. The first, in August, was a tough one: Hot, humid, and hilly. Wearing his Boston Red Sox baseball cap backwards (a leftover from T-ball season), Josh ran the race like a veteran: a nice even pace while taking in water on the run at the two aid stations. At both aid stations he took off his cap and asked me to pour cold water on his head. I wish I had a recording of the giggle he let out both times–a sound a parent could never forget. Josh never broke stride until the last half mile, when he told me his stomach hurt. At that point, he saw the finish line and broke into a sprint, leaving his poor father to eat his dust.

The second race, in September, Josh improved his 5K time by almost five minutes. After a steady first mile he caught a glimpse of another runner who was in his age group (14 and under!), and again began to sprint. I thought that certainly Josh was going to burn himself out shortly, but to my surprise, he maintained this accelerated pace for the remaining two miles of the race. I spent 16 minutes watching the red letter 'B' on the front of his cap (remember, he wears it backwards) bouncing up and down quicker than I'd ever seen. Josh crossed the finish line, and looked at me with the widest eyes and asked 'daddy, did I win a trophy?' It broke my heart to tell him that he finished 7th in his age group, behind four 14-year-olds, one 13-year-old, and a 12-year-old. But after I poured a cup of water on his head and heard his little giggle, I knew everything was fine.

The third race, in October, Josh was dead set on winning an award in his age group (again, 14 and under). He had trained really hard for this race. In fact, a week before the race, we went to a Cub Scout picnic. As I was responsible for cleaning up afterwards, Josh 'waited' for me by running back and forth for almost 40 minutes along a 200 yard walkway. He had run as much as five miles in practice and would proudly report his training times to me before he had a chance to catch his breath (he has a one-mile route in the neighborhood he runs about three times a week–the run always has to start and finish *exactly* at the mailbox). On race day, with his cap on backwards, Josh started the race a bit too quickly for his little legs, especially considering it was an uphill segment of the course. Three minutes into the run, he was already breathing as hard as I've ever seen him breathe. I could tell by the redness in his cheeks that he had overextended himself too early, but he managed to slow down long enough to regain his breath, his energy, and his desire. He caught his second wind in the middle of the race, and with a half mile to go, he said something I had never heard him say before. 'Dad,

I think I have to walk.' About one second after I told him there was nothing wrong with walking, I found myself looking at the bouncing red 'B' once again. I was amazed at the pace at which he completed the race from that point on. He managed to take 30 seconds off his fastest 5k time, and finished 2nd in his age group. On the way back from the race, Josh asked 'dad, am I going to be on time for my soccer game?'

Like I mentioned earlier, I know a lot about endurance; but I'm learning even more from my six-year-old son. I've never seen anyone with a stronger resistance to quitting. My understanding of endurance was on a more physical and mental level. Josh has shown me that endurance comes from the *heart* as well. Oh, the things we learn from the young …

One thing I've noticed over the past six months: Josh no longer calls me 'daddy.' He now refers to me as 'dad.' On the morning of his 3rd race, I asked him why he doesn't call me 'daddy' anymore, and he said 'dad, I don't want to sound like a baby.' It looks like we've both come a long way these last six months. I've learned how to put my heart into endurance running and Josh has developed in leaps and bounds physically and even more so emotionally. My little boy doesn't seem so little anymore.

I guess I won't be hearing his little giggle when I pour water on his head anymore either. I sure hope he continues running and wearing his Boston Red Sox cap … backwards, of course.

Epilogue: Children have an uncanny knack for making their parents proud. In most cases, they have no idea they are doing so. The proudest Josh has ever made me was something he said in private to my good friend Al Barker when he was only seven years old (something Al–God bless him—reminds me of often):

'When I grow up, I want to be just like my dad.'

Josh

<u>Passion</u>

I have lots in common with my youngest son Josh. Running, a love of sports played with a ball (football, basketball), a dislike of sports played *without* a ball (hockey, boxing), and a fairly frenetic energy level. My oldest son Justin is another story. Besides both of us having a pretty good jump shot with a basketball and sharing the same address for 20 years, we don't have too much in common.

I tried to get Justin interested in running at an early age, exposing him to such high-profile races as the Peachtree Road Race and the Cotton Row Run. Was he impressed? Yes. Was he impressed by the *running?* Absolutely not. What impressed him were the crowds, the many refreshments, and any non-running items added to the 'spectacle' of the race itself (helium balloons, face-painting clowns).

Justin did, however, show an interest in other things. And by interest I mean *obsession*. When he first started elementary school, he was fascinated by sharks (after seeing 'Jaws'—numerous times). Whenever he saw a body of water (a lake, a river, a lobster tank at the grocery store), he asked if there was 'a shark in there.' Imagine his disappointment when we told him there wasn't. He decided that when he grew up he wanted to be around sharks: study them, hunt them, care for them—it didn't matter. For a few years it was 'shark this, shark that' up until the time that …

His interest in sharks was replaced by an interest in horror movies. It didn't matter that he was still so young that he couldn't see the *really* scary ones. Nor that when he *did* see the really scary ones, he'd always cover his head with a blanket or go into another room while asking 'did his head come off yet?'* (*A scene he remembered from the first time he ever saw a really scary one). Once we told him that 'his head came off' (meaning the really scary part was over), he'd rejoin us to continue watching the movie. Then afterwards he'd brag to his friends about sitting through 'the scariest movie ever.'

When Justin hit his teen years, music replaced horror movies. Hip-hop, hard rock, rap, punk—Justin went through stages. He's in one right now, but I'd be hard-pressed to guess exactly which stage he's in right now (but I'd guess hard rock—for the third time). In a way he reminds me of *me* at the same age, although Black Sabbath and Alice Cooper have been replaced by bands like Hip Replacement and Seven Deadly Shins (four guys, one of them with a wooden leg). It's rare to see Justin without his stereo blaring in his room or without his CD case in hand.

Justin's now at a point where he will be deciding what he'd like to do with the rest of his life. Whatever he decides, I wish him the best, and I hope he's as passionate about his chosen profession as he has been about sharks, horror movies, and music. *Passion*—I wonder where he gets it?! Something for me to think about tomorrow when I go running for—hey, will you look at *that*—my 10,000th day in a row!

1986 Barnesville Buggython–Justin's 'first race

Melissa: A Story of a Champion*

I went to Warm Springs one hot summer night in June of 2001 to run a race sponsored by the Roosevelt Warm Springs Institution for Rehabilitation. The Institution works with 5,000 people annually with various disabilities. The race was to raise money for the seated and mobility clinic; in other words, children and young adults confined to wheelchairs.

Prior to the 10K race, a shorter race of 2K was held for the youngsters who were clients of the clinic. I watched one little girl who couldn't have been more than 10 years old nor weigh more than sixty pounds push the tires on her wheelchair so hard that she almost won the female division of the race. She finished a close second to a young lady who was much older, bigger and stronger than she was. But I promise you she didn't go down without a fight, struggling so hard on that final uphill with everything she had in hopes of passing that one last competitor.

After all the wheelchair-bound children had completed their race, the 'able-bod-ied,' as the starter called them, competed in theirs. The field wasn't too deep, and I managed to with the Men's Masters division.

At the awards ceremony, trophies were awarded to the winners of the wheelchair race first. 'Melissa,' as I discovered the tiny girl's name to be, was called to the stage to receive her award. Melissa wheeled up the ramp to the stage to receive her second place trophy, six inches of metal and marble which made her break out in a big smile. I noticed her mother in the crowd with a smile even bigger than her daughter's.

Afterwards, awards were presented to the 'able-bodied,' and I was called to the stage to receive my trophy which was–and I am not exaggerating–three feet tall! It made me think about the effort I put out for *my* race, and then about the effort Melissa had put out for *hers*, and I realized who the TRUE champion was. I looked where Melissa and her mother had been in the audience but didn't see them. I went to some of the people in that vicinity and they told me Melissa and her mother had left. Fortunately they were able to point me in the direction they had headed.

I found them just as the mother had gotten Melissa seated in the back of their van, and noticed Melissa was still holding onto her trophy for dear life. I intro-duced myself and said I had won the Master's competition, and asked Melissa if she would do me the honor of accepting MY trophy, as HER effort that evening had been much greater than mine and that she was the *real* champion. Melissa broke into the biggest smile I have ever, and I do mean EVER seen and she immediately pried the engraved plate off of her trophy, did the same to mine, and placed HER plate on her *new* trophy! I felt honored that Melissa accepted, and I knew by the tears running down her mother's face that she was OK with it as well.

I asked Melissa if I would see her at the race next year, and she told me she would be and that *she* was going to win a trophy for *me*!

And do you know what? I've already selected a spot on the mantel for it.

This story originally appeared in the February 2002 issue of the Running Journal. Unfortunately, the Warm Springs race was not held the following year.

Your Pace or Mine

Since I've never been a 'genetically fast runner' (my term), my rewards aren't always in the form of trophies, plaques or medals. For me, the best rewards are when I am able to lend my support to a fellow runner by pacing them to a particular goal, and to share in their enjoyment and satisfaction when they reach it. Given the choice, I would rather pace someone to a particular performance than race it on my own and win a personal award. I've been really fortunate to share in many of these 'intangible rewards' in my running career.

In fact, I paced someone in 36 of my first 100 marathons. On several occasions, I paced for more than a single runner. Following are some of my more memorable pacing experiences:

Charlotte (NC) Observer Marathon, January 1982

I paced Paul Anderson to his first–and only–marathon finish. Around the 20 mile mark Paul was tiring quickly, and he asked me to run ahead, get the car and return to the course to pick him up as he 'wasn't going to be able to finish.' I ran ahead, finished, and simply waited another 15 minutes or so until Paul crossed the finish line. As Paul was running towards the finish line, he spotted me in the crowd and cursed me every step of the way those last 300 yards. Later, after he had accomplished his goal of finishing a marathon, he couldn't thank me enough. Actually, that last sentence is a lie: he continued to curse me for *weeks* after the event. But I know in his heart he was thrilled because that's pretty much all he talked about ('finishing a marathon') for many months afterwards.

Atlanta (GA) Marathon, November 1987

My training partner, Ed Rush, wanted me to pace him to a sub-3:30. The race wasn't particularly memorable, but we did manage to run 3:25:13, a P.R. for Ed. As we walked through the finish chute together, Ed cramped up and leaned on me for support–all 6'5" and 250 pounds of him. Needless to say, I wasn't able to offer much 'support' and we both toppled to the ground. Later, once Ed's cramping subsided, he was delirious with his performance. So much so that it was his last marathon … *ever.*

Atlanta Marathon, November 1993

After training with Valerie Reynolds for six weeks, she decided she wanted to qualify for the 1994 Boston Marathon, which would require her to run a 3:35 qualifier. She chose the difficult Atlanta Marathon, and asked if I would pace her. Val was very impressive in her first marathon effort in a while; in fact she spent the last six miles focusing on the 'next woman' and doing whatever it took to pass them, which she did—time after time. Her 3:30:24 assured her a spot in Hopkinton the following April.

Tybee Island (GA) Marathon, February 1997

Al Barker asked if I would pace him to a 3:10. I agreed, and was glad I did, as Al ran incredibly well. Around the 22-mile mark, Al asked me to run ahead to see if 'the guy in front of us' was in his age group. I caught up with the 'guy' and found out he was and gave the appropriate signal to Al. Feeling pretty good, I ran ahead and finished in 3:03:53, good enough for 7th place overall. Al finished in 3:07:28, well under his goal and 11th place overall (but unfortunately second in his age group as he never passed the 'guy').

Chickamauga (GA) Marathon, November 1997

I met Earl Tyler of Macon along the course. He asked me what I was trying to run and I told him I'd like to 'cruise to a 3:20 or so.' Earl mentioned he needed to run a 3:25 to qualify for Boston, and asked if he could 'tag along.' We ran the majority of the race together, although I 'sprinted' the last mile to break the 3:20 mark. Earl was a couple of minutes behind, qualifying for Boston by several minutes.

Museum of Aviation (GA) Marathon, February 1998

Sue Bozgoz, a Major in the US Army asked me to pace her to a 'sub 3:10 or so.' We actually had a pretty good run together, never forcing the pace and never in doubt of hitting our time objective. We ran the marathon in 3:08:29, and Sue was not only the top female finisher, she was also the top military finisher, beating the fastest military man by over 20 minutes. I also managed to win the Men's Master's title with my effort, an unexpected surprise for a pleasant run.

Grandfather Mountain (NC) Marathon, July 1998

My friend Richard Penland and I ran this demanding course in a solid 3:30:19 (the severe uphill of the course adds about 20 minutes to one's 'normal' marathon finishing time). This marathon was memorable as the cover photo of the September 1998 issue of *The Running Journal* featured a photograph of us running the race together (*look it up!*).

Chickamauga (GA) Marathon, November 1998

My friend from Macon, Earl Tyler, introduced me to a friend of his, Thomas Jones, and asked if I would pace Thomas to a 3:30 to qualify *him* for the Boston (for future reference, I have never said 'no' to this type of request so I'll skip that part from now on). Thomas ran well, although we were right on schedule for our 3:30 goal for most of the race. In fact, the last two miles we needed to pick up the pace slightly to beat the 3:30 mark. Around mile 25, I told Thomas that I was going to sprint ahead as I needed to 'water some trees.' After two minutes of sprinting, I pulled up next to a tree to take care of business, and 15 seconds later I looked to my left and–*Thomas was standing next to me doing the exact same thing!* I wrote this in italics because Thomas couldn't afford the additional time it took for him to water some trees! Of course, I could see the demanding pace was taking its toll on him, both mentally and physically, so I didn't say anything. When we resumed running, however, I picked up the pace even more. Thomas, like the trooper he is, never complained and stayed with me step for step. We crossed the finish line in 3:29:14, earning Thomas a spot in the elite Boston field. I turned to congratulate him, but the alert medical crew immediately put Thomas in their ambulance and took him to a local hospital. I found out later that he was given fluids intravenously as he was dehydrated from his hard work. I saw him at Boston the following year, and before long, he was doing full-distance triathlons and ultramarathons.

Callaway Gardens (GA) Marathon, February 1999

By chance, I ran into Nancy Stewart at this event, and she asked me if I would pace her. She wasn't sure how fast she was capable of running, since she wasn't familiar with the marathon distance. Nancy ran an incredible (first-time marathon of) 3:10:38, and used her performance as a stepping stone to the Boston Marathon where she and two of her Atlanta Track Club teammates captured the Women's Master's Team championship.

Shamrock (VA) Marathon, March 2000

What started out as an 'easy' marathon for Valerie, Al, Kelly Murzynsky and I turned into a substantial effort on the part of Kelly and I. Fighting an incredible wind, Kelly and I pulled away from Valerie and Al and ended up with a negative split marathon. In fact, each of the last six miles was faster than the preceding mile. Kelly and I finished in 3:17:32; for her, it was a sign of good things to come.

2000 Shamrock Marathon—with Kelly, Valerie and Al

Tallahassee (FL) 50K, December 2001

Kelly and I ran together, although she 'edged' me out by one second at the finish. Her 3:57:31 earned her the women's title, and a second place finish overall. I won the men's Master's title with my three-fifty-seven-thirty-**two!**

Callaway Gardens (GA) Marathon, February 2002

I met Gary Griffin of Tallahassee for the first time around the two-mile mark, introducing myself when I saw his 'Gulf Winds Track Club' singlet. We inadvertently ended up running the remaining 24 miles together, talking most of the way (actually, Gary did most of the talking, and I did most of the listening). I finished in 3:22:40, breaking away from Gary in the last ½ mile so I could pass someone who looked like he was in my age group (I managed to pass him, and it turned out he was in my age group). Gary finished a few seconds later, and said it was his fastest marathon time in 10 years. Excited by his performance, Gary made a trip to Boston in 2003 via this qualifying effort.

Peachtree City (GA) 50K, November 2002

Kelly and I ran together, and Fred Johnson of Tallahassee–a friend of Gary Griffin's–joined us somewhere along the course. The three of us stayed together for 29 miles or so until fatigue caught up with me. Fred went on to win the men's master's title (guess who finished second?) and Kelly the overall women's title. Me? I was just glad our first-time event was a success: we had six runners finish the race in less than four hours (and if someone–I won't say who–had run 13 seconds faster, we would have had seven!). What can I say; being the Race Director took its toll on me.

Tallahassee Marathon, February 2003

Although the event was rained out (actually, 'thunder-and-lightening'ed out' is more like it), Fred Johnson and I ran the marathon course anyway. The lead cyclist even agreed to stick around to lead us (as it was a new course for the event). We ran the entire race together and finished in a 'tie for first' in a time of 3:21:20.

Chattahoochee (GA) 10K, March 2003

Paula May asked if I would pace her to 41:30. Actually, what she said was 'I'd like you to pace me to 41:30, if you can still run that fast.' That being said, Paula (and I) ran well, finishing in 40:38. Not only did Paula win her age group and set a P.R., she also set the Georgia state record in the 10K for her age group! In September, Paula asked me to pace her in the Macon Labor Day 5K. We ran 19:40, a time that earned Paula the women's overall title. Better yet, I could still manage a 19:40 5K six weeks after Badwater.

Finally, my favorite pacing adventure:

Forest Park (GA) 5K, October 2000

I didn't officially enter this event, as I was only running to pace my son Josh (age 15 at the time). Not only did Josh run well, finishing in 21:11 (on a course slightly longer than 3.1 miles), *he won the race!* To put his accomplishment in perspective, consider I 'won' my first race when I was 27, by running a local church-sponsored four-miler in 26:21. Normally, anytime you finish ahead of everyone else in a race, you consider it a win. However, leave it to me to find one (my aforementioned four-miler) that finishing first didn't necessarily mean winning:

There were absolutely no awards nor any recognition of the 'winners' at the pancake breakfast after the race, and while everyone was eating pancakes, a runner walked in and said loud enough for everyone to hear that he showed up late but ran the course in 25 minutes.

Let me correct the first point, as now someone was getting all sorts of recognition and pats-on-the-back for 'winning' the race, but it most certainly wasn't me.

I'll end by saying that not all of my pacing has been successful. To date, I have failed to help three fellow runners qualify for Boston (and they know who they are). In time, I hope all three qualify, and I look forward to pacing many more fellow runners in the future. Just as long as it doesn't require me to run too fast; after all, I'm not a genetically-fast runner (right, Paula?).

Once Around the Block

By Valerie Reynolds

A marathon is a marathon. They are all the same–26.2 miles. But somehow, the Boston Marathon seems to be different. Is it the crowd support? Is it the qualifying? Is it the tradition that was established in 1897? I've heard it called the "greatest running experience next to the Olympics." I've read books about it. I've heard hundreds of stories of experiences running in the Boston Marathon. Most of all, I've heard many goals of 'running the Boston Marathon." Perhaps, that's the part that makes it so special–the stories, the experiences, the goal setting and the expectations of what it means to run in and finish the Boston Marathon.

For me it all started while I was in college. I slogged my first 26.2 mile adventure in December 1982. Just one month later, three days after my 23rd birthday, I would talk to my dad for the first time I can ever remember. I was two the last time he saw me. "I'm a student at Georgia Tech" I told him the first time we talked. "I'm majoring in computer science and I've got a job. I've been putting myself through school for almost five years now," I added. Initially, I didn't know what to talk about. "I'm a runner. I just ran my first marathon last month." Maybe that will impress him, I thought. "Have you run in the Boston Marathon?" he asked. "No, but I want to. Maybe someday," I told him. Someday soon, I hoped. Talking to him the first time was interesting. The only thing we had in common was genes. I didn't know what to say about our missing past so I concentrated on today and the future.

In our next few conversations, the Boston Marathon came up several times. For a non-runner, he seemed to know quite a bit about it–the length, Patriot's Day, the noon start time, even some of the winner's names. I listened carefully as he meticulously told me detail after detail about the Boston Marathon.

In our next few conversations, a trip to Massachusetts (Agawam–a small town outside Springfield) for our first meeting was planned. I had received pictures of him and his wife so I knew what they looked like. He found a road race we could go to so he could see me run. When I came in second overall, I could see the excitement on his face. It didn't matter that it was a small race. The camera clicked away and captured many "Kodak-winning" moments. For the rest of the weekend we visited his friends and people stopped by his house to meet me. Each person was told of my "almost win" and to this day, the trophy I won that day is the most gazed upon trophy I own. I saw a spark of interest in him that weekend but didn't realize until much later the impact it would have on both of us.

We kept in close contact during that time. He always asked the three basic questions about school, my job and running. However, my current classes and the "he said, he did's" of work weren't nearly as interesting as running. It was something we could discuss and as an active person, it was something he could almost relate to. I visited him again for Christmas that year. He bundled me up one day for a run in the freezing cold, and I mean freezing with a minus 15 degree wind chill. He went with me one day on the bicycle when I ran. Finally, one evening after a long day of visiting and shopping, I decided to go for a run. Out of the blue, I asked, "Hey dad, why don't you go with me? Just once around the block?" "Sure," came an almost immediate response. "I can do that. Just let me go get some sneakers on," he added. And in sneakers and sweatpants we very slowly slogged around that block where he lives. "That was okay," he said as we got back. I continued on, wondering if he really thought it was okay. The next evening, as I got changed to run, I asked again. "Hey, dad, you want to go again—once around the block?" The immediate response was "Sure!" and within minutes, he was decked out in sneakers and ready to go. Our slog around the block was uneventful. I'm not sure we even spoke during it. I would leave the next day. After spending the previous four Christmases alone with nowhere and nobody to spend it with, there were many things I wanted to say. Watching and listening to his interest in my activities and me was new and different and I wanted to thank him. But, somehow, I didn't feel comfortable saying anything.

The next few months were very interesting. The phone calls increased as he told me of twice around the block, three times around the block. Barbara, his wife, spoke of him wearing out the streets on the block. I send him issues of running magazines so he could "read up" and buy some running shoes. I began to realize the impact of that "spark of interest."

During the next several years, there were many changes in my life: graduating from college, moving, getting married, moving again, changing jobs, getting out of shape, getting back in shape, and starting a business. He never missed asking about any of my interests. Through it all, we found our common interest to be our running. He had dropped the block routine and was now wearing out a path alongside Main Street as he trekked it up and down every evening. He had added road races to his plate of activities. We were always discussing a new race, distance or event, race times, the food after a race, and of course, t-shirts. His times continued to improve. The Boston Marathon continued to occur every year without me. He always read about it in the paper and if I didn't bring it up, he would tell me about it. I received newspaper clippings in the mail (I guess he thought we didn't have newspapers in Georgia). However, I always looked forward to them and read every single one. Every so often, I would ask him if he wanted to run a marathon. "I don't know. We'll see," he would say. With that response, I knew someday he would and I would be able to share that with him.

In 1989, the pressures of growing a business, lack of motivation, a failed attempt at a marathon due to strep throat, and negative influences from my spouse took its toll. I quit running. I never intended to. It just happened. Phone calls with dad became one sided. I didn't have any times to report or races to tell about. We discussed my business venture and his work, but something was missing. That common bond that sparked us both, for me, was gone.

Running became more difficult to even discuss during this time. I missed it terribly. I maintained my streak of Peachtree Road Races. Around the 4th of July of every year, I would tell him of my adventure down Peachtree, running it many years with little or no training. It would get harder and harder with each passing year. Every year I would try to maintain my running afterward. However, each year I would give in to the stresses of work and spousal discouragement.

Dad continued to improve and do very well. He called one day in 1991 to tell me he had been accepted into the New York City Marathon. I hadn't been running at all. It would be too late to even try to get in. Anyway, my adventure through the five boroughs of NYC in 1985 turned out to be one of the worst running experiences of my life and I vowed never to do it again. In fact, I had not run a marathon since then. I knew I would run again, someday. However, I would miss his first marathon. I'll catch the next one, I thought.

After completing his first marathon and settling back into racing, his times improved dramatically again. He called one day and announced he had run a 10K in just over 40 minutes. "Wow, that's better than mine," I told him. I was really impressed. I was excited for him and sad for me at the same time. I didn't have any running accomplishments of my own to share with him. Meanwhile, they still held the Boston Marathon that next year without me.

In November 1992, he ran the Rhode Island Marathon, missing his qualifying time for Boston by only seconds. "Are you going to run another marathon before the end of the year to try to qualify for Boston?" I asked. "No. Maybe next year," he replied. I knew he would qualify in his next marathon attempt. Would he end up running Boston before I did?

I started thinking about running a lot more in early 1993. I don't think there was any one specific catalyst at that point. Rick, a running friend of mine, had a serious "heart to heart" with me one day—"All work and no play makes Valerie a dull girl" he had said. Maybe it was "Wishing Upon a Star"–an article I clipped out of a running publication on goals and the Boston Marathon that made me say "next year." Whatever it was, on April 19th, 1993 I set my watch to go off at noon. As I sat in my office at noon, the people in my work world were totally oblivious to my dreams or even what that day meant to me. I would return to running, I decided. It would give me the strength I needed to make the changes in my life I needed to make. I ran that day barely making the .4 mile loop around the pond behind my house. Little did I know that in six days my perspective on life would change forever.

It was a Saturday night just after dark–April 24th. Bill, my husband, had a massive heart attack that involved an entire team of EMT's and several doctors before the night was over. He would be revived several times throughout the evening. Eventually, a miracle drug would turn the situation from a worse case scenario into a positive prognosis. How fragile life can be, I thought. Because of his second chance at life, I hoped Bill would do some of the things he talked about doing for years. I knew he would. If only he could just accept my running as something I enjoyed and wanted to pursue. More passionately than ever, I would tackle my dreams. Dad and I talked several times during this period. "I'm going to do some of the things I've always wanted to do" I told him. "I'm started back running and this time I'm really going to stick with it no matter what."

On May 11th, I would start slogging around the pond three days a week. After all, Peachtree was coming again–my 13th Peachtree. There was a benefit race on June 5th. I would try to make it through the 5K distance. Could I get to three miles in three weeks? I would try. I knew Teri, my neighbor, would run with me and help me.

June 5th came quickly. I would finish the run in the slowest time I had ever run a 5K race. I won't write it down. I called dad to tell him of my accomplishment. He was glad I was running again. I better set a goal. Certainly I wanted to finish the annual Peachtree 10K again this year as in the past 12 years. However, a goal beyond that is what I needed. It would have to be Boston. No more putting it off. After all, dad will probably qualify this year. I would also try to qualify. I would also set a longer-range goal that day–something that would take two or three years to achieve. I'll run lots of marathons, I thought. Perhaps an ultramarathon. I'll break 40 minutes for the 10K. As I pulled out my old running logs and reviewed them, I thought about some of my previous goals. Yes, everything I had ever dreamed about I would do. A plan would be necessary. For now, Boston would be long range enough.

The return was slow. I finished Peachtree only slightly better than the previous couple of years. I called dad. "Yep, I finished another Peachtree," I told him. He ran a race that day too. How exciting! We were back to talking about running again.

The return to running was more exciting than ever. I appreciated my running more because I realized how important it was to me. I returned to the local club's Saturday morning fun runs, began to meet a group on Sundays and made lots of new friends. Meanwhile, dad heard about everyone and everything. He made plans to run the Rhode Island Marathon again. This year, he had an entire group of people he had never met wishing him well. I tried to determine which marathon I could run to qualify. It would have to be after the first of the year. I needed at least six months of running behind me before I ran a marathon. Meanwhile, on November 7th, dad ran the Rhode Island Marathon in a time of 3:24:36, easily qualifying for the Boston Marathon. Wow! He did it! I was excited for him. Now, it was my turn.

With the Atlanta Marathon only a couple of weeks away, Scott, my new training partner, would convince me to give it a try. After all, it was right here in Atlanta. It wouldn't involve a trip anywhere and he would run it with me to pace me. I couldn't pass it up but I didn't want to decide until the week before. I was very apprehensive about it. After all, it had been nine years since my last marathon. "OK," I told him. "I'll give it a shot." On Thanksgiving Day, a conservative approach would be the order for the day I decided. When Scott asked what I wanted to run that morning, "How about eight-minute miles?" was my reply. Three hours 30 minutes and 30 seconds after the gun sounded, we would cross the finish line in what would be the best marathon experience I had ever had–a "first marathon" experience. I easily qualified with almost 10 minutes to spare. However, that time was not nearly as impressive as the seconds it took me to call dad upon returning home. "I qualified!" I practically shouted to him over the phone. For almost an hour, he patiently listened to every detail. Finally, the Boston Marathon would be held and we would both be there.

During his Christmas visit, we made our travel plans for Boston. After the first of the year, our phone calls increased as we discussed our training runs and recent events. I was making some major changes in my life that were not very pleasant. Bill had recovered from his heart attack. It had been a year but he had not made any changes in his attitude. Going out for a simple run became a major obstacle.

I decided I wouldn't live my life like this. In mid-March, I moved out and filed for a divorce. After years of hiding this desire to be fit, I could finally run or workout whenever I wanted.

Running was fun again. Dad heard it all. It took only seconds to call him after returning home from a local 10K. "Hey dad, I broke 40 minutes in the 10K!" I announced without even a Hello. "Holy smokes!" he said. It wasn't what he said but how he said it that I will never forget. "Are you going to run the marathon with me?" he asked. "I'll see how I feel that day" I told him.

April 18th came very quickly as my training increased to never before seen levels. My new running friends–Scott and Al along with myself overwhelmed each other with "running" enthusiasm. The Boston Marathon was affectionately called "Christmas in April." The pre-race hype was everything I had expected and then some. I had been working too many hours and was concerned about being too tired. Should I run with dad or should I try to run a good time? We would all start together–dad, Scott, Al and I. I decided if I saw dad at any point after a couple of miles, I wouldn't pass him, I would stay with him and we would run it together.

As the gun sounded, Scott, Al, dad and I said our last good lucks. Dad took off. He was ahead of me the last time I saw him. The cheering of the crowd along the way was awesome. However, within the first five miles, I was beginning to have problems with my toes–my shoes were too small. Where was dad? Had I passed him? I was comfortable with my pace but by 16 miles my toes were really hurting. I still had not seen him. I must have passed him and not noticed. It was during the 18th mile way up ahead on a hill that I first caught glimpse of him. As I caught up to him at the 19-mile mark, I leaned over and said "Hey dad. How y'a doin'?" A surprised look came over his face. This was perfect I thought. I would finish with him. It was meant to be.

He had gone out too fast and his pace was beginning to slow. We slogged along together barely talking. The slower pace was a relief. However, my toes were going to ache at any pace. Dad was depleted. I could tell. Into the 25th mile, he stopped to walk. "You go on ahead." he said to me. "No way, dad. I'm going to finish with you." I told him. We clocked an 11:16 mile. Yes, it was a marathon horror story, but I would stick with him and we would finish together. Even though my toes were aching, I was beginning to feel semi-recovered by this point and I concentrated my efforts on encouraging him. As he started to run again I put my hand in the small of his back and pushed him up a slight incline. He was brave to be so depleted and run nine minutes for that last mile. "You're my hero, dad!" I told him as we rounded the corner toward the finish line. Yes, we finished hand in hand together. As we walked through the finish chutes, he was still wobbly; he announced to everyone he saw "This is my daughter. We finished together." I was real proud of him. Probably like the pride a parent feels for their child's accomplishments.

As we got to the end of the chute, he turned around, gave me a kiss and a big long hug and said "I love you. I couldn't have done this without you." As we hugged in the midst of a sea of people I realized he was right. Perhaps not for the reason he was thinking. He had guts and determination and I knew he would finish the full 26.2 miles that day. He didn't need me to help him finish. My contribution came one cold winter evening in 1983 when I asked him if he wanted to go once around the block with me. Perhaps it was his pride in me for winning the first marathon just one week later that kept him circling around that block every night. Or maybe he was looking for something we could share and build memories together. "I love you too, dad." came my response as a lump formed in my throat. I realized then that I will never look at the years that we didn't have together, but instead be grateful for what we do have as a father and daughter.

For me, there will be other races for PR's; there will be other marathons; there will be other running goals to accomplish. It took us 11 years to get to the Boston Marathon. To run in and finish our first Boston Marathon together as father and daughter is certainly one of the highlights of my life. After all, isn't that what the Boston Marathon is all about–the expectations, the goal setting, the experiences and the stories? For me, this was a dream come true.

Thanks, *Pacemaster!*

By Kelly Murzynsky

I have a really nice running watch. A chronograph, actually. My thoughtful husband bought it for me the summer I started running with Scott. I'm fairly sure that you can store billions of splits and information in it but I've never needed to ... because I run with the Pacemaster, Scott. He always knows the pace (or at least he pretends to) no matter where we are, what course we're on, or what mile marker we've just passed. This in turn has made my really nice running watch obsolete.

You see, Scott has run half my marathons (and both my ultramarathons) *with* me. Side by side the entire way—keeping up with our pace, storing it in *his* watch and passing on the relevant information to me. I always wear my really nice watch, but strictly as a fashion accessory (it goes with my outfit).

At least once or twice a year, I set out to prove to myself that I am *not* 'Pacemaster dependent.' So I confidently register for a marathon that I am certain Scott is *not* planning to run. About a week before the race I begin to wonder if maybe I should have invited Scott and panic whether or not it's too late! After the doubt, panic and anxiety are under control, I pack my really nice watch and hope it will do its job as well as the Pacemaster. If I think sensibly and if history is a reliable predictor, I convince myself that I'll be fine. After all, without Pacemaster, I came in second at the Napa Valley Trail Marathon, and won both the Greater Cleveland Marathon and the Blue Angel Marathon. I also ran my personal best at the Steamtown Marathon—*without* the Pacemaster. Not too bad with just a watch (a really nice one!).

Next on my schedule is the Durango Marathon. Sure, I'll have to travel all the way to Colorado to run without the Pacemaster. But when I'm standing on the starting line wearing my really nice watch, I'll thank Scott for teaching me how to use it.

A Record to Be Reckoned With

By Fred Johnson, A.K.A. 'The Crapmeister'

I first met Scott Ludwig at the Peachtree City 50K in November 2002. Along with Kelly Murzynsky, the eventual women's winner, the three of us ran the race together. Then again, at the 'unofficial' Tallahassee Marathon the following February (officially, it was postponed due to inclement weather. However, Scott and I and several others ran it … anyway. *Un*officially, we tied for first.), he dragged me along in spite of my numerous pit stops, which clearly added minutes to our finishing time. However, I'm getting a little tired of all the fanfare one has to endure while running with an endurance icon like Scott. If I hear one more person ask about his 28 year running streak or his Master's win at the 2002 24-Hour

Championship, I may lose it. Some may say I'm jealous, but all I want is my just due. The bottom line is that I've taken more 'number twos' during runs—in more exotic places—than any runner alive. But no one cares about this accomplishment and that bothers me ... *a lot!* Never has anyone said to me 'My God, you're Fred Johnson and you've crapped during runs all over the world!' Clearly, Scott's streak is an incredible feat, but taking a dump in a minefield in Bosnia must be equivalent to gutting out miles day in and day out for a quarter century. There's a reason some mines are called 'nut busters.' I mean, you step on one and the device bounds three feet in the air (about waist-high on most males) and explodes.

I've been a soldier for 18 years and I have been afforded the opportunity to run in some pretty neat places. And because I'm more than a little 'regular,' I've been forced to 'pit stop' during most all of my runs. A sample of some of my more prominent 'numbers twos' follow: I'll leave it up to you whether I deserve a place in the record books.

Tuzla, Bosnia-Herzegovina

This was the location of the aforementioned minefield incident. Needless to say, Bosnia is full of mines. During a run with a Croatian buddy of mine, I had to go. Well, if you're like me, when the feeling comes you can't think about anything else. I'm sorry, but you may be talking to me and I'll nod my head as if I'm listening, but I'm actually looking for a place to go and won't hear a word you say. That's exactly what happened. I told my Croatian friend Pjec that I had to stop. I then made a bee-line straight into an open field. With Pjec yelling 'no,' I bypassed a sign I couldn't read, and I went to squat. Pjec then came to the edge of the road and said 'Fred, you're in a world of sh#&.' I answered 'no kidding,' digging toilet paper out of the key pocket in my running shorts. He said 'no, I'm serious; that sign says we're in a minefield.' Talk about instant constipation. Fortunately, my footprints where I entered the minefield were visible and I retraced my steps out. If I weren't so near retirement, I wouldn't be telling this story because if one of my bosses gets wind of it, they'll boot me out for sheer stupidity.

Quito, Ecuador

Of all the places I've 'number two'd,' Quito is where I felt most comfortable. The reason is that I could stop, drop trouser, and no one would pay me any attention. I stayed in downtown Quito and the only place I could run without risking my life was the park across from the hotel. Suffice to say, people in Quito are downright *mean*. However, in their meanness, they are very open in doing their 'daily duty' and I appreciated that. While running around the park, I got lured into running with a group of students from the university. This was after a night of eating fish head soup and drinking beer with a name I couldn't pronounce, so I was primed for more than one 'pit stop.' As the urge came upon me and I debated 'to go or not to go,' the runner in front of me promptly stopped, dropping his skin tight running shorts and doing his business 10 strides in front of me. Dodging his droppings, I directed myself to the nearest tree and did the same. It was at this point I realized my runner's plague was international.

Paris, France

It was really an uneventful 'pit stop' along the Seine, but it makes the list only because the French are crapping all over us now after we bailed them out of two wars.

Vicinity Tapline Road, Saudi Arabia

Tapline Road is near the Iraq boarder and it is where I spent a month or so before the Gulf War. Running in Saudi Arabia was tough for many reasons, but I was committed to run every day to stay fit. The most difficult part of running there was that I had to do it in my uniform and equipment. I could ditch my weapon with a guard, but the rest of my uniform had to remain intact. In addition to my uniform, I had to wear a flak vest, helmet, boots, and a belt with suspenders that carried canteens of water. I didn't run far or very fast, but I ran every day. My runs in Saudi Arabia rank as my best in spite of the constraints. I started the runs right before daybreak and I would run toward a series of rocky hills in the distance. I timed the runs so I could watch the sun come up over the hills. Of all my morning runs spanning over 20 years of running, the sun was never more magnificent. I would run out for about 10 or 15 minutes and then turn around and run back to camp. The other good thing about running in Saudi is that you could pretty much 'pit stop' anywhere. In this particular instance, that became my problem. After several cups of good Army coffee, I started on my trek. Right at the moment the sun finished cresting the hills, I had to go. Good timing, but the moment came over me fast. I quickly took off my suspenders and vest and in doing so my helmet came off. Since I was in the middle of the desert, all I had to do was squat. However, unbeknownst to me, my helmet had settled right underneath me. When I finished, I discovered I had unloaded inside of my helmet.

Garmisch, Germany

Honestly, I felt guilty 'going' in Garmisch. This city, near the Austrian border, ranks as the second most beautiful place I've ever run. Because I was so enthralled with Garmisch's beauty, I actually 'held it,' while my better judgment told me to go. All of us have been there—tightened glute muscles; short, quick steps; forward lean; eyes darting, looking in every direction for a restroom. I ran like that for two hours which, in itself, has to be some sort of record. But because of my discomfort I wasn't enjoying the splendor of the Bavarian landscape as much as I could, so I decided it was 'time.' However, there was a problem: I was running along a 'fusweg' (German for 'foot path'—consider me cultured!) in an open field with absolutely no cover. Not to mention there were a bunch of folks on the path walking or running in both directions. Fortunately, in the distance, I spotted a barn that appeared abandoned, except for a couple grazing cows. I did my best version of a sprint, jumped the fence behind the barn, landing in what I thought was mud. I did what I had to do and went to kick off the 'mud' from my shoes when I noticed it wasn't mud at all—I had landed in cow dung. To make matters worse, a farmer and his wife were watching me, laughing themselves to tears.

Peachtree City, Georgia

My 'dump(s)' in Peachtree City rank in the top ten because it was the venue of my first ultramarathon, as well as my introduction to Scott and his crew. I came to the Peachtree City 50K with no expectations other than finishing the race, hopefully in a reasonable time. That goal changed when I linked up with Scott and Kelly and got caught up in the moment. Unfortunately, I was plagued with an overactive bowel for most of the race. As a result, I had to make a 'pit stop' every (4.7 mile) lap and then sprint to catch back up with them so I could maintain their pace. I believe this fartlek effect contributed to my running a pretty good time and ousting Scott in the last two miles. I know it bothers the heck out of him that I won that Master's title (and received a miniature golf cart for my efforts, which ranks as the nicest award I've ever won). I didn't deserve it because Scott is a much better runner than me, but I attribute the victory to the five cups of coffee before the race and the Krystal burgers I ate the day before. Having said that, I believe this racing strategy is worthy of mention in a prominent running publication.

Looking Over My Shoulder

By Paula May

Written on the eve of her 50th birthday

I'm fast approaching one of those 'threshold moments' in a runner's life: the move to a new age group. A *big* one. <u>FIFTY!</u> Grandmasters. Old.

Scott tells me I should write something profound, figuring I've gathered so much wisdom in these oh-so-many years. It's the least I can do, he says, since we're even putting on a 50K 'fun run' three days after my 50th birthday, commemorating my change to 'grandmaster' status. This run will be my first distance beyond the marathon. I know: 50 miles at age 50 would have been more dramatic, but 50 *kilometers* is *doable!* True DARKSIDERS always do what they say they are going to do, and since I don't want to jeopardize my status with the group, attempting a 50K seems like a safe bet.

I'm a firm believer that who/what/where we are in this life is a direct result of all the choices we make. Certainly the same can be said for the kind of runner you are.

Anyone who watches 'Oprah' on Tuesdays knows who Dr. Phil McGraw is. Dr. Phil tells us that we have all ended up where we are right now in this life because of the impact of certain pivotal people and defining moments in our lives. These people and events are all part of the factors that have led you to make the choices that have brought you to this point in your life.

Next month I'll be 50. Not many women run every day; fewer race competitively and even fewer do so after turning 50. So how did I get to this rare place? Who were these pivotal people that brought me to this extraordinary place for a female half-centurion? I looked back on my last 24 years of running and realize that there were indeed 'pivotal people' who influenced my choices to run, race and to make them essential parts of my life.

Growing up in the 1950's and 1960's meant that opportunities for female sports programs were at best limited, almost nonexistent. That was before Title IX and certainly well before Title IX made any impact. In my high school a girl could play basketball or be a cheerleader. There were only eight spots on the cheerleading squad; 150 girls would try out. Not that I consider cheerleading a sport, you understand. So, I did no physical exercise until I started running in the late 1970's when I was already 26 years old.

That was when I met my first pivotal person; the one who actually influenced my decision to begin running. His name was **Tim.** Tim was a commodities broker who also ran. His goal was to run a marathon. Part of achieving his goal was also running the Peachtree Road Race. He invited me to watch him and 10,000 other runners one 4th of July. I walked from my apartment on 26th Street up to Peachtree Street to watch the event and was immediately overwhelmed. I was amazed that this mass of humanity would have such a profound effect on me. At that moment I was changed forever—*I wanted to be one of them!* As I stood on the sidewalk, tears streamed down my face. I was inspired that so many people would work so hard to reach their goal of finishing the challenging 6.2 mile course. These were real runners to me and I became one the very next day. I knew I could do this. From that day forward, I never stopped running. I didn't see Tim much after that. I did call him 18 months later to tell him I ran my first marathon in Atlanta. Tim still had not run his; I don't think he was all that happy to hear from me.

Then I met **Schelly**. She and I sold Cheez Doodles. Schelly is my good friend who did all those long training runs for the marathon with me. Without Schelly to keep me company, make the hours go by faster and to celebrate with afterwards, I still might have done it, but it wouldn't have been *nearly* as much fun. Schelly moved back to Minneapolis and stopped running, but she did keep smoking.

I was officially a part of the running boom. I ran every race I could find for a few years, collecting my t-shirts as my prize. I raced almost every weekend, sometimes on both Saturday *and* Sunday. There wasn't nearly as much information available on training (outside of Jim Fixx's book), so racing served as my speed work.

Then I met **Laura Murphy,** captain of the Atlanta Track Club Women's competitive team, at the Stone Mountain 5-Miler. Laura gave me the confidence to take my running to a higher level. She asked me to join the team (well, I *might* have asked *her*). More importantly, I remember thinking that Laura believed I could run with the fast girls. Her positive encouragement made it easy for me to believe that with the support of the women's team I could accomplish loftier goals. And I did. Those few early years on the women's team were my first opportunity to be part of a team. For women, and some men, those opportunities were rare at the time. I became a competitive runner.

After lots of speed work and a few more marathons and P.R.'s, marriage, pregnancy and child rearing became bigger priorities and my running regressed, but I managed to maintain 'jogger' status. I raced occasionally during those years when it seemed like I was always pregnant (I had three daughters, all age five or younger), which proved to be much harder than training for a marathon.

I still picked up a plastic trophy here and there, but usually because no one else showed up for the race that was in my age group. I even ran my P.W. ('personal *worst*') while pregnant with my youngest daughter.

Moving from Atlanta to Peachtree City, a runner's Mecca, was certainly a defining moment. There probably isn't a better place to run than the 80 miles of golf carts paths throughout the natural beauty of Peachtree City. Enter **Bill Anderson**, pivotal person #4. Bill is an accountant, extremely attentive to detail who is able to spout off any data you care to know (and some you *don't* care to know), especially with respect to local runners. I don't have to maintain a running log; I just ask Bill. Bill can tell me my time—splits included—from the Labor Day Road Race in 1998. He can also tell you his times, as well as everyone else just ahead of him or just behind him. I count on Bill for data retrieval. Bill and I met at church and fortunately for me, every time he saw me he asked me to run with him and his group. Bill's tenacious and for that I am grateful. After about three years of asking me to come out and run, I finally decided to take his advice and stop running alone. Of course, now that others were watching, I had to start running *well* again. My competitive nature wouldn't allow me to simply jog. Oh no—now I had to get back to work! The group Bill ran with was serious, so *I* had to get serious. I ran with Bill when it was his *easy* day and my *hard* day. Bill always runs one step ahead of you and keeps you on your toes.

Bill opened the door again for me to run well and Val pushed me through the 'marathon' door—the more the merrier. **Valerie Reynolds** is pivotal person #5. Val was running extremely well and was a great inspiration to me, as well as a staunch supporter. Val's easy-going nature and her 'go girl' encouragement made it easy for me to work hard again and get into position to rejoin the ATC

Women's competitive team. So I did rejoin after a hiatus of well over 10 years! I also started to train for marathons again—something I had sworn off years ago. All the marathon training and marathon talking just sucked me back in and now I can't imagine *not* being in the place where I'm always training for one. I like it here and I plan to stay here as long as I can keep it up.

Through Val I met her closest running friends, **Al Barker and Scott Ludwig.** Between the three of them, they had run over 200 marathons. So *if you run with them,* you *run marathons* (and pretty much any one you choose, they'll do it with you). I love the comment Val made to some poor soul who had no idea about their history of marathoning when asked which marathon she will use to qualify for Boston:

'Any one I want.'

Al and Scott stay in marathon shape year-round by running at least one 20-miler a week. They are certainly the final pivotal people who have contributed to the runner that I am now.

Al is an optometrist; but running, racing, traveling (primarily to races) and painting tell more about Al than what he does for a living. I believe Al lives to run, runs to race, and travels to races and take photographs so he can paint. More importantly for me, Al is pivotal person #6 because he will run with me anytime, any day, anywhere. Al will also travel to a race with me under these same conditions. Al will run with me slowly when I can't keep up with Scott and Kelly Myrzynsky, or when I'm too tired to run any faster. He will never let me run alone. Al will always run with me when I ask, is always on time, will run long or short, slow or fast. He never lets me down and is a good conversationalist on those long runs. We have a lot of chuckles about how good we look for our ages and what awesome shape we are in and how the fat people must hate us when we run by. Al and I always manage to pick up 'hardware' in our age groups at races. No one could ask for a better running companion and friend. Hopefully, Al and I will be running until the days we die, and I plan on another 50 years at least. I know Al does too.

The older I get, the more important I realize it is to have a good sense of humor. My 7th and final pivotal person is **Scott,** who has added another dimension to my running. Scott takes his running very seriously, and has made me realize we can't take *ourselves* (or anyone else, for that matter) too seriously if you want to have fun. Scott has a quiet, dry sense of humor. It's hard to laugh out loud while you're running, but Scott can make it happen. Scott has run almost 100 marathons and has a 24-year running streak going. If that isn't serious enough, he's planning on the Badwater 135 Ultramarathon in July of 2003. As DARKSIDERS always do what they say they'll do, Al and I will be there to provide support (fortunately I'm a trained medical professional).

Scott will also run with me anytime, any day, any place—as long as it's 3:30 a.m. during the week and at least 20 miles on Sunday. He'll pace me in a marathon on Saturday and then pace Kelly in one on Sunday (which she'll *win!*), and then he'll run again on Sunday night because he stopped at Dairy Queen after the second marathon. He used to be fat … need I say more?

If I want to do 800 meter repeats at 3:00 minutes (I wish I *could*), Scott will run just ahead of me at a 2:59 pace *(exactly!)*, so that if I stay on his tail, I'll accomplish my goal. He has an uncanny sense of pace (probably from those 87,000+ miles he's logged) as well as distance. At any point in the run he can tell you your exact distance run and where to cut off the course if you only want to do—say 16.4 miles—that day. He and Bill have a lot of common when it comes to details (but I realize there's a HUGE difference in their running philosophies; Scott promotes quantity while Bill favors quality … but I understand Bill has never beaten Scott in a race. Go figure.).

Scott, as all the pivotal people I have met since moving to Peachtree City, has enriched my running experiences dramatically. I know I am on the lunatic fringe with Scott, but it's a lot of fun our here on the DARKSIDE. We are not ordinary and our lives are full.

Baby Steps

By Stephanie Sudduth

Why do I run? There are many answers, but they are probably not the same for most of you who are reading this book. I told Scott that I would agree to write because I felt that those of us who are more 'casual' about their running are underrepresented in these pages—although we *do* make up the majority of people who run.

I began running when I was 30 years old. I went to the doctor and was told that I, being 5'2" tall and weighing 220 pounds, had dangerously high blood pressure. This scared me enough to take action. To put my size in perspective, Scott says that he is 5'10" tall and began running because he was overweight—at 195 pounds! I began walking every day for an hour. As I started to look and feel better I started adding in some running, and soon I was doing a lot more running than walking. At this time my husband Anthony, who is in the military, was a big runner. When I started, he was actually training for the Marine Corps Marathon. He talked me into running my first 10K with him and assured me he wouldn't leave me in the middle of the race. So I signed up for the Cobb Classic 10K. On Labor Day, 1997 I ran my first race! It was great and I was hooked.

I ran *every day* after that! I always ran an hour or more and would stress if something interfered with my running. My family told me I was obsessed (they hadn't met Scott yet). 'Mommy, lay with me and let's watch a movie,' my youngest son Alex would beg. 'I'm sorry, honey, mommy has to go for her run. I'll be back soon,' I would reply. Off I'd go feeling a little guilty but also feeling justified that I was improving my health so I would be around to be his mother for many more years. What's an hour out of my day to do something for myself? My weight dropped to 135 pounds, which was the smallest I had ever been. My health improved and I looked and felt great!

Then on October 31, 1997—almost two months after my first race—Alex was diagnosed with leukemia. We made many trips back and forth to the doctor and spent countless nights there. Needless to say this significantly hindered my running and I slowed down quite a bit. I began to stay home and watch movies with Alex. I ran when I could and I even took days to walk with friends. I gained back some of my weight but I was no longer consumed with my running. I began to learn to enjoy running as well as *not* running. Scott talked me into running the Brooks Day 10K and I managed to win a first place trophy in my age group (by the way, Scott did *not* take home a trophy of any kind). These days I still try to get in a daily run and I continue to enjoy running. However, my main goal has shifted to running in order to balance out my beer consumption. I figure if you drink light beers (96 calories) I need to run one mile for each beer I drink. So far this 'arrangement' has been working out pretty well.

Unfortunately my husband never got to run the Marine Corp Marathon. His flight was supposed to leave the day we found out Alex had cancer. He had to call his running group and tell them to go ahead without him, and he hasn't run since. I'd love to have him go for a run with me but he says not to bother him—he'll run when he's ready. Alex passed away on April 17th, 2001, almost two years ago. In June I went to San Diego to run the Rock n' Roll Half-Marathon with Team in Training (they only allow Team in Training members to run the half; everyone else runs the full marathon). My best friend, Joyce Rivera and I both ran in memory of Alex. Although we didn't have the best 'time' or set any records, we did something worthwhile and meaningful. I guess we *did* have the 'best' time.

This year we are planning the 2nd Annual Huddleston Hustle 5K and Kid's Fun Run (last year it was called the 'Run for Alex'—and to Scott and I, it always *will* be), held at Huddleston Elementary School (where Alex went to school) and run in the memory of my son Alex. The money we raise from the event goes to buy books for the school's media center. The books are put in a nook that is called 'Alex's Corner.' Last year the school bought $4,500 worth of books! This year we hope to surpass that amount. Scott said that he has never seen as many kid's in a fun run as he saw at the inaugural Run for Alex. I feel really good about encouraging children to start running.

My main point is that I still consider myself a runner. Although I may not *look* like a runner, I still feel like a runner and I still enjoy running. At least I'm doing *something!*

Farewell to a Friend

Now I know what it feels like to be hit with a ton of bricks.

My wife called me with the news that Paul, one of my best friends from high school, had passed away unexpectedly. Paul's wife Debbie had called Cindy with the tragic news, only five days shy of my 50th birthday. Paul, who was my 'little brother' in my fraternity during college, was only 46.

Debbie asked if I would speak at Paul's memorial service, which was to be held on December 16th at Blue Springs State Park in Orange, Florida. Paul had been a park ranger in Florida for the past 24 years, and his fellow rangers wanted to honor him in the park where he first met Debbie some 13 years ago. I told Debbie I would be honored.

I thought about what to say for several days, and remembered I still had the traditional fraternity 'paddle' Paul gave me in 1976 when he became a brother and selected me to be his big brother. It was still in the attic—in the exact same place it had been when it managed to dodge countless garage sales and charity donations over the years. I decided to use the paddle in my speech at the memorial service.

I flew to Jacksonville and drove Paul's mother Shirley—who I hadn't seen in over 20 years—to the service. The two hours passed quickly, as Shirley filled me in on too many details of Paul's adult life to remember. What I do remember is what a terrific person he turned out to be. I was touched when Shirley said things to me like 'you were the one who got him started in golf' and 'he learned so many of his good habits from you: saying please and thank you, saying yes sir and no sir, and holding open the car door for a lady. Paul was always so impressed how you always would hold the car door open for Cindy.'

When we arrived at Blue Springs, I knew immediately why Paul loved it so: what a beautiful park! The service was held in a small cottage next to the spring, and I was impressed by the park ranger staff, all neatly dressed in their green uniforms. Several of them spoke at the service, and it was obvious that they all respected, honored and loved Paul, both professionally and personally.

Towards the end of the service, I was called upon to speak. I had wondered for several days if I would be able to get through it; after all, I had practiced aloud several times during my morning run and I had difficulty each time finishing (the speech, not the run). But when I got in front of everyone and began talking about the good times Paul and I shared during the 1970's—in high school, in college, and during the summer of 1973 after my parents moved to Virginia and Paul and Shirley allowed me to spend the summer with them so I could be close to Cindy—I was suddenly reliving the moments as if they were yesterday. I spoke of the many rounds of golf we played in all kinds of weather *(the weather that people are amazed I run in today? Paul and I used to golf in that weather!)*. I spoke of the time Paul proudly told me he made the JV tennis team, challenged me to a Saturday morning tennis match, and I squeaked by him in our nine-set match by scores of 6-0, 6-0. 6-0, 6-0, 6-0, 6-0, 6-0, 6-0, and 6-0—only to be challenged to a rematch the next day. I spoke of how Paul, who hated his naturally curly hair (the kind men hate and women love) so much that each morning of the summer I spent with him and Shirley, he would wash his hair and put on a hat to 'flatten' it dry before leaving the house. I spoke of the time—right after I started running—that Paul accompanied me to the track to run a timed mile and finished a mere 50 seconds behind my 5:49 ... his face turning the brightest shade of red imaginable in the process.

I ended my speech by talking about Paul following in my footsteps at the University of Florida and joining my fraternity and selecting me as his big brother. I opened my speech by stating that my parents never gave me a little brother, and ended by repeating my opening statement and adding 'but that was OK, because Shirley and Gene Allen gave me one.' I then picked up the paddle Paul had given to me 28 years ago and was about to read the inscription when the strangest thing happened: all of the oxygen was suddenly sucked out of the room. I couldn't breathe, and when I made eye contact with Shirley, I could no longer speak.

It took about 30 seconds to regain my composure, and I picked up the fraternity paddle, showed it to everyone and read the inscription in what had to be the longest three seconds of my life:

To Scott. Thanks. From Paul.

I hugged Shirley, who was sobbing silently, and asked her if she would like the paddle. She looked at me with the widest eyes and said sweetly 'Oh, could I? I remember how proud Paul was of that paddle and how he wanted to give you something really special.' I told her I would be honored if she would accept it. She did, and I was.

Paul's widow spoke after me. I thought the worst was over, but I was wrong. Debbie spoke about all the little things she'd miss that Paul did, like speaking to their pet dog Choo-Choo and taking Debbie for a ride on his motorcycle. But when she added 'how Paul always held the car door open for me,' I flat out lost it.

At the end of the service, one of the park rangers asked us to visit the springs to try and see the manatees before we left. After all, 'Paul would have wanted us to.'

Once I (yet again) regained a semblance of composure, I walked towards the springs—thinking how proud I was of Paul and that I had been a part of his life.

Paul had made a difference, and in some small way, I'd like to think I played a part.

On the way to the springs I asked a ranger about the manatees. He told me there are usually 25 or so in the mornings, but once crowds gather they're hard to see. Nonetheless, I still walked to the springs and when I got to the dock, the largest manatee I have ever seen slowly—gracefully—effortlessly—swam by silently underwater.

As it did, I silently said farewell to Paul one last time.

CHAPTER SEVEN
CROSSING OVER ... TO
THE DARKSIDE
Testing the Limits

I am incredibly proud to be the President of the Darkside Running Club. The members are the finest runners—and people—you would ever hope to meet.

If you're looking to join a running club that is comprised of dedicated ... and talented runners who are also amazingly supportive, encouraging, motivating, dependable, and down-to-earth, look no further. You've found it.

By the way, they all have a wonderful sense of humor as well. To do what we do, you have to.

Once you get to the last page of this chapter and are ready to join me and the gang, you'll know where to find us.

In this chapter:

- Running Clubs ... Proceed with caution!—Be careful when you decide where you pledge your allegiance. You may not realize what you're getting into.

- Exactly what is the Darkside?—Learn how it all began (consider this your history lesson).

- The Birth of the Darkside—We finally decided to form a club and make it official.

- A Quick Peek inside *absolutely true ... Tales from the DARKSIDE*—Once you're a member of the Darkside Running Club, this is a taste of what you can expect.

By the way, to join the Darkside Running Club, visit our website, www. darksiderunningclub.com for a membership application!

Running Clubs ... Proceed with caution!

I've been a member of numerous running clubs and organizations. However, with the exception of the Darkside Running Club (one that Al Barker and I founded in the mid-90's), I haven't had much success with them. In fact, to be quite honest, I have discovered that when it comes to being a member, I don't have the 'right stuff.'

Florida Track Club

My first experience with a running club was in 1978 in Gainesville, Florida. With a whole two months (and over 60 miles!) of running under my belt, I met up with members of the Florida Track Club (with boasted of members such as Frank Shorter, Barry Brown, and Jeff Galloway) one Tuesday evening for a three-mile run. We met on the University of Florida campus, and someone spoke up and announced which route everyone was to run. Being new to the group, I knew I would have to follow someone else. I figured it wouldn't take me long to find the slowest runner in the group—someone I could latch onto to get me through the run. I was right, as it didn't take hardly any time at all to find the slowest runner in the group. Me. Within the first 90 seconds of this so-called 'group run,' I found myself all alone, jogging aimlessly around campus trying to act like I knew what I was doing and where I was going. I eventually returned to the spot where we began our 'group run' only to find every car, bicycle and gym bag long gone. I couldn't even find anyone in order to pay my membership dues and become a member of the club.

Jacksonville Track Club

My next experience with a running club was in 1979 in Jacksonville, Florida. After graduating from college, my wife and I were working in the Jacksonville area and I decided it would be in my best interests to join the club that hosted the famous River Run every March. I attended a monthly meeting in a hotel conference room in downtown Jacksonville, signed up to be a member of every possible committee a running club could have, and to this day have not received a follow up phone call or letter (and now that we're in the 21st century, an E-mail) asking for my help.

Atlanta Track Club

Immediately after moving to Atlanta in July of 1979, I went to a local running store (which—coincidentally—was owned by Jeff Galloway) and bought a pair of shoes and mentioned to the young man behind the counter that I wanted to join the Atlanta Track Club. The young man seemed genuinely interested—even intrigued—and asked me what my 10K time was. I proudly told him 40 minutes (remember, at this time I'd been running less than a year) and for the longest time I couldn't understand why he didn't seem impressed. After I joined the ATC, I realized that the men's open competitive team boasted runners who could run 10K in 31 minutes. I also realized why the young man behind the counter didn't seem impressed.

I remain a member of the ATC and am proud to say that I was a member of the men's masters competitive team from 1994 until 2003 (once my Badwater training began and I lost a lot of my speed, I found myself no longer able to meet the qualifying standards for the team. An interesting side note is that these standards were for distances of a marathon or less—I tried to 'debate' that in 2003 I was a nationally-ranked 24-hour endurance runner and won the men's masters 24-Hour National Championship in 2002, so I should still be 'fast enough' to run competitively for the team. Unfortunately, it didn't hold water, and I was relegated to 'inactive' status.).

Getting back to the competitive team, I was proud of some of the things I accomplished with the ATC:

- Being a member of the Men's' Masters Championship Team at the 1995 Marine Corp Marathon (my time was 3:02:26).

- Being a member of the 4th place Men's' Masters Team at the 1997 Chicago Marathon (2:57:38).

- Being a member of the Men's' Masters Teams at the 1995, 1996, 1999 and 2000 Boston Marathon (and achieving team finishes of 11th, 28th, 14th and 43rd, respectively).

- Being a member of the Men's' Masters (unofficial) World Championship 100 X 1 Mile Relay Team (my split was 5:22, which was the average for all 100 legs of the event).

- Being top-seeded (which meant I was able to 'rub elbows with the Kenyans—at least during warm-ups) at the Peachtree Road Race from 1994 through 2002 (with a personal best of 36:56 in 1996).

Peachtree City Running Club

In May of 1990, Cindy and I moved to Peachtree City. One year later I joined the Peachtree City Running Club. In fact, I joined the club on May 11. I remember the date exactly, as it was (a) the day of the Brooks Day 10K, which I ran with several members of the PTCRC, and (b) the day I tried to sign up for the PTCRC 1,000 Mile Club. I say *tried* because I was told by the 1,000 Mile Club coordinator that to be eligible for the 1,000 Mile Club, you had to (a) run 1,000 or more miles from one club Christmas party to the next, and (b) sign up for the 1,000 Mile Club by May 1. As I 'missed the deadline' by 10 days, I was not eligible to sign up this year—I even offered to start from zero on that day.

Ironically, in November of 1994 I was elected President of the PTCRC. After taking office at the Christmas party, I did my very best to turn a club that billed itself as a 'social club with a running problem' (as members liked to boast) into a '*running* club.' One of my clearest memories of my Presidency was running 33 races during the year (including a win in a 50K race) of my Presidency (1995)—most of them on Saturdays, of course—only to discover that once my one-year term as President was over (interesting side note—Presidents of the PTCRC can serve two terms if 're-elected.' To this day, I believe I still remain as its only 'one-year President'), members had been a bit 'negative' towards me for not showing up at the Saturday morning club 'fun runs' (a short 10K, followed by a rather large breakfast more suited to someone who had just run a 50K). The fact that I was running my tail off at races all over Atlanta week after week—wearing a PTCRC singlet and thereby representing the club—didn't seem to carry much weight. A new President was elected in December of 2005 (I dropped out of an election for a second term) and to this day the club remains 'a social club with a running problem.'

Don't get me wrong: the PTCRC is comprised of a lot of really good people doing a lot of really good things, and I have many fine memories from my days with them. In fact, I believe my son Josh was the first 9-year old to ever earn the coveted 1000 Mile Club jacket.

Note: Several of the articles contained in this book originally appeared (albeit in slightly different form) in the official newsletter of the PTCRC, The LEGacy, in the early 1990's (which may explain why a couple of them sound a bit dated).

United States Streak Running Association

In 1994 George Hancock, a runner in Pennsylvania, developed a list of the top streak runners in America. When his first listing was published (fall of 1994), I found I owned the 9th-longest consecutive days running streak in the USA. Twelve years later, I have managed to work my way up to … 36th place! This group of streakers formed an official club, the USRSA, just after the turn of the century, and if you have $20—and a streak of one year or more—you can be a member.

Gulf Winds Track Club

After meeting up and running with Gary Griffin at the 2002 Callaway Gardens Marathon, and after hearing Al's tales of the 'good old days' with the Gulf Winds Track Club of Tallahassee, Florida, it was inevitable that I would one day become a member. It's turned out to be a rewarding venture, as I've met many dedicated and talented GWTC runners: Fred Johnson, Gordon Cherr and of course, Gary Griffin. Al has retained his membership after being away from Tallahassee for so many years—the GWTC instills that type of loyalty in a person.

I've been fortunate enough to run the Tallahassee Ultra Distance Classic (consisting of both 50K and 50 mile options) six times and have a pretty good track record:

- An overall victory in the 50K in 1998
- Two masters championships in the 50K (2001 and 2005)
- Two masters championships in the 50 miler (2003 and 2006)

- A 7th place finish in the 50K in 2004

On a personal note, it's a good feeling being a University of Florida Gator and doing so well in the home of our rival Florida State Seminoles.

Knowing the Race Director of the 2003 Tallahassee Marathon (Gary!) proved invaluable, as the race was canceled due to lightning and thunder storms. However, after pleading with Gary to let those who wanted to do battle with the elements run the marathon, he allowed those of us who still wanted to compete (maybe 18 or so) to do just that—and Dana Stetson volunteered to ride the lead bicycle. Fred Johnson and I managed to tie for the 'championship' in a modest time of 3:21 (my one and only marathon 'win' ever). I've had a lot of success running GWTC events, particularly in the ultra arena.

It only seems fitting that I remain a member of the GWTC—and that many of its members are also members of the Darkside Running Club—as I used the 1994 Tallahassee Marathon as a qualifier for the Boston Marathon (at the insistence of Al and Valerie Reynolds, who had already run a qualifier). The three of us ran the 1994 Boston Marathon together, and shortly thereafter we laid the foundation for the Darkside Running Club.

Georgia Ultrarunning and Trailrunning Society

My membership in the Georgia Ultrarunning and Trailrunning Society (GUTS) is more of a 'reciprocal membership' agreement I have with its President, Janice Anderson. Janice, one of the most talented trail ultrarunners in the country and former President of the Atlanta Track Club, has always supported my feeble efforts at trail-running and over the years I have been a participant in many of her 'Fat Ass 50K's' in various topographically-undesirable-to-me locales around Atlanta (Stone Mountain, Kennesaw Mountain). When GUTS was formed by Janice and her trail cohorts, several other ultra events were added to the club's arsenal, including the Silver Comet Ultra Run 50K and 100K. In the 2006 edition of the 50K, I managed to set a Georgia State age group record. The surface? Concrete bicycle trails (not trails!).

Janice was also instrumental in helping to make the Darkside Running Club's Peachtree City 50K the host of the first Georgia State 50K Road Race Championship (in only the race's second year of existence). One year later we were honored to host the National 50K Road Race Championship—where the fastest road

50K of the year in America was run—and thanks to the exceptional fund-raising talents of Darksider Andy Velazco, $3,000 in prize money was offered to the top runners in the event.

Darkside Running Club

The one club in which I truly, truly belong. No excuses ... no whining ... everything is possible. I am proud of all of the members, as their passion for running is as strong as mine.

Exactly what is the DARKSIDE?

The prelude to the official formation of the DARKSIDE Running Club (in December of 2001) took place in the fall of 1993. Al Barker, Valerie Reynolds and I discovered that we shared a love for marathons as well as a passion for running long distances—*frequently!* I paced Valerie at the Atlanta Marathon on Thanksgiving Day 1993, her goal being to qualify for the Boston Marathon for the first time. Val ran incredibly strong that day—considering we had only been doing long runs together for six weeks. Al ran Atlanta also, and they decided they would be going to Boston in April. They also decided that *I* would be going as well. I reminded them that I did not have an official qualifying time, so they decided I would run the Tallahassee Marathon in February to earn a ticket to Boston.

I qualified at Tallahassee, and Al and Val ran it as well (as a training run). The weekend in Tallahassee was short and precise: we drove to Tallahassee Friday night after work, spent the night, ran the marathon, and returned home Saturday afternoon—all accomplished in less than 24 hours. Thus the phrase *'business trip marathon'* was coined. There would be many more to follow.

Through the years, we've maintained our friendship and our mileage, and between the three of us we have well over 250 marathons. Not to mention quite a few ultras as well.

The principles of our friendship and our running served as the foundation for the DARKSIDE. Specifically, they are:

- *A passion for running: the longer the distance the better.*
- *A desire to stay in marathon shape year-round.*

- *Competition.*

- *Camaraderie.*

- *Pushing and motivating each other to excel.*

- *A keen sense of humor.*

- *Dedication.*

- *Not taking yourself seriously.*

- *A love of marathons ... and beyond.*

- *Believing that nothing is outside the realm of possibility.*

Ten years later, all ten of these principles are still in tact.

Welcome to the DARKSIDE.

1994 Boston Marathon—with Al and Valerie

The Birth of the DARKSIDE

Our regular group of Sunday 20-milers got together for a Christmas dinner at the home of Paula May and Eric Huguelet one Friday night in December of 2001. Following dinner, we officially formed the DARKSIDE Running Club. The original four members were Paula, Al Barker, Kelly Murzynsky and I. Eric (Paula's husband) and Joe (Kelly's husband) were to be known as the DARK-SIDE Ladies' Auxiliary, with Eric as President. I was selected (honored!) to be the first President of the DARKSIDE.

We formed our own set of rules and regulations that we decided could be (a) changed on a whim and/or (b) made up as we went along. Some of the 'rules' that have withstood the test of time:

- No excuses and more importantly no whining.

- When presented with the choice of several distances (at a race), select the longest one.

- Run a race in the *shirt from that race* and face serious consequences.

- Live by the slogan *'If you don't make eye contact, it never happened.'**

*Interpretation: if you engage in a questionable behavior—i.e. public urination, changing from running clothes into dry clothes while standing next to your car after a run—if you don't make eye contact with another person, as far as you or anyone else knows, *it never happened!*

- Facts only—no boasting—report on your running credentials/race results *only* when asked.

- It's never too early/late/hot/cold/(insert excuse of choice here) to run.

- No bailing out on group long runs (*unless* you say you're *going to* before the run begins).

- No name dropping (*'me and Uta,' 'I was telling Billy Rodgers,'* etc.) or race dropping (*'at Gasparilla,' 'going up Heartbreak Hill,'* etc.).

- Relays are for those who can't do the whole thing by themselves.

- Leave trail running to mountain goats.

And the most important of them all (which has gotten more than one of us in trouble):

- **Once you *say* it, you've got to *do* it!**

We have managed to have a lot of fun with these over the years, and we make it a point to notate any 'infractions,' like when Paula, Al and I were in line for the porta-john just before the start of a marathon and Paula said (loudly enough for several runners to hear) 'I'm cold; I wish I'd brought my Boston jacket along' (Rule violated: No race dropping.).

We are excited about what our small band of runners has established, and are quite proud of our membership. We have many incredibly talented runners on board, as well as several novice runners who are working their way towards their own individual goals. The membership is spread all over the country, and we remain connected though our newsletter and the internet. It's not uncommon for Darksiders from three or four different states to show up at the same race; when it happens, we're sure to hang the 'Darkside Distance Team' banner prominently at the event.

In 2002 the first quarterly issue of our newsletter, *absolutely true ... Tales from the DARKSIDE* was published. I may be slightly biased, but I believe it's the most entertaining, informative and motivating running periodical today. But don't take my word for it:

- *Your newsletter has too many highlights to mention. It is a serious slice of journalistic heaven.*–Gary Griffin
- *Your newsletter reflects what runners really talk about.*—Fred Johnson
- *I laughed until tears were running down my face.*–Mary Lane Johnson
- *I enjoyed looking through your newsletter and got some laughs. Neat publication; well, maybe d-a-r-k publication. But weird is good. All the best.*–Bruce Morrison, Editor of *The Running Journal*

In 2002, the first Peachtree City (Georgia) 50K was hosted by our club. Subsequent events added to our repertoire were the Darkside 8-hour Run (established in 2003), the Darkside Marathon (established in 2005), and the Way Too Hot 50K (established in 2006).

In 2006, our website was created–and is being expertly maintained–by one of our members, Doug Cassiday. Feel free to visit us by going to:

www.darksiderunningclub.com

Who knows? You may be one of us.

A Quick Peek Inside:

absolutely true ... Tales from the DARKSIDE

The official newsletter of the Darkside Running Club is published quarterly. In each issue you'll find articles from a variety of authors, as well as photographs and race reviews from all around the world.

The regular features include:

- The Starting Line–The introductory comments by the editor (me!) outlining what's in store in the current issue.

- Speed Kills–Race results from the members (including finishes of note; i.e. 1st in age group, first overall, personal best). Note: 'Kills" can be read as a noun or a verb–reader's choice.

- The Finishing Kick–Final comments by the editor summarizing the issue as well as what to look forward to during the next three months.

- The Runner's High Photo Gallery–Photographs submitted by members from races, training runs, etc. Occasionally, photographs tend to be somewhat 'creative.' For example, you never know when Al Barker my be superimposed running with the Kenyan front runners at the Peachtree Road Race.

- The DARKSIDE answers your Questions–We firmly believe that so-called 'expert opinions' to running-related questions are nothing more than that–opinions. We firmly believe that opinions are like butt holes; everyone has one. With that in mind, we began providing our own opinions to questions we ran across in more prominent running periodicals. However, after two years of answering (I'll summarize here) 'shut up and run' to most of them, we realized that the following is a composite of pretty much *all* of the questions we ran across:

  I really want to qualify for Boston, but I've got several problems I need your help with. First of all, I hurt pretty much all over my entire body when I run. What can I do to make it not hurt so much? Once I can run injury-free, I know the 20/30/40 (pick one) *miles I run each week will be enough to get me in marathon shape, but I really hate doing 20-mile runs—they're just too long. What other training can I do that simulates a 20-miler? Will cycling help? By the way, did I mention that where I live it's too hot/cold/humid/arid* (again, pick one) *to run long? As for speed work: it makes my plantar warts irritable and results in an ugly phlegm in my throat. Could you just recommend a training program that will allow me to qualify for Boston without running too many miles/doing any speed work/doing long runs/causing my body to hurt* (pick pretty much all of these)?

- The FLYING PENGUIN Awards—Every month this coveted award is given to any DARKSIDER who does something noteworthy, presumably for something to do with—but not limited to—running. A few winners include:

  - Todd Davison (December 2002) for qualifying for Boston in his first marathon.

  - Al Barker at age 56 runs an impressive 19:14 5K—only six days after running the Boston Marathon (April 2002)

  - Paula May sets a Georgia women's state age group (50-54) 10K record (March 2003).

  - Kelly Murzynsky wins the first two ultras she runs—the Tallahassee 50K and the inaugural Peachtree City 50K. (December 2001, November 2002, respectively). Note–Kelly later wins the next two 50K's she enters (again, in Tallahassee and Peachtree City), making her four-for-four.

  - Susan Lance, in her first competition longer than 41 miles, runs 107.4 miles and finishes as the 5th female at the USATF 24-Hour Championships in San Diego (November 2004).

  - Paula May finishes two races in the same hour–and wins both of them (May 2005).

  - Lloyd Young, age 82, establishes national age group records for 50 miles, 100K and 24 hours at the FANS 24-Hour Run (June 2005).

  - Craig Snapp and Debbie Ciccati both run personal highs of 643 miles each in one month (August 2005).

- Danielle Goodgion runs her 2nd lifetime ultra at the Darkside 8-Hour Run–a mere one week after running her 1st lifetime ultra (April 2006).

- Brenton Floyd wins his first ultra (Darkside 8-Hour Run), completes his 300th lifetime marathon/ultra (Knoxville Marathon), and finishes his 1st 100-miler (Umstead). He also celebrates turning 21 years of age (April 2006).

- Prince Whatley celebrates the completion of his first 50 mile run in Tallahassee by running the accompanying marathon the very next day (December 2003).

- Andy Velazco raises $3,000 in contributions to fund the prize money in the Peachtree City 50K, which is serving as the National 50K Championship (May 2004).

- Sandy Geisel completes the Western States Endurance Run, and appears on the cover of the DARKSIDE newsletter (June 2003)!

- 'Brain FART*leks*'–An occasional special feature that highlights anything strange, unique or downright noteworthy in the world or running. A few examples:

  - Sandy Geisel ran only two of the four laps of the Atlanta Fat Ass 50K, or as she referred to it, the 'Half Ass.'

  - Andy Velazco has an entire article in the July/August 2003 issue of *Marathon and Beyond* summarizing his crewing efforts at Badwater in 2002 (where he paced the participant for 90 miles).

  - Eric Huguelet was so excited about winning his first race award (at the Run for Alex 5K) that he went home and built shelves (plural) for his award (singular).

  - At the Peachtree City 50K, the head of the Georgia Chapter of the USATF spoke with Race Director Scott Ludwig two times on race day: once to say 'good morning' and once when runner Sue Sinclair was bitten by a dog on the course to scream 'YOU BETTER TAKE CARE OF THIS ... NOW!!!' as if he was 10 years old. Actually, we exaggerate: he screamed at Scott as if he were eight years old.

- Quarterly Race Calendar–a truly unique calendar–compiled regularly by Al Barker–as it contains a variety of (usually marathons or longer) distances in a variety of locales all over the country. What makes it truly 'unique'? The chances are excellent that a Darksider will be participating in them.

- Darkside Profiles–Get to know the members of the Darkside Running Club 'up close and personal'.

- The Cover–you never know what to expect on the cover of the news letter. Past issues have included:

  - Sue Sinclair, the runner mentioned earlier that was bit by a dog in the Peachtree City 50K

  - Andy Velazco, pictured in the middle of Death Valley during his participation in the Badwater Ultramarathon

  - Yours truly, in a race to the finish with Heathcliff the Cow in the 1994 Tallahassee Marathon.

  - Susan Lance's arm and leg, both sporting fresh injuries sustained from falls she experienced doing what she loves most–running trails.

  - Gary Griffin, Fred Johnson, and yours truly after completing the first–and only–Posey's 50K Run.

  - Sandy Geisel competing in the Western States Endurance Run (she finished!).

  - Al Barker competing in the Western States Endurance Run (he didn't).

  - Al Barker with his good friend, Bill Rodgers (yes, *that* Bill Rodgers).

  - Al Barker with his good friends Gordy Ansleigh and Cowman A-Moo-Ha

- The Articles–As mentioned earlier, the articles are submitted by the members of the club, and for the most part, 'what you see is what you get.' By that, I mean that I don't reject anything from the members: if it's submitted, it gets printed (although all are subject to a little editing and/or modification). Not only are the members talented runners, they are talented writers as well. Here are a few examples of their writing styles. We'll call them:

Literary Splits

Did I mention I'm in better shape than most women half my age?
-50 year old Paula May, in reference to her exercise regimen

Did I mention I'm in better shape than most women twice my age?
-60 year old Al Barker, in reference to his exercise regimen

Running a marathon makes the turkey taste so good.
-Al Barker, in a newspaper article about his running the Atlanta Marathon on Thanksgiving Day

How many runners does it take to run Hood-to-Coast? Twelve Atlanta Track Club Masters or one Scott Ludwig.
-Mike Popick, discussing how to put a team together for the 195 mile relay

Our exclusive interview with Frank Shorter wasn't 'exclusive.' Actually, it wasn't even real, as we made it all up.
-Editor, making a correction from a prior issue

Remember, we welcome any submissions (photos, articles) for this newsletter. We can make use of just about anything; we even used an article from *Runner's World* for something useful—rolling it up and swatting a fly.
-Scott Ludwig, sharing his special affinity for a rival publication

Any one I want.
-Valerie Reynolds, veteran marathoner, when asked which marathon she would use to qualify for the Boston Marathon

Running an ultra is not like a walk in the park. It is like a day in hell.
-Normer Adams, after completing the JFK 50 Mile Run

Compared to other races, it was probably the most enjoyable race that I have ever run.
-Normer Adams, adding to his previous comment after the JFK 50

I will never run that freakin' race again.
-Scott Ludwig, after completing the JFK 50 Mile Run

You can check out, but you can never leave.
-Keith Wright, after spending a summer training with the core Darksiders and returning to his home in New Jersey

Darksiders know that moonlight running is best. It's cooler, there's no traffic at 4:00 a.m., and at that time of day, no one will have called or come by to spoil your running plans.
-Paula May, giving her opinion on the best time of day to run

Run early, before you actually wake up.
-Keith Wright, giving his opinion on the best time of day to run

Imagine running a quarter mile at 75 seconds. Now do 100 of them without stopping. You'd STILL finish a half mile behind the leaders.
-Larry Rawson, while broadcasting the Boston Marathon

The word 'Darkside' is appropriate for the group for two reasons: (1) it is not like your ordinary local running club, and (2) the members do a great bit of their training in the dark (literally).
-Scott Ludwig, describing how the Darkside Running Club got its name

Once you say it, you gotta do it!
-Darkside regulation

Whining and excuses are forbidden.
-Darkside regulation

Maintain enough mileage to allow for guilt-free food (or drink) binges.
-(maybe the most important) Darkside regulation

Get bigger shoes, dumbass.
-Kelly Murzynsky, offering advice to a runner suffering from black toenails

The fact that you even asked this question say there's no hope for you. Learn to play the accordion instead.
-Al Barker, answering an inane question posed by a beginning runner in Runner's World

Sell crazy someplace else. We're all stocked up here.
-Al Barker, responding to yet another inane question posed by a beginning runner in Runner's World

When the aliens come, they're going to eat the fat ones first.
-Al Barker, explaining why he runs

Starting off too fast in a race and slowing down later results in a positive split performance (first half faster than the second half). More appropri-

ate terminology for it would be 'premature acceleration.'
-(We'll say) anonymous

We're always looking for new runners to 'cross on over' to the Darkside, so they too can capitalize on the things we consider a privilege to enjoy—health, fitness, camaraderie, passion, enthusiasm, dedication, and knowing that these things make any goal possible. We're even able to make the rather extreme goals sound reasonable.
-Scott Ludwig, discussing what the Darkside Running Club is all about

On a particularly cold morning, Al couldn't understand why his ski cap wouldn't fit over his head. Turns out he had taken a cat sweater out of the closet, not his ski cap.
-Scott Ludwig, on Al Barker getting ready for a winter run

Put me down for a turd.
-Al Barker, returning from a visit to the desert and reporting to Badwater crew chief Paula May, who was monitoring everyone's 'intake and output' during the 135 mile event

The last wine station, one of the busiest, was also serving raw oysters.
-Andy Velazco, reporting on the peculiarities of France's Medoc Marathon

Long day after long day after long day—things that never would have been possible or would have been considered inane became commonplace.
-Gary Griffin, discussing his string of ultra performances in the middle of 2002

On top I saw the snow and couldn't resist doing 'snow angels' in the middle of summer.
-Sandy Geisel, commenting on her activities after the first 3.7 miles of the 100 mile Western States Endurance Run

The temperature was 119 degrees Fahrenheit—in the shade—at 2:00 p.m.
-Andy Velazco, on the conditions in Furnace Creek two days before the Badwater Ultramarathon began

The two hazards we were warned about never materialized, which were (a) watch out for rattlesnakes warming themselves on the road after dark and (b) watch out for local rednecks riding around after midnight

throwing beer bottles at you.
-John Saunders, discussing comments from the Race Director at the Bethel Hill Midnite Boogie

A friend once told me 'after your first hundred (marathons), you will just begin to learn how to be a long distance runner.
-Andy Velazco, after finishing his 100th marathon

So, in no particular order, Pennar offers: bird excreta, occasional 100+ degree heat indices, zero shade, and a 4:00 a.m. start.
-Gary Griffin, on the appeal of the Pennar 40-Mile Run

I would not have dreamed of attempting a 100 day streak of running had it not been for the sick, degenerate example set by Sir Scott of the Darkness, and I am certain that this helped me to reach a new level of endurance and self discipline in my training.
-Prince Whatley, discussing one of the factors contributing to his PR at Nashville's Country Music Marathon

I can believe a guy ran a 2:05 marathon; I can believe a guy ran 26 minutes for 10K, but ain't no way I believe that Andy Jones kept his pace under six minutes a mile for all 41.2 of those Strolling Jim miles.
-Carl Laniak, discussing the hilly course at Strolling Jim

Reminiscent of the dirty haze surrounding 'Pig Pen' from the Charlie Brown comic, the flies formed a dense cloud around Scott and Gary.
-Fred Johnson, discussing the conditions at the Posey 50K in Tallahassee

When I arrived at that glorious finish my watch read 3:33:30 and I had tears in my eyes.
-Gary Griffin, on his finish at the Boston Marathon

The Darkside newsletter is what runners REALLY talk about ... not that garbage in *Runner's World.*
-Fred Johnson, discussing his views on Tales from the Darkside

I hate *Runner's World.*
-John Saunders, on his application for membership on the Darkside

I never got to break the tape at the end because they couldn't hold on to it.
-Kelly Murzynsky, discussing her victory in the extremely windy conditions at the Blue Angel Marathon

As I watched the traffic go by, I could see motorists shaking their heads as they saw this tall, skinny Jersey boy running in a driving rainstorm. I pointed to my chest, and muttered, to no one in particular, 'Hey, I am a DARKSIDER!!!"
-Keith Wright, running in difficult conditions getting ready for the Boston Marathon

I understand that the extreme conditions in this race, including but not limited to temperatures in excess of 130F, wind, dust, high altitude, and radiant surface temperatures in excess of 180F, make the risk of dehydration, altitude sickness, significant skin damage, blistering, heat exhaustion, heat stroke, traffic accident, renal shutdown, brain damage and death possible.
-Warning to entrants on the application for Badwater

You know you're on the Darkside when you only plan vacations where there is a weekend race.
-Paula May, explaining one way of knowing you've 'crossed over'

You know you're on the Darkside when you are wearing running clothes in all the photos in your album.
-Paula May, explaining another way of knowing

A little less whining and more technical information would have been nice.
-Al Barker, reviewing the book To the Edge by Kirk Johnson, a Badwater veteran

ZZZZZZZZZZZZZZ
-Scott Ludwig, reviewing the movie Chariots of Fire

I look back on it with both horror and gladness.
-Gary Griffin, thirteen months after crewing at Badwater

Running is often difficult … it is hard to breathe, it makes you sweat a lot, and your legs ache and burn and they get tired.
-Gary Griffin, remembering why he runs

As the South Africans say, you have to run at least one Comrades in your life; but to really know the course you have to run it both ways.
-Andy Velazco, after finishing Comrades and thinking about running it again next year when it is run in the opposite direction

Around mile 53 I blew lunch in front of my crew and lost my pasta dinner and anything else that was in my stomach.
-Mike Brooks, recounting a highlight from running Badwater

In the ultrarunner world, Badwater is the Holy Grail.
-Andy Velazco, Badwater veteran and 2004 Badwater crew member

Run every run like it is your last.
-Keith Wright, on his personal philosophy about running

When you step off that concrete, you're in Alabama.
-Stranger to John Saunders as he was looking for the 'Run to Alabama' finish line along the Silver Comet Trail

I ended up with 22 stumbles and three actual falls, and the three falls were quite spectacular.
-Paula May, commenting on her Hot to Trot 8-Hour Run

We didn't finish last, however, so we can be thankful for that.
-Mary Lane Johnson, after completing the Summer Beaches Run

I fell off a bicycle once, and it was standing still.
-Al Barker, recounting his athletic prowess as a youth

Why is it so much easier to get into a routine of sitting on you're ass than it is to get into exercising?
-Stephanie Sudduth, lamenting after a self-imposed break from running

I've never been handled.
-Paula May, when asked who her favorite handler is

I think they deliberately call it a 5K instead of what it really is; 3.2 miles.
-Rick Ryckeley, writing for a local newspaper about his participation in the Panther Prowl

Today was a day that required walking the uphills. And by uphills, I mean the flats, too.
-Al Barker, after battling the heat in the 2004 Boston Marathon

Years from now, people will look back on this race and we'll be remembered as heroes.
-Prince Whatley, talking about the 2004 Boston Marathon finishers

It's not a run if you don't go anywhere.
-Scott Ludwig, discussing his views on running on treadmills

Any run that requires me to use my hands to advance is no longer a foot race.
-Scott Ludwig, after running—and climbing—the Oak Mountain 50K, a notorious trail run

Don't you feel better after you take a day off?
-Countless people to Scott Ludwig after they find out he's run every day for over 28 years

That sure sucked.
-Scott Ludwig, after dropping out at Western States at mile 62

Scotty's feet were hanging off the bed about fifteen inches from my face. If you have never seen his feet, consider yourself of good fortune. Most of his toenails are black, his toes look like they have been hammered and shaped by some crazed artisan, and they stick out in every direction imaginable at the same time. Some of his toes were covered in what appeared to be electrical tape, others in duct tape, that much was clear.
-Gordon Cherr, waking up on the motel floor following a short night's sleep after Scott's Western States failure

Carl Laniak gave it to me because he thought I looked fast before a race started. Boy, was he wrong.
-John Saunders, explaining how he got the nickname 'Speedhog'

When you can't run a 10K at the same pace you once ran your marathon PR, your racing career is over.
-Scott Ludwig, reflecting on his loss of speed

What is anal glaucoma? Essentially, it means that I just don't ever see my ass running fast again.
-Scott Ludwig, adding to the previous comment

I was pretty much a bloody mess.
-Gary Griffin, commenting on the aftermath of the Mountain Mist 50K

Strap a twelve pound bowling ball on your back and run a timed mile at the track.
-Scott Ludwig, suggesting how to determine the effects of weight gain on one's running

Believe in yourself; you can do more than you think possible.
-Janice Anderson, offering advice to other runners

I love the way the running articles 'tell it like it is' as compared to other running magazines that gloss over all the 'real stuff' that happens when you run.
-*Mary Lane Johnson, on why the Darkside newsletter is her favorite running publication*

In my estimation, the distance was closer to 57 kilometers or so.
-*Scott Ludwig, following the Oak Mountain 50K*

2003 was different, as I did 17 doubles (52.4 to 62 miles in two days). Those weeks I only did a three mile run on Wednesday—I needed to recover.
-*Brenton Floyd, describing a 'typical' week of running*

The most important thing I've gained through my association with the Darksiders is a group of friends who believe in and practice friendship.
-*Susan Lance, on being a member of the Darkside Running Club*

Run, bitch.
-*Obviously intoxicated bar patron to Prince Whatley as he ran by at 4:30 a.m. on a cold Tuesday morning along the sidewalks of New York City*

After reading the article about 'what makes one a Darksider,' I realized that deep down I am a Darksider as well.'
-*Jonathan Beverly, editor of Running Times, after reading an issue of absolutely true … Tales from the Darkside.*

I noticed that this year Mr. Beverly entered the Boston Marathon but failed to finish, most likely a result of the extremely unfavorable heat. Sorry, Jonathan; your DNF rules you out as a Darksider. A *true* Darksider would have completed this year's Boston Marathon … crawling on their hands and knees just like the rest of us.
-*Scott Ludwig, commenting on Jonathan Beverly's previous statement*

The part about Jonathan Beverly failing to meet Darkside standards because of his Boston DNF cracked me up. I dropped out of that race (in 2003) myself, so I guess I'm screwed as well.
-*Kevin Beck, Senior Writer for Running Times*

Eat less. Move more. Don't smoke.
-*The entirety of Al Barker's condensed version of a self-improvement book*

It took me a solid twelve days before I was rid of the virus that my 'friends' at work began referring to as 'Ebola.' Actually, I lost so much blood during those twelve days that they weren't far from the truth.
-*Scott Ludwig, recounting a bad experience while suffering from E coli 1057*

I'm expecting to see an Adonis bathed in a golden light. He will be a man with a perfect physique, and catlike movements, like a leopard stalking game. He will be surrounded by adoring ultra marathoners, answering their questions, deciding their race strategies and approving their regimes and generally holding court about the fine points of ultra-marathoning.
-*Jim Bonds, anticipating his first meeting with Scott Ludwig*

To say his mechanics are piss poor is putting it mildly. I wouldn't bet on him finishing a two mile run with a tailwind—without stopping for a breather … or a smoke.
-*Jim Bonds, moments after meeting Scott Ludwig and seeing him run for the first time*

You don't have any elite men in the field yet? Well, you have one now.
-*Scott Wolf telling Peachtree City 50K Race Director Scott Ludwig of his imminent entry in the event (note: Mr. Wolf did not enter)*

It's all in the head, and if there's nothing in the head to begin with, it's that much easier.
-*Craig Snapp, explaining his philosophy of running*

In July of 2001, Brenton became the youngest person to run a marathon in all 50 states and D.C. when he completed the Snow Mountain Marathon in Winter Park, Colorado. It was time for him to slow down, so he only did 21 marathons that year.
-*Betty Burrell, discussing the accomplishments of her 16-year old grandson Brenton Floyd*

What made the day distinct wasn't what Bob Ray did, but what (he) didn't do for the first time in 13,885 days.
-*Mike Klingaman, describing the day that Bob Ray decided to end his consecutive days running streak of over 38 years*

He had my total focus, attention and interest until he said his body was 'ripped like a prizefighters,' which—unfortunately—was on page 4.'

-Scott Ludwig, expressing his thoughts on Dean Karnazes' autobiographical book, Ultramarathon Man: Confessions of an All-Night Runner

I am getting happy feet watching the runners go by.
-Gordon Cherr, while observing runners circling a two-mile loop during a 50-mile ultramarathon

I have an entry for next year's Florida Ironman. I need to learn to swim.
-Andy Velazco, optimistically expressing a personal goal

'Ya gotta want it bad, Sarah, ya gotta want it bad.'
-Rob Apple offering advice to Sarah Tynes on what it takes to finish the Vermont 100 Mile Run

As much as I wanted to finish that run, missing the cut off after only 24 miles was almost a relief in some way … a mercy killing.
-Al Barker, after being pulled from the tortuous 2006 Western States Endurance Run

I'm telling you if I could have eaten aluminum and pooped out a can of beer I would have.
-Danielle Goodgion, recalling what she would have done to help Scott Ludwig as his pacer at the 2004 Western States Endurance Run

I am working on my speed and will return to ultra runs after I turn 85, when I enter into a new age group.
-Lloyd Young, 83, looking ahead to 2008

I want to be just like Lloyd when I grow up.
-Al Barker, 61, commenting on the running prowess of Lloyd Young

If my mother knew what I was doing, she would be turning in her grave, but the exercise would do her good.
-Charles Cohn, 75, discussing his prowess for completing long-distance events

99.9—the percentage of the total time elapsed between miles 20 and 30 that either Gary Griffin or Scott Ludwig spent whining to the other about how miserable they felt.
-Gary Griffin, analyzing a 50-mile ultra in which he and Scott both competed

I've literally seen more doctors in the past five months than I have in the previous 35 years. It would be one thing if they were all for one or two ailments. But they were for a variety of problems: tics, foot infections, e coli, cuts requiring sutures, and water on the knee. There were others as well, but I kept them to myself as I didn't want my doc to think I was a hypochondriac.

-Scott Ludwig, recalling a particularly difficult time towards the end of 2006

CHAPTER EIGHT
RUNNING IN THE DARK
The Mystique of the Ultra

The largest 10K in the country has over 55,000 runners. The largest marathon in the country has over 40,000 runners. The largest ultra in the country has slightly over 1,000 runners. However, most ultras have a small, intimate field of several dozen runners.

Several dozen driven, determined, and incredibly dedicated runners.

In this chapter:

- Anything Over 26.2 Miles Ain't So Bad—I ran my first ultra—a 50 Miler at Stone Mountain Park—and it elevated my love for running to another level.

- Something I Always Wanted to Do—Running the width of the state of Georgia—all 280 miles of it—had never been done before. I wanted to be the first to do it, even if I only had three years of running under my belt.

- A Relay? In the Mountains?—I hate running in the mountains, and relays are for runners who can't do the whole thing by themselves. So why am I here?

- 19:31:10—Once upon a time there was a runner who wanted to run 100 miles. What did he do about it? He entered a 24-hour endurance run.

- Something I Never Want to Do Again—Ten years later, and still no one had run the 280 miles across the width of Georgia. Since I now had thirteen years of running under my belt, why not give it a second shot?

- At Long, Long Last—Winning my first race was a huge moment in my running career. Hey, aren't you listening: WINNING MY FIRST RACE WAS A HUGE MOMENT IN MY RUNNING CAREER!

- 'Strolling' Jim?—I Don't *think* so!—It was supposed to be a nice, easy 41 mile jaunt through the country roads of Tennessee. The best laid plans ...

- 24:00:00—My second attempt in the 24-hour endurance run. This time I made it to the finish line.

- Wakulla Springs Ultra Redux 2003 (by Gordon Cherr)—What's more fun than a 50-mile jaunt on a cool, brisk Saturday morning in December? Pizza and beer on Saturday night, and a nice, easy marathon Sunday morning.

- Renegade—Once again, it was supposed to be a nice, easy 41 miles jaunt through the country roads of Tennessee.

- Come Sail Away—However, I never do anything 'nice and easy.' This Strolling Jim was no exception.

- Olander Memories—Some of my finest ultra memories were made on the 1.091 mile loop of Olander Park in Sylvania, Ohio. I'll miss not having the opportunity to make more.

- Ultras (Road surface only)—A chronological history—by distance—of my two dozen years of ultras.

Anything Over 26.2 Miles Ain't So Bad

If you have never attempted an ultramarathon (by definition, anything over 26.2 miles), I can understand why the title above wouldn't make much sense to you. However, if you *have* attempted and/or completed an ultramarathon, then you know *exactly* what I'm talking about.

I can see by the collective blank look on your faces that most of you aren't on the same page. For that matter, I'm not sure you're even in the same *book*.

Perhaps I can clear this up for you. Following are several tidbits that led me to reach the conclusion I revealed to you in the title of this piece—that anything over 26.2 miles ain't so bad.

- A true marathon of 26.2 miles is considered for the most part a 'race." Anything *over* that distance is considered an 'endurance run.' To finish an ultra with the same body and mind that you started with is one of the many measures of success in an ultra.

- It is very acceptable—and highly recommended—to eat and drink as much as you need/want/crave during an ultra. Unlike a marathon, you should feel no guilt if you stop running at any time to replenish. Stopping to rest is permissible as well.

- Speaking of running, should you walk during an ultra, remember that this is the *norm*, not the *exception*. Again, no guilt required should you stop running and feel a need to walk for any reason. In fact, in the latter stages of some ultras, the simple act of walking is a challenge.

- Talking to other 'competitors' is highly encouraged. Actually, anything you can do to keep your mind occupied while you cover 30, 40, 50+ miles is highly suggested.

- Bathroom breaks really don't interfere with your overall time, especially when you calculate your 'pit-stops-to-miles' ratio is only 1 to 15 (O.K. those of you who know me know my ratio is more like 1 to 5, but I make up for them by trying to eat and run at the same time).

- The cardinal rule of ultrarunning: WALK THE UPHILLS!! Where else do you find an athletic event with a recommended strategy like *THAT!!!???*

- The 'competition' in an utra is always thinner than in any race of 26.2 miles or less. Of course, 'competition' is probably not the correct word. With very few exceptions, participants in an ultra are really not 'competing,' but merely 'surviving.'

- Once you complete an ultra, you are not physically exhausted as you would be had you run an all-out race of a shorter distance. Speaking from experience, a 5K *race* takes more out of me than a 50K ultra (note: a pace for a 50K is about 28 percent slower than a pace for a 5K. If you run a 5K at an 8:00 minute/mile pace, expect to run a 50K slightly slower than a 10:00 pace).*

*Addendum to note: Be advised that this is merely a 'rule of thumb' and is most definitely NOT supported by scientific research. It is merely an educated estimate on my part.

- Success in an ultra marathon is more mind over matter than anything else. Slow or fast twitch muscles, carbo-loading, interval and fartlek training, racing flats, negative splits—fuggetabowdit. Just lace up your shoes and make sure you have enough to think about for several hours.

- When tackling an ultra remember one word:

PATIENCE

Get used to the idea that you're going to be there for a while. And along the way, make sure to 'stop and smell the roses.' You'll be glad you did.

Where else can you find an athletic event that you can be successful at while eating—drinking—walking—talking—even answering nature's call?

Interested, are you? If you're thinking that I might be right after all—that anything over 26.2 miles ain't so bad—maybe an ultra is right for you.

Something I always Wanted to Do

I became fascinated with ultramarathoning early in my running career. I ran my first marathon after only four months of running and moved on to my first ultra three years later. In the winter of 1982, I, along with 17 other adventurous souls, started a 50-mile race around the base of Stone Mountain (10 five-mile loops). After some sound advice from a veteran ultra runner early in the race (walk the uphills or pay the price later) I had no trouble completing the race, finishing in 7:28:20 … good enough for 6th place. I decided right then and there that the longer the race, the better off I was. I was, indeed, an ultrarunner (or at least I had the potential to be).

Then I made another decision: to run an ultramarathon that no one had ever run before. Inspired by the efforts of two southeastern runners who had run across not only states but entire countries as well, I decided I would run width-wise across the state of Georgia, from Columbus to Savannah (crossing the state from west to east). I knew that one of the aforementioned runners had run Georgia from north to south, but no one had ever run west to east (or east to west, for that matter). I hoped to be the first. Here was my chance to complete an ultra that had never been attempted, let alone completed.

The preparatory stage of my forthcoming journey was enjoyable. Initially, I looked on a map of Georgia to find an "out of the way" two-lane road that ran from one side of the state to the other. Georgia Highway 280 fit the bill. I could start at the Georgia-Alabama border in Columbus, GA and finish along the coast in Savannah. I drove the route two months prior to the actual run, which I had scheduled to begin on Saturday, October 30 and end on Saturday, November 6. I plotted every conceivable landmark, water stop, mote/hotel, convenience store, gas station, and town on my route. If it existed on Highway 280, it was on my map. Every mile was indicated so that I would be able to monitor my progress along the way. My goal was to run between 33 and 38 miles a day, allowing me to complete the 280 miles in approximately eight days.

The week prior to my run was enjoyable as well. Getting all my supplies ready— three pairs of running shoes, numerous changes of running attire, toiletries, canteen, cash/credit cards, medical supplies and lots of Vaseline—added fuel to my already burning fire. I couldn't wait to get started. I had it all planned: My wife Cindy would drive me to Columbus on Friday, October 29 and after a good night's sleep in a hotel near the start I would begin my cross-state trek early Saturday morning. All systems were, as they say, 'go.'

One small detail before I move on to the run itself. Early in the afternoon on Friday October 29–the day before the run–Cindy asked me how many people were aware of my imminent adventure. When I told her 'just a few close friends and co-workers' (I had to take a week's vacation for my run), she said I should let the Atlanta Track Club know what I was up to. (Very) Reluctantly, I phoned their office and told someone there of my plans. When the voice on the other end of the telephone concluded our conversation by asking the inevitable 'why,' I merely said that it was something I always wanted to do. Little did I know how these words would come back to haunt me.

The evening of October 29, Cindy and I drove to a small hotel in Columbus where I would get what would prove to be my last good night's sleep for a month. The plan was falling into place nicely. Cindy would lead/follow me in our van the first two days of the run, allowing me to progress without having to carry a 20-pound pack on my back.

The first thing I did on **DAY ONE** (Saturday, October 30) was decide to run 50+ miles each of the first two days, taking full advantage of not having to carry the backpack. I awoke around 5:00 AM and decided to get started right away. As the hotel was merely a half mile from the Alabama/Georgia border, I walked to my 'starting line.' My trek officially began at 7:10 AM. Cindy met me around the 22 mile mark later in the morning with a dozen of the finest doughnuts I have ever had the pleasure of devouring. I ended up running 58 miles that first day, finishing slightly past Plains. Fortunately, the weather was fairly cool, and I made it through the day with few, if any problems (*detectable* problems, anyway). I stopped running that first day at 6:30 PM. At this point, I wondered if I underestimated my ultrarunning prowess and questioned whether or not I could complete my run in six days, maybe less.

Awakening the morning of **DAY TWO** (Sunday, October 31) I was glad to discover that I only had a few aches and pains, and lo and behold, no blisters! Immediately, I decided my goal was another 50+ miles for the day. Beginning the second day's run at 7:30 AM. I was pleased to find another day of cool weather awaiting me. With Cindy at my beck and call to tote my supplies and provide me with liquids in a moment's notice, I felt on top of the world. I managed 46 miles for the day, ending up in Cordele and bringing my two day total to 104 miles. Heck, I'd be in Savannah by Thursday for sure. Maybe I should have run the *perimeter* of Georgia instead ...

Sunday evening brought me closer to reality than I had been in two days. After dinner, Cindy took off with the van, heading back to Atlanta as she had to be at work the next day (apparently she didn't tell *her* co-workers about the adventure). I was faced with my 20 pound handicap (the backpack) for the remaining 176 miles, and food and drink were no longer available upon command. I decided to relax in the hotel that evening and enjoy the *Atlanta Journal and Constitution* before nodding off to sleep. As is my custom, I immediately flipped to the sports section and, to my dismay, found the following headline deep in the bowels of Section E: **'LUDWIG TO RUN ACROSS STATE.'** The article went on to describe what I was doing and even quote me as to why I was doing it.... because it was 'something I always wanted to do.'" The first thought that crossed my mind was that the person *responsible* for my unwanted infamy had just deserted me less than an hour ago. My second thought was that I had better complete my run or face the imminent consequences of a highly-publicized *failure*. My third thought was that my legs didn't feel nearly as 'peppy' as they had a mere 24 hours earlier....

For the sake of argument, let's call the first two days of my adventure 'the ecstasy.' Logically, what would follow then would be 'the agony.' Well, I'm here to tell you that truer words were never spoken. I got out of bed the morning of **DAY THREE** (Monday, November 1) with a pair of knees that felt as if the bones, tendons and muscles inside had been fused together during the night. Being an optimist, I figured that once I got out on the roads, all my soreness would work its way out of my creaking joints. Stepping out of my hotel room at 6:30 AM, I was aghast to find the temperature approaching 80 degrees on *the first day of November!* Again, the optimist in me remembered all those long training runs in July and August in temperatures approaching 100 degrees. There was no need to let little problems like stiff knees or warm weather make me alter my game plan at this point.

I ended up the day 38 more miles down Highway 280, finishing up in Abbeville around 5:00 PM. Not only were my knees screaming at me for relief, I experienced what must have been second degree sunburn and several blisters approximately the size of a quarter on the bottoms of both feet. I checked into a hotel, took a bath, got dressed and walked (*hobbled*) to the local convenience store in search of medical aid. I knew I was in trouble when I asked the clerk at the counter where I could find the town doctor. She replied 'We had a town doctor once, but he died.'

I needed help but didn't know where to turn. I didn't want to call Cindy for fear of hearing an 'I told you so.' So I turned to someone who was always there for me: my parents. I called them (collect) on the store's pay phone and when I told them of my dilemma (like I said earlier, not many people knew about my run before the article in the newspaper. My parents, who live in Virginia, knew nothing about it ... until now), my mother's reply was drowned out by my father's laughter on the other line. I managed to gather 'Epsom salts' from the oft-interrupted conversation, and proceeded to purchase some at the convenience store. I went back to the hotel room, took an Epsom salt bath, and went to bed around 7:30 PM, confident (*praying!*) that a good night's rest was all I needed …

I woke up around 5:00 AM on **DAY FOUR** (Tuesday, November 2) feeling like a heavyweight prizefighter had used my legs for punching bags during the night. I left the hotel room at 5:45, placed the backpack across my (now) sunburned shoulders, and ever-so-painfully stepped off the curb and out onto the highway. The weather was still warm and before long I realized I had done nothing for those water blisters on the bottoms of both feet. Being a former Boy Scout, I was prepared for an emergency of this nature. I had several sterilized needles in my backpack. I pulled off the side of the road, removed both shoes, and punctured and drained all seven blisters. Yes, *seven*.

This may come as a surprise, but four hours and 17 miles later I had convinced myself that my healing prowess had been inadequate. I literally hobbled the duration of my run on day four, and after 159 miles of ecstasy and agony, I decided that I (at least *half* of me–the lower half) had had enough. I called my friend Bruce, who just happened to be on vacation as well, and he (bless him) drove to an isolated spot along the side of Highway 280 in Milan and rescued me from myself.

It was painful for the next two weeks to wear shoes and my running over the next 12 weeks suffered as I was forced to a hobble after several miles each day. My knees took a long time to forgive me. I explained to them in lieu of all my training and preparation I had failed to realize what running on one side of the road for that extreme a distance would do to them. How did I know that the small slope on either side of the road would have such a drastic effect on my knees? Eventually, maybe I'll forget about it also. I'll bet it would help if I got rid of my course map.

Eventually, who knows—I just might try it again …

After all, it is something I always wanted to do.

A *Relay?* In the *Mountains?*

I guess the easiest and safest answer is simply 'because it was there.' The question is 'why did you run in the 1991 Georgia Long Distance Relay?'

The Georgia Long Distance Relay is a 124 mile journey through the mountains of north Georgia run primarily through the still of the night. I guess there are other answers to the question, such as 'for my own personal satisfaction' or 'to prove I have what it takes' or even 'to share in the team goal of going the distance.' Whichever one you believe, I'm sure each one of them sounds just as plausible as the next. However, all of them are lies.

I did it because I had a 'brain fart.' Pure and simple.

A 'brain fart,' also known as a cerebral flatulation, is when your heart is in the right place but your brain goes in the other direction. For example, you're asked to bring home a gallon of milk on your way home from work. You stop by the grocery store, proceed to pick out a nice bottle of wine to enjoy with dinner, and maybe a pint of ice cream for the kids—without *once* thinking about the gallon of milk you stopped for in the first place. Sound familiar? A brain fart!

Now that we have that established, it's easier to understand why I said 'yes' when I was asked if I wanted to run. My heart was asking why *anyone* would want to spend the entire weekend inside a mini-van full of sweaty runners, each one required to run three separate mountainous five-mile legs approximately five hours apart—which is *just enough time* for your body to become totally stiff from the prior five-mile leg while *not being enough time* to recover either physically or mentally. Naturally, while this debate was silently taking place inside my heart, my brain allowed my vocal cords to utter 'yes.' A brain fart of the highest magnitude.

Well, the Relay is now in the past. It's over, the team did well, and my body (and mind) has totally recovered. It provided me with a lot of fond memories, and the satisfaction of participating in a highly successful team venture of this proposition felt incredible.

In hindsight, I'm glad that I said 'yes' and if anyone asks me why I did it, I'm saying I did it for personal gratification.

Of course, we all know better.

19:31:10

8:05 a.m., Saturday, September 17, 1988. Slightly warm, a bit on the muggy side. Rain is imminent. As I stand beside 91 fellow competitors on the white strip marking the beginning and ending of the 1.01 mile track circling the Atlanta Water Reservoir, I wonder why I'm here and even *considering* what lies ahead … and ahead … and ahead.

The gun sounds, and I'm off at a brisker-than-I-had planned 7:15 minute per mile pace. I keep this pace up for a little over two hours, dropping back to a 7:45 pace for the third hour before checking in with a Georgia Tech grad student for his project 'Does Lung Function Limit Performance in a 24-hour Ultramara-thon?' The project requires me to inhale and exhale as hard as I possibly can into a plastic tube for five minutes every three hours. I would soon learn that I was a fool for volunteering for this study, as this intense breathing was much more difficult than the run itself. Plus, every time I did it I lost 15 minutes, and stopping every three hours gave my body the opportunity it needed to allow rigor mortis to set in, making it that much more difficult to get started again.

Forgive me, as I have not yet told you what I had gotten myself into. I'd enter The Athletic Congress' 24 Hour Endurance Run National Championship. Why? As you've read on these pages before; why *not*?

The format for the run is to run counterclockwise for four hours, reverse direction and run clockwise for four hours, etc., for the duration of the 24 hours. The theory is if you ran in *one* direction for the entire time one leg would end up shorter than the other. Let me be the first to tell you that in the latter stages of the event (*especially* after the sun when down), changing directions was all you had to look forward to!

Aside from the research project I (like a fool) had volunteered for (well, not a complete fool, as I got a free submerge-your-body-in-a-water-tank body fat test for taking part), the race went well. I was on the leader board the entire time I was competing, at one point climbing as high as 7th and usually holding steady around 11th. One other problem: remember the imminent rain? After several rain showers, I was down to my last (of three original) pair of dry shoes. My wife Cindy came by around 8:00 p.m. Saturday night and was kind enough to take the two pairs I wasn't wearing to a local laundromat to dry them. Sounded like a good idea, right? Maybe if they weren't dried *at three hundred freakin' degrees!* Both pairs seemed at least a full size shorter when I wore them again. Eventually, I would lose the big toenail on my right foot–not that big a loss, really; at least both my legs were the same length after the event!

Cindy and our two sons went to sleep in my van (parked right next to the track) around midnight, at which time I had already logged 86 miles (I figured the lung experiment 'cost' me about seven or eight miles already). At 2:30 a.m. Sunday morning I caught my second wind, and started back running miles at a sub-8:00 minute pace. I covered nine more laps between 2:30 and 3:35 a.m. before finally calling it quits after 100 laps, which equated to (officially, according to the TAC) 101 miles 294 yards. My official race time was 19:31:10. It was an odd experience for me, as (1) it was the first race I did not actually 'complete,' (2) when I removed myself from the race I had just caught my second (?) wind and–believe it or not–felt really strong, and (3) I had again climbed to 7th on the leader board. But at that point I could care less about being in 7th: I just wanted *to stop running!* Apparently, my brain had finally talked my body out of competing any longer. I told my lap counter I was finished, packed up my gear, got in the van and drove home (yes, *I* drove!). I went to bed that morning around 4:30 a.m. without benefit of a bath, a solid meal, or even (gee, I wonder why) a goodnight/congratulatory kiss from Cindy. The bath came six hours later, the meal even later sometime Sunday evening, and the kiss about 10 days later (the recovery time my body needed before I could run–or do anything *else* for that matter–without pain).

About two weeks later, I received a bronze medal in the mail from TAC. Apparently I had finished third in my age group (and 27th overall). The medal had the words 'National Championship' embossed on it but it failed to identify the event, although a runner is pictured beneath the TAC logo. I had achieved the goal I had set for myself: <u>*one hundred miles!*</u> As I recall, I ran the extra lap in case my lap counter missed one of my laps.

Why am I talking about something that happened so long ago? Like I said earlier, this is the only race in my running career that I didn't complete. It just so happens that this year's event will take place September 14-15 in Olander Park, Ohio ... and I just happened to sign up. Why? Why *not?!?*

Something I Never Want To Do Again

Back in 1982, almost 10 years ago to the day, I attempted to run across the state of Georgia, 280 miles along Highway 280, because it was 'something I always wanted to do.' You may recall that my attempt ended after 159 miles in the small town of Milan simply because my knees would no longer support my body weight. As I write this on November 1, 1992, I can finally say that the first run I ever failed to complete has now been completed. That's right—I have finished my self-proclaimed 'Run Across Georgia,' and I can say without a doubt, it is 'something I never want to do *again*.'

It all started about four months ago when I was solicited to be a part of my company's annual United Way campaign. In these tough economic times, the United Way Committee realized they would need several fund-raisers to meet the corporate goal. Naturally, bake sales, golf outings and T-shirt sales were all agreed upon as being part of the campaign. I casually mentioned that I would be willing to try my Run Across Georgia as part of the campaign IF the company would (a) give me the week off to do it (what the heck, I figured—I still had my 'course map') and (b) pay for my expenses. To my amazement, the company agreed. 'Agreed' is probably an understatement: the company was willing to consider me a 'loaned executive' (to the United Way) for the week, agreed to pay all my expenses incurred during the run, gave me my choice of a fellow employee as a support crew (his expenses were included, too; PLUS *he* got a week off with pay as well), and had a poster printed promoting the event with me in Reebok (which provided me with shoes and running attire) gear superimposed over a map of Georgia. Officially, JCPenney Catalog, Reebok, and the United Way were sponsoring the event and calling it '280 on 280' (as in 280 miles on Highway 280) with the catch being for individuals to 'sponsor' my run with a donation per mile. (By the way, when I was asked to submit a proposal for my idea, I quickly jotted down '280 on 280' as a title and the powers-that-be *loved it*. Go figure)

The official dates for the run were Sunday, October 18 (to leave Columbus) through Saturday, October 24 (to arrive in Savannah). So at precisely 7:30 a.m. (didn't want to be late for my first day of 'work') on the 18th of October, not quite 10 full years after my inaugural failure at this attempt, I set out in my new Reebok attire with my sights set on the east coast of Georgia.

At this point, I could provide a step-by-step account of the run, but that would be too lengthy (not to mention *boring*), considering I took approximately 350,000 steps to complete my journey. Instead, I will give you a synopsis of the highlights and lowlights of the adventure. You can decide for yourself which are which:

- Total length of the run–280.1 miles (the run finished in front of the Savannah DeSoto Hilton, an agreed-upon site for other JCPenney employees to meet at the end of the run.

- Total number of minutes actually spent running–2,661, or 44.4 hours.

- Average pace–(exactly) 10.0 minutes per mile *(honest!)*.

- Total ounces of fluid consumed during the run–996 (62.25 pounds).

- Total weight lost during the run–8 ounces (my one-man crew lost 10 pounds!).

- Injuries incurred during the run–pulled right thigh muscle, left leg shin splint, blister on left big toe, toenail lost on right big toe, severe sunburn/windburn of face (even with sun block and lip balm), cramps in arch of right foot. Not bad, considering.

- Average starting time each morning–7:45 a.m.

- Average quitting time each evening–5:15 p.m.

- Average length of 'work day' (remember, I was receiving my regular salary)–9.5 hours

- Average 'bedtime' each evening–9:00 p.m. (yes, I missed most of the World Series).

- Total number of miles ran per day–50, 40, 43, 45, 45, 44, and 13 (I could have finished the run in six days, but I had to finish on Saturday to 'meet' a group of people from JCPenney along with Cindy and my two sons).

- Total number of uphills I walked–*all of them* (and there must have been over 150 of them. Did someone tell me south Georgia was *flat?*).

- Total number of downhills I walked–zero (mistake!).

- Total number of times a vehicle tried to be 'cute' and run me off the road–three (one was successful; which reminds me—add a bad cut on my right lower calf to my list of injuries).

- Best use of supplies to alleviate a pain–on the 3rd day I took a leftover painkiller (from a previous dental surgery) with a beer to deaden the pain in my right thigh. Would you believe it *worked?*

Answer to the question 'will you ever do it again?'–Refer back to the title of the article.

One thing is certain: it sure feels good knowing that I have now completed the only run that ever kept me from the (albeit 'imaginary') finish line. It's time to move on to bigger and better goals, like finish painting the fence that I've been working on all summer long. I doubt *that* would give me any shin splints.

Note: My one-man support crew, Steve Banks, took over three hours of video-tape of my run across Georgia. Occasionally I'll watch it, remembering what Steve told me the first time he reviewed the film: 'I hate to tell you this, Scott, but you looked considerably worse each day of the run.' Imagine that.

'280 on 280' in 1992–Catching my breath

<u>At Long, Long Last</u>

After over 350 attempts dating all the way back to November of 1978, I finally did it.

I don't care if there were only 30 other participants.

It doesn't matter that the weather was so cold and windy that it would irritate a penguin.

It's not important that it was conducted over a distance that only a *mother* could love (O.K, so this one doesn't exactly make sense. Still, you get the point.).

I don't even mind that it went by the name 'Fat Ass.'

Come to think of it, it doesn't even bother me that most of the 30 participants *ran* like penguins (a slow waddle—believe me, this one makes sense).

Ladies, gentlemen, and fellow runners, the words you are reading are being written by the 1995 Atlanta Fat Ass 50K Champion. And I've got the trophy (well, actually it's a big rock stuck on a plaque) to prove it.

The time: 7:00 a.m. The place: Stone Mountain Park. The date: Sunday, January 8, 1995. The weather: low 30's, with a wind chill making it feel like the North Pole. The course: one mile around a parking lot, then six five-mile loops around the base of Stone Mountain.

I felt adequately trained for the event. My two foremost opponents were the weather and boredom. My two training partners, Al and Val, were also running the event, although they were using it as a training run. To combat the boredom, I had two 'aces' up my sleeve:

1. I knew that at some point I would lap Al and Val (which would enable me to say 'hello,' which, when you're running alone for almost four hours, is quite exciting); and

2. My wife Cindy was going to join me around the start of the 4th lap to pace me on her bicycle ('oh boy, someone to talk to!').

While running the first three laps, I was looking forward to seeing Cindy around the 16-mile mark. When she wasn't there, I figured I could handle one more lap by myself … alone. At the 18-mile mark I passed Al and Val (at their *13*-mile mark), and if I remember correctly, grunted as I passed by. There went my first exciting moment! After the 4th lap, still no Cindy, so I figured I could handle one *more* lap by myself … still alone … but knowing that she would be there to pull me through my 6th and final lap. After the 5th lap and 26 miles, *still* no Cindy. Well, now I knew I was on my own for the duration, and the only thing I had to look forward to was the finish line.

I haven't yet mentioned that, except for the first 10 seconds of the race when Al sprinted by me ('hey look everybody, I'm leading the race!'), I had been leading the race the entire time. As the race was run *around* the mountain, I had no idea whatsoever how close anyone was to me. I wondered if my three 'nature calls,' which cost me a total of 75 seconds (yes, I timed them) would come back to haunt me. I had two close calls my final lap, as two runners tried their best to pass me, but after leading for 29 miles, there was no way I was going to let them pass me *now!* Although I successfully held them off, it wasn't until later I found out they weren't even participants in the race. Oh well, it was more a matter of pride, anyway (I *hate* being passed—even on training runs).

I would be remiss if I failed to mention how extremely cold I was during the race. I would have mentioned it sooner, but I'm fairly certain my brain just recently thawed out. Let me just say this: on my final three laps, I picked up two cookies each time at the aid station to get some needed calories. Of the six cookies, one made it into my mouth, and maybe half of it was eaten. My mouth and jaw were too cold to chew and my nose was so stopped up that I needed to breathe—deeply—through my mouth. Put the two together, and you can picture the cookie crumbs flying everywhere. After I crossed the finish line, one of the three race officials filled out my finish card for me. Not only could I not write, I couldn't even grip the pen.

I watched the 2nd place finisher cross the line a little over three minutes behind me (like I mentioned earlier, I had no idea how far of a lead I had. You could have told me three minutes or three miles, and I would have believed it. After all, we started the race in the dark, and everyone was so bundled up I never really saw any faces).

I decided to get in Al's car to warm up while I waited for him and Val to finish. Al had given me his car keys (figuring I'd finish in front of him), and after fumbling with them with ten frozen fingers I managed to get the door open. I climbed inside and turned the heater on, shivering for a good 20 minutes. I changed into my warm-ups and went back to the finish line and asked about an awards ceremony. The head official, who throughout the race had been my biggest fan and supporter, told me that runners could get their awards when they finished. I asked for mine, and my biggest fan asked me innocently enough 'what place did you finish in?' Apparently I was sitting in front of the car heater during my 15 minutes of fame.

He presented me—O.K., he *handed* me my rock (symbolic of Stone Mountain), I ate a few frozen M & M's, picked up my official Fat Ass t-shirt and finish certificate, and walked back to the car in total anonymity.

A champion at last.

'STROLLING' JIM?—I don't *think* so!

I first ran the Strolling Jim 40 Mile Run (which is a misnomer, as the race is actually 41.2 miles) in 1998. Here's my biggest mistake: *driving* the course the day before the race made me think the 'hills weren't all that bad.' *Running* these same hills, however, turned out to be pure hell. My wife Cindy was going to meet me at the 15-mile mark on her bicycle to lend her support as my crew. With the mindset that the 'hills weren't all that bad,' I was running a 7:15 minute mile pace when I met up with her. Not bad, except for one small detail: I had already hit 'the wall' ... and ironically I still had a full marathon remaining. Fortunately I had Cindy to help me through it. Unfortunately, Cindy found it impossible to negotiate the hilly terrain fast enough to keep up with me. I finished up the last 26+ miles pretty much alone, except for the occasional runner that *passed* me. O.K., so there were quite a few of these 'occasional runners.' I finished up in five hours and 56 minutes—not too bad for a first-timer who wasn't part mountain goat. I vowed not to return, although deep down inside I knew if I did and ran a more conservative pace I could improve on my time.

My vow not to return ended five years later, as I selected the 2003 edition of the Strolling Jim as the perfect course for a long and hilly training run in my preparation for July's Badwater 135. I want to emphasize the word 'Strolling,' as my intention was to run a slow, even pace in an effort to get my legs familiar with running long distances over hilly terrain. My **first, foremost, and _only_ goal/priority/objective** was to **complete the distance** ... no matter how long it took. As I had a 10 hour drive from Ponte Vedra, Florida to Wartrace, Tennessee the day before the race, this goal seemed extremely sensible.

The race began promptly at 7:00 a.m., and a contingent of 15 or so runners took off at a pretty fast clip. I, however, was not one of them. My thighs felt as if they were asleep, thanks to yesterday's ten hour drive. Of course, I was comfortable knowing my plan was to take it slow and easy. However, it wasn't three miles into the race when a **second goal** came into play. The lead female runner pulled alongside me and asked me three questions: (1) do you have a crew? (2) do you have any fluids? (3) do you have anything to eat? Once I responded 'no' to all three, she verbally assaulted me with comments such as 'there's no way you're going to run this race under six hours' and 'you're going to cramp up in a big way before you get to the finish line.' I told her I would be fine by drinking the water along the course every three miles or so. She told me I was crazy. **Goal #2 (and 2B): Finish under six hours and finish in front of this female runner.**

Soon afterwards, a runner from Ohio, Dave Corfman, pulled up alongside me. We struck up a conversation and proceeded to run the final 36 miles of the race together. It's unusual to run that long with one person in a competitive event, but we were on the same 'wave length' all day long. When he felt like surging, so did I. When I thought it appropriate to walk up a hill, so did he (we began calling this practice 'smart hill,' as in running the hills intelligently). We even managed to pass five other runners (while being passed by none) during this time. Eventually we finished together tied for 8th place, but Dave got a finish card before me so I technically was 9th (not that it mattered to me; after all, this was a training run).

Two things about my run with Dave: (1) prior to running with me he had run with the female runner who had berated me earlier. Apparently she is a nationally-ranked ultrarunner (a point she made perfectly clear) who always ran this event 'around five hours and 45 minutes.' (2) As I mentioned earlier, we passed five runners while we ran together. This second point brings me to my **third goal,** for which I can thank my friend Gary Griffin, which was to **'beat (a certain runner).'** As this certain runner was in the initial lead pack early in the race (back when my legs were still asleep), I doubted I would see him again. I was wrong, as he came into view with a little over a mile left in the race. He had a good ½ mile lead on Dave and I, but it appeared we were slowly but surely closing the gap. As we hit the last corner, I told Dave the finish was only about 400 yards away. I asked him if I thought we could 'kick' and catch him, and we decided it wouldn't be in our best interests. I agreed, only to change my mind 200 yards later and tell Dave 'I'm sorry, I just *have* to' (kick and try to catch him). Dave went with me step for step (we were obviously still on the same wavelength) and we caught that certain runner with about 80 yards to go. He managed a slight kick, but gave up with about 40 yards to go, finishing a few seconds behind Dave and I.

Seconds after I completed my place-of-finish card, I jumped in the car and headed back to my hotel room in Shelbyville (about 12 minutes away) to get a quick shower, pick up my son Justin and check out of the room. Which reminds me of my **fourth goal,** which, if prioritized, would actually have been my *first* goal, which was to **do all of these things by 1:00 p.m.,** as that was the latest checkout time I could convince the hotel manager to give me. Keep in mind the race began at 7:00 a.m., I ran it in 5:52, and it was 12 minutes back to the room.

Your math is correct: I walked into the room at 1:04, only to find Justin on the phone with the hotel manager who was calling to ask why we hadn't checked out yet. I took the phone and said I'd be out of the shower in three minutes, and fortunately I wasn't charged for another day (maybe because Justin was checking us out of the room while I was showering, which briefly distracted the manager).

Justin and I stopped back by the finish line in Wartrace to enjoy the post-race barbeque (a tradition!) before heading back to Peachtree City (*another* 4 ½ hours on the road!). I'm glad we stopped, for three reasons:

1. I was starving, and the barbeque was actually pretty good.

2. The female runner approached me and said 'I can't believe you finished under six hours' and asked 'How did you do it without any support?' To which I simply smiled and didn't say a word. I didn't find it necessary.

3. That 'certain runner' was complaining to everyone within earshot (keep in mind we had been done running for over 45 minutes at this point) that 'runners just don't do that in ultras' (i.e. kick at the finish) and he 'didn't hear them (Dave and I) coming up behind him.' When I heard the latter, I simply said we were in 'stealth mode' and we were silent because 'obviously we weren't even breathing hard.'

Sometimes the races which you *plan* to be uneventful turn out to be the *most* eventful, not to mention rewarding. Like the 2003 edition of the Strolling Jim.

You probably noticed I didn't mention the 'female runner' and 'that certain runner' by name*. I thought that would be mean. I will, however, list the results of the first 12 finishers. I consider it my obligation to you the reader:

Runner	State	Age	Time
Tim	AL	40	5:00:04
David	TN	51	5:01:07
Stan	AR	39	5:05:30
Dink	AL	37	5:07:12

DeWayne	AL	38	5:12:37
Tom	OH	40	5:18:46
Dogman	AL	42	5:42:27
Dave Corfman	OH	40	5:52:16
Scott Ludwig	GA	48	5:52:17
Richard	GA	53	5:52:20
Carl	GA	21	5:55:40
Chrissy	AR	42	6:02:13

*You can do the math, can't you?

24:00:00

12:15 p.m., Saturday, September 14, 2002. Slightly warm, a bit on the muggy side. Rain is imminent. As I stand among 167 fellow competitors behind the starting line of the 1.091 mile path circling the lake in Olander Park in Sylvania, Ohio, I wonder why I'm here and even *considering* what lies ahead. Actually, that last part's a lie: I know *exactly* why I'm here and (for the most part) what lies ahead …

If you recall, I mentioned previously that the 24 Hour Championship in 1988 was the only race I didn't 'complete' (as I failed—albeit intentionally—to run the entire 24 hours). This year I would make amends. After all, I felt I was more than ready as:

- I had averaged 90 miles per week over the past nine years (without ever taking a day off for rest).

- I had averaged 4 ½ hours sleep (weeknights) and 5 ½ hour sleep (weekends) per night over these same nine years.

- I had run myself to 'exhaustion' on more days than I care to remember. Or should I say more days than I'm *able* to remember.

- I had practiced my 'forever' pace (you know—the one you can lock into and run so easily that you feel like you can hold it *forever?*) with great success for the past three weeks.

- I couldn't get the words of Gary Griffin out of my mind, as he told me in February to run in this event and 'make yourself known in the ultra world.'

Yes, I felt more ready for this event than any athletic competition I've ever participated in. At 12:17 the horn sounded, and all 167 of us were off, each with our own goals to achieve and reasons for being here. I've told you mine.

As I'm well aware, talking about the actual *running* of an event—*any* event—has been proven to be the single most boring subject matter on the planet (*look it up!*). So, let me offer you some of the 'highlights' of the next 24 hours:

- Kevin Setnes, a world-class ultra runner and captain of the USATF Men's 50K National Team, was participating in the event. He, like six other runners in the field, was a former champion of this event. As each runner is allowed to set up their own 'aid station' along the course, I set up my cooler on a card table next to a chair I shared with a fellow runner (David Sowers, who would be an integral part of my 2003 Badwater adventure). Directly across the asphalt from me were two large canopies, three huge beverage dispensers (one full of—are you ready for this—*bottled spring water* which was emptied into one of the dispensers one bottle at a time), enough fruit to supply the entire field … for a week, six chairs and three volunteers (groupies?). I saw Setnes beneath the canopies and figured it was headquarters for his 50K team. Well, I was half right; it was *his* headquarters. At one point during the race Setnes was leading (there was a leader board which was updated every hour, although in this particular instance, I knew he was leading because I asked him and he told me he was leading). Early Sunday morning, Setnes dropped out of the race (he had taken ill), and you'll never believe who kicked his tail! That's right, Mr. Cooler and Card Table (with a Shared Chair).

- The female winner, Ann Heaslett, didn't make it to the awards ceremony, as she was rushed to the local hospital immediately after the event and treated for dehydration. In all likelihood, I should have joined her.

- For the first several hours, my name didn't appear on the aforementioned leader board (which listed the top ten) and I just knew I should have been listed. Each time I passed the scorer's tent I said 'check your standing; you're missing me!' Finally, my name was added (at the 9:20 p.m. update, only eight hours late!), and according to the 'live' internet broadcast of the event '*unknown* Scott Ludwig continues to move up and look strong.' So much for Gary's advice of making myself 'known' in the ultra world. Coincidentally, except for my name being in the official standings each hour, I was never mentioned again in the narrative which accompanied the standings.

- With two hours to go, the runner I shared a chair with reminded me that the race paid prize money for the top five finishers. Guess what position I was in at the time–fifth! I spent the final two hours looking beneath my name on the leader board (as I had the entire race) and actually managed to pull myself into fourth place during the last 120 minutes.

- While I was officially the fourth place finisher (as you had to be a member of the USATF to actually compete), the overall 'winner' of the event was the greatest ultra runner in the world, Yiannis Kouros of Greece. While I was pleased with my 129.1 miles, Kouros managed to 'lap' me more times than I care to remember.

- Prior to the event, participants were asked to guestimate their mileage (comparable to a runner's taboo of asking prior to a race 'what time are you trying to run?'). This information was posted on the official website, and I'm proud to say I was one of twelve males who exceeded their guestimates (I had guessed 125 miles). Five females managed to exceed their guestimates.

- At 1:00 and 3:00 a.m. Sunday morning there were two incredibly strong rainstorms (complete with thunder, lightning, high winds and course flooding). I should have stopped (there were many runners who hid beneath some of the large trees lining the course–you can insert your own 'dumb runner' joke here), but I kept on running only to finally change shoes around 4:00 a.m. when the rain had stopped and the course flooding had subsided. The combination of 129 miles and four hours of 'wet shoe running' cost me both big toenails two months later. But it was worth it (did I mention 4th place paid $175? Or that the cost of the trip was almost $500?)!

- I ended up only nine miles out of first place. Like I said earlier, I never looked above my name on the leader board except occasionally to see how far I was behind Kouros. However, in retrospect, I don't think I lost the race–I simply ran out of time. I felt incredibly strong the last three hours, even lapping Kouros once during the final hour (OK, he stopped to change CD's in his Walkman, but I still passed him!). There's no doubt in my mind that if I had another four hours, I could have made up those nine miles. When's that 48 hour championship, anyway?

- Kouros lapped me for the first time as I was finishing my 6th lap (around the 10K mark). I got my revenge 22 hours later (see previous entry above).

- No, I didn't sleep during the event. In fact, I woke up race morning at 7:00 a.m. and didn't take a nap until I got back to the hotel room around 4:00 p.m. Sunday. Around 6:00 p.m. I attempted to eat dinner. Attempted.

- I was close to dehydration after the event. In fact, the medical personnel chased me around with a bag of glucose, but they didn't know who they were messing with (someone with an incredibly strong aversion to needles). I tried eating a hot dog, and managed to force down one bite. The awards ceremony was a blur, but I did manage to stand up through it without assistance! That's more than I can say for 3rd place finisher Steve Godale, who had to be propped up.

- I finished 29 miles ahead of the first male finisher at this year's Badwater 135 ultramarathon. Why was this significant? Just thinking ahead.

- I managed to beat seven of the nine previously-mentioned former champions in the field. I remember how intimidated I was as they were introduced at Friday night's pre-race meal. Was.

- I enjoyed running a couple laps with the editor of *Ultrarunning*, Don Allison, as he and I and another runner passed a few miles dissing (I mean 'discussing') *Runner's World*. Their idea, not mine (but it sure could have been).

- Speaking of *Ultrarunning*, the editor himself wrote a three page article on the event. No, I wasn't mentioned in the article (merely listed in the results) at all, destined to remain an 'unknown.'

- Ray Krowelicz, bless his heart, referred to me as the 'south's newest phenom to the ultra ranks' in *the Running Journal*. Where else can you be a 'phenom' at age 47? Ain't ultrarunning great?

- I almost forgot: ***I won the 2002 USATF 24 Hour Male Master's Championship!***

All things considered, I have to admit that I couldn't have been more pleased with my performance. I was never tired or sleepy, was able to successfully lock into my 'forever pace' when I needed to, spent the vast majority of the 24 hours passing other runners (while seldom being passed, if you factor out the Greek runner), and did not suffer any injuries of consequence (although it took almost three months for me to have any 'zip' in my legs). I was right when I said earlier that I was 'more than ready.' After all, I'd been training for nine years.

The Numbers Game

- 12,535–miles run by all competitors
- 500–approximate ounces of fluid I consumed
- 175–prize money (in dollars) for my 4th place finish
- 172–most mileage for any runner
- 162–runners completing fewer miles than me
- 129–miles I ran
- 118–laps I completed
- 75–average number of miles per runner
- 40–number of times I was 'lapped' by Kouros
- 38–total runners with 100+ miles
- 24–hours I spent running
- 19–hours I needed to reach 100 miles
- 13–fewest miles by any runner
- 11:09–my average pace per mile
- 9–miles I finished behind the USATF champion
- 5–my overall place of finish
- 4–my USATF finishing place
- 3–pounds I lost during the event
- 1–my overall Master's ranking
- 0–times the thought of running and/or quitting crossed my mind

Wakulla Springs Ultra Redux

By Gordon Cherr

(Author's note: Gordon is a resident of Tallahassee, a long time member of the Gulf Winds Track Club, and a really nice guy. He offered both his home and his service to Al Barker, Prince Whatley and I during the second weekend in December 2003 as the three of us participated in the Tallahassee Ultra Distance Festival.)

They gathered at my home after a long Friday night drive from Atlanta, drawn here for the Ultra. First my long time friend and running buddy Al Barker. Al is a bit new to the ultra scene, having recently finished his first 50-miler, and now being accepted into the field for the Western States 100 next June. Then Scott Ludwig. Scott is anything but new to the ultra scene, a veteran of more than 100 marathons and numerous ultras, he was recently 6th at the Badwater 135 (miles!), run from the furnace of the floor of Death Valley to the frozen reaches of Mount Whitney Portal at nearly 8500 feet. Scott is also a streak runner, and if I'm not mistaken, he has not missed a day's run in more than 25 years. And their third training partner, Prince Whatley.

They came into my home, unloaded their gear, thanked me for my hospitality, and said goodnight. Wake us up at 5:30. Three totally different personalities on the verge of a great challenge ... the 50 miles of the ultra! All three look drawn and tired, and I had forgotten just how the thought of 50 miles can weigh so heavily on one's psyche even before the first step has been taken on race day. I mean, its not sweat off my brow, I am only going to help these three meet their demons, assist with food and drink, and maybe jog the last few miles as a pacer if someone is fading hard near the end. Being a glorified cheerleader is not stressful. At least I do not expect that it will be. Good night, Al.

Scott was another story. We sit in the darkened kitchen, drinking decaf and chatting the way long time runners do. Of shared friends and experiences, of aches and pains, of hopes and dreams, children and wives and jobs. Of anything BUT the relentless challenges of the next day. Ultras are so complicated. The further the distance, the more that can and will happen. You can train diligently with great intelligence and plan and improvise, hydrate and eat, but you don't know anything until it's over. Every ultra is a learning experience and ultra runners are always on the learning curve, or so it seems. I do not know Scott well. In fact, I do not know him at all, but after the miles we will share tomorrow and all is said and done, I will know him well enough. It will be my gain for sure, and I will be honored to call him 'friend.'

Prince is a total stranger, and obviously blessed with the gift of gab. He is, as it turns out, a salesman by trade, and that trade fits him well. He has the bulky, well-muscled legs of a power lifter, not the slim aerodynamic legs of a long distance runner. But, if I have learned anything about ultras, it is that good ultra runners come in all shapes and sizes. No one is to be discounted on looks alone. And if you could peer into their chests you would find that one shared commodity. They all have heart, and plenty of it. Guts. Backbone. Drive. Determination. Heart. Prince will be breaking new ground tomorrow; he hasn't gone the distance previously, not even close. I can read uncertainty (not fear) in his eyes, but when tomorrow comes, Prince will have a great triumph.

The day dawns early and we are at Wakulla Springs by 6:00 a.m. for the 7:00 a.m. start. Many friends I know, other still to be met later that day—race workers, lap counters, husbands, wives, children and dogs all mill about in tense anticipation.

I have parked my pickup next to the start/finish line where laps will be counted. Al, Scott and Prince know the drill and have brought provisions sufficient to feed an army of runners. You don't know what you might need, so you bring it all. Gatorade, water, Endurox and some magic potions that I don't even ask about. Pretzels, fig newtons, Gu, Carboom, crackers, Cheez-its, a mountain of clothes, sunscreen, bodyglide, Vaseline, and more shoes than you might see at a running store. The back of the truck looks like a poor man's makeshift smorgasbord, and before the day is done most everyone who runs the race, whether 50K or 50 miles, stops by for a handout. Not that there isn't plenty of other food here. Race Directors Fred and Margarite Deckter know how to throw a party, and soon after the horn sounds I find myself gorging on bananas and oranges, cookies and cakes, bread and peanut butter, and a hot cup of coffee, courtesy of the Wakulla Springs Lodge.

But the gun does go off and the runners are gone, heading out into the dark on what will be a very long and painful day for most. I'm thinking that Scott should do well in the 50-miler; I can only hope the best for Al and Prince. I know that Al wants to run about nine hours or so. Prince, a realist today, only wants to finish upright.

Each lap at the ultra is 2.07 miles and the start/finish line is a great place to grab a chair and watch the race, and mostly the gradual disintegration of many runners as the day progresses. Some will be there running before first light until after the roads are completely dark and deserted. Moving, always moving ahead. That's the key. Easier said than done. One personal drama or another, usually several at the same time, are unfolding, all day long and into the night. It is impossible not to cheer for someone trying so hard for so long, putting up with the grind, running and walking after the physical body shouts 'quit' at the top of its lungs, but the heart and the head say 'keep on.'

The first 50 mile runner is completing the first lap, and it's Fred Johnson. Fred is an accomplished and experienced ultra runner. I have the good fortune to run a bit with Fred and Dana Stetson on a few of their 5:30 a.m. jaunts on the golf course in Killearn. We run in the dark with flashlights and headlamps and we often find ourselves humming the theme song from 'Coal Miner's Daughter' when we run on those dark mornings. Fred has talked a bit about this race. He was disappointed with his performance last year–he calls it 'paralysis by analysis'– and I figure that he has another plan for this year. I mean, you don't finish an ultra without a plan and Fred is big on plans, and right now Fred is cruising along at about 7:45 per mile. He keeps this up for the first few laps and by lap three or four I find myself yelling at Fred to calm down and slow down too, because I think that he is going out way too fast and a crash is coming, maybe in another two or three hours, but it is inevitable at this pace.

Scott is running an easy second in the 50-miler, at about an 8:30 pace. Outwardly he looks cool and collected but this tells me nothing because even when he is wasted, as I will later see, Scott is cool and collected. I am getting happy feet from watching the runners go by. I can't stand to watch and not join in, but I promised Al and Prince that I would pace them through the last two or three loops, although that isn't going to be for maybe seven more hours. But on one lap Scott asks me to pull out some fig newtons for him the next time around and then when he next appears, he asks me to join him for a while. I'm only too happy to oblige.

We run the next six miles at that easy 8:30 pace, talking about this and that. Mostly we discuss how Fred is looking. Fred is putting about a minute on Scott every loop and he looks good. But in my opinion, Fred is going to crash after about six hours if he doesn't come to his senses quickly and Scott knows how to go the distance. Scott makes the conscious decision to hang where he is. Experience dictates a waiting game. Actually ultras are dominated by finishing, and real racing is mostly nonexistent. Scott confides in me, even at this relatively early stage, that physically he is fine, but he doesn't feel mentally prepared for today's effort. But he is going to hang in there and see what is what in several hours. 'Several hours' … the perspective of an ultrarunner sure is skewed.

I notice Gary Griffin. Gary is coming off some major injuries and is not sure where he is. I mean, he signed up for the 50K, but started with the 50-milers, who start about 1,000 yards behind the 50K group. I guess that he is just used to starting there and he goes there out of habit. Gary is looking kinda puny when he comes by and I ask him if he wants some company. I can see that Gary is having a rough patch after about 20 miles and I hope that a little companionship will help him see his way to the other side. Rough patches are as common in ultras as they are in almost every race and every workout. It is hard to believe that you will come out of the other side when you feel so crappy and you are fighting yourself to not stop and quit. But the fact is that if you make it through a rough patch, you will actually come out the other side feeling stronger than you thought possible. For a while anyhow.

When he sees and hears me, Gary breaks into that big country boy smile of his and says 'of course, with you my friend' and thoughts of walking are shelved for the time being. Off we go at his pace, talking about this and that and after a few more miles Gary says that he will go another lap too, because that will be one lap closer to home and maybe he'll feel better, and maybe he'll get another lap done, and then another and he might actually find the finish line. Indeed, when it is all over Gary does finish on his feet–and running, not walking–in about 5:10. And then he feels so good and full of running that he runs a few more laps for good measure, cheering and encouraging the others. See, experience in knowing that you can run or walk even when your body is badgering you to stop, and that it will get better, can make all the difference. After countless miles and hours, Gary knows this, and with a little help for a few miles, he came home the winner that he is. Good effort, Grif! No, not a good effort, rather a *great* effort.

Meanwhile, the day is wearing on and the runners are wearing out. I am watching Fred and Scott, and Fred has continued to lead, and not only lead but stretch his advantage. When Fred puts about two miles on Scott, he actually comes up behind and could lap him, and I have a sudden realization that barring absolute and utter collapse, Fred is going to win this race. All he has to do now is keep Scott in his sights, and soon the two are running together, which they continue to do until the last few miles when Scott begins to pull away, but is unable to meaningfully close the gap.

Fred, I am sorry that I doubted you this day. Your race plan was executed flawlessly, and you ran with great determination and style. Fred deserved this win, he earned this win, and his indomitable spirit was apparent to everyone who watched the 50-miler, Great race, Fred.

Scott had a great race as well. He runs a PR of 7:26 and it is impossible to be sad with that effort. He has no complaints and looks as calm now as he did before and during the race. Sitting in my beach chair, he is smiling and encouraging the others who still have so many more mile and hours to go. I can't imagine why he is not sound asleep at this point, but he looks fresh, if that is possible. He and Fred are chewing the fat about something, and I'm guessing that someone is discussing dinner. As it turns out I am later proven correct.

Laps are passing and people are coming and going. Al and Prince have hung together for nearly 36 miles. I can't stand it any longer and I jump in with them. Prince is yakking nonstop, and then he is trying to perform mathematical calculations in his head. Anything to get through the next few miles. He does not seem physically tired as much as being mentally tested, although I know that after 36 miles surely he is a bit winded. As for Al, he is too quiet and I know my friend does not feel well at all. He complains of an upset stomach, and as I get to the smorgasbord on the rear of the pickup truck he begins to gorge. I think that this is a very bad idea on a queasy stomach after about 38 miles, but Al will have none of it. Prince grabs a Carboom and some salted pretzels and says he will wait. But it is obvious that he needs to go now, at his own pace, and I tell him to go, I will finish up with Al. As it turns out, Prince does go, and he goes strong too for the remainder of the race. He looks good, and smiles for the next 12 miles and kicks some booty in 9:27. What a great effort, Prince. I bet you are still smiling. I know that you are still talking!

As for Al, he stuffs fig newtons and Cheez-its into his mouth, some double caffeine GU and drinks some Endurox. Then he goes looking for some fruit and snares a banana or two and down the hatch they go. Then more handfuls of Cheez-its and more Endurox and soon we are walking and then running, and I am hoping to be out of range when Al finally barfs this up. He is going through a rough patch now and I question whether he will make it. All thought of nine hours is gone; Al is on survival mode now.

We run along at about an 11 minute per mile pace and I am trying to talk to him about anything and everything. Being a pacer is not as easy as it seems. You are relatively fresh and your charge is not. You can't go too fast, but you need to keep him moving at all costs. Talking encouragement, talking trash, telling jokes, anything that you can think of. The miles are passing slowly for me, and I have only been out here for 16 miles. What about Al; he is on mile 44 by now. I remember that when Al is tired, really tired, his right foot slaps the pavement and makes a loud sound when he runs. Right now both of his feet are going 'slap, slap, slap' and we both start to laugh about it, and I can't believe that he is laughing after 45 miles. And I can't believe that he hasn't ralphed up all the junk that he ate at the last stop, too, but he tells me that he is actually feeling better now that his stomach has calmed down. Hey, maybe just maybe he is going to make it after all.

Al and I have four laps to go, about eight miles. We are trash talking about everyone we know. Under his breath, Al is cursing out everyone else on the course, hoping that no one else will run him down from behind. Then we are discussing the Western States 100, which has accepted him, but as it turns out instead of questioning his sanity about thinking of running 100 miles, Al now wants to discuss his training. Soon we are down to six miles and things begin to look manageable except that it is getting dark out and there aren't any street lights out here. I never thought to bring my headlamp or flashlight.

And it is getting weird, too. At the far end of the course, a motorist who is lost and wants directions to Woodville accosts us. I give him directions and he asks what we are doing. I tell him that Al is running 50 miles. His mouth just flies open and he says 'Fifty miles … fifty miles … fifty miles–are you guys crazy?' Why, yes, we are, thank you! We continue on our way. Then we are down to two laps when we pass a disheveled, elderly-looking woman in the fading light of the parking area. She looks at us in the eye and says 'keep your shoulders back and your head up, keep your chin off your chest and run tall' and then she disappears towards the lodge. Now, I have only been running for 20 miles, so it is a bit too early for hallucinations. I ask Al if he saw that, and he says that he saw her too. OK, we are still OK.

Just one lap to go and Al has emerged through the far side of the funk that earlier plagued him, and we are rolling now. The beginnings of a smile of satisfaction starts to cross his lips and the running, believe it or not, starts to feel almost effortless. We make one more obligatory stop at the tailgate smorgasbord and soon we are running what seems now to be a 2.07 mile victory lap. Not 20 minutes ago the thought of another two miles seemed painfully insurmountable, but now I feel the beginnings of a good runner's high setting in. I remember very little of that last lap except to applaud Al when he crossed the line to the whistles and clapping of those few remaining race workers and runners, who stayed to see him through to the end. Ten hours and eleven minutes. A job well done.

Dinner was at Momo's Pizza. Although we had run 222 miles amongst the five of us, we still could not finish one of those enormous wagon wheel pizzas, with 'everything' on it. Several pitchers of beer didn't hurt, either (for medicinal purposes only, I assure you). Al was almost dead asleep in his chair. Prince was still talking. Scott and Fred were quietly discussing running the Tallahassee Marathon the next day and trying to talk Prince into running it with them. For no particular reason I feel like a proud mother hen.

As it turns out, Scott ran the marathon the next day in 3:58. Prince ran 4:23. Fred logged a few more miles with them before coming to his senses. And Al went to the Wakulla Springs Lodge for a breakfast of eggs, sausage, grits, toast and coffee and he cheered them all on until he fell fast asleep in a lawn chair.

Renegade:

Putting the 'war' in 'Wartrace'

Oh, Mama, I'm in fear for my life from the long arm of the law.
Law man has put an end to my running and I'm so far from my home

I had every intention of making this year's Strolling Jim 40 Miler a true, relaxing 'run in the country.' However, it turned out to be anything but.

As a prelude, here's a posting on the ultrarunning website that appeared a couple days after the event–I believe it was posted by the Race Director:

About 10 or 12 years ago we added the trek in the Strolling Jim starting out two hours before the regular race. The idea was to provide a chance for super slow runners to run the race and get done in time to party at the finish line with the other runners.

It turns out that the trek holds a fascination for those who have no business in the trek. This year–for the second time–a trekker, who HAD NO BUSINESS RUNNING THE TREK duked it out with the actual winner over the last couple of miles, eventually nosing him out at the finish.

But that runner was not alone: about half the trek field came in among the top runners creating a major nuisance in scoring.

Next year the trek will be restricted to runners over 60 years of age, or with special approval by me. It is my intention to dole out the trek numbers personally. Needless to say, contenders will not be trekking.

I don't have any real heartache with those who entered just to beat the sun, although they were a little too fast for the trek, but the idiot who beat the winner …

My questions, for the listers out there is:

> *What is going through someone's mind …*

> *First, for a six hour runner to enter the trek AT ALL, when it is specifically requested that anyone with the least chance of breaking nine hours NOT run the trek.*

> *Second (and this in the one I really don't get), why the hell would you race and beat the actual winner to the finish line?*

If the guilty party is on the list (author's note: I'm not–a friend forwarded this message to me), *you don't have to admit it to the list (I know your name and didn't include it here), I would really like to know what you were thinking.*

What was I thinking, he asks? Read on …

Come Sail Away

I'm sailing away, set an open course for the virgin sea
I've got to be free, free to face the life that's ahead of me

Al Barker, Susan Lance, Danielle Goodgion and I decided to enter the 2006 Strolling Jim 40 mile run in beautiful Wartrace, Tennessee as a training run for this year's Western States Endurance Run. Susan and Danielle have agreed to be our pacers–Susan for Al and Danielle for me–and we agreed to run all 41.2 miles together with the same effort Al and I expect to expend this summer as we tackle the mountains of the Sierra Nevadas. Seeing as 'the Jim' is run on rolling country roads, we didn't expect anything noteworthy to happen. Our intent was to spend a beautiful spring Saturday morning enjoying each other's company, experimenting in eating along the course, practicing with our fuel belts, and–in my case–taking as many photographs as I could along the way.

Sometimes, however, what should have been a calm, relaxing, non-noteworthy morning in the country turns out to be much more than that. This was one of those mornings.

The Strolling Jim offers a 'trekker's' start time of 5:00 a.m. (the regular, competitive race begins at 7:00 a.m.) for those who need the earlier start that allows them to finish at a decent hour. Ordinarily, the slower runners and/or walkers opt for the earlier start. However, as the four of us had tickets for a concert in Peachtree City later that night at 8:00 p.m. (Styx!), we opted to begin running at 5:00 a.m. Susan and I had used the trekker's start two years prior for the same reason, and the timing of it worked out very well. Our goal was to finish in 7.5 hours or less, which would give us plenty of time to get to our seats in the amphitheater to hear 'Blue Collar Man' and 'Come Sail Away' (the latter could have been our theme song for our run–our soothing, relaxing run through the country).

As I had been running fairly well lately, I had told Al, Susan and Danielle that if I felt good after getting through the hilly portion of the course known as 'the walls' (ending at mile 34), I was going to push the pace for the final seven miles. After almost six hours of conversation, food, drink, and many 'summer vacation photographs' (a reference to the fact that I never appear in family vacation photos as I am always the photographer), I did in fact 'feel good' after 34 miles. My timing couldn't have been worse, as right after I informed Al and Susan that I was going to 'gun it' (Danielle had fallen slightly back a few miles earlier), I noticed the two leaders of the *real* race about 300 yards back. The two leaders happened to be (arguably) the two finest ultrarunners in Alabama, and they were bearing down on Al and me as if we were hardly moving. I decided I would try holding them off as long as possible, and when the true leader of the race was about to pass me I would take a photograph of myself with the leader directly over my shoulder–I wanted to use it in the Darkside newsletter with the following caption: *Scott held off the eventual winner of the race for 37 miles.*

Two miles later I was still 'in the lead' (remember, I had a two hour head start on the boys from 'bama). Around mile 36 the leader's wife–who was driving a van in support of her husband–was along the side of the road and said to me 'you're running pretty fast for a trekker.' I told her that I wasn't trekking–I just had to be somewhere later that night.

Then, two more miles down the road and I still hadn't been passed. I couldn't imagine what was taking them so long; surely at least one of them should have left me in their wake by now. I encountered the wife once again, and this time she said to me (with plenty of attitude): 'It ain't over 'til it's over.' I thought to myself, 'Here I am out for a comfortable run through the countryside on a beautiful spring morning wearing a water belt (which I never wear when I'm competing ... actually which I never wear *ever* unless I'm doing some serious preparation for Western States) with a camera in my hand and this _____ is giving me a hard time. What the hell??!!'

At this point I was still ahead of everyone in the race and I decided since I was still in this position after 38 miles I was going to make it a challenge for anyone to pass me. I picked up the pace a bit, and I found Gary Cantrell (the founder of the race) at the '5K to go' mark and he handed me a feather. I asked him what it was for and he merely shrugged. I thought that it was a Strolling Jim tradition for the first person to reach this point–whether they are a competitor or a trekker–to be handed a feather which would in turn cross the finish line with the eventual winner. I also had heard that a trekker had *never* crossed the finish line before a competitor in the 27-year history of the event. Two years ago when Susan and I ran together we had noticed Gary driving by us several times late in the race–appearing a bit nervous that two trekkers were out in front of all of the actual competitors. When Susan and I were passed by the leader at the 37-mile mark, Gary looked relieved. When I passed Gary *this* year, he had a smirk on his face. I had no idea why.

At the 39-mile mark, I encountered the wife a third (and what proved to be final) time. This time she offered this gem: 'Oh, you're carrying a feather. Do you think that will make you *fly?*' It was at this point that I decided that there was no way in hell her husband—or anyone else, for that matter—was going to pass me before I got to the finish line. With half a mile to go, I heard one of the 'bama boys' shouting encouragement at the other in a valiant, albeit futile attempt to get him to catch me. However, I managed to run a 21:16 for the final 5K which proved to be fast enough to get me to the finish line first. Almost.

As I approached the finish line, one of the volunteers jumped out on the course and 'met' me about five feet from the finish tape. He screamed at me to 'stop' short of the finish line. I managed to stop, although I staggered slightly as my legs were a bit shaky after running 41 miles. Imagine that. When I staggered slightly, it was my misfortune to stagger *forward,* as this caused the volunteer to shove me in the chest with both hands and scream 'You're not allowed to cross the finish line!' Then he turned to a volunteer recording finishing times and screamed at her to notate my time as *'nine hours ... give him nine hours'* (the minimum time allowed a trekker in the official results). However, the way he said—no, screamed it—was more like he was condemning me for having the audacity to get to the finish before those actually racing the course. I threw the feather (yes, I was still holding it) to the ground in disgust (how's that for an effective gesture—a feather to the ground!) and walked past the finish line just outside the actual finish chute. The time on my watch indicated I had covered the course in 6:47:59.

About a minute later one of the 'bama boys' crossed the finish line. He was the winner of the 28th annual Strolling Jim 40 Mile Run. Eventually, everyone who crossed the finish line throughout the day was a winner. There was only one loser on this beautiful spring morning in Tennessee. As runners and trekkers alike shared in the post-race barbecued chicken, the winner's wife was in a corner eating a bird of a different feather—crow.

Come sail away.

Olander Memories

When I read that the Olander Park races in Sylvania, Ohio would no longer be held, I felt saddened by the loss. The event and its staff—both of which I have come to appreciate tremendously—has treated me like a family member since the moment I took my very first step (there would be approximately 435,000 more) on the legendary 1.091 mile path around the magnificent lake in the middle of the park—a park that (deservedly so) gets more than its fair share of use by the people of Sylvania.

I had the distinct pleasure of participating in three National Championships on the course where—according to the entry form—'the participants are treated like royalty.' The entry form told the truth, a direct reflection of the tremendous work of Race Director Tom Falvey and his staff. Although I only had the pleasure of participating at Olander three times, the memories will last a lifetime:

September 2002–National 24 Hour Championship

My running pal Gary Griffin told me to go to Olander 'to make a name for myself' in the ultrarunning community. At the point in the race where I worked my way into the top ten on the leader board, a live webcast referred to me as an 'unknown.' Ultimately I ran 129 miles and finished 4th overall male and earned the title of National Masters Champion in the process.

September 2004–National 100 Mile Championship

My first attempt at a *pure* 100-mile race. I finished in 18:23:18, good for 10th overall male and 2nd in my age group. Since I ran this event a little less than two months after running Badwater, I was very satisfied with the performance. Also, seeing my friend Gary finish his first 100-miler at Olander was a treat.

September 2005–National 100 Mile Championship

My third attempt (and my first since a failure at the 2004 Western States Endurance Run) at a pure 100-mile race. I finished in 21:34:34, good for 12th overall male and 3rd in my age group. Also, seeing my friend Susan Lance finish her first 100-miler at Olander (and Gary his second) was a pleasure.

Next September, I'll miss flying to Toledo and driving the 15 minutes it takes to get to the town of Sylvania. I'll miss eating spaghetti and drinking (usually too much) beer on Friday night at the pre-race dinner. I'll miss talking my running friends into giving Olander 'a try.' I'll miss passing out sometime Sunday morning following an exhausting 'day at the track.' I'll miss talking to the many runners, volunteers, crew members and spectators lining the course. Most of all, I'll miss seeing my good friend Tom Falvey.

When I heard the news about the discontinuation of the Olander races, I sent Tom a note, which read:

Tom—say it ain't so.

I read in the November 2005 Ultrarunning that Olander will be no more. I was really said to read that the race will no longer take place on the traditional second weekend in September due to dwindling participation and financial difficulties. But I certainly understand your predicament.

I have many fond memories of Olander, and it always brought a special smile to my face when I received your confirmation E-mail for your events with the words 'I hope you win' at the end of the note.

You always managed to treat every participant as if they were the most important person on the course, and you took the time to get to know each and every one of us. For that, you will always have the respect and admiration of the many members of the Peachtree City, Georgia based Darkside Running Club who have run in your events through the years.

Speaking for all of us who learned a lot about running, about life and about ourselves in the 'Yankee Stadium of ultrarunning,'

<u>*We hope you win.*</u>

Scott Ludwig
Olander participant–2002, 2003, 2005 (representing 329 of the best miles of my life)

2005 100 Mile Run in Olander Park—with Al, Susan and Gary

<u>Ultras (Road surface only!)</u>

(I think I finally found my niche!)
Listed chronologically and by distance

Distance	Date	Location	Time	Place of Finish
31 miles (50K)	Jan 1995	Atlanta GA	3:48:23	1
31 miles	Dec 1998	Tallahassee FL	3:44:58	1
31 miles	Dec 2001	Tallahassee FL	3:57:31	3
31 miles	Nov 2001	Peachtree City GA	4:00:12	7
31 miles	May 2003	Tallahassee FL	4:10:00	T-1

31 miles	July 2004	Lancaster SC	5:45:50	18
31 miles	Dec 2004	Tallahassee FL	4:32:45	7
31 miles	Feb 2005	Atlanta GA	4:54:20	NA*
31 miles	Jul 2005	Lancaster SC	5:05:54	7
31 miles	Dec 2005	Tallahassee FL	4:09:49	2
31 miles	Feb 2006	Atlanta GA	3:56:58	4
40 miles	Jun 2003	Pensacola FL	6:02:56	5
41.2 miles	May 1998	Wartrace TN	5:55:06	21
41.2 miles	May 2003	Wartrace TN	5:52:16	9
41.2 miles	May 2004	Wartrace TN	7:44:55	NA**
41.2 miles	May 2006	Wartrace TN	6:47:59	NA**
50 miles	Feb 1982	Atlanta GA	7:28:25	6
50 miles	Dec 2003	Tallahassee FL	7:26:58	2
50 miles	Dec 2006	Tallahassee FL	7:52:47	3
100 miles	Sep 2003	Sylvania OH	18:23:18	14
100 miles	Sep 2005	Sylvania OH	21:34:34	18
24 hours	Sep 1988	Atlanta GA	101 miles	27
24 hours	Sep 2002	Sylvania OH	129 miles	4
24 hours	Nov 2004	San Diego CA	111 miles	12
24 hours	Nov 2005	San Diego CA	114 miles	18

135 miles	Jul 2003	Death Valley CA	36:32:46	6

NA*—Unofficial Time
NA**—Trekker's Start

2004 San Diego One Day Run–The Edge of Exhaustion

CHAPTER NINE
MAGIC AND ME

When our boys, Justin and Josh, were young, our family adopted a female black lab puppy that we named 'Magic.' She got her name because at that time (a) I was an amateur magician, (b) the boys liked the Orlando Magic basketball team, and (c) their favorite basketball player was Magic Johnson. Plus, the fact that her fur was black added a nice touch to the name ('black' Magic).

In the late 1980's, I would take Magic for a 1.5 mile run each morning before I went out for my solo run afterwards. After several years, the distance was reduced to one mile, then a half mile, and finally a five-minute walk along our street (after all, during that time she had become a senior citizen). Magic didn't have the greatest running form, nor did she possess any degree of speed. In many ways, she was much like me.

But her enthusiasm for getting out the front door—much like mine—was as strong as it ever was. As long as she was willing, I was more than able.

In one of the early issues of the DARKSIDE newsletter, Magic wrote about what went through her mind during one of her morning jaunts. The article became one of my dad's favorites, and he encouraged me to ask Magic to write regularly about her 'dog's life.'

In this chapter:

- What's Going on Down There?—It's quite obvious that Magic's brain is busier than her four legs when she goes out for her morning walks.

- What's Going on Over There?—Visits by 'Gramps' meant two things: lots of extra walks and lots of extra food. Magic loves her Gramps.

- What's Going on Out There?—In June 2002 Justin found a stray white kitten on a road in Brooks, Georgia. Maui* became the sixth member of the Ludwig household, as well as Magic's best friend (although Magic won't admit to that).

- What's Going on In Here?—One morning in June 2003 dad saw a newspaper ad featuring a black kitten wanting to be adopted. That very same evening, Molokai** (Molly) became the seventh member of the Ludwig household. This, of course, made Magic the 'minority member' of the family (four humans, two cats, one dog).

- Looking Over My Hind Quarters—Magic reflects on the people who have had significant impacts on her life.

- Separated from my Shadow—Magic led a healthy, happy life for almost 14 years, but that didn't make it any easier for dad to say goodbye.

Maui was given his name as my parents just returned from a ten-day trip to the island of Maui to celebrate their 25th wedding anniversary.

**Molokai was given her name as my parents wanted to stick with the letter 'M' for naming the pets.*

<u>What's Going on Down There?</u>

By Magic Ludwig

Every morning dad's routine is the same: waking up, drinking coffee, putting off taking me for a walk as long as possible while reading the newspaper, eventually giving in and taking me for a walk (a 'run' in my younger days), feeding me, going for his daily run, shaving, showering, dressing and heading off to work.

Dad says he does a lot of thinking when he goes for a run. About work. About what to write next. Wondering why he drives on a 'parkway' and parks on a 'driveway.' You know, important stuff like that.

What do I think about? Follow my train of thought as dad takes me for my morning walk ...

ALLLLRIGHT! Free at last ... gotta pee gotta pee gotta pee ... can't go there ... went there yesterday ... gotta pee ... gotta find a spot ... HERE ... ahhhhh.... how did I ever make it through the night? Hey, what's that rabbit doing in my yard ... HEY RABBIT ... what's the deal ... hey, I'm talking to you ... yeah ... that's right, you BETTER run ... gotta go check out where the rabbit was ... man, it's hell dragging this guy around by his leash ... come on, dad, stay WITH me! ... wow, this smells nasty! ... darn rabbits ... which reminds me: gotta pee gotta pee gotta pee ... now where is that great spot I found yesterday ... oh yeah, by the hydrant on the corner ... gotta hurry ... gotta hurry ... gotta hurry ... oh yeah ... wait, this is more than pee ... oh YEAH ... wow, and I thought the rabbit's business smelled nasty ... hey, who's that barking? ... must be that Lipshitz dog cooped up in the garage again ... poor sap ... man, it's great to be outside ... which reminds me: gotta pee gotta pee gotta pee ... wonder where Lipshitz's dog pees? ... hey, while I'm here, I may as well use his yard! ... how do you like THEM apples, Lipschitz's dog? ... man, life is good ... sleep-eat-drink-which reminds me ... gotta pee gotta pee gotta pee! There, much better now ... I'm THIRSTY! ... gotta get home so I can get some water and rest while dad goes running ... then when he gets back I can go pee some more ... guess I'll nap in the meantime ... man, life is good ...

What's Going on Over There?

By Magic Ludwig

It amazes me how Copernicus' view of the solar system was important, as it allowed sensible consideration to gravitation. Which reminds me of Kepler's laws of planetary motion and Galileo's ... hey, who's that on the front porch? Can it be ... can it be ... YES, its' GRAMPS!!!! Oh boy oh boy oh boy! Come on in, Gramps, I'll be right back with my leash! Yessirrees time for a walk ... it's always time for a walk when Gramps comes for a visit! Awwright, here we go. Yes sir, follow me–I'm gonna show you all the spots I've marked. This street is MINE! Wait-a-minute … back so SOON? Darn.

Now where was I? Oh yes: the prejudice shared by Rationalism and Empiricism is that man does not know things directly but grasps only their impressions. Rationalism is concerned with the impressions made on the intellect, but … hey is Gramps heading for the refrigerator? You betcha! Oh yeah, gimme some of that baloney! Throw a slice of that bread my way. Go ahead and drop a few potato chips on the floor … I'll get 'em. There we go … I can always (munch munch) count on Gramps (munch munch) for a couple of Pringles. Hey, Gramps is tearing up a piece of baloney … allRIGHT!! Who's your doggy? Here it comes … GOT IT! Wait-a-minit … finished already? Is that ALL? Darn.

I'm reminded that the absences of dogmatic sectarianism in Leo Tolstoy and his indisputable humanity was due above all to his capacity … wait, Gramps is making a move off the couch! Time for another walk … so soon??? He's lifting one leg and–what was that NOISE??? A low-flying airplane? Wait, why is Gramps putting his leg back down?!? And WHAT is that gawd-awful smell? And why isn't Gramps getting my leash or heading to the refrigerator? Oh, NOW he's getting up … that's it, head out to the garage and get my leash. After all, it's been, what-15 minutes since our last walk? I could always water a bush or two. Hey, why is Gramps going to the bathroom? And there's that noise again … and that SMELL!! What's going on? And why am I sitting here with *no leash* and *no potato chips*?!? Darn.

Come on, Gramps. You can do better than this. Man, what IS that smell?

<u>What's Going on Out There?</u>

By Magic Ludwig

Let me begin by telling you that, for the most part, my life is pretty routine. For example, I can tell you exactly where I'll be and what I'll be doing (or more precisely *not* doing) each and every moment of each and every day. For example, every Tuesday at 11:30 a.m. you can find me sleeping on the floor in the master bedroom. That's what makes the day I'm going to tell you about so different. That, my friends, is the day I became a *hero*.

The day started off as normal. The alarm went off at 2:00 a.m., and dad reset it for 2:40. At 2:42, dad let me out into the backyard (my *empire*) to 'take care of business.' So far so good, but this is where things get different. From my spot on the deck I spotted an ominous white object (OWO) near the northern perimeter of the back yard. As any guard dog worth her salt will do (so I'm told), I began barking, freezing the OWO dead in its tracks. I knew if I barked long enough (as shorter barks merely signified I had spotted a squirrel) dad would come outside to see what had caught my attention.

I was right. By 2:44 dad was on the deck asking me what I was barking at. Once he caught a glimpse of the OWO, he jumped off the deck and headed straight for it, barefoot and all. I mention 'barefoot' because the backyard—*my* backyard—is a veritable minefield (if you know what I mean). But that didn't stop my dad. Nosirreee, not even when he stepped in several of my 'monuments' in his pursuit of the OWO. It's a shame dad accidentally stepped in a couple of my master-pieces, particularly a little creation I was quite proud of and had named 'Mount Everest.' In practically no time, dad had the OWO *in his hands*! And then pro-ceeded to *bring it inside the house*! What was he thinking?!? And what *was* this OWO?

Once inside the house, I saw that the OWO was none other than the latest addi-tion to our family—Maui the cat. *Omigod, what have I done?!?* I was actually responsible for rescuing the only thing on this planet that truly gets under *my fur*. Its obvious dad had no idea how long it took me to convince Maui to jump out that window that was accidentally left open last night!

I realize my job is to follow dad everywhere he goes. Unfortunately for me, the cat believes his job is to do the same for me. Where I go, Maui goes. What I eat, Maui eats (yes, even my dog biscuits … the crumbs, anyway). When I drink, Maui drinks. That darn cat is constantly (and literally) under my feet. When I go out to the backyard, Maui sits at the glass door—watching … waiting. It creeps me out, man! When dad pets me, Maui jumps in his lap. When Mom gets home, Maui runs through my legs to get to her first. While I patiently wait by the table during dinner for table scraps, Maui jumps on the table and helps himself.

And what is it with that cat constantly trying to bite my tail? In fact, the other day Maui started biting my ears! Please don't tell me I had the opportunity to end this misery and threw it away by barking!

But wait a minute … here comes dad with a dog biscuit for me. This is unusual: dad knows I don't get a biscuit until we finish our morning walk at 3:24. But he gives it to me anyway! And now he's calling me a hero for 'rescuing' Maui. Heck, I didn't even know the OWO was a cat, let alone Maui. All I saw was a white blur on the other side of the yard–my yard! That, my friends is the reason I was barking.

And that, my friends is the day I became a hero.

Rats.

What's Going on In Here?

By Magic Ludwig

Just when I've gotten used to that little white WOF (waste of fur) Maui, my parents go out and bring home yet another cat! And they bring it into my house! I've got to be honest here: I am literally beside myself.

Over the past year, Maui and I have learned to respect one another's space and privacy. We each have our own 'territory,' as well as specific 'visiting rights' with both mom and dad. We even have our daily routine that we've managed to perfect over the past six months. For example, each morning:

- Once dad wakes up, Maui gets a treat, and I go for a walk.

- After the walk, I get a biscuit. Maui eats the crumbs.

- Maui and I hang out in the bathroom while dad shaves and showers (me on the floor, Maui on the stool).

- Dad feeds us after his shower.

- Once Maui and I are full of our own food, we finish off the food in each other's bowls.

- Maui and I nap until mom wakes up, at which time we beg for (some more) attention and/or food.*

  *(*Mom always knows we've already eaten. Rats.)*

Maui and I had become quite accustomed to this sequence of events, and now a wrench has been thrown in our well-oiled engine. She's tiny, she's black and she goes by the name of Molly (I hear its short for Molokai. I hope my parents aren't getting a cat for each of the Hawaiian Islands).

At first, Maui spent most of the day chasing Molly all over the house showing her who was in charge. But Molly never backed down. I was just grateful that the two of them were keeping me out of it. But eventually, Molly began to hold her own with Maui (who is roughly twice her size), and turned her attention to something bigger—me!

The things that Maui did a year ago—chase my tail, bite my ears—Molly started doing! All I want is to be left alone, and now this! I'm pretty sure my age precludes me from having to put up with this kind of treatment: I'm going to check with the AARP (American Association of Retired Pets) as soon as I finish writing this to see if I have any recourse.

Not that I have any compassion for cats, but Maui is getting short-changed in this deal as well. Not only does he have to share his cat food and cat treats with the NKOTB (New Kitten on the Block), he has to share his litter box with her! Talk about humiliation! One time Maui was in the litter box 'taking care of business' and Molly hopped in beside him to do the same. Boy, you talk about pressure! I don't know how Maui managed to finish, but he did. Of course, Maui totally ignored mom and dad for the next three days. But I agree with him—they deserved it.

I know that in time Maui and I will incorporate this newly-acquired WOF into our routine (or should I say we'll 'adjust' our routine—taking Molly into consideration). For now, however, that kitten just gets under my fur.

I've got to admit, though, Molly is a pretty cute kitten. For example, she tries to drink from the faucet like Maui (who puts his head to the side and laps at the water), but Molly always puts her head directly beneath the stream of water and as the water is saturating her head, she licks at the water that rolls over her nose past her mouth. A little slow, but cute.

Maybe I'll give her a chance after all. Just a small one, you understand, but a chance.

Looking Over My Hind Quarters

by Magic Braelinn Ludwig

I saw in the newspaper that a 95-year old man just broke the world age group record in the 100-meter dash by running the distance in 22 seconds. It made me realize that since I will be turning 14 (human) years old this Thanksgiving, at this point in time, I am 95 years old in dog years.

I just finished reading Paula May's piece about the people who helped shape her running career. It was called 'Looking Over My Shoulder." It made me think about all the lives that have influenced me over the years.

What do these two things have to do with anything, you may ask? It made me realize that I owe it to you, the reader, and to myself, the aging warrior, to put some things down in print for you to enjoy and reflect upon. Think back to the people who shaped my running career–and my life–will accomplish both. But where do I begin?

My brothers, Justin and Josh

I was welcomed into the Ludwig family over 13 years ago by nine-year-old Justin and six-year-old Josh, who for the first month or so wouldn't allow me a moment to myself. I remember the first weekend I spent with them ... winter blessed us with about six inches of snow on the ground and we played outside in it. The snow touched the bottom of my stomach so I had to hop–exactly like a rabbit–to move around in the front yard. I remember when dad and my two brothers spent an entire Saturday building a small 4' x 4' pen for me in the garage, and when they placed me in it I proceeded to hop right out of it. They must have forgotten they named me Magic.

My Gramps, Bip

In my youth, I loved taking long, slow walks. When my Gramps came to visit, I could count on three or four walks a day–some lasting as long as 40 minutes! I couldn't wait for Gramps to get off the couch, because I knew one of four things was about to happen, and three of them meant good things were in store for me: (1) he was going for a walk which meant I was going for a walk, (2) he was getting something to eat, which meant I was getting something to eat, (3) he was going to sleep or to take a nap, which meant I was going to sleep or take a nap, or

(4) he was going to the bathroom which meant I was going to wait outside the bathroom door for him and make him feel guilty because he didn't do (1), (2), or (3).

My Friend, Valerie

I was an outside dog for the first five years of my life. One spring, my dad's running pal, Valerie offered to let me stay with her and her two dogs Tyler (a golden retriever) and Tara (a standard poodle) for three weeks so that she could housebreak me. I had a great time, and Tyler and especially Tara and I became really close. Outside of two or three 'accidents,' the housebreaking was a success (sorry about that, Valerie). When my dad came back to pick me up after three weeks, he was amazed to find Tyler, Tara and I lounging in the living room wearing our matching bandanas. We looked like three desperados, but I could tell my dad was happy that I would be coming home to live with him, Mom and my two brothers on the inside of the house instead of outside in the yard. I know my dad always felt guilty during heavy rains when I would seek shelter by digging in the dirt next to the house, trying to stay dry beneath the overhang on the roof. I know my dad always feels bad when he thinks back on the days when I was banished to the backyard.

My Brother, Maui

Maui, the white cat Justin found on the road in Brooks, Georgia, has been a part of our family for three years. At first, it would irritate me the way Maui would chase my tail and bite it once he caught it. Maui was a real pain in the ass. But over the years, we've become really close, and I know by the way Maui follows me around and shadows my every move that he really cares for me. Although I don't show it (in fact, I do a really good job ignoring him) on the outside, I really love that cat. He doesn't chase my tail very often any longer, and he knows I'm not quite as agile as I was three years ago, but every so often he will paw at my snout or ears. I know that's Maui's way of saying 'Magic, you've still got it!'

My Sister, Molly

Molly, the black cat my dad adopted two years ago after he became intrigued by her photograph in the local newspaper, took up where Maui left off. Once Maui decided to respect my space, Molly decided to invade it. After two years, the novelty that is me has worn off a bit, and Molly is starting to spend more time chasing Maui around the house. That's good news for me–Maui and Molly play while I get to nap, and once Maui and Molly are tired and need to rest I get to nap some more. The way God intended.

My Mom

My mom has always been there for me. She always manages to land all the 'less than desirable' dog duties. You know, like 'hiding the dog pill in the piece of bread' and 'cleaning the sleepy stuff out of the eyes' and 'cleaning up after any and all of the dog's inside-the-house accidents.' You know–all the fun stuff. The unique part? She has never complained about any of those things. Not once. From the very first day when she allowed me into her home and called me 'Miss Mag,' I knew I was a part of her family. Now if I could only get her to weaken when I intensely stare at her eating dinner–silently ... patiently begging for a bite or two. That's my mom for you–a real rock.

My Dad

My dad is the farthest thing from being a rock. If I hit him with my big 'baby browns' (eyes) while he's eating, I know it's only a matter of time before part of his meal is mine. Here's something I don't think anyone but my dad knows: in the late 1990's I had a five-year running streak of my own. Each morning, my dad would take me for a 1 ½ mile run though the surrounding neighborhoods before he went out for his regular run. It didn't matter if dad was only running eight miles or a marathon–he would still take me out for my run first. Towards the latter part of my streak, the runs became a combination of running and walking, and then became mostly walking, which then became one mile and later a half mile and now simply a five-minute walk up and down our street. After all, I'm not a puppy any more. But I still have my figure to worry about!

The best times of my life now are when my dad stays home with me. Whether he's watching television, taking a nap, taking a shower, reading, writing ... whatever he's doing, I'm right there with him. He calls me his 'shadow,' which in some crazy way is appropriate, since he's always tripping over me ('tripping over his own shadow!'). My favorite season is the fall, when dad and I watch our beloved Florida Gators play football on the television in the den ... just as long as he pets me every now and then.

Epilogue

I've had a great life, and I really have loved and appreciated all the many people who have been a part of it. Al, Kelly, Susan, Paula, Jan, Bruce, Stephanie, Gran, Hope, Billy, Eric, Prince—thanks for being a part of my life. I know when you come to visit my dad and mom, you do so just as much to visit me—that can be our little secret.

As for my five-year streak, my dad says he sees a Boxer every morning walking a three-mile route with its owner around the neighborhood. I bet that Boxer is out to break my record. That *bitch*.

Separated From My Shadow

I can't remember a time when I didn't have my constant … dark … and most of all, loyal shadow at my feet. Shadows are oftentimes taken for granted … sometimes to the point of neglect. But I, for one, always felt a small degree of comfort and satisfaction knowing my shadow was there by my side—through thick and thin … no matter what—to offer its unflappable support and silent encouragement to weather whatever storm came my way.

For many cold winter months, my shadow—cast by the moon, not the sun—was right by my side during my early morning runs. Runs I would finish by 5:00 a.m. with temperatures in the high 20's, without ever hearing a whimper or whine from my shadow.

For (too) many years of busy, busy days at work, I wouldn't even have the opportunity or presence of mind to notice my shadow until I got home from work and unlocked my front door and found it—as always—right by my feet, serving up the usual amount of comfort and support.

For countless Saturdays in the fall, I would sit in front of the television in my living room doing what I do best—watching college football. My shadow seemed to enjoy these days best, as it didn't require any effort at all to stick by my side (since I didn't seem to move very much throughout the day).

Then one day I looked down by my feet and my shadow—no, a *part* of me—was gone. My constant, dark and loyal shadow was no more. While I found comfort in knowing that I never took my shadow for granted, I am saddened by the fact that I will never feel that same degree of comfort and satisfaction knowing my shadow is there by my side–through thick and thin ... and no matter what–to offer its unflappable support and silent encouragement to weather whatever storm comes my way.

Magic Braelinn Ludwig
1991-2005

Magic

CHAPTER TEN
RUNNING THROUGH HELL

Badwater

Running in the 2003 Badwater 135 Ultramarathon is unquestionably the pinnacle of my running career. In fact, I originally wanted to run in the 2002 edition, but in order to ensure I reached my lifetime goal of 100 marathons (which I would not attain until the 2003 Boston Marathon), I waited until 2003. Knowing how difficult and demanding Badwater is, I feared that I might do permanent damage to my body and/or psyche which would preclude me from running marathon #100.

My patience paid off. It allowed me time to focus on and train for Badwater for the better part of two years. Looking back, I doubt I could have done it with anything less.

In this chapter:

- Sand Wars Episode 1: Attack of the Phantom Race Director—If you thought training for Badwater would be difficult ... if you thought competing in Badwater would be impossible ... just finagling an invitation to the 'big dance' proved to be quite a challenge.

- Sand Wars Episode 2: Return of the Dedi(cation)—With 15 years of base mileage, 10 years of heavy mileage, two years of concentrating primarily on ultra distances at a slow, steady pace, and six months of centering my running on the sole purpose of completing the event, I was ready to tackle Badwater. That is, if anyone is ever really 'ready to tackle Badwater.'

- Sand Wars Episode 3: The Desert Strikes Back—Seven days in July 2003 that will forever be remembered as the 'crown jewel' in my running career. Sharing the adventure with five runners who have meant so much to me and my running made it that much more memorable.

- Scott's Badwater Statistics—Summarizing the Badwater experience with numbers: lots and lots of numbers.

- Congrats to the Crew (by Paula May)—Badwater Crew Chief Paula May offers her thanks to the crew for a job well done. In all honesty and sincerity, they were every bit as essential to the success of 'the mission' as the runner.

- The Badwater Ultramarathon Experience (by Gary Griffin)—Crew member Gary Griffin offers his perspective of Badwater, illustrating how demanding it is to serve on a crew for this extreme event.

- Come Hell or BADwater (by John Kissane)—John Kissane gives such an excellent account of our Badwater adventure, you'd have thought he was there.

- Final thoughts about Badwater—If you even think you might be interested in tackling the toughest footrace on the planet, consider this required reading.

- Badwater Takes Center Stage–Documentaries! Books! Magazines! David Letterman, for crying out loud!

- Living to the Point of Tears (by Al Barker)—Crew Member Al Barker eloquently recounts the Badwater experience.

- A Note of Thanks—From the runner to the crew.

- Post-Badwater Cool down—After running Badwater, a quick 100-miler seven weeks later should have been a piece of cake.

The Badwater Ultramarathon is a 135 mile invitational running race starting in Badwater in Death Valley (elevation 280 feet below sea level) and finishing at the Whitney Portals on Mount Whitney (elevation 8,360 feet).

The course runs through Death Valley—where runners could face temperatures reaching 130 degrees—and over three mountain ranges with a finish on the highest mountain in the contiguous United States.

Runners are required to make their presence known at five checkpoints along the course: Furnace Creek, Stovepipe Wells, Panamint Springs, Darwin, and Lone Pine.

Badwater is recognized as 'the toughest footrace on the planet.'

Deservedly so.

Sand Wars: Episode I

Attack of the Phantom Race Director

It's taken 21 months to get to this point, but it was worth the wait. I think.

I became interested in running the Badwater 135 Ultramarathon right after Father's Day, 2001, as my wife Cindy gave me a copy of the video 'Running on the Sun,' a documentary of the 1999 race. I instantly became fascinated with the event, and read a book written by one of 1999's participants, Kirk Johnson. Watching the video and seeing the varying degrees of pain, anguish, and suffering, I realized I was extremely familiar with all of it (excluding the runners getting fluids via an IV–which, by the way, is grounds for disqualification in the event).

I decided that once I completed my 100th marathon (projected to be Boston 2003–which wound up being accurate), I would give it a shot. I had already met three Badwater qualifying standards (two 50-mile races, one 100 mile race, one 'extreme' event–which was my 280 mile run across Georgia in 1992), but I felt I needed to 'pad' my resume. After all, when I told the Race Director in 2001 that I had run 80+ marathons, he told me 'I don't care how many marathons you've run.' When I asked if met the qualifying standards with two 50 milers and one 101-miler, which was done in a 24-hour event, he said 'check the website.' Pretty helpful and encouraging guy! So I entered the 24-hour National Championship in September 2002 and ran 129 miles, an achievement I felt would guarantee acceptance into Badwater.

Let me clarify 'acceptance.' First of all, you have to pay (a non-refundable) $50 just to have your application reviewed by the Race Director. Entries are available on-line on January 2 of the year of the event. I began filling my entry form out at 11:00 a.m. EST that day; it took me a full hour. Later I found out I was the 17th application received. As 68 applications were submitted on January 2nd, I didn't think it would take long to reach the Race Director's target of 100. Once 100 entries were received, 75 runners would be 'invited' to compete. I figured I'd hear in the very near future if I was in or not. I figured wrong.

January 11–this was the first day I expected to receive word from the Race Director. Paula dropped me off after we returned from a marathon in Warner Robbins, and I asked her to wait while I checked the mail. Nothing. Damn.

January 29–According to the Badwater website, there are 97 applications on file. The Race Director wants to get 100 before he makes his decisions. Damn.

February 3–98 applications. Nothing in the mail. Damn.

February 4–One of the entrants donates $1000 to the official charity and gets an automatic invitation. The Race Director advices all applicants that 'you too can be automatically invited' by donating $1000.' There are no takers. The wait continues. Damn.

February 14–100 applications. Finally.

February 25 (or there abouts, I'm losing track)—the Race Director states that the invitations will be sent out this week. Damn.

February 26–One applicant withdrew. Two were 'automatically invited' (the second being the so-called Mayor of Badwater, Ben Jones, who was pretty much already invited, as the Race Director asked him to be the first 70-year-old to compete in Badwater). That leaves 97 applicants for 73 spots. Damn.

March 1–I received a congratulatory phone call from Gary Griffin. His friend Jeff Bryan had gotten a rejection E-mail from the Race Director the day before. As I had not, Gary assumed I had received confirmation. Gary assumed wrong. But he gave me hope.

March 3–The Race Director sent an E-mail saying invitations were mailed out on February 28. Should be any day now.

March 3, 5:00p.m.–I'm in! I saw #7 on the 'Entrant Contract' which basically states that I realize I may die in the event. All that for only a $250 entry fee! Damn.

March 4, 5:44 a.m.–The check is in the mail. We're going to Death Valley! Hot damn!

2003 Badwater Application

Number of Years Running–25
Number of Marathons and 50K's–102
Qualifying Standard(s)–
1998 24-hour National Championship, Atlanta, GA–101 miles (19.5 hours), 27th place
2002 24-hour National Championship, Olander Park, OH–129 miles (24 hours), 4th place
1982 Stone Mountain 50 Miler, Stone Mountain, GA–7:28:25, 6th place

2000 JFK 50 Miler, Boonesboro, MD–8:00:19, 56th place
1992 Run Across Georgia–280 miles in 6 days

Previous Badwater Racing Experience–none
Previous Badwater Crewing Experience–none
Previous Badwater Clinic Experience–none

My Badwater Prediction–Under 40 hours. I base this prediction on my successes in 24-hour runs, as well as the base mileage I have (87,300 miles over 25 years, including an average of 90 miles/week over the past nine years). I've got a streak of 24+ years, and am accustomed to running in the heat and humidity of Georgia and Florida. I've also run successfully in the climates of Las Vegas (3:02 marathon) and St. George, Utah (2:48 marathon). PLUS: I've got a fantastic crew lined up to assist me, and they've even got a catchy slogan: 'Just CREW It!'

My Weirdest Experience–I attempted to run solo across the state of Georgia (from Columbus to Savannah), a distance of 280 miles, in the fall of 1982. I pulled up 'lame' on the 4th day (after 159) miles, as my left shin was on the verge of a major stress fracture from running facing traffic the entire time (i.e. the nap of the road took it's toll). I called a friend of mine in Atlanta to come 'rescue' me as I lay on the side of Highway 280 for four hours until he arrived.

Note: I attempted this run again in the fall of 1992 with a support crew of ONE and MADE IT! Six days–280 miles–and more chilidogs and onion rings than I care to remember!

My Most Challenging Race Experience–The JFK 50 Miler in 2002. I am not accustomed to running on trails (I do most of my running on the streets in my neighborhood at 3:30 a.m. in the morning), and the 13 miles on the Appalachian Trail (AT) almost did me in. I was in 23rd place ENTERTING the AT, and 47th when I EXITED it. Somehow, someway ... I managed to hold my position until the end of the race. Not bad, considering I basically WALKED the 13 miles of the AT ... I don't know how you can run on loose rocks, piles of leaves, slippery slopes, etc ... unless you're a mountain goat.

Why I Run Ultras–I've been successful at them over the years (I kind of sensed this in high school because in 10th grade, I could run the 600 yard run faster than anyone in my class that DIDN'T throw up afterwards). Running 5-10 percent slower than I do in marathons makes an INCREDIBLE difference in what I'm able to accomplish over distances of 50K and up. As I'm getting older and losing my speed, ultras are more and more appealing to me.

Why I want a slot on the starting line of the 2003 Badwater Ultramarathon–I'll run my 100th marathon at Boston this year, and running Badwater this July would be the 'crown jewel' in my running career. Plus, I've been focusing on this race ever since I received the video 'Running on the Sun' for Father's Day 2001 and then read the book written by one of the participants from 1999. In fact, I gave my five crew members a copy of both for Christmas, and they've already watched the video (SEVERAL times!) and read the book … and taken notes.

Personally, I think about Badwater every day: some days I don't know how I can run the 135 miles across Death Valley and up Mount Whitney, and then there are days when I think I have a chance to win it. It sure would be great to find out which thought is closer to reality. I picture the finish at Mount Whitney at the end of my run each day, and imagine how great it would be to complete Badwater.

My Other Ultrasport Experience–none

Media that I will represent or write for–I believe the Atlanta newspaper, the *Atlanta Journal-Constitution,* will be interested in covering it. In the January 1st edition, they listed my hopes of running Badwater in their special 'New Year's Resolutions' sections.

Media that will cover my experience in this race–I'm not sure at this time (although I doubt it). See previous answer.

The Charity that I will represent and raise funds for is–the Alex Sudduth Memorial Fund, which benefits the children's ward of Egleston Hospital in Atlanta. Alex was the seven year old son of my next door neighbors (Stephanie and Anthony Sudduth) who lost their son to leukemia two years ago. Stephanie and I organized a race in Peachtree City last year, the 'Run for Alex 5K, 'in his memory (held in April, Alex's birth month). We are making it an annual event.

Do I speak English–yes
Does my crew speak English–yes

<u>*Will I hike Mount Whitney after the race*</u>–(hell) no

<u>*Here is my athletic resume*</u>

87,000+lifetime miles
Have run everyday since November 30, 1978
Run across the state of Georgia–280 miles
600 lifetime races
Masters Champion–2002 24-hour National Championship
Member of the Atlanta Track Club Men's Masters Competitive team
Editor of the *Absolutely True … Tales from the DARKSIDE* (a local 'underground' running newsletter)
Marathon PR of 2:48:41
10K PR of 36:14
5K PR of 17:12
50K PR of 3:44:58

Sand Wars: Episode II

Return of the Dedi(cation)

First, let me explain about the title of Episode II. It's been a long time since I've been this excited about a race … at least one in which I want to do well. Badwater has given me a renewed sense of dedication and purpose, something I've been missing of late.

The following recounts my preparation for this year's Badwater Ultramarathon. Hopefully, it has given me 'what it takes' to complete the 135 miles from Badwater, California *(Death Valley!)* to the portals of Mount Whitney.

Base Mileage and Conditioning

Fortunately, the regimen I've put myself through over the past 24+ years has made this my strongest area. Particularly these past 9 ½ years, as I've averaged over 4,700 miles annually and survived on an average of five hours sleep per night. These, along with pushing myself to the point of exhaustion more times than I care to remember, are the primary reasons I even considered tackling Badwater in the first place.

Diet/Eating Habits

Admittedly my weakest area, especially when you consider the following:

- My brown-bag lunch at work has been the same every day for 24 years: bologna and cheese sandwich, Ruffles potato chips, Little Debbie Fancy Cakes, and a Diet Coke. I call it my 87-cent lunch (I did the math).

- Five years ago vanilla ice cream was a *daily* treat, although three years ago it became a *3-time-a-week treat*. Recently it's down to once or twice a week (depending on my weekly mileage).

- Vanilla cake with vanilla frosting is my biggest weakness–especially when the frosting overpowers the cake itself. Everyone I know (family, friends, workmates) all know this, and they all make a special effort to make it known to me when there's one around. Some–actually most–even 'save' me extra frosting.

- I could survive on fast food and pizza if I had to. I know this for a fact, as I did it during college (not counting my freshman year when I survived on Pop Tarts and cans of spinach).

- I know what vegetables and fruit are, but I'd be hard pressed to recognize more than 4 or 5 by sight (particularly since I've been told that potato chips are not vegetables).

Fortunately for me, my DARKSIDE teammates developed a diet for me that I began in earnest on March 3. I began on that day as I still had not received my acceptance into Badwater, so I decided to put the 'cart before the horse' and go ahead and start my diet anyway. Believe it or not, that afternoon, I received my invitation in the mail. Some of the highlights (poor choice of noun) of my 'new and improved' eating habits:

- My brown-bag lunch at work is now turkey or tuna on wheat bread (no mayonnaise!), veggie crisp chips, Little Debbie Rice Treats and a Diet Coke. Back in March I experimented with different types of bread and chips, but I found myself continually ruling them out as most of them tasted like cardboard. I've learned to enjoy–make that tolerate–this current menu. I forgot to mention that initially I was trying vanilla wafers as a dessert but found that I had to eat an entire box of them before I was full.

- I've had three hamburgers since March 3: on Al's birthday, the night of the Doobie Brother's concert (I had to grill hamburgers and hotdogs for 10 people, and it would have been a crime if I didn't have at least one of them!), and on the 4th of July. Also of note: not one single serving of anything from the 'fried' food group since March 3rd.

- I've eaten in many fast food restaurants over the past four months but have always ordered either a chicken (grilled, of course) sandwich or a salad. Prior to March 3rd, I had never eaten a salad–or for that matter, grilled chicken–in a fast food restaurant.

- In the early days of this new diet, I allowed myself one 'splurge' meal per week (normally after my long run on Sunday). Over the past two months, I've felt too guilty to splurge. So I haven't (what's wrong with me?).

- I love sweets. This diet has limited me to the following 'sweets': jelly beans, Rice Krispie Treats, vanilla wafers, and frozen yogurt (I may have strayed a couple* of times in March when pieces of vanilla cake with vanilla frosting 'appeared' on my desk at work, however). *(by a couple, I mean 8 or 9 times. OK, 12)

- I've said sentences I've never said before in my life, such as:

   In place of French Fries, could I have a salad with my sandwich?

   Could you fix that without mayonnaise?

   (A the doughnut shop drive through) I'll have a plain bagel please.

   (At a Mexican restaurant) I'll have the #24–there's no meat in that, right?

   (To anyone offering me vanilla cake with vanilla frosting) No, thanks.

   (After running 40 miles) I'd like two veggie burgers, please.

However, I've got to admit that I do feel better after four months of 'eating right.' Stomach problems have almost been non-existent, and I actually find myself craving salad (sometimes, not always). And best of all, my belt now fastens one notch more to the right (so does my wristwatch for that matter). I may have only lost four or five pounds, but I've lost quite a bit of my circumference.

High Mileage

I selected the eight weeks from Monday, April 21 (date of the Boston Marathon) to Sunday, June 15 (Father's Day) for some high mileage. I targeted five ultramarathons during that time to get acclimated to running long distances, forcing my body to recover quickly, and pushing myself to exhaustion (figuring I would be doing a lot of Badwater in that condition). My longer runs during this period follow:

Date	Miles	Comment
Monday, April 21	54	Boston Marathon 'out-and-back'
Saturday, April 26	20	Training Run (with Kelly)
Sunday, April 27	21	Training Run (with Al, Paula, Eric)
Saturday, May 3	41	Strolling Jim 40-Mile Run
Sunday, May 4	20	Training Run (A/P/E and Prince)
Sunday, May 11	23	Training Run (A/P/E/P)
Saturday, May 17	31	Posey's 50K Run (with Fred and Gary)
Sunday, May 18	20	Training Run (A/P/E/P)
Saturday, May 24	24	Training Run (A/P/E/K)
Saturday, May 31	52	8 Hour Track Run (A/Prince/K)
Saturday, June 7	40	Pennar 40-Mile Run (with Gary)
Sunday, Jun 8	20	Training Run (A/Prince)
Saturday, June 14	25	Training Run (A/Paula/K)
Sunday, Jun 15	20	Training Run (A/P/E/P)

Even though I only ran 805 miles during these eight weeks, I was satisfied that I averaged just over 29 miles for the 14 days listed above (note: the other 42 days I averaged 9.4 miles–'rest' days). As I mentioned, my goal was to push myself to exhaustion, and I managed to do just that. As approximately the 30-mile mark on my fifth (and by design final) ultramarathon during this time (Pennar), my body pretty much told me that it had enough (although I would have liked for it to hold out for another 10 miles!).

I used the 8-Hour Track Run on May 31st to experiment with liquid replacements and to focus on–quite frankly–being bored for extended periods of time (like I may find myself at Badwater). I did learn several things with respect to hydration and energy/calorie replacement:

- My body will require (a minimum of) 40 ounces of fluid per hour. I averaged 18-20 ounces per hour (water, Gatorade, Sustained Energy and Diet Coke) during my eight hours on the track, and the last hour proved to me that wasn't enough. I haven't run through Death Valley before, but figuring eight ounces of fluid for every mile, 40 ounces an hour sounds about right.

- Why Diet Coke? This workout reminded me I use it to curtail nausea during long runs.

- Sustained Energy, which (honest-to-God) tastes and even smells like swamp water, is almost palatable if you mix in Crystal Light (*thanks for the suggestion, Paula*). By the way, the Sustained Energy drink is for calorie replacement during endurance events. It sure would be a crime to be drinking 'swamp water' to the tune of 300 calories every eight ounces.

- I detest running with a bottle in my hand. That's where my support crew will come in handy (please forgive the pun–totally unintentional).

One last thing: for the 30 days leading up to Badwater, I didn't consume any beer, wine, or liquor. Fortunately, the three days prior to these 30 days was a 'guys golfing weekend' in Montgomery, Alabama. After that, I'm not sure I even *wanted* any more beer, wine or liquor for 30 days (with one exception: I would have loved a beer immediately after the Peachtree Road Race. It's been a tradition–for 24 years now–to polish off two or three beers before 9:00 am on the 4th of July. On the other hand, it was nice not having my usual 'hangover by noon' this year).

Supplemental Training during the High Mileage Stage

A while back noted ultrarunner Ray Krowelicz said he used long–distance *driving* (as in a car) as a training device for endurance events. He mentioned that often-times it is more difficult to stay awake and focused while driving than it is while competing in ultradistance running events. With that in mind, I approached all of my driving during these eight weeks as Badwater training, which included:

> **Friday, May 2:** 10 hour drive to Wartrace, Tennessee (which allowed me 6 hours sleep prior to Strolling Jim).
> **Saturday, May 3:** 4 ½ hour drive to Peachtree City (immediately after Strolling Jim).
> **Friday, May 16:** 4 ½ hour drive to Tallahassee (for the Posey 50K)
> **Saturday, May 17:** 4 ½ hour drive to Peachtree City (immediately after Posey's)
> **Saturday, May 24:** 5 ¾ hour drive to Jacksonville Beach
> **Monday, May 26:** 6 hour drive to Peachtree City
> **Friday, June 6:** 5 ½ hour drive to Pensacola (for Pennar)
> **Saturday, June 7:** 5 ½ hour drive to Peachtree City (immediately after Pennar)

Eight trips and the equivalent of almost two days (46 mind-numbing hours, to be exact) behind the wheel. Every little bit helps!

With this 'base' of cross-training behind me, I decided to branch out into other areas:

Swimming: I tried swimming 350 yards every day for a week. I'd tell you how long each 'workout' lasted, but you'd either (a) laugh or (b) not believe me. Actually, you'd probably do both. Anyway, I noticed my legs had absolutely no life in them during my morning runs following a swim. I felt it appropriate to cease and desist immediately. The lifeguards will have to find some other method of entertainment.

Weightlifting: The hardest part of my weightlifting 'workouts' (I have got to quit using quotation marks around that word—it may give you the wrong idea) was removing enough weights off the barbell once my son Josh finished using them. I would take off more weight than I would leave on the barbell to work out with. Once I made the weights me-friendly, I would do three or four sets of 10 bench presses ... with ample* rest between sets (*ample being as long as it took to read one section of the daily newspaper. I've never noticed how fascinating the obituaries are).

Walking: Eric and I walked 12 miles the last Saturday in June. We began by walking at the track, so I could get a 'feel' for my walking pace. Walking normally, I timed a mile in 14:47. I walked another mile using my trekking poles: 14:55 (must have been the added weight!). I walked one more track mile what I thought was my fastest pace yet: 14:51. I must be getting tired. Eric and I then walked another nine miles over really hilly terrain. I learned that (a) trekking poles will be helpful going up mountains and will be a detriment on flat and downhill terrain and (b) I should wear sandals or shoes with the toes cut out when I travel downhill (as my toes were constantly striking the front of my shoes). One last thing I learned: someone who is not used to walking should not begin a walking program by walking 12 hilly miles. If you do, your butt cheeks will be incredibly sore the next day.

I continued walking in the afternoons during July (still doing my running in the mornings), but didn't count the mileage towards my weekly tapering targets. Periodically, I would do my daily run and walk in one session; I found it much easier to run first, and then walk as opposed to walk first then run. Insignificant? Maybe. But in one short month, I managed to lower my walking pace/mile by over 20 seconds.

Tapering

Although my body needed the rest, this was the toughest part for me. After running to exhaustion for the better part of the last 10 years, intentionally cutting back on my mileage was hard to do. I started my tapering phase five weeks out, hitting weekly mileage (in order) of 80, 70, 60, 50, and finally 30 while maintaining my weekly long run of 20+ miles (except for the final week). Note: I didn't count any *walking* distance in my weekly totals.

Up until the week before Badwater (the 21 mile week), I still managed to maintain my 20 mile run every Sunday. Except for the weekend in Montgomery, where I ran 22 miles Saturday instead.

Heat Training

If there's one thing I heard about Death Valley, it's that experiencing the heat is like sticking your head in a hot oven or blowing a hairdryer directly in your face. That being the case, my crew strongly advised that a little heat training would be in order ... especially since I do most of my running in the dark (*i.e. out of the sun!*).

I began my heat (adaptation) training four weeks before Badwater. The first day I ran seven miles in the morning wearing a T-shirt and windbreaker. While I wasn't noticeably hot, I did manage to perspire enough so that I had to 'wring out' the T-shirt when I finished. In my mind the key was getting the heat *index* in the ballpark of Death Valley, since I didn't think I'd see temperatures in the 120's in Georgia.

Over the next 28 days I experimented with different combinations of attire; as long as I could 'work up a sweat' (not too difficult in Georgia in the middle of the summer), I felt it was productive.

Kelly arranged for me to use the sauna at her gym for the 10 days prior to our departure to California. I 'maxed out' at 180 degrees (the highest I could get the sauna to go—also the highest temperature I could *bear!*). I read that someone trained in a sauna at 211 degrees (one degree less than the boiling point of water). A couple times in the sauna I put my face about 18 inches away from the rocks (the source of the heat). Considering I singed my eyebrows, I have to assume the temperature had to be close to water's boiling point.

Physical Inventory

I'm sure it was mostly mental, but I noticed my aches and pains grew as the number of days before Badwater shrank. I even went to a doctor during the last week in June to see if he could do something about my 39-month-old numb right thigh. If you knew what I thought of doctors, you would realize how desperate I was.

I figure most of my pre-Badwater aches and pains were all in my mind, and once I ran the first mile in Death Valley they would all disappear. In case they don't, I want you to know what I believed to be wrong with me during my tapering stage:

- Tooth ache
- Cracked crown
- Sore neck, right side
- Stiff upper back and shoulders
- Numb spot in right side of chest

- Right thigh (still!) numb; possibly spreading to right knee and right shoulder
- Bone spur in ball of left foot
- Stress fracture re-occurrence in left shin
- Pain in right ankle
- Ugly toes (*perpetually ugly toes*)

Advice from the Experts

I ran into several Badwater veterans who weren't hesitant to offer some free advice, such as:

'*Have different shapes of fluid bottles as you will get mentally tired of holding the same shape in your hand at some point during the event.*'–David Jones, former Badwater Champion

'*Don't do anything stupid like running in a sauna or hooking yourself up to a dryer. You don't need to pull a tire behind you for training because you aren't doing that at Badwater.*'–Mark Godale (referring to the scenes shown in the 1999 Badwater documentary 'Running on the Sun'). Note: Mark competed that year and ran 29:50.

A few more from Mark Godale:

- *Get a good crew with an ultra background*
- *Have your crew stop each mile and give you water and ice for under your hat*
- *Many sleep the first night. That is a mistake–it's cooler running at night than during the heat of the day.*
- *Pouring water over your head is a big mistake–it could run into your shoes and make your feet wet. Use baby powder on your feet–I didn't have a single blister.*
- *Take goggles–in case of a sandstorm.*
- *Good things to eat: soup, peanut butter, mashed potatoes.*

'*Running in the southeast is a big advantage as you get used to running in heat AND humidity.*'–Mark Henderson, Badwater Veteran

A few more from Mark Henderson:

- *In Death Valley the heat radiates from 360 degrees—wear white and DRINK!*

- *I wore Teva Trail Sandals and a good sock. Kept my feet cooler and blister free.*

- *Demonstrate patience and discipline early to conserve your legs for the long haul.*

- *Bring a variety of things to eat and drink—maybe things you don't normally eat during races, as there's no Wal-Mart close by.*

'Don't do it.'–David Jones

'Enjoy the journey. Be happy out there. It'll be a great experience.'–Mark Henderson

'The crew needs to train like the runner. The pacers will be out there quite a while, and they need to train for the conditions. The crew member who is driving the van also needs to drink frequently and stay hydrated; it's a dry heat, and you won't even notice that you're losing precious fluid.'–Andy Velazco, 2002 Badwater crew member and 2003 Badwater participant (from his article 'The Glamorous Life of an Athletic Supporter', *Marathon and Beyond*, July/August 2003 as well as from a meeting he conducted with my crew and I in February).

'The runner is going to need a strong crew to make all decisions for him once the race starts. The runner's opinion of not needing something is irrelevant. The runner won't feel like eating or drinking, so just give it to him/her and make sure it's consumed.'–David Sowers, veteran Badwater crew chief (from a meeting he conducted with my crew and I on April 26).

A few more from David Sowers:

- *The crew must be physically and mentally prepared for hardships as this event eats up crews as it does competitors.*

- *Water should be bought figuring 20 ounces per hour per person. The water will be used for drinking, eating and washing.*

- *The real race doesn't begin until Stove Pipe (mile 42).*

- *Buy ice and gas every chance you get.*

- *A crew member with sunburn, blisters or becomes dehydrated has just become a liability.*

And a personal favorite from David:
'Never say how bad Scott looks or get into a pity party with him. He is going to have some very low points and will piss and moan; just change the subject and try to figure out if it is a fuel/hydration issue or if he is just a (we'll go with) pansy.'

Final Thoughts about Tapering

A thought occurred to me during my tapering phase: *'I'm spending more TIME preparing for Badwater during my rest (tapering) period than I was during my high mileage period.'* How can that be, you may ask.

Consider, during the high mileage period, running 100 miles a week took approximately 800 minutes. Add in the time for my requisite weight training and the total grows to 806 minutes a week.

Now, during a randomly-selected tapering week (we'll go with the 50 mile week):

- 50 miles of running takes approximately 400 minutes.

- Walking three miles per day (21 miles per week) takes approximately 315 minutes.

- Spending 45 minutes in the sauna five days during the week takes 225 minutes.

Adding these up totals 940 minutes a week … *WITHOUT* weight training added in! So much for 'rest.' I'm actually spending almost 20 percent MORE time 'resting' for Badwater than I was training for Badwater.

This tapering phase has not only made me feel more tired than I did during the 100 mile weeks, but I've been a lot hungrier as well (my metabolism couldn't change *that* fast could it?!!)!

Final Thoughts

I feel like I've done my homework. I've run hard (and easy, when the schedule called for it), I've (re)learned to walk, I've cross trained (*Weightlifting! Swimming! Golf!*), I've improved my dietary habits, I've worked on heat-acclimation, I've tested all my gear (sandals, hats fuels/fluids, etc.), I've gotten a wealth of advice (from books, magazines, Badwater veterans), and I've tapered more than I've done in the past ten years.

But most of all, I feel ready for two very distinct reasons:

I've got a very positive mental attitude about Badwater.

I have the utmost faith and confidence in (and appreciation for) my Badwater crew.

It should be memorable. I hope my crew and I will 'enjoy the adventure.'

Sand Wars: Episode III

The Desert Strikes Back

Seven Days in July. **'Badwater Week.'** And what a week it was.

Friday, July 8 (-4 days)

Paula, our crew chief, held the final DARKSIDE crew meeting at her house. Gary, Al, Paula and I. Josh? Had to work. Eric? Went to the Braves game. Priorities, you understand.

We went over our final gear check and chronological plan for the upcoming week. It appeared we had our game plan firmly in place. All that remained was the execution. Of the game plan, that is (not *me!*).

Years of training and months of planning were about to be put to the test. We believed we were ready. And willing. And yes, able. We'd find out soon enough.

Saturday, July 19 (-3 days)

Delta takes us from Atlanta to Las Vegas (by way of Dallas). I'd like to say an uneventful airplane ride, but that would be a lie. As I had been heavily hydrating the past several days, I finished off a 20 ounce bottle of water just before boarding the plane. After sitting on the plane for 30 minutes (we still had not left the gate), I realized I had to urinate. Desperately. Just as I was about to visit the restroom, the pilot announced we were ready to take off and to please be seated. OK, I could wait until we were in the air.

However, we crept along the runway, making my particular condition magnify in urgency. When the pilot announced that we were '4th in line for takeoff,' that was it for me. I jumped out of my seat (figuring I had time, since planes take off at two minute intervals) and headed to the restroom, despite the flight attendant 'reminding' me that the pilot asked that we be seated. I told her I couldn't wait any longer.

While I was inside the restroom, I heard the flight attendant (obviously on the phone to the pilot) saying 'I'm sorry, sir, he said he couldn't wait any longer and ignored me.' Terrific; two years of dedicated Badwater training down the drain 'cuz I know once I exit the restroom I'll be escorted off the plane. The pressure was so intense that I wasn't even able to urinate. Upon exiting the restroom, I was relieved (figuratively, not literally) that the flight attendant merely assaulted me verbally (as if I were an eight year old) about disregarding the pilots instructions. I apologized and told her it wouldn't happen again. Later, once we were in the air, I returned to the restroom, where I was finally relieved (literally, not figuratively).

Once we landed in Las Vegas, we rented our 14-passenger van, dropped off two of the seats (we needed storage space!) at the house of a friend of Paula's, and made a final shopping trip (cooler, meals, water, miscellaneous items) to Walmart. Finally, we checked into our hotel for some much needed rest (I slept 12 hours–something I haven't done since college).

Sunday, July 20 (-2 days)

Gary, Eric, Paula and I went for a short run in Vegas. We noticed we were perspiring–something we weren't expecting considering (a) we were running a nine-minute per mile pace and (b) there's no humidity in Vegas. What implications did this hold for Badwater?

We loaded up the van and made the 2 ½ hour drive to Furnace Creek, where we were welcomed by temperatures hovering around 120 degrees. **Welcome to hell.** Once we settled into our rooms, we drove out to the starting line in Badwater, where it was even warmer. Driving back to the hotel, we let Josh out of the van two miles out so he could test the conditions.

Gary and I waited for Josh, anxious to hear his report. However, he didn't need to say a thing: the color of his cheeks said it all. They were BRIGHT RED, approximately the color of a ripe tomato. Later that night, Josh and I went to the pool to cool off. Or so we thought. The water temperature had to have been in the 90's, and the air temperature was still close to 110. Surely the conditions would improve by Tuesday (race day).

The rest of the evening was spent raiding the hotel's ice machines and wondering whether or not Al (he was flying to Las Vegas this evening and renting a car) would be able to find us in Furnace Creek. He did. A good omen, perhaps?

Another nine hours of sleep for me; a good investment for what lies ahead.

Monday, July 21 (-1 day)

A short run to start the day, followed by a visit to the hotel's breakfast bar. Actually, breakfast *buffet* is more like it. Fresh fruit, cereal, breakfast burritos, eggs, bacon, sausage, hash browns, English muffins, biscuits and gravy, pancakes, apple fritters, juices, coffee, soda, water ... good timing, as the crew and I were able to load up on some much-needed calories. After all, we would be living on fig newtons and pretzels for the next two days.

We made a trip to the Furnace Creek Visitor's center at noon to pick up my race number. We met Jay Birmingham, the first man to officially 'race' from Badwater to Mount Whitney over 20 years ago. He autographed a copy of his book about his feat, *The Longest Hill*, for me. I met Chris Kostman, the Race Director, and had my pre-race 'mug shot' photo taken. Three hours later my crew and I would return for the pre-race clinic.

Imagine 300 people in a room ... for almost three hours ... weak air conditioning ... and temperatures outside over 120 degrees. Sound like fun? Sounds like pre-race conditioning, if you ask me. I can't remember the last time I was that hot (wait–yes I can, it was yesterday!). But you get the picture. We were all familiar with most of the information presented in the clinic–race rules, race history, etc. A short video of last year's event was shown, focusing on Pam Reed's historic finish (the first female winner of Badwater!). Pam was back to defend her title, and she was assigned to my time group (10:00 a.m., the other two groups starting at 6:00 a.m. and 8:00 a.m.). Pam, deservedly so, was presented with a plaque in honor of her accomplishment. At the end of the clinic, all runners were invited

Scott Ludwig   239

on stage to be introduced to everyone else in the auditorium. It was so hot on stage my knees started to perspire. Drops of perspiration were literally saturating my shoes. More pre-race conditioning, I assume. Twenty painful minutes later, we were free. Unless, of course you opted to attend the foot clinic. Which we did. Fortunately, Paula felt comfortable that she knew how to take care of my feet should problems arise, but she and Gary attended anyway. Me? I went outside to get Marshall Ulrich's autograph for a friend of mine. Plus, it was cooler outside than it was in that damn auditorium …

We ate dinner as a crew one last time before tackling the beast. The crew gave me a card wishing me well, with a personalized message from each one of them (Josh had signed with the insightful message 'Your son, Josh.' That eliminated any possibility of me confusing him with all the other 'Josh's' in my crew.). Early to bed: 9:00 p.m. The game plan was for me to sleep until 6:00 a.m., eat breakfast at 6:30, and then nap a few more hours before we headed to Badwater at 8:55. Great plan.

Tuesday, July 22 bleeding into Wednesday, July 23 (0 days)

Great plan, but terrible execution. I was awake at 1:05 a.m., and absolutely could NOT get back to sleep. I was, however, ready to eat at 6:30 a.m. (although it killed me to make another pass through the breakfast bar and only eat two pieces of French toast, some eggs and a few pieces of melon). Such a deal for $8.50. Next on the schedule? A short nap. If a short nap means lying on the bed staring at the ceiling for 90 minutes, then my 'nap' was a success. At 8:55 a.m. I was *more* than ready to go. It was time to get this show on the road, or as one of the support vans had written on both sides, to 'shut up and run.' My crew and I boarded the van at precisely 8:55 a.m. and headed over to Badwater, semi-oblivious to what lie ahead. Soon enough I would be *totally* oblivious to just about everything.

We arrived at the starting area on schedule, just in time for the Race Director to call all runners to the 'Badwater sign' for pre-race photos. If standing directly in the hot sun for 20 minutes (*'hold the banner up a little bit higher … now lower … just a bit higher … now hold it … and smile!'*) just before the race is about to begin is a good idea, then this was certainly a 'good idea.' However, if sitting in the shade and hydrating for those final minutes before the starter's pistol goes off at 10:00 is a better idea, then this was a bad idea. You decide.

We assembled at the starting line around 9:58, listened to the starter's instructions, stood silently for the National Anthem, and shook off any remaining pre-race jitters. At precisely 10:00 a.m., we were on our way to a destination some 135 miles away.

First checkpoint—Furnace Creek (18 miles)

Pacing was prohibited in this segment, so my crew provided me 'pit stops' every mile or two (depending on how I felt). At first, the entire crew would tend to me at once (imagine being mugged by five people armed with spray bottles, water bottles, wet towels, and sun-block—it's the best description I can offer). Soon enough, they would develop an 'assembly-line' rhythm that was much more efficient and effective. I ran with Pam Reed, the defending champion, for ... oh, let's call it four miles ... before she pulled away. I was content to run alone, not wanting to expend valuable oxygen by making small talk with any of the competitors. My sole focus was to move forward ... at all costs. I reached Furnace Creek in 3:02, an average 'pace' of 10:06 per mile. I changed shorts, shoes and socks as they were totally soaked with perspiration and water.

Second Checkpoint—Stovepipe Wells (42 miles)

Gary was my first pacer, and he opted to run this entire 24-mile stretch so that he could develop a *feel* for this event. As we got close to Stovepipe Wells Gary and I both got to experience what 130 degrees *feels* like. For weeks leading up to this event we had heard the analogy that the heat 'feels like putting your head inside a hot oven' or 'is like blasting a hair dryer directly in your face.' Gary and I and the rest of the crew can now say that is *exactly* what 130 degrees feels like! It was so hot the palms of my hands felt like they were on fire (due to the heat radiating off the road surface). I continually asked Gary to splash water on my hands to cool them off. A crew member for another runner said they put a thermometer on the blacktop road and it read 141 degrees. The soles on Gary's (brand new!) shoes began to separate, as the heat was melting the glue holding them together.

Occasionally a desert wind would blow across the highway. If you're thinking this served to cool us off, you would be mistaken; these desert winds felt like blasts from a roaring fire, and the best thing I can say about them is that they didn't singe my eyebrows. Even if it felt like they did. We completed our second leg in 6:28, an underwhelming pace of 16:10 per mile. At least we were getting ready to 'cool off' by heading up to Towne's Pass.

Third Checkpoint–Panamint Springs (72 miles)

OK, so maybe heading up to Towne's Pass isn't such a great thing after all. A seemingly endless (18-mile) climb to 5,000 feet. Eric accompanied me for this portion of the course, and the only analogy I can make is that is was similar to walking up flights of stairs for the better part of five hours. Now's probably not the best time to mention that I detest walking up stairs. I experimented with trekking poles, but it was difficult to say if they were more of a help or a hindrance. Once we reached the summit, I changed into my running sandals (actually, the crew changed them for me) so that my toes would not 'bang' the front of my shoes on the down hills. (I would repeat this for the duration of the event on the down hills.) The rest of the crew alternated pacing me once we reached the summit, before Paula took the final stretch right before the checkpoint to allow the other crew members to use our hotel room at Panamint Springs to shower and/or take a quick nap. I mentioned to Paula that I was debating whether or not I should stop at the room, and finally decided that I did want to take a quick shower and a short nap so that I could psychologically divide the remaining 63 miles into a 'different day' from that of the first 72 miles. We completed the third leg in 9:04, a robust 18:08 per mile pace.

Intermission

Somewhere around 4:30 a.m. Paula and I entered our room at the Panamint Springs Resort. If 'resort' means 'Norman Bates Motel,' then yeah, this was a resort. I took a quick shower (I forgot to remove my watch, so once it got wet it became so fogged that it was of no use for the remainder of the event). I lay down and managed to fall asleep, and the next thing I knew Paula was out of the shower. She lay down on the other bed and said she was going to sleep for 'five minutes.' As we had no alarm clock, I was afraid to fall back asleep for fear that we would not wake up in 'five minutes' and sleep away valuable time. In approximately 90 seconds Paula bounced up and said 'Let's go!' She never fell asleep. I found out later that my sleep consumed a whole 60 seconds. Fortunately, in my mind, I did fall asleep, and I could now mentally 'divide' the race into two different days.

Fourth Checkpoint–Darwin Turnoff (90 miles)

Eric was called back to active duty, as the next 18 miles were uphill–*all of them!* There was very little terrain that was even remotely runnable. Eric did a superb job keeping me motivated, focused and hydrated during this period. We even managed to pass a few other runners (climbers?) during this portion of the course. Eric (rightfully so) reprimanded me when I broke one of my racing guidelines ('no wasted motion') by taking a few steps backwards to see a wounded bat on the side of the road. The fourth leg took 6:22, an it-could-have-been-worse 21:13 per mile pace.

It was during this stretch that my crew and I realized just how difficult it could be to consume 300 calories per hour during an ultra event such as Badwater. Up until now, I was taking my Sustained Energy (SE) drink (flavored with Crystal Lite lemonade) for the bulk of my calories, occasionally eating pretzels, jelly-beans, or peanut butter to round out my 300 calories per hour. But at this point, I was starting to gag at the thought of drinking any more SE. Paula asked me what I would like to eat, and I replied 'popsicles.' Al made a quick trip in our "spare" car to find some. When he returned we were disheartened to find that after eating two popsicles, I had consumed a whopping ... 30 calories! At that point I began eating small portions: three pretzels, four jellybeans (*'how many calories now?'*), two bites of peach Jello (*'how many NOW?'*). Unfortunately, I had to take 'a swig' of SE to round out my 300 calories. Gag.

Fifth Checkpoint–Lone Pine (122 miles)

I don't know who was looking forward to this 32-mile stretch more: my crew or me. After seeing me walk for the better part of 30 miles over the last 48 miles, they were ready to run ('run' in this case meaning 'get this thing over with'). Paula (our downhill specialist) took the first pacing assignment, and before I knew it we were off at an 8:00 minute pace. I would pick out 'targets' from which to run from and to, and would continue this practice over the next 32 miles. With the exception of Eric who we were 'saving' for the final 13-mile climb up Mount Whitney), Paula, Gary, and Josh got excited and broke a pre-race request of mine ('don't tell me how my fellow competitors are doing') by mentioning I was in 8th place.

Being this late in the race, knowing where I stood wasn't such a bad thing, as holding my place and finishing in the Top Ten at Badwater was certainly a realistic expectation at this point. An expectation I was fairly comfortable with, until Eric told me around mile 115 that there was a runner up ahead, and I should be able to catch him in four or five miles. Josh was my next pacer, and I asked him if he wanted to catch the other runner NOW. He did, and so did I. We sprinted approximately a mile where we caught and passed the runner, one who I had last seen over 100 miles ago. Eric unofficially timed our mile in 8:15, but it felt like a sub-6:00. Gary took the next leg, and Eric mentioned there was yet another runner about a mile ahead who I could catch in four or five miles. Gary and I shuffled along until we spotted this runner in the distance. As I did with Josh, I asked him if he wanted to catch the other runner now. He did, and so did I. We took off at a 6:00 minute pace (or 8:15 if you believe Eric) and caught him within a mile. Adding insult to injury, we caught him on an uphill. At mile 120. Ouch. (We found out later this particular runner finished an incredible *nine hours* behind us) Josh took the final two-mile stretch into the checkpoint in Lone Pine, where we found out we were now in 6th place.

Paula had prepared some Raman noodles for me, the first food I had in 36 hours that remotely resembled an actual meal. It was heavenly. All five bites.

Sixth Checkpoint–Mount Whitney (135 miles)

As Josh will be quick to tell you, I was absolutely dreading the final 13-mile leg to the portals of Mount Whitney. And rightfully so: after 122 miles of desert and two mountain ranges, making a runner cover these final 13 miles uphill was just plain mean! Eric was once again my pacer, and he did everything in his power to keep me focused, positive, and hydrated. I managed to stay focused, positive and hydrated–for seven miles. At that point–six miles from the finish line–I fell backwards, barely maintaining consciousness. I asked for some more Ramen noodles, but Paula had nothing to heat them with except for the radiator of the van. The noodles warmed–slightly–but they were extremely 'crisp.' Paula, Gary and Al provided shoulders to (literally) lean on, as there were a few moments I nearly fell off the side of the mountain. Paula was force feeding me Gatorade and Gary was continually splashing my head and shoulders with ice cold water. I asked one of them to slap me in the face, but they wouldn't do it. I guess they thought a slap might knock me totally out, which would put a serious cramp in completing the journey. I continually asked Josh 'who was behind me' thinking that–surely–someone would be passing me in my limited condition. Unfortunately, if someone *did* make an attempt to pass me at this point, there wasn't a thing I could do about it. Fortunately, no one did.

2003 Badwater–Climbing Mount Whitney with Eric and Paula

The last two miles seemed endless, as we wound around the mountain with no end in sight. Cars were passing us in both directions, many shouting words of encouragement as we neared the finish line. At least I think we were nearing the finish line. Occasionally I would find myself walking more side-to-side than forward, a victim of fatigue, exhaustion, and (I'm convinced) oxygen deprivation (we were at altitude, remember?).

Eric drove the van ahead to take his video camera to the finish line officials, hoping they would film us as we 'triumphantly' completed our mission. He agreed to meet us at a point one mile from the finish, where the six of us would congregate and run the rest of the race 'as one.' When we caught a glimpse of Eric in our headlamps, it was a bittersweet feeling as *thankfully*, we only had a mile to go, but nonetheless *we still had a mile to go!*

After what seemed like another hour, we saw the lights at the finish line (it was now just after 10:30 p.m.). The six of us ran (assuming 'ran' means 'shuffled sort of fast')–with our heads held high–through the finish line banner, officially signifying the successful completion of our journey. Hugs all around! Chris Kostman officially told us that we finished in 6th place and we were the 3rd place male finisher. Not bad for a bunch of Badwater rookies. The sixth leg had taken 4:10 to complete, a 19:14 per mile pace. Not too shabby when you take into account the last two miles consumed a full hour.

I sat down in the official finisher's chair–surrounded by my wonderful crew–for some final photographs for the website. I literally looked like death warmed over, but I couldn't have cared less.

We enjoyed our journey, and we were successful. We couldn't have asked for anything more.

2003 Badwater–Smiles all around: it's over!

Thursday, July 24 (+2 days)

My crew–God bless 'em–join me for a three-mile run (gotta keep the streak alive!). Afterwards, a little housekeeping on the van followed by an incredible lunch at the pizza parlor across the street from our hotel, the Dow Villa. Josh and I split a large cheese pizza, but we eat less than half of it (Josh because he ate everything on the late-night menu at the hotel's diner last night; me because my stomach had apparently shrunk over the past two days). I spent the afternoon limping back and forth across the street to the laundromat to wash some of the dirty clothes Josh and I had generated this week. I met the wife of a Badwater entrant (Art Webb, the 211 degree sauna guy) at the laundromat, and she told me her husband was still on the course. (We passed him on our way back to Las Vegas the next morning; he was at the half-way point of the course) as he was experiencing some difficulties (he did eventually finish, however).

All Badwater participants and crew members were invited to a pizza dinner at a local elementary school that evening. We spent a lot of time talking with Pam Reed (who successfully defended her title, by the way) about her performance and her training. She said she has to run three times a day, as she has to manipulate her running around her demanding schedule as a mother of three. I invited her to our 50K race in November, and she said she'd run (she didn't) if I'd return the favor and run her race (I didn't either) in December.

After dinner, a short video of this year's race was shown. As my luck would have it, there was a special feature on each of the top *five* finishers (I finished 6th, remember?). Regardless, it was well made and very inspirational (up to the point that it *didn't* convince me to run it again).

Following the video, Chris Kostman hosted the awards ceremony. He asked all runners who failed to complete the course to stand, and they were given a rousing ovation for 'having the guts to try.' Very deserved. Then, all finishers were called to the front of the room to receive their finisher's medal and, for those finishing under 48 hours, the coveted belt-buckle. We posed for photographs—I've never been in front of so many flash bulbs before—and then Pam and men's winner Dean Karnazes were asked to say a few words. Chris closed the evening by referring to all of us as part of the 'Badwater Family.'

A pretty nice honor.

Post Script: On Friday, we made the drive back to Las Vegas. Obviously, we 'retraced our steps' along the same route we started three days ago in Badwater. If I hadn't already decided I would never run the race again this would have done it for me. I realized that yes, the heat was a huge factor in my performance, but the mountains were much more significant. We stopped in Stovepipe Wells for a drink, and the heat— only slightly over 110 degrees today—still felt like we were sticking our heads inside a hot oven.

Friday night, w enjoyed a crew 'victory dinner' at the Pink Taco in Las Vegas. Afterwards, Paula, Eric, Al and Gary returned to the hotel for some much needed rest before our 6:00 a.m. flight to Atlanta the following morning. Me? I had promised Josh that if I was still able to walk after the race–at this time I barely 'qualified'–I would take him to see the casinos before we returned to Atlanta. The four hours Josh and I spent–at MGM Grand, New York New York, Mandalay Bay, Excalibur, Luxor–I wouldn't trade for anything. Josh was so impressed with the large casinos, the bright neon lights and the endless 'eye candy" the city has to offer. But for me, walking on two severely blistered feet was a true test of my pain threshold (I'm sure I exceeded it somewhere during the night). We finally got to bed just after midnight, allowing me two hours sleep before I had to get up for one last run with Gary before we all headed to the airport for our long-awaited (and triumphant) return to Atlanta.

And yes, you read the previous sentence correctly.

Scott's BADWATER STATISTICS

(an * indicates an approximation)

Total Inches Ran	8,515,584
Total Minutes Ran	2,192.77
*Total Steps Taken	193,360
*Total Calories Consumed	11,000
*Total Calories Consumed via actual FOOD	500
*Total Calories Consumed via Sustained Energy (gag)	10,500
Total Distance Covered (in miles)	134.4
Total Distance with a Pacer (in miles)	117.4
Total Distance without a Pacer (in miles)	17
*Total Distance RAN (in miles)	90
*Total Distance WALKED (in miles)	44
*Total Number of 'Pit Stops'	100

*Number of Pit Stops resembling a Chinese fire drill	2
*Number of incredibly efficient Pit Stops	98
*Total Pounds of Fluids Consumed	100
Total Time (in hours)	36:32:46
Bib #	20
Average Pace per Mile	16:19
Total Pounds of Weight Lost during the Race	10
Overall Place of Finish	6
Number of Women ahead of me	3
Number of Men ahead of me	2
Total number of shoes/sandals/socks worn	3/2/10
Number of blisters on my feet	4
Number of blisters on my feet that HURT	3
% slower than Pam Reed, overall winner	28%
Quickest leg in relation to Pam (Furnace Creek)	16% slower
Slowest leg in relation to Pam (Stovepipe Wells)	44% slower
From 2002 backwards, place of finish my time would have placed me in 13 previous Badwaters	
	6, 7, 9, 8, 4, 3, 2, 2, 3, 3, 3, 4, 4 (1990)
Number of Times I thought about Quitting	0

Number of Times the Crew thought about Quitting	0 (tough bunch!)
Number of Badwaters in my Future	0
Number of Hallucinations	0
Number of Hallucinations I expected	3 (at least!)
Highest temperature reported on the course (in degrees F)	133
Highest recorded temperature on earth ... *ever!*	134
# of Runners in the Race	73
# of Runners who Completed the Race	46
% of Starters who Completed the Race	63%
% of People receiving Medical Aid who were crew members	40%
% of DARKSIDE crew members who received Medical Aid	0
Youngest starter's age	31
Oldest starter's age	70
# of Men who started the race	57
# of Women who started the race	16
# of Men who completed the race	31
# of Women who completed the race	15
% of Men who completed the race	54%
% of Women who completed the race	94%
*Distance I covered when Pam crossed the finish line (in miles)	105

*Distance I had remaining when Pam fin-   29.4
ished (in miles)

Number of Significant Items in this List   0

BADWATER ELEVATION PROFILE

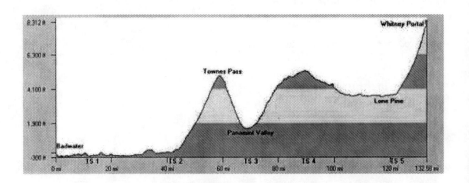

Checkpoints–Distance–Elapsed Time–Pace per Mile

Checkpoint	Distance	Elapsed Time	Pace per Mile
Furnace Creek	18	3:02	10:06
Stovepipe Wells	42	6:28	16:10
Panamint Spring	72	9:04	18:08
Darwin Turnoff	90	6:22	21:13
Lone Pine	122	7:27	13:58
Mount Whitney	135	4:10	19:14

Making the cover of Ultrarunning (I'm #20)

Congrats to the Crew

By Paula May

Hello, DARKSIDE Crew:

Skinny Bitch here with the last word.

I'm very proud of everyone's contribution to the Badwater mission. An awesome job for a bunch of rookies (or even veterans, for that matter). We may have started out a little rocky with a few squirts of sun block in Scott's eyes and looking like the Keystone Kops for those first 17 miles, but we caught on and had the pit stops down to a science by the time we were on the home stretch.

We got Scott through it with minor damage: a few (huge!) blisters and battered muscles, but no gastric upsets or injuries which would have ended our Badwater quest quickly.

Sorry about all that barking … but you guys sucked it up and responded in true soldier fashion in order to help Scott accomplish the feat he had before him. Everyone performed critical, necessary tasks that resulted in a successful race for Scott and a satisfying experience for the crew.

Josh—I know your dad is as proud of you as I am for being a great team player, always having a positive attitude, being available to run, pacing your dad through some of those difficult hot miles before Lone Pine, and being my go-fer. There were so many tedious tasks that I needed done, and you were always there to handle them. I'm so glad you were part of the crew.

Al—You were my main 'go get me' guy. Smart idea to get the back up vehicle; to make those runs to the closest town to get me ice, popsicles, and fig newtons. And of course, being available to Scott as pacer was invaluable. And you get the prize for comic relief with 'put me down for a turd.'*

Gary—Where you got the energy and stamina for pacing Scott through some of the most difficult, hot, early miles I will never know. I know Scott and the entire crew appreciates that you hung with him to brave those 133 degree temperatures before Stovepipe Wells and then again when the temperature rose on the second day on the road to Lone Pine. Those 60 miles you ran would have left me wilted and worn out to the point I wouldn't have had much left for everything else my role as 'Skinny Bitch' required. Your eternal optimism and support for Scott was uplifting to us all.

Eric—The number two pacer in terms of mileage! Your energy on the uphills leading out of Stovepipe and again out of Panamint and yet again on the Whitney Portal Road was a blessing, coming at a time when Scott needed your sense of humor and encouragement. I was very proud of you for stepping up to take on this difficult part of pacing. And early on you remembered to say 'yes, dear.'

Everyone worked together to get the job done well and I know Scott as well as I appreciate the hard work and sacrifices made by the DARKSIDE Crew. Thanks for letting me be the chief; you were all excellent Indians.

Fondly,

Skinny Bitch (**Paula**)

Paula and the crew maintained tedious, detailed records of everyone's intake and output throughout the event. At one point Al walked out into the desert, and when he returned to the Crew he—in his best John Wayne hitching-up-his-pants impersonation—proudly delivered his classic (and oft-repeated) line.

2003 Badwater–Celebrating the finish!

"Yeah.... but it's a dry heat."

The Badwater Ultramarathon Experience

By Gary Griffin

The Badwater Ultramarathon bills itself as the most prestigious and most difficult of all ultrarunning events, and it can make a pretty good argument for such status. It begins at the lowest point in North America, Badwater, in Death Valley National Park, some 280 feet below sea level and proceeds through some 40 miles of harsh desert, over two mountain ranges, across another 25 miles of desert valley, and finally up Mt Whitney, the highest point in the continental U.S. That encompasses nearly 13,000 feet of climbing before finishing at the Whitney Trailhead at 8,360 feet. To make it even more fun, the race is run in July, which is statistically the hottest month of the year in Death Valley, where the average daily high temperature is 115 degrees. "Yeah," you say, "but it's a dry heat". That's what I thought, too. No problem. I'm from Tallahassee, Florida where the act of walking from one's carport to the back door in the summertime requires one to carry a water bottle for hydration and thrice-a-day showers to stay fresh are commonplace amongst those of us that don't hole ourselves up in an air-conditioned, hibernating state until the first signs of fall on Columbus Day. Besides, a Florida ultrarunner won the Badwater race twice in the mid-90s and I took that as a sure indicator that training in the southeastern US prepared one for whatever some arid desert could offer up in the way of a hostile environment. Oh, you silly, silly boy....

So, why am I telling you all of this? Because by an odd twist of fate, I found myself involved in the 2003 edition of Badwater, and it was an experience that I will never forget. Relating it to you all will be difficult, as such experiences always are when we have traversed the normal bounds of activity and found ourselves at some point where few have had the opportunity to go before. My opportunity began with that aforementioned twist of fate that involved a determined and talented runner with a dream....

The Runner

While on a teaching assignment in Atlanta in the spring of 2002, I ventured over to the Callaway Gardens Marathon one fine Sunday. Along about mile two I found myself running next to a congenial fellow who was easy to talk to, and humble. He had run a 3:08 marathon the day before over at Tybee Island, and had no trouble running alongside me that day at Calloway for some 23 miles as I ran my fastest marathon in many years. At mile 23 he sprinted on in, but before that we had engaged in a non-stop review of races we had been part of and our hopes for the future. It just so happened that this fellow had won our Tallahassee 50K at Wakulla in 1998, had run our Tallahassee Marathon, and most strikingly was a streak runner. Now I generally am not overly impressed with streak runners, for I don't think that the act of running every day for an extended period is a particularly healthy thing, and may even hint at obsessive-ness and a lack of attention to other aspects of life that are important to me when I pick my friends. This guy was different, though. He was nonchalant about his streak, which began in November 1978, and which had averaged nearly 10 miles a day. He maintained a serious job as a J C Penney manager in Atlanta, was a family man, and active in organizing local races that benefited charitable causes. I liked that. Besides, he ran alongside me that day when he could have run off and left me, and encouraged me to my best marathon in years. It was when he donned a pair of Zubaz athletic pants after the run that I knew I had a lot in common with this guy, for I thought that the pair I owned were the only ones still in existence. (For those not in the know, Zubaz were a very fleeting fashion statement in the late 1980's, seen only on college sidelines during football season, and were a crazy concoction of swirling stripes on baggy pants with elastic bands at the ankles.) Well, this guy had a pair from his alma mater, the University of Florida (a hated rival of my University of Miami Hurricanes), but the Zubaz connection helped us overcome that obstacle. In the course of sharing our dreams that day, this fellow mentioned that he was approaching 50, and that before he reached that milestone, he wanted to run a little race called Badwater. The fellow's name was Scott Ludwig.

We kept in touch, as he lived in nearby Peachtree City, and maintained a tie to Tallahassee as a member of the Gulf Winds Track Club. Besides, he was turning his running career more and more towards ultrarunning. He entered the US 24-Hour Championships in Olander Park, Ohio in September 2002, and I told him to "make his mark in the ultrarunning community". He did so by finishing 4th overall and was the first master with a total of 129 miles. Shortly after that he applied for the 2003 Badwater Ultramarathon and asked me to be a part of his crew, and to assume the role of "spiritual advisor". When my wife Peg and I went to Death Valley the next month, I brought him back a block of salt that makes up the ground at Badwater and a photo of the small white stripe at the end of the road at Mt Whitney that signifies the finish line. There was never a doubt in my mind that his footprints would find their way to both of them.

The Course

Like Scott, Badwater had been a dream of mine as well. Every ultrarunner has thoughts of Badwater, for it truly offers as foreboding a challenge as any footrace on earth. Even the most-talented of racers will dismiss it, for it is truly a "fringe event," and many will argue that it is more adventure racing that a road race. In 2002, Badwater was won by 40 year-old Pam Reed, a mother of three, who trounced her nearest rival by five hours. A gentleman at the Mount Whitney store told me last October that from that point forward, Badwater would be a race. Pam Reed's victory brought never-before seen publicity to the event, and several US newspapers and CNN were covering the 2003 edition. A video of the 1999 race entitled 'Running on the Sun' was gaining popular acclaim as more and more people were learning about this race across the burning California desert to Mt. Whitney. As a member of Scott's team for 2003, I had listened to advice from seasoned Badwater participants, read an abundance of instructional material, had seen the video, and had driven the course. I thought I knew what I (and the rest of the team) was in for. Friends, I had no clue.... Until you experience Death Valley in the summer, you have no idea. It is like no other place I have ever seen. It resembles what I would expect on the surface of the moon–barren and appearing lifeless for mile upon mile upon mile. And oh, the heat. Our trip last fall found us basking in 90-degree highs that were tolerable enough that we hiked and ran and lived to tell about it. The nights were even pleasant, as many desert nights can be once one escapes the intensity of the summer months. But Badwater is in July, and this is the place that has recorded the highest temperature ever recorded in the US–134 degrees, and has an annual rainfall of less than two inches. This is truly one of the most hostile environments on earth, and it was here that Scott had chosen to run 135 miles. For anyone that is counting, that is five marathons and a 5K cool down.

The Crew

No one runs Badwater alone. Well, almost no one. A fellow by the name of Marshall Ulrich from Colorado has run the event several times, and traveled the route one time towing a rickshaw-like cart with all of his supplies. Scott opted instead to assemble a team of friends of varying talents and to rent a large van in which to keep all of us and his mountain of supplies. I was proud to be a part of this team, as it included another current Gulf Winds Track Club member and a former Tallahassee resident named Al Barker. Besides being a very talented marathoner (he's run near 3:10 at age 58, and has several sub-3 hour marathons at Boston) Al is an optometrist and a regular training partner of Scott's. Our Crew Chief was Paula May, the 50-54 Georgia age group record holder at the 10K, and a talented marathoner. Besides her strong organizational and leadership skills, she brought a wealth of medical knowledge to the team as an experienced physician's assistant in anesthesia. Her husband, Eric Huguelet, was not only our filmmaker (someone had to record this for posterity!), but also a strong runner and an even stronger walker who would lead Scott up the wicked inclines from the valley floor and finally up the 13 tortuous miles of Mount Whitney. Paula and Eric also are regular training partners of Scott's and make up the core of the growing Darkside Running Club under whose banner Scott would run the race. Finally, there was Scott's 17-year-old son, Josh. Josh must have been having an extremely boring summer back home, or just really wanted something out on the far edge to write about in his 'How I Spent My Summer Vacation' essay.

The Race

Badwater racers are selected based on their credentials. One makes an application to Badwater, stating why they want to run and what it is that they have done that qualifies them to be a potential finisher. Interestingly, a wealth of ultramarathoning experience is not required, as one entrant this year was participating in his first ultra. He was, however, a five time leading finisher in the Hawaiian Ironman, and a recent finisher in a triple Ironman. Such insanity gave him a slight edge over individuals that peppered their applications with tales of 100-mile runs and stories of nights spent sleeping inside saunas to build up their heat readiness. Ultimately, 75 were chosen to toe the starting line at Badwater last Tuesday morning, with three evenly divided waves going off at 6 a.m., 8 a.m., and 10 a.m. Those that finished in less than 30 hours had a legitimate chance to win, while those finishing in less than 48 hours won the coveted Badwater belt buckle. The official cutoff time was 60 hours, which is a long, long time to be out in Death Valley.

Scott went off at 10 a.m. with the other elite runners that included last year's winner Pam Reed, the veteran Ulrich, 10 time finisher Scott Weber, former record holder and trans-America runner Jay Birmingham, and Canadian Monica Scholtz, an elite finisher of over 25 100-mile runs.

Due to the potential for crowded road conditions, crews are not allowed to pace their runner for the first 18 miles between the start at Badwater and the first checkpoint at mile 18 at the Furnace Creek Ranch. Conventional wisdom and hard statistical evidence has shown that patience pays and speed kills in the early grueling stages of Badwater and that those who are still moving by the second checkpoint at Stovepipe Wells (mile 42) have an excellent chance of making it to Whitney within the cutoff time. Scott went out with last year's winner Reed and a group of several others and then settled into a comfortable sub-nine minute pace in the first leg. Temperatures at this time were already near 120 degrees, and the first signs of a hot desert wind were coming across the salt basin at Badwater. He arrived at Furnace Creek in approximately three hours, whereupon I joined him for the 24-mile leg to Stovepipe Wells. It is the memory of these next 6+ hours that will forever be etched in my mind when I recall this incredible event. During these 24 miles we encountered the unceasing near record 130 degree heat that I trust will be as close to a near-death experience as I want to get. The intensity of the heat and the wind made it virtually impossible to stay well-hydrated.

While the crew tried to get Scott's core temperature down at mile intervals by wiping him with ice cold towels and by constantly giving him ready-chilled shirts to wear, I was at times carrying a water bottle in each hand and another in my pack to get us from stop to stop. One was to keep him hydrated, one was to constantly squeeze onto his head and neck, and one was getting fluid into me if I had the presence of mind to do so. While the crew would minister to Scott at the stops, I would do what I could to assist them while at the same time realizing that I had to get my own core cooled off and hydrated. It was an interesting experience, and one that has made me question if tackling the event as an entered runner will ever be in my future. By the time we arrived at Stovepipe it was 7:30 p.m. I was as tired and in need of a break as I have ever been. Meanwhile, he had been in the desert for eight and a half hours, was not a single foot above sea level, and still had 93 miles ahead of him. But, as the sun was getting low, he had reached a point that 11 of the 75 either failed to reach or would not go beyond.

The next 18 miles were all uphill, climbing to 5,000 feet at Townes Pass, the intermediate point between Stovepipe and the third check station at Panamint Springs (mile 72). We took turns through this stretch, with Eric doing most of the uphill walking and Paula encouraging Scott to run the steep 8-mile downhill towards Panamint Valley and the final two miles to the checkpoint. I was with Scott on the uphill leg at 10:30 p.m. under the clear desert sky and we were told that the temperature was still 110 degrees! I never thought I could be in 110-degree heat and feel comfortable but after the mind-altering experience of the previous afternoon it was very much the case.

Sometime after midnight we agreed that Josh and I should go ahead to Panamint Springs and check into the room that Scott had reserved for the purpose of getting some rest and a shower before facing the long second day of heat. We would sleep for an hour or two, and then relieve Eric and Paula so that they could do the same. Scott was expected to arrive around daybreak. As soon as I lay down I realized things were not as they should have been. Not only were my legs twisted grotesquely by cramping muscles, but also I was extremely nauseous. There was no air conditioning at the so-called 'resort.' and the room was extremely hot. Josh was so tired that he fell asleep, but my fear over what was happening to me and the nausea kept me from doing the same. We had been told that the act of a crew member going down in such a remote area can mean the demise of your runner, and all I could think of was that I needed medical help and it was likely to take me out of action. Scott, meanwhile, had another 60+ miles ahead and another day in the desert. After throwing up, I went immediately to the check station to see about some medical advice. I was told that all of the medics were back at Stovepipe treating downed runners and crew there, and that none were available. I described my dilemma (which included not having urinated for 16 hours) to one of the race volunteers and he told me that I simply was in serious need of sodium and water and that if I could get some in me I would have a chance of being able to continue. Although the symptoms clearly supported such a diagnosis, I was shocked that could have actually been the problem, as I had been eating sodium tablets every half-hour while running and drinking very heavily all day. Evidently, neither had been sufficient to deal with the brutal conditions that I had been in, and it was apparent that in my focus on keeping Scott cooled and hydrated that I had not taken care of myself as I should have. I immediately ate two '*Succeed!*' caps and drank the last two liters of bottled water at Panamint, which were graciously given to me by a worker at the all-night outdoor bar. As a team, our problems were further compounded by the fact that Panamint and Stovepipe were both out of ice, and the only place to restock was in Lone Pine, some 50 miles away. Although I immediately felt better after the tablets and the water (I couldn't have ever felt any worse I don't believe!), I offered to go to Lone Pine for the ice and other supplies. The two hours out of the heat and more water returned me to normal, and I was able to hook up with Scott and the team by the time they were only a few miles out of Panamint.

The dawn brought some milder temperatures as a blessed overcast sky moved in, and we rotated two-mile shifts as Scott moved towards the Mile 90 checkpoint at Darwin. He had worked hard during that 18-mile stretch and other than some bad blisters, was looking and feeling strong. He's a remarkably determined runner that never lets the inevitable ultrarunning 'bad patches' affect him; furthermore, he is a strong finisher in all endurance events and seems to be at his best when his rivals are struggling. Well, his competition this day was struggling and his focus was on 'relentless forward motion' and the finish at Whitney. The scoreboard at Darwin had him in about 10th place when he arrived at 10:30 a.m., and it was at this point that we again set out into the 32 miles of high desert known as Owens Valley leading us to Lone Pine, the last stop before Whitney. I had been warned back at Panamint that the previous day found temperatures of 110 degrees in this area and sand storms, but I kept this from Scott so as to not discourage him. Perhaps as much as meeting your runner's physical needs, the pacer and crew need to encourage and keep nothing but positive thoughts in the head of the runner. Fortunately for us, the temperatures remained in the low 100's and although the sun came out and the wind blew, we encountered no dust. Scott ran incredibly well, reeling in three of his fellow competitors during this stretch. He arrived at Lone Pine at 6:30 p.m. in 6th place overall, and had only the 13 mile uphill trek to the Whitney Portals ahead of him. He knew going in that this portion was basically un-runnable and that even the top finishers are reduced to a leg-numbing hike at this point. Nonetheless, he worked hard all the way to the top, maintained his position, and gloriously crossed the finish line at 10:32 p.m., some 36 hours and 32 minutes since the start, some 135 miles away.

The repeat winner was the amazing Pam Reed, in 28 hours and 27 minutes. I had the chance to spend some time talking to her at the post-race dinner and her crew chief was a tremendous amount of help to me before the start, with his advice on the importance of keeping our runner as cool as possible. For those of you out there with a disdain for long training runs, Pam has managed to win this affair two years now with no training runs longer than 20 miles. By her own admission, she is just an average marathoner, but manages 100 miles a week into her busy life by running as much as four times a day. Like Scott, she is methodical, patient, and has an easy stride that never changes in spite of miles and miles of tiring running.

The Lesson

The Badwater experience was a remarkable time. It showed me the incredible harshness of nature in an environment that is not conducive to any sort of life–much less that of running 135 miles. It showed me that those who put their bodies and minds to the test in this perhaps ultimate of ultrarunning events are normal, hard-working, family-oriented, caring people who simply have a desire to conquer a tremendous challenge. It also was a case study in getting along with others under the most trying of circumstances–extreme heat and discomfort, confinement in close quarters for over 36 hours, and no sleep. It all came about because of a singleness of focus and a determined effort to do everything we could to see the talented Scott Ludwig be the best that he could be and attain his Badwater goal that he had voiced to me in our first meeting 18 months prior. He finished in 6th place in a field that included on this day the very best in the world that were willing to put themselves to the test. As a crewmember, I was deeply honored to be there, and am proud of him not just as a friend but also as a member of Gulf Winds Track Club. There may be others from GWTC that leave their footprints in Death Valley–Jeff Bryan and Fred Johnson have voiced their desire to see what the fuss is all about. The night before leaving for Badwater I had told Peg that I may give it a run next year. When I called her several days later from Lone Pine following my experience in the desert and the Panamint Springs motel room that 'maybe' had become an emphatic 'No!' But, as is often the case in ultrarunning, it always gets better. It got better that morning and that afternoon, and on Whitney that night. Never say never. But—never listen to anyone that tries to tell you, 'It's a dry heat!'

The Day After

When Scott was accepted into Badwater several months ago, the real question in my mind was not whether or not he would finish, but whether or not he would then let the streak die a peaceful death. After all, he had reached the mountaintop, both literally and figuratively, and the burning question in my mind was, "How could he possibly run the day after Badwater?" Well, that was a very silly question on my part. Those on the crew that have known Scott far longer than I assured me that he would run his mandatory minimum of three miles on Thursday. Sure enough, less than 12 hours after finishing atop Whitney, we were all gathered in the motel parking lot for day number 9,000 (more or less) of what is one of the 35 or so longest running streaks in the U.S. I feel certain, however, that none of those ahead of him have ever run Badwater. Like I say, though, he's really a fairly normal individual....

Come Hell or BADwater

By John Kissane

(Originally appeared in the *Georgia Runner*, September 2003)

Drive through Peachtree City, Georgia at 3:30 on a random weekday morning and what do you suppose you'll see? Well, most likely not much in the quiet, peaceful community just southwest of metropolitan Atlanta. But, depending on where you drive at the hour, you may catch a glimpse of a lone runner, making his way along a darkened city street or heading out of town. 'Whoa! Someone's jut ripped off the 7-11!' you might say to yourself. However, you'd be wrong: it's only Scott Ludwig, Georgia's top ultradistance runner.

'One thing about Scott is that if he says he's going to do something, he's going to do it,' says Paula May, a fellow Peachtree City resident and one of Scott's

long-time running companions (on weekends, that is). 'It's just his determination,' continues Paula. 'He just does what he says he's going to do.'

A couple years ago, Scott decided he had to run the Badwater Ultramarathon, a
torturous 135-mile event that traverses California Death Valley, climbs up and
down several mountain ranges, and finishes at an attitude of 8,360 feet on the
slope of 14,494-foot Mount Whitney. This July, true to his word, Scott not only
ran Badwater, but he finished an outstanding sixth overall, in 36 hours, 32 minutes and 46 seconds. It was a long, hard journey, one that actually began some 25
years (and a bit more than 88,000 miles) ago.

Scott credits two of his graduate school professors at the University of Florida
with getting him started in running. He had put on weight during college days
and the pair of instructors, distance runners both, convinced him to try it. Scott's
wife Cindy, to whom he's been married for 26 years now, also encouraged him to
run, but, of course, no one imagined the extent to which he would pursue the
sport.

What happened was that Scott took to running like a fish to water. He completed
his first run in early 1978 and on November 30 of that same year began a running streak that is still going strong. He will hit 25 years without missing a day
later this fall, one of the top two or three dozen running streaks in the world.
Scott ran his first Peachtree Road Race in 1979 (the year that he and Cindy
moved to Atlanta) and he hasn't missed one since. To date he has run more than
600 road races. Although he focused on 5K's and 10K's during the early years,
Scott ran his first ultra, the Stone Mountain 50-Miler, back in 1982. That same
year he also attempted a solo run across Georgia, from Columbus to Savannah. A
shin injury forced hi to abandon on the fourth day, after 159 miles, but in 1992,
Scott made a similar cross-state run, successfully completing a 280-mile route in
six days.

After moving to Peachtree City in 1990, Scott became even more serious about
his running, and about the marathon. He has averaged 90 miles a week during
the past ten years and has completed nine or ten marathons each of the past seven
years. This April he ran his 100th 26.2 miler at Boston (after first running from
the finish to the start, to make it a 52.44-mile Badwater training run; more on
that later). Completing 100 marathons had been one of Scott's major goals, and

he wanted to do that before Badwater. 'I figured if I ran Badwater and blew up I might never run again,' he says, 'so I wanted to get the100 in first.'

An interesting (or perhaps 'mind-boggling' is a better choice of words) aspect of Scott's running is his routine of running about 3:30 every weekday morning. He's done it for years out of necessity, due to his job as Warehouse Department Manager at the J.C. Penney Catalog Center. The facility closed for good on August 15 of this year and Scott will be moving on to another job. Will he continue the early morning running schedule? Only time will tell.

Scott's desire to run the Badwater Ultramarathon dates to Father's Day 2001 when Cindy gave him a video documentary of the 1999 race. 'I watched it' he recalls, 'and they showed everybody in all kinds of distress and I said been there, been there, been there.' And I said to Cindy 'I'm doing this race.' And she says 'No you're not.' And right then I worked out a timetable where I'd get my 100th marathon at Boston in 2003 and then try to get into Badwater, and it worked.'

There's a world of difference between the Badwater Ultramarathon and your typical running event. For one, just getting in takes work, as it is an invitational race that accepts a maximum field of 100 athletes. Applicants must meet strict entry criteria and complete detailed application forms, providing documentation of qualifying race results.

Then there is the Badwater course, which is unthinkably difficult. Starting well over 200 feet below sea level, just two miles east of the lowest point in the western hemisphere, the first 40 miles of the race are run through Death Valley. During this portion of the event, the terrain doesn't present that tough a challenge but the heat does an admirable job of making runners miserable. Consider this: when the air temperature topped out at 133 degrees at mid-afternoon on July 22 during this year's race, the heat coming off the asphalt roads was probably in excess of 200 degrees. So, even in you think you're running along OK in those conditions, you're still toast!

At a point known as Stove Pipe Wells, the climbing begins in earnest, as to get out of Death Valley runners must complete a 5,000-foot, 17 mile ascent to Towne Pass Followed by a 1,200-foot descent to the bottom of Panamint Valley. Once accomplished, the next test is a climb to more than 5,000 feet and the Darwin Turnofff, going over the Argus Range. From there it's on to Lone Pine at

122 miles, where runners must face the last, and perhaps the most grueling section of the race: the ascent to Mount Whitney Portals at 8,360 feet.

Scott began his 'serious' training for Badwater on March 3 when he received the official race invitation in the mail. 'By serious,' Scott explains, 'I mean I started over-dressing, hanging out in saunas, and I ran five ultras in a seven-week window to get ready for it.' The first of these was Boston, where he ran from finish to start, turned around, and ran the race itself to record his 100th marathon finish. Next, in early May, it was the Strolling Jim 40-Miler in Wartrace, Tennessee, followed by a 50K put on by some of Scott's friends in Tallahassee, Florida (an opportunity to run in the heat). On May 31, Scott ran for eight hours on the track in Peachtree City, completing 52 miles with a group of friend taking turns accompanying him for several laps at a time. Finally, Scott returned to the Florida heat on June 7 to run the Pennar 40-Miler. Of particular importance was that recovery time was less lengthy with each ultra, so Scott knew he was progressing nicely. 'I recover pretty quickly anyway,' he says, 'but all of those paid off when I went out to Death Valley.'

In addition to all the training one of the keys to Scott's success at Badwater was putting together a crack support crew that did everything from taking care of him during brief, but frequent pit stops, to running with Scott during many sections of the race. The group included crew chief Paul May and her husband Eric Huguelet, Al Barker, Gary Griffin and Scott's younger son, 17-year-old Josh. All played key roles, none more important than Paula who, as a medical professional, monitored Scott's fluid intake and output and kept hydration almost a non-issue.

The only problem in fact, was that Scott developed blisters on the balls of his feet in Death Valley, but Paula's skillful taping kept them intact. 'I was worried that they would tear open and he just wouldn't be able to run,' recalls Paula. Fortunately, that did not happen. Scott used three pairs of running shoes during the race and two pairs of running sandals, which he wore on the downhill sections. Most of his diet during the ordeal was consumed in liquid form, about 100 pounds of it, and he experienced no stomach difficulties.

The Badwater field was divided into three time groups with a staggered start format. Scott was in the last group, which set off at 10:00 a.m. on Tuesday, July 22. Late that afternoon, nearing the end of the Death Valley portion of the race, Scott learned the temperature had hit a race-record 133 degrees. 'I got the first of two second winds when I heard that,' he says, 'I don't know why.' Despite the record-setting heat, Scott claims the second day, mostly in the mountains, was tougher. 'You get used to the heat after a while,' he says, 'but the mountains are endless.'

Scott's crew was working hard as well. No pacing was allowed during the first 17 miles, but at that point, Gary began running through much of the remaining desert portion with Scott. In the mountains, it was primarily Eric who accompanied Scott on the uphill sections, while Paula did duty on the way down. Al and Josh ran with Scott as well, especially during what Scott describes as his '32-mile fartlek run' from the 90-mile point to the 122-mile Lone Pine checkpoint. 'My crew took turns taking two miles at a swing,' he explains. 'We'd run maybe a half mile, walk a hundred yards, and run some more. We picked off three people during that stretch.' However, at Lone Pine whatever 'fun' Scott and crew were having during the fartlek came to an abrupt end.

'Finishing on Mount Whitney, that's just mean,' he says. 'If you finished in Lone Pine at 122 miles, that would be a good race. But all you can do the last six miles is walk, it's so steep.' Scott completed the last several hours in complete darkness, adding to the difficulty. 'It was pitch black up there, you can't see anything,' he recalls. 'And you keep seeing lights, hoping it's the finish, but it'll be another car coming down the mountain. Your mind is shot by that time so you're just dying to get to the finish.'

And finish he did, in a remarkable sixth overall. Scott's crew was elated but hardly surprised. 'Scott is just one of those guys who will not quit,' says Paula May. 'For so much of the race he was in a lot of pain, a lot of agony, but he never complained. And I knew he wasn't going to quit unless he just fell down and literally passed out.' Scott received one of the coveted Badwater Ultramarathon belt buckles for finishing in less than 48 hours, something only ten race finishers achieved.

After hearing his amazing story, I found myself wondering what Scott Ludwig will do next, so I had to ask. Given his 9,000+ day running streak, I wasn't expecting him to say, 'Oh, I'm done running for a while. I'm building a shuffleboard court in my backyard.' However I'll admit, I thought he might speak of taking a break from the long stuff. I was wrong. By the time you read this Scott will be days away from running the USATF 100-Mile National Championships in Ohio, and in October he'll travel to St. George, Utah to pace Eric Huguelet's attempt to qualify for the Boston Marathon. In November, Scott will be helping out on the 2nd annual Peachtree City 50K. Finally, in December there's a 50-miler in Tallahassee, Florida, with a possible marathon (a race that was rained out last February and rescheduled) the following day. 'If we can still walk,' as Scott puts it.

Scott Ludwig's ultimate running goal, at this point anyway, is the 2004 Western States Endurance Run. Although considered the Granddaddy of ultradistance events, the 100-mile Western States probably isn't the equal of Badwater in terms of difficulty. But it's a trail event and 'I really hate trails,' Scott admits. 'But my friends give me a hard time about not running them,' he says, 'and everybody always wants to know if you've run Western States. So I'd like to run it next June, and then I might call it quits on the weird stuff.' I think 'might' is the key word here. In other words, I'm not holding my breath!

Author's note: There were many articles in local newspapers and magazines covering our Badwater adventure. John's article is the only one that had completely accurate information about the adventure and completely accurate quotes from my crew and me.

Final Thoughts about BADWATER

After 25 years of base preparation, two years of dedicated training and six months of *deadly serious and specific fine-tuning*, my Badwater dream came true. Without a doubt, it is the single greatest accomplishment in my running career, and I'm fairly certain it will remain that way. Obviously, it could not have been done without the teamwork and determination of my crew. Paula–I couldn't have asked for a more determined and dedicated crew chief. Al–who has lived the Badwater dream as long as I. Gary—there is no bigger cheerleader or optimist in the universe. Eric–I'll never forget how you came through on the mountains when I desperately needed the support. And Josh–I can't tell you how glad I am that you were a (very integral) part of our grand adventure. I will forever be indebted to all of you. And I'll never forget our week in Death Valley.

Will you do it again? I was waiting for Chris Kostman to ask me this very question as I sat in the finisher's chair at the Whitney Portals. Unfortunately, my brain was too scrambled to come up with a clever way of saying 'no way in hell.' Fortunately I never had to, as he didn't ask. But if he did ask me, I believe I would have simply said 'once is enough.' As I write this several weeks later, I know in my heart (and <u>soles!</u>) that this is the right decision. The training, the expense, the logistics, the time requirements, and the sacrifices of both the runner and the crewmembers towards a goal of finishing Badwater are astronomical. The chances of everything coming together–are small. Doing Badwater again would be pushing my luck, as I believe our team did it damn near perfectly the first time.

However, if anyone has followed my Badwater 'trilogy' with an inkling of giving it a try somewhere down the road, here are several pieces of advice to consider before you attempt to take on Death Valley:

Train on the mountains Running in the heat of Death Valley was nothing compared to the miles and miles of ascent after Stovepipe Wells. Whether you run or walk the mountains isn't important; what is important is that you acclimate yourself to–essentially–*climbing!* Running the steps in a football stadium, walking up several flights of stairs, exercising on a Stairmaster–these all would serve the purpose as well. Simply put, you MUST be ready to move your body *uphill!!*

Tie bandanas around your ankles Although it is dry heat, you will still be sweating, and by no means do you want your feet to get wet. I discovered tying bandanas around my ankles helped to keep some of the perspiration away from my feet. Unfortunately, I discovered this *after* I had small blisters forming on the balls of each of my feet. Fortunately I had a crew chief who was masterful at taping my feet so that I could continue running (or walking, as the case may have been). Between Paula's taping and the bandanas, further damage was kept to a minimum.

Attire suggestions The white desert hat and sun reflecting long sleeved shirt that come so highly recommended by race officials? Not necessary. I wished I had started the race in a Cool-Max T-shirt (soaked in ice water) and a simple baseball hat (with plenty of sun block on my face, neck and ears). I started the race in the desert hat and long-sleeved shirt and thought I was going to suffocate during the first few miles. Interesting fact: although my crew and I used sun block throughout the event, we still expected to have a few spots of sunburn. Between the six of us, we had *none.*

Do a good job of protecting your lips. Some of us really had bad sores on our lips a couple of days after the race. Don't hesitate to use plenty of lip balm or chapstick throughout the event (that includes nighttime hours as well!). The arid climate will do a number on your lips if you're not careful.

Consider two support vehicles (not just one). If nothing else, this serves as 'insurance' should one of your vehicles wind up stuck on the side of the road. It was reassuring to know we had a backup vehicle should a problem arise with our primary vehicle (fortunately we never did). Additionally, the extra vehicle can be used by crewmembers to run errands (popsicles, anyone?) or to seek some much needed 'relief' (sleep, shower, food–SOLID food, etc.).

Refresh yourself frequently during the event. My crew had an ice-cold washrag ready for me at each pit stop. I used it on my face, the back of my neck, my thighs and my knees. It was the closest thing to a bath I could find, the cooling effect was much needed (and appreciated), and it kept my legs as 'fresh' as possible. Also, occasionally gargling with mouthwash (per a suggestion by Gary) worked out well, as it was both refreshing and helped get whatever taste (salt, water) or feeling (*parched throat*!) I wanted to eliminate.

Wear running sandals on the descents**!** I can't recommend this enough. The first time Eric and I crested a mountain and began heading downhill, my toes began striking the front of my running shoes. I instantly asked my crew to get my sandals, and for the remainder of the race wore those (Nike Straprunners) for all the descents. Thankfully, I didn't have any problems with my toes throughout the event. Side note: the sandals may come in handy for several days after the event as well, as your feet–if they're anything like mine–will swell (wider not longer), and any shoes you attempt to put on will be a little snug.

Solicit advice from an experienced crewmember. We were blessed to have the advice (and wisdom) of David Sowers, who had been Adam Bookspan's crew chief at Badwater on several occasions. His experience and recommendations proved invaluable towards our success at Badwater. You can read all about how to prepare for and compete in this event (and believe me when I say that my crew and I read *everything* in print about the race), but there's nothing like hearing it 'from the horse's mouth.'

If you're interested, it just so happens I know a few 'horses.' Five of them, as a matter of fact.

Badwater Takes Center Stage

If nothing else, the 2003 Badwater Ultramarathon extended the notoriety of the race originally generated by the documentary *Running on the Sun*, which chronicled the 1999 edition of the event. A 1999 Badwater rookie, Kirk Johnson, discusses his trials and tribulations in his book *to the Edge: A Man, Death Valley and the Mystery of Endurance*.

In her autobiography, *The Extra Mile: One Woman's Personal Journey to Ultrarunning Greatness*, Pam Reed discusses her 2002 and 2003 Badwater victories. Later, Dean Karnazes writes of his first attempt at Badwater (a DNF—did not finish—in 1995) in his autobiography, *Ultra Marathon Man: Confessions of an All-Night Runner* (apparently wordy book titles are common amongst long-distance runners).

Pam Reed appeared on *Late Night with David Letterman* less than a week after her 2003 Badwater triumph. Letterman did his homework, as he asked all the right questions, making the interview both interesting as well as humorous. A few examples:

(After Pam tells him the temperature reached 133 degrees)
'I was reading that they (the runners) can't have aid stations along the route because people waiting for the competitors in the sun and the heat would die.'

(After Pam tells him that women may be better suited to distance running than men because they're able to have children, and mentally can go through a lot of pain and there's definitely pain involved in running the race)
'I see; but you did not give birth during the race?'

(After Pam tells him she was awarded a belt buckle for her win)
'Good Lord, sign me up. Where do I get in this? A new belt buckle ... are you kidding me?

Later, *ESPN Magazine* featured an article about Chris Bergland, who finished two places ahead of me at Badwater. The article, 'The Road to Hell,' describes what Chris was experiencing at various checkpoints along the course. Let's see how Chris did, and for the sake of comparison, let's see how I did at similar points during the race (mine will be presented in *italics*):

Mile 00, Elevation—282 feet

CHRIS: As he drives to the start line in Death Valley–Eminem's 'Lose Yourself' pumping on the stereo–Bergland is eerily calm. (Considerably less so is his rookie support crew: big sister Renee, little sis Sandy, bud Bobby and one Magazine writer.) Before the 10 a.m. gun, he rushes to perform his final rites: tying his shoes and clearing out his bowels.

SCOTT: *As he drives to the start line in Death Valley, Scott looks anxiously along the course for fellow DARKSIDER Andy Velazco, who started his race at 8 a.m. His rookie support crew–Chief Paula, her husband Eric, buds Al and Gary, and son Josh– eventually spot Andy running towards Furnace Creek and wave and scream vigor- ously. They realize later that if they had opened the windows, Andy might have actu- ally seen or heard them. Before the 10 a.m. gun, Scott performs his final rites repeatedly; specifically, 'watering' various places near the starting line.*

Mile 17.4, Elevation—165 feet

CHRIS: Bergland is troubled by a charley horse in his right knee (suffered on the flight to California) and a cracked rib (he collided with a bicyclist the month before). But so far, he's cool with the 128 degree heat; he trained in a sauna lead- ing up to the race. 'Is it hot?' he asks, as he tears through Furnace Creek in first place.

SCOTT: *Ludwig is troubled by the white hood and long-sleeved shirt which came highly recommended for Badwater. It's obvious that the outfit is a scam, and Scott realizes he is better off running with a T-shirt and baseball hat. Once the 'recom- mended' gear is removed, Scott is cool with the 128 degree heat.*

Mile 41.9, Elevation 0

CHRIS: The crew keeps Bergland doused in water, helping him fight off the now 130 degree sun. Chris reports that he feels no heat inside his body, just a warm glow from how well the race is going. But at mile 51, he yaks up his apricot energy bar. A mere gag, he insists. It looks nasty either way.

SCOTT: *The crew keeps Ludwig doused in water, helping him fight off the now one-hundred-and-thirty-<u>one</u> degree sun. Scott reports that the hottest parts of his body are the palms of his hands, as the heat is radiating off the surface of the road. Scott hasn't thrown up (nor will he later) although the crew is taken aback by the nastiness of the blisters of his feet.*

Mile 72.3, Elevation 1,970 feet

CHRIS: As night falls, Bergland, still running in first, joyfully croons 'Up Where We Belong.' The temperature hovers at 110 degrees. He pounds downhill, pleased with his speed. Then as he ascends his second major hill, sleep deprivation and darkness take over. The lights on the slope produce a mirage effect, teasing him into a constant 'almost there' mindset. The peak is farther than his brain has anticipated. The miscalculation sinks his spirit.

SCOTT: *Night has already fallen, but Ludwig is still running. Paula joins him running the downhills, and she appears to be pleased with his speed–considering Scott has spent a substantial amount of time walking the uphill stretch out of Stovepipe Wells. Scott and Paula see the peak in the distance, but the lights on the slope produce a mirage effect, making the destination appear closer than it actually was. The miscalculation ... well, the miscalculation pisses Scott off, actually.*

Mile 90.1, Elevation 5,050 feet

CHRIS: Bergland says he still feels lucid, but deep into the night, the switchbacks on the pitch-black road make him feel like he's in a fun house. Fallen rocks distract him; the camber of the road abuses his legs. Chris can't decide whether to walk or run. He hears that 2002 Badwater champ Pam Reed–close on his heels–is struggling too. He slows to a walk. Elation fades. Dejection sets in.

SCOTT: *Ludwig is lucid, but early in the morning the switchbacks on the pitch-black road make it feel like he's not advancing (as he's spending more time going left-to-right and then right-to-left). Scott has no problem deciding to walk. He hears that 2002 Badwater champ Pam Reed is virtually a light year ahead. Scott could care less.*

Mile 111, Elevation 3,600 feet

CHRIS: As the sun rises, Bergland stops without warning, pulls down his shorts, as he delicately puts it later, 'Everything in my intestines comes out in one explosion.' After trailing for 111 miles, Reed overcomes Chris. But he continues to chug along until another 'accident' fills his shorts with what says feels like burning acid. His sisters change him and wet-wipe him clean.

SCOTT: *Chris did <u>WHAT???!!!</u> Scott realizes if he encounters similar difficulty, he is on his own. He knows this to be true because his crew told him so before the race started.*

Mile 115, Elevation 3,600 feet

CHRIS: Bergland has collapsed in the back of the support SUV, his face moth white, his lips a cadaverous blue and green. The crew fears a fatal heatstroke. But his temperature vacillates from 97 to 101.3 degrees, out of serious danger. Chilled Coke cans to his groin and armpits have him chattering–and covered in goose bumps. A medic tells him to relax, rest and continue. He's back on his feet 40 minutes later.

SCOTT: *Scott catches his second wind and begins the best stretch of his race, passing three other runners in the process and moving into sixth place. Unfortunately, Pam Reed has already crossed the finish line. Fortunately, Scott is in no danger of heat-stroke, as the weather has been fairly pleasant with temperatures hovering between 105 and 110 degrees–out of serious danger. Chilled Diet Coke to his throat prevents nausea.*

Mile 122.3, Elevation 3,610 feet

CHRIS: Thirteen miles from the finish, his spirit is broken. Resting made his leg swell. Falling behind punctured his will. The altitude has made his lungs feel 'small and synthetic' and bloated his body to an old Elvis-like puffiness. But he clings to a 9/11-inspired motto: 'Stay Strong: We are New York.' Five hours later, arms raised to the sky, he crosses the finish line in fourth place.

SCOTT: *Thirteen miles from the finish, he dreads what comes next–13 miles straight up Mount Whitney. He clings to consciousness–barely–and five hours later, arms (barely) raised to the sky, he–along with his rookie crew–crosses the finish line in sixth place.*

The Aftermath

CHRIS: An hour after the race, his crew helps him into his hotel bed. He is too tired to eat much. Or move. 'I feel like I've been ripped in half,' he says. Three weeks later, his legs are still numb, four toenails have fallen out and he's removed a piece of skin from his blistered foot so large that it would make the JACKASS gang queasy. A month later, he has nightmares about his surreal breakdowns. Yet he dreams of competing next year–and conquering hell.

SCOTT: *Ten minutes after the race, the entire crew (except Josh) has downed a beer. Scott, in fact, is already on his second one. However, he is too tired to eat. That didn't stop his crew from going to the diner, where Josh ordered everything on the menu (After surviving on energy bars and Fig Newtons for over 36 hours). Meanwhile, Scott went to sleep and during the night got up to 'water' the toilet and blacked out on his way back to bed. Falling face forward, he was lucky not to strike the desk, television, or frame of the bed. He was not so lucky in that he landed face down directly on the center of his forehead. Three weeks later, two toenails have fallen out and he has removed three pieces of skin from his blistered feet which–if patched together–could provide the sole of an entire other foot. A month later, he sleeps as well as he ever did, knowing that he would not be competing next year. After all, hell had already been conquered.*

Finally, the October 2003 issue of *Ultrarunning* **features Badwater champion Pam Reed on the cover.** Inside the issue you will find an account of my Badwater adventure that I was more than happy to write for my friend Don Allison, the magazine's editor and publisher, who has done more to promote the unique sport of ultrarunning than anyone I know. I imagine as a favor to me he also featured another runner on the cover of that issue lurking over Pam's shoulder and wearing race bib #20: *me!*

The Badwater Ultramarathon, the toughest footrace on the planet, was elevated to an even higher status by the 2005 and 2006 victories by Scott Jurek, a seven-time winner of the legendary Western States Endurance Run. I imagine in the years ahead, it will continue to intrigue and captivate the imagination of runners everywhere. As well it should.

Living to the Point of Tears

By Al Barker

I wanted to live deep
And suck out all the marrow in life
And not when I come to die,

Discover that I had not lived.
• *Henry David Thoreau*

Badwater 2003 has come and gone. The event that had been on our minds so often for the past year was over in a 'quick' 36 hours. And now, as I have time to reflect on all of it, one thing that stands out is the reaction of others to 'how I spent my summer vacation.' *'You're going where?' 'You're doing what?' 'You must be crazy!'* But the truth is, I never saw it that way. When asked to help, my answer was an immediate 'yes.' To have a small part in helping a friend complete the most difficult ultra marathon on the face of the earth was what I considered an honor. That's the way I like to live.

I've always admired people who do things that are about and beyond the ordinary. Things that add dimension to life. Some are actors. Some are artists and scientists, and some are athletes. They all have one thing in common. A common bond that gives their lives meaning. That one thing is passion. Their lives are so much richer for it. They are lucky indeed.

In planning for the trip we tried to consider all the possibilities. Death Valley is one of the hottest and driest places on earth and we would be there in the hottest time of the year. That, added to the length of the course with the long ascents and descents, amounted to something that is hard to imagine.

I had read all the books and seen all the documentary films on the race as well as the area in general, but all this pales in comparison to the reality of being there and seeing it. To stand at Badwater, 280 feet below sea level, and watch those people begin a run that will end 134.4 miles later at Whitney Portal (8,360 feet) is enough to humble anyone.

We seemed to do almost everything right. Paula, our crew chief, planned everything meticulously over the preceding several months. We sweated. We paced. We laughed. We measured our input and output to perfection. We even made side trips to get needed stuff while Scott just kept running. And running. Of course, all that paid off at the end as we gathered around him for the much-deserved finish line photo.

At the post-race dinner, I had a chance to talk to Pam Reed, the overall winner of both this year's and last year's race. She looked the part: small, compact, very fit and also very gracious. Being curious as to how she trains, I asked her the burning question about her typical running week. After casually describing what seemed like an impossible task, she followed with *'I just like to run,'* almost apologetically, as though she felt the need to justify such a lifestyle to me. I'm sure she has been in this situation countless times before, getting that 'you've gotta be kidding' look from those who can't relate to her. I did, however, understand her and I was truly impressed.

I also saw Andy Velazco at the post race dinner. His beaming grin was hard to miss. He had that look, as did all the other finishers, of peace that comes with such an accomplishment. He didn't need to say anything. It's understood. I envy him.

There was never any question in my mind as to whether or not Scott would finish. After ten years and about a zillion miles, I know him pretty well. I knew he would push himself almost to the point of tears and never complain. Passion! Scott's strength comes from somewhere deep inside. He just simply knows that he can do it. No excuses! After all, anyone who can run for 25 years without missing a single day has something that few of us possess. And so far I was not surprised to see him push himself to the max to complete what he had set out to do. Great job, Scott!

Being a part of that, even in such a small way is one of those times in life that I will never forget. Someone once said that *'going for a run with good friends is one of life's greatest joys.'* And what a run it was!

And now in the aftermath of an event that will never seem quite real, as we savor the memories, the big question looms before us. How do you top this? Where do we go from here? What happens tomorrow? I have no idea. But isn't that the beauty of it?

A NOTE OF THANKS

To Paula, Eric, Gary, Al and Josh

I will never be able to tell you how much I appreciate the support, encouragement and dedication you willingly provided to make our trip to Death Valley a successful one. I doubt I will ever be able to put into words what completing Badwater means to me, but know that whenever I think of it, a part of me will always remember that you were there for me during the 'toughest footrace on the planet.'

You guys are the greatest.
Scott

Post-Badwater Cool down

(Otherwise known as the USATF 100-Mile Championship)

I had promised one of my Badwater crew members, Gary Griffin, that if I was still able to *walk* after completing Badwater, I would go with him to the USATF 100-Mile Championship in Olander Park, Ohio (the scene of last year's 24-Hour Run) as he attempted this distance for the first time. Why not? After Badwater, 100 miles on a flat surface should feel like more of a *sprint* than an endurance run. AND I would have a little over seven weeks of recovery behind me after Badwater.

The race was scheduled for 10:00 a.m. on Saturday, September 13. The month leading up to the event I had averaged 100 miles a week (so much for tapering). So on Monday, September 8th I decided to *truly* taper—but in the long run, tapering turned out to be the *least* of my problems.

Monday, September 8th

I ran 11 miles at a slow pace. After all, following four 100-mile weeks this felt pretty easy. I'll start my true taper tomorrow.

Tuesday, September 9th

I ran eight miles at a really easy pace. By Saturday, I should feel pretty fresh. That is, until my wife got 'the phone call' at 9:30 p.m.

Her friend Jan had a flat tire on I-285, a busy interstate circling Atlanta. Jan, alone and frightened (rightfully so, as she was in a 'bad' section of town and the 18-wheelers were flying by her just a few feet away), asked for our help. By 10:15 p.m. Cindy and I found her car—warning lights flashing—near Exit 7.

I proceeded to loosen *four* of the lug nuts on the flat tire; unfortunately, the *fifth* lug nut needed a 'key' that was nowhere to be found. After searching the car four or five times, we called AAA for a tow truck. As fate would have it, we found the 'key' just after we made the call. I got the tire changed, and we drove back to the automotive tire center near home and left her car via the overnight drop box. Our mini-adventure was over by 1:30 a.m.

Actually, for *me* the 'adventure' was just beginning. I didn't realize it at the time, but when I loosened the lug nuts (which were on REALLY tight) I pulled something in my right shoulder blade. I didn't realize it until Wednesday morning when I had a tough time getting out of bed.

Wednesday, September 10th

My shoulder is killing me. I figure running might do it some good. Nine miles at an easy pace felt pretty good; no problems with my shoulder whatsoever. That is, until *after* I finished running. The moment I stopped, the pain in my shoulder blade kicked in. It appears that the only time I won't be in pain is when I'm running (if you can explain that), which works out well with a 100-miler coming up this weekend.

Maybe a good day's rest will do my back good.

Thursday, September 11th

So much for that theory. A good day's rest on Wednesday, but yet another tough time getting out of bed today. Surprisingly, running 13 miles with Kelly and Eric felt pretty good, and my shoulder didn't bother me at all. After our run, I helped Eric haul off some lawn waste to the local landfill (it took about six hours), and while I was actually *working* my shoulder felt fine. However, on the rides to and from the landfill I felt like a knife was sticking in my shoulder blade. Not a good sign for this weekend.

Gary drove up from Tallahassee and joined us for dinner. I told him of my dilemma. He asked me the obvious question ('Do you still want to run?'), and I told him the thought (of *not* running) never crossed my mind. Gary knows me better than that, but I imagine he asked it out of courtesy to Cindy (although in actuality *Cindy* knows me better than that as well).

Friday, September 12ᵗʰ

Once again, getting out of bed was tough. The four easy miles, however, weren't. The ride on the airplane, though, was *extremely* tough. I should have warned the lady next to me of my dilemma, because I spent the 90 minutes of the flight positioning and repositioning every 20 seconds or so. I never could find a position that minimized the pain in my shoulder.

When we got to Ohio, Gary and I stopped for lunch. I had two glasses of liquid painkiller (a welcome 32 ounces on draft), and later that night at the pre-race dinner I had three more cans of the same. Now I had *two* ways of minimizing my pain: running and beer. Fortunately, tomorrow I would have plenty of time to minimize my pain (via running).

Saturday, September 13ᵗʰ

Although the race was to start at 10:00 a.m., I was wide awake at 1:08. I never did get back to sleep, as I could find absolutely no position that would minimize the pain in my back. At 7:00 a.m. Gary woke up, and I told him that if I were wise I would take a doctor's advice (I'm guessing at this point as to what he/she might say) and 'take two aspirin and relax the entire day.' But instead, I'm going to try and run 100 miles.

At 10:00 a.m. my journey has begun. I will be pain-free for the next 18 hours, 23 minutes and 17 seconds.

Sunday, September 14ᵗʰ

I sleep in our rental car until it's time for Gary to finish. I walk over to the finish line to take a photo of Gary finishing his first 100-miler, and we return to the hotel for a quick 90 minute nap before we have to head to the airport.

At 11:00 a.m., we're ready to leave the hotel. I was in *serious* agony at this point (my back was screaming *bloody murder* and both of my big toenails were dangling after last night's 'fun'). But the worst part is: between Gary and me, *I was in the best condition to drive to the airport!*

Once we returned the rental car, we struggled with our luggage, and managed to make it to our gate in time for our 12:55 p.m. flight home. This time, I forewarned the gentleman sitting next to me of my condition, and told him that I would be 'adjusting' my position in my seat every 20 seconds or so. I did ('adjust') but it made absolutely no difference. My body was paying me back (rightfully so) for what I had just put it through. Gary was kind enough to buy me a can of liquid painkiller on our flight.

Once we landed in Atlanta, I wished Gary a safe drive back to Tallahassee. I offered him a room for the night, but he wanted to get back home as he had to work the next day.

Cindy met me at the airport and (thankfully!) drove home. Somehow I managed to unpack and throw my dirty clothes in the washer, but I wasn't able to do the other things I normally do when I return from an out-of-town race: read the newspapers, check the mail, dry my clothes and put them away, etc. The *only* thing I was able to do was lie on the couch (and reposition every 20 seconds) and drink a few more bottles of liquid painkiller.

Postscript

My right shoulder blade continued to plague me for several days after the event. For whatever reason, the only way I could make the pain stop was by running. Running with two severely sore hamstrings, I might add.

I found out later that I had finished 14th overall and 2nd in my age group at the 100-Mile Championships. To be honest, I couldn't have cared less. My shoulder wouldn't let me.

Chapter Eleven
Running off the Road
The Curse of the Trail

I honestly can say I gave it an honest shot. In fact, several honest shots.

That being said, I can honestly say that I hate running on trails. I realize that to some runners, trails are nirvana. To me, trails are hell. Pure, tortuous and evil hell.

But don't let me influence you. Feel free to decide for yourself. After you read this chapter, of course.

In this chapter:

- It Seemed Like a Good Idea at the Time—I helped a friend celebrate his 50th birthday by accompanying him to the JFK 50-Miler. I hope he enjoyed it more than I did.

- A Necessary Evil—Training for the 2004 Western States Endurance Run forced me to run some trail ultras for practice. This one proved to be the worst of the lot.

- Beautiful Disaster—The Sierra Nevada Mountain Range is beautiful—absolutely breathtaking. The route through them that was the 2004 Western States Endurance Run, however, was a disaster.

- Beauty and the Beast Part I—As fate would have it, for the second straight time my name was selected via lottery to run in the (2006) Western States Endurance Run. Perhaps with a better training plan, this time would be different.

- Beauty and the Beast Part II—A second chance to complete the only race I failed to finish. This had to be the one, as there certainly was not going to be a third time.

- Beauty and the Beast Part III—Badwater or Western: Which was tougher? The answer may surprise you.

- Western States: A Pacer's Perspective (by Danielle Goodgion)—My wonderful pacer offers her perspective on our jaunt up and down (but mostly up) the mountains.

- A Chronology of all my TRAIL RUNS—A finite history of the fourteen runs that made me cry 'uncle.'

It Seemed Like a Good Idea at the Time

The race from hell has a name and it is the 2000 JFK 50 (Mile Run). In almost 24 years of running road races, it is the *first* race I have vowed to _never_ run again (something usually stated immediately after finishing a difficult race, only to change one's mind when the race rolls around the following year). Well, it's six years later and nothing's changed: I repeat—I will _never_ run that freakin' race again! Why? Let me count the reasons why:

Reason #1

The race starts innocently enough in a small town where you run along a street (mostly uphill) for three miles. I was told you need to make a move early as once you entered the Appalachian Trail at the three mile mark you had to run 'single file' (due to the narrowness of the trail); therefore, the position you were in when you *entered* the trail would be the same when you *exited* the trail at 16 miles. Boy, did I prove *that* theory wrong!

I entered the trail in 23rd place (yes, a volunteer was counting). When I exited the trail a mere 13 miles later I was in *47th* place. Granted, if I was adept at running on mountains (say, like a mountain goat) I could have held my position. However, since I was desperately afraid of falling (I basically 'hopped' for 13 miles from rock to rock and—fortunately—*most* of the rocks I chose to land on didn't *move!*), I repeatedly 'pulled to the side' of the trail and allowed other runners to pass. In fact, when I left the trail, a volunteer told me my position (I dropped 24 spots on the trail) and mentioned that 'hey, here's one who's *not* bleeding!' Lucky me.

Once I left the trail, I had to cross a railroad track to get to the 26 mile path along the canal. Of course, a train was approaching from my left and a volunteer was holding his hand up telling me to stop. Naturally, I sprinted across the track, because if I *did* stop (a) I'd have to wait five minutes for the train to pass and I'd cramp up really bad, and quite possibly decide to call it a day right then and there and (b) since I was intentionally disobeying a volunteer, I thought I had a *really* good chance of getting disqualified (unfortunately, it didn't happen)!

Reason #2

Now I'm running along the canal, and I am bored silly. For 26 miles, the scenery *never* changed! Water to the left, trees on either side of the path, and once in a while … *another runner!* There was talk from others of the prestige of (a) breaking eight hours and (b) placing in the top 50. All I wanted was for this adventure from hell to be over. I couldn't give a rat's ass about 'top 50' or eight hours. I didn't stop at the numerous aid stations because I didn't want to spend any extra time on the course, even if it was to do something necessary like replace the calories I had burned. No way, just let me keep going to get it over with.

After a while I was in a 'trance' *(try looking at the exact same scene for four hours!)*, and I tried to lock on to a runner in front of me. I was so mentally disconnected from running at one point, I had to focus on imitating what *he* was doing so I could do the same … and all I'm talking about is putting one foot in front of the other. Yes, I was a *goner!*

Reason #3

After 42 miles the course changes to winding, hilly country blacktop. Fortunately for me, I finished while the sun was still out. Others weren't so lucky. The roads were *so* winding and hilly that it would be really dangerous to run on them at night: no road shoulder, no traffic control, and *no lights!* Fortunately, I was finished before the sun set. Others weren't so lucky. I ran the final 12 miles with a female competitor from Ohio, who had several ultra wins to her credit. At first *she* had her sights set on breaking eight hours, but as we climbed the final hill and saw that an all-out 400 yard sprint was needed to reach that goal, we settled on a quick shuffle and finished in eight hours and 19 seconds (actually, she beat me by one second … as if that mattered). I wound up in 56th place … as if that mattered, either. All I know was: I was *done* and I *wouldn't be back.*

A Necessary Evil

I approached the 2004 Oak Mountain 50K (in Pelham, Alabama) with (a) an open mind and (b) as a training run for June's Western States Run. By now I trust you know I have a disdain for trails, but since I'll be spending at least 24 hours on them in June, I started this race as a prelude to the big event in California.

For your consideration (and calendar planning in the future), I will review the race in the formatted presented in the book *The Ultimate Guide to Marathons* by Dennis Craythorn and Rich Hanna.

Course Beauty: To me, the entire course looked the same–dirt, leaves, roots and rocks. If one dared to look up and to see their surroundings, one could count on taking a spill, ranging from a simple fall to the ground all the way to a 500 foot 'drop and roll' down the side of the mountain. My running partner, Al Barker, experienced (fortunately) two of the former. I was lucky enough to not 'eat dirt' at all, although I have no idea what Oak Mountain State Park looks like–aside from the dirt, leaves, roots, and rocks I mentioned previously. Score (on a scale of 1-10)–2.

Course Difficulty: Having to navigate a right-angle drop to a waterfall and then having to climb—hand over hand–up the other side is indicative of the difficulty of the course. Someone mentioned to me that navigating the decline was better than the alternative–navigating the *incline*–but I stated that I wasn't so sure of that, as I had never seen anyone fall *uphill* before. Also, the course wasn't an accurate 50K (31 miles)–in my estimation, the distance was closer to 57 kilometers or so. Score–10.

Appropriateness for First Timers: Al and I approached the race with no aspirations for a competitive time. Good thing, as we only finished 10 minutes under the nine hour cutoff. While the event was not appropriate for 'first timers,' Al and I noticed a large number of those around us late in the race were doing their first ultra. Many of them were carrying backpacks, wearing cross-training shoes, and exhibiting other forms of 'newness to the sport' that made Al and I feel humbled. At least they *would* have made us feel that way had we given a rat's ass. Score–1.

Race Organization: The race started on time and the course was fairly well marked … for a trail run. However, the volunteers seemed clueless as to 'what lied ahead,' as Al and I would frequently ask what we could expect next. The perfect example was at the last aid station (26 miles, but probably closer to 29 miles) where we were told by volunteers that the finish was 'downhill and on the road to the left.' Al and I turned left onto the road running downhill, only to be screamed at by a backpack carrying rookie who informed us we needed to retrace our steps and turn RIGHT and then go UPHILL on the TRAIL. Also, there was no ice at any of the aid stations, and as the temperature was in the low 80's, the fluids were all warm and the bread in the peanut butter and jelly sandwiches was 'toasted' (apparently Tupperware is a luxury item at Oak Mountain). To make matters worse, the aid station at 17 miles was out of fluids. Apparently, race organizers didn't expect as many runners to pass by the 17-mile aid station as the other five or six aid stations along the course. Score–2.

Crowds: Aside from the fact that no one–NO ONE–had a clue as to the distances anywhere along the course (Al and I heard 'one mile to go' from cyclists and hikers and volunteers for at least 40 minutes towards the end of the race … and yes, we *were* moving), the crowds were supportive. I'm sure that for the runners that gave a rat's ass, that mattered. For me, I couldn't have cared less if they were throwing rotten eggs at me. I just wanted off the freakin' course, OFF the trails, and IN the car heading back to Atlanta where I could once again run on the safe and sound asphalt trails of Peachtree City. Score–3.

Summary: This is the second race I've competed in that gets my "Never Again' stamp of disapproval (the first being the JFK 50). I'm sure Western States will be the third.

Beautiful Disaster

How do I feel after training for (OK, maybe not *training*, but certainly *worrying about*) the 2004 Western States (WS) Endurance Run for seven months?

How do I feel after spending over $1500 for an event I didn't even complete?

How do I feel after investing five days of my life (which I'll never get back) to travel to California to run (well, mostly *walk)* only 62 miles of a 100 mile event?

Humbled ... embarrassed ... but mostly RELIEVED!

Relieved that I can now speak of it in the past tense.

If that's the case, you're probably wondering what led me to Squaw Valley at 5:00 a.m. on a cool, crisp morning on June 26, wearing unfamiliar running garb—trail shoes, fanny pack, water bottle—and staring at a 4.7 mile climb up the side of a freakin' mountain.

Al Barker, that's what.

After Badwater last summer, Al expressed an interest in doing something 'out of the ordinary.' So he talked me into entering the WS lottery via the 'buddy system' and to his delight and my dismay, our names were selected.

Before I knew it, Al and I, along with our support crew of Susan Lance and Gordon Cherr, were on a flight to San Francisco. Upon arrival, we rented our 'support vehicle' (a Cadillac—only in California, folks!) and drove east to Truckee, where we stayed for two nights prior to the start of the race and got acclimated to the elevation.

The day before the race, Al and I checked in with race officials who slapped a fluorescent yellow band on our respective wrists with our name, race number, weight and pulse (mine, ordinarily 52, registered at 64; Al, ordinarily 50, registered at a whopping 86 ... he was admittedly 'nervous'). The altitude did strange things to our bodies, elevating our pulse and blood pressure and inhibiting our ability to *breathe*.

At the official pre-race meeting, instructions were given to runners and crew. The top male and female runners were introduced, as well as half of the 1300 volunteers responsible for the event (well, maybe not *half*, but it seemed that way in the hot sun).

Noted ultrarunner Ray Krowelicz sat next to me at the meeting and told me I'd do well and that I'd have no problem with the course ('it's runnable'). I told Ray I was terrible on trails and feared the worst. Guess who proved to be right (hint: it wasn't a 'noted ultrarunner') in the long run—if you consider finishing 62 miles of a 100 mile event 'long.'

I left two drop bags with the volunteers to be delivered to Michigan Bluff (55.7 miles) and the Rucky Chucky River crossing (78.1 miles). The plan was for Gordon to pace me from the allowed checkpoint (Foresthill School, 62.0 miles) to the finish. At that time it would be around nightfall (my calculation derived with 'noted ultrarunner's' help), and he would bring my flashlight and headlamp. We expected that I would hit 62 miles around 8:00 p.m. (although Ray thought I'd make it by 6:00). The only thing we were *all* right about was that when I hit 62 miles it would still be Saturday. Barely, as it turned out.

We all ate our 'last meal' at Subway (none of us barely saying a word) and were all fast asleep by 6:30—eight hours before our 2:30 a.m. wakeup call. At 4:00 a.m. race morning we were at Squaw Valley eager to get the show on the road. After Al and I made our final pit stops (five for Al; one for me), we were at the starting line for the countdown to the start. It took us 25 seconds after the starter's gun to get to the starting line so we could begin—WALKING for the next 4.5 miles up to the Escarpment, going from an elevation of 6200 feet to an elevation of 8700 feet. Al and I experienced 'sausage fingers' (swelling caused by altitude pressure) and realized—in a field of 444 runners—there were only 20 or so runners behind us.

Once we reached the summit, we turned a corner, *ran* for the first time, and came across our next 'opponent'—a huge patch of ice! Al went in front of me and slipped, and when I put out my hand to stop him, I did a cheerleader-quality split, hyper-extending my right knee and pulling my left groin in the process. Terrific, and only 95 miles to go!

Next, I found myself running alone (what happened to Al?) on an eight-inch wide path with razor-like shrubs attacking my legs from both sides. Am I having fun yet?

Not to worry: things only went downhill from there (and when I say 'downhill,' I means lots of *UP*hill). I felt like I was Indiana Jones: fending off five attackers only to turn the corner to face TEN attackers … then, after defeating *them*, being chased by a rolling two-ton boulder.

I saw Gordon and Susan at Robinson Flat (24.6 miles) which, as it turned out, was the brightest spot in my day. It lasted all of twelve seconds. I gave Gordon my fanny pack (thus sacrificing one of my two water bottles) as it was bouncing and tearing a hole in my back. I would rough it from that point with my remaining handheld water bottle which, as it turned out, was a big mistake.

The next thirty miles offered some beautiful scenery; I was actually moving so slowly on occasion that I had time to enjoy it. The view, that is … not the event.

The three canyons between Last Chance (43.3 miles) and Michigan Bluff were without a doubt the beginning of my end. The climb up Devil's Thumb (the first canyon) required a climb of 1,600 feet in only 1.7 miles, and required traversing 37 switchbacks (which caused me to flashback to the hellacious switchbacks on Mount Whitney at the end of Badwater last summer). The second canyon, requiring an 1,800 foot climb in 2.8 miles to Michigan Bluff (but only seven switchbacks … seven loooooooong switchbacks!) led me to Michigan Bluff. I stopped to have my big toes examined and tended to, as they were both tearing apart due to my altered foot strike caused by my accident on the ice. When I took off my left shoe, the medical team was horrified by the condition of my big toe. Unfortunately, they were 'ooing and aahing' over damage to my toe incurred at Badwater *last summer*—they didn't even notice the toenail was tearing apart from the cuticle! A video team taped the whole 'repair' process (for an upcoming documentary, I understand); the duct tape was a nice touch. I only had to have a large blood blister lanced and taped on my right big toe.

As I was feeling a lot of pain in my thighs, my calves, my back, my … well, my BODY, I also asked for a massage. The masseuse couldn't believe how stiff my legs were, but she managed to loosen them up to the point that, when I stood up, they actually felt refreshed. However, my toes (and now my right heel) were still hurting. Terribly.

Did I mention the sun had now set and it was dark? Or that I was still seven miles away from Gordon ... and my flashlight? Or that I still had one more canyon to negotiate?

I borrowed a small penlight (from Chris of Tucson—God bless you, Chris) to use through the third canyon, requiring a 6.3 mile journey. When I got to the bottom of the canyon, it was pitch black. The penlight, emitting a beam of about four feet, was difficult to navigate by, but I managed to finally make my way to the Foresthill School checkpoint (62.0 miles).

Did I mention that I noticed a runner update board in Michigan Bluff and that it indicated Al had dropped out at 43.3 miles (appropriately named Last Chance)? Or that if I knew I would be rescued I would have dropped in my tracks and waited for the rescue team? Or that any semblance of desire to finish this damn race was now gone? After all, this was Al's dream (not mine), and the event combined two of the four things I hate (the four things being hiking, camping, hunting and fishing—you can figure out the two I'm referring to). Or that, in an effort to move out of the way of a participant who wanted to pass me, I lost my balance, slipped on pine straw, fell backwards, and struck my head on a boulder? I decided I was in hell. I couldn't wait to make it to Foresthill ... to call it a day. Literally, a *day!*

I walked with Chris and his pacer (I found out later pacers were allowed after 8:00 p.m., not at mile 62 as we thought—which meant Gordon *could* have joined me at Michigan Bluff and I would have been spared the use of the penlight) the last 1.7 miles to Foresthill. A volunteer walked with us, encouraging Chris to complete the event. She stated that 'the hard part is over at 62 miles' and that the course was 'technical' (the kiss of death for me) right before the river crossing. Thank God she wasn't aware I had no intention of continuing, or she would have directed her comments to me as well as Chris. I simply walked along in silence, acting as if the thought of quitting never entered my mind.

Upon arriving at Foresthill School, I couldn't locate Gordon, so I asked a volunteer to find him for me ... while I sat in a lawn chair. I told the volunteer I might drop out of the race, but I'd tell her for sure in a moment. I weighed in and realized I had lost six pounds in the last 19 miles. I also realized I had not consumed a single calorie during that time (all I had consumed was water; lots and lots of water). Then I saw Gordon running across the parking lot—attired in the appropriate gear, wearing his headlamp, holding my lights in his hands, and most disturbing of all, EAGER TO RUN! I asked Gordon if he would be disappointed if I called it a day. After all, Gordon had trained and prepared for his 38 mile stretch of the WS course ... and he'd been waiting for several hours to take center stage. Gordon told me I looked pretty beat up, and he would understand if I dropped out (God bless you, Gordon). I walked back to the volunteer and told her 'number 134 is dropping out of the race.' With a nod from the volunteer, it was over. I was officially out of WS.

The next four or five hours was a blur, but suffice it to say that I slept in five different spots during that time: in a volunteer's vehicle for the ride from Foresthill to the finish line, on the sidewalk next to the finish area, in a volunteer's vehicle in the finish area parking lot, in our support Cadillac, and in a hotel room (note: the original plan didn't call for a hotel room, as Al and I were supposed to be running during the night).

The four of us woke up the next morning and returned to the finish line, where we witnessed many accomplishing what Al and I could now only dream of doing—finishing WS! I saw Chris from Tucson finish, and was proud of him for doing so. After all, I knew volunteers had required him to gain weight before leaving two checkpoints and at Foresthill he was so cold that I left him lying on a cot underneath two blankets, certain that his race was over. Like Ray Krolewicz the day before, I was wrong.

I spoke briefly with Don Allison, the editor and publisher of *Ultrarunning*, and he seemed to have a hard time believing he was talking to the same person who finished sixth at Badwater eleven short months ago. Like I tried to tell Ray yesterday, I'm terrible on trails. Maybe 'terrible' is an understatement.

Sunday afternoon, the four of us went running (although I wouldn't call what Al and I were doing *running*). After our run, Al and I spoke with the famous 'Cowman,' who told us he was writing a book on his life. I thanked him for getting me national exposure on ESPN during coverage of the 1987 Boston Marathon (I was running next to him, and cameras were always looking for 'the runner with the horns on his head'). We then saw Monica Scholz, who played leap frog with me at Badwater last summer (although she eventually finished in front of me). She was excited with her WS performance, as she 'finally' finished in the top ten. She was set to return to Badwater in two weeks, and we wished her well and told her we'd follow her on the webcast (Note: Monica went on to being the first female finisher—and third overall—at Badwater in 2004).

We saw local legend Tim Twietmeyer, working with several young boys to clean up the field where only moments before the grand finale of the WS had taken place. He is also the only runner I saw cross the finish line during my 'nap' on the sidewalk the night before.

Now that it's over, I have no regrets. Just an overwhelming sense of relief—relief that I'll never run another trail as long as I live.

Al is another story, however. This morning—only eight days after our beautiful disaster—he told me he's going to try WS again someday. Susan wants to try it too.

I, however, am staying where I belong. On the roads.

Beauty and the Beast (Part I)

As fate would have it, I entered the lottery for the 2006 Western States Endurance Run (so much for staying on the roads) via the buddy system with my good friend and training partner Al Barker. For the second consecutive time, we managed to beat the odds and were selected to be on the starting line in Squaw Valley at 5:00 a.m. on Saturday, June 24. As the lottery was held in December of 2005, that meant I had a little over six months to 'get (trail) serious'—which was exactly the same amount of time I had to get ready for Badwater three short years ago.

I decided to return to many of the things that worked for me then (why ruin a good thing?), while supplementing my training and preparation with a few variations specific to a venture on the trails (which I felt was absolutely essential, having been primarily a 'road runner' my entire life).

Here's a capsule summary of those six months:

The Edge of Exhaustion*
(*There's nothing I fear more, and no place I'd rather be)

Although I had vowed (yet again) to reduce my mileage in 2006, I realized that I needed to actually *increase* my mileage—training to the virtual edge of physical exhaustion once again—if I were to stand a chance against the demands of the 100-mile route through the mountains of the Sierra Nevadas. I resumed my **95 miles per week** regimen which, when supplemented with a job that requires 50+ hours per week as well as enough jobs around the house to make Bob Vila anxious, managed to tire me to the point of nightly blackouts around 7:30 p.m. in my recliner. Excellent—this was just what I needed.

In a ten-week span from mid-January through late March, I managed to run **six marathons** (five of which I actually put forth a substantial effort) and **three 50K's** (two of them being on trails, and a third—on concrete—in which I set a state age group record). In other words, I wasn't merely 'logging miles;' I was running relatively hard (something I hadn't been doing since Badwater three summers ago). The first weekend in May, my Western States pacer—Danielle Goodgion—and Al and his pacer—Susan Lance—ran the Strolling Jim 40 Mile Run together as a final long-distance tune-up. We did reasonably well, all finishing comfortably in around seven hours.

I also 'stayed the course' with my **regular long training runs**: in a five-month window from January through June, I had fifteen runs of 20 miles or longer, with four of them being 31 miles or longer. I was doing my homework.

As for the training 'supplements' I referred to earlier, I turned my attention to the **trails**. As I mentioned, I ran two 50K's on trails (Kennesaw Mountain, Georgia and Oak Mountain, Alabama), two races I'm familiar with but don't particularly care for (they're not on roads, remember?). Additionally, I ran the Bartram Trail in North Carolina (22 miles) with Al in April, and the Pine Mountain Trail (again, 22 miles) in Georgia with Gary Griffin in May. During my run with Al, we maneuvered along the route with what we called 'Western States effort,' advancing as if we were going to be doing 100 miles. We completed the route in a little less than six hours. Perfect. During my run with Gary, I gained some valuable insight as to how trails should be run. Two things Gary taught me—that would pay off for me in June—were 'look ahead and plan your next three steps' and 'trust the rocks' (I have always had a tendency to do everything in my power to avoid landing on a rock when I run—probably my bad experience in 2000 on the Appalachian Trail at the JFK 50 Mile Run in which most of the rocks I opted to land on wobbled, causing my ankles to periodically twist wildly from side to side). Running that day with Gary gave me a lot of new-found confidence.

My final trail run was a **night time** return to the Pine Mountain Trail with Al, Danielle and Susan two weeks before Western States. We ran ten miles on the trail after the sun went down to test our headlamps and handheld flashlights on the trails. Although we were on the trails for three hours, we considered it a success.

The other supplement? **Hills!** Plenty of them—numerous ¼ mile and 4/10 mile hill repeats and a particularly hilly 12-mile training route with Al and/or Danielle.

Aside from the running …

I returned to Paula May's prescribed **pre-Badwater diet** on January 2, and stuck with it fanatically for six months. This happened to coincided with a 101-day weight-loss contest at my place of employment which I won by losing 19 pounds (just over 12 percent of my body weight)—ultimately dropping my weight to a mere 136 pounds. And as I did three years ago, I did not consume any beer the last 30 days before Western States (which was probably more of a superstitious reaction than anything else).

The last two weeks before Western States, I incorporated a lot of **walking** into my daily running regimen (while reducing my weekly mileage as a taper). I knew I would be doing a lot of walking in the mountains, and wanted to get a sense of my 'walking motion' to feel less awkward (I've always hated to walk—it's so much easier to *run*).

For probably the first time in my life, I kept a bottle of **water** on my desk at work and would refill it many times throughout the day (usually at the end of one of my many visits to the restroom). Did I fail to mention that I even incorporated **running with a water bottle** on some of my training runs, something I've *never* done?

My wife Cindy surprised me with an anniversary gift (our anniversary being six days before Western States) of a gift certificate for a **full-body massage**, which I took advantage of four days prior to the race. I've always read that a massage is recommended the week prior to a major athletic endeavor. If that's true, this was absolutely the time for it.

I watched Al's video, **'A Race for the Soul,'** which chronicles an earlier edition of the Western States Endurance Run. On the third viewing (which was sometime during the first week in May), it 'took,' and I began to actually visualize myself crossing the finish line. In contrast, the first time I saw the video 'Running on the Sun' (which chronicles the 1999 edition of Badwater), I knew instantly that one day I would cross the finish line on Mount Whitney.

My final preparation, of course, was to **prepare for the event mentally**. Obviously, the first hurdle is visualizing success. After that, a game plan—which requires the utmost in patience, perseverance and mind over matter—has to be formulated. My game plan revolved around five elements:

- *Enjoy the course and the camaraderie.*
- *Don't push; take what the course gives you.*
- *Patience. Patience. Patience.*
- *Focus on the positives; block out the negatives.*
- *Keep moving.*

Last-Minute Anxieties

Considering I was running well, was feeling reasonably healthy, and was at my lightest weight since I was 13-years old, I was feeling pretty good about my chances of finishing Western States, which until now had been the only major blemish on my running career (the aforementioned failure at Western in 2004).

But just when things are going good …

Sunday night, June 18 (six days before Western States, and the evening of our 29th wedding anniversary … not to mention Father's Day)—I ask Cindy to take a look at the 'scab' on the back of my left thigh, as it's been there for quite a while and I just can't seem to get rid of it. Cindy politely informs me my 'scab' is actually a well-fed tick, who's been feasting on my blood for at least a week (assuming I picked it up in Pine Mountain on the night training run the weekend before).

As I'd been feeling achy all weekend, I figured I had Lyme disease, and that most likely my last six months of training would be for naught. I visited a doctor (which indicates how desperate I was) the following day. He calmly removed the tick and said he doubted I had Lyme disease, and my weekend jaunt through the mountains was still a 'go.' I felt good dodging this last-minute bullet. An omen, perhaps?

Let's hope so. I have to be in Squaw Valley in five more days.

Beauty and the Beast (Part II)

Not to put any pressure on myself, but wanting to make it to the finish line of the Western States Endurance Run had become my own personal version of Captain Ahab's elusive Moby Dick … Arnold Palmer's never-achieved U.S. Open championship … Superman's Kryptonite, for that matter. Mind you, trail running has no appeal to me, and I have no false aspirations of ever being proficient—hell, I'll settle for *competent* these next 100 miles—on the trails.

Up until two years ago, the only run I failed to complete was my initial attempt in 1982 at running across the state of Georgia. Ten years later, I gave it a second try and was successful.

Now, two years removed from my initial failure at Western States, here I was again in Squaw Valley with two days to make my final preparations—both physical and mental—to give it a second (and absolutely *final*) try. Al, Susan and I had two days to eat, rest, strategize, and rest some more. (My pacer, Danielle as well as her husband Bill would see me Saturday morning at Robinson Flats, approximately 30 miles into the race.) In fact, the two days before the race I slept for ten hours and seven-and-a-half hours, respectively—record amounts for me. Race morning Al and I woke up at 3:00 a.m. and headed for the pre-race breakfast/bib number pickup literally next door to our room at the Squaw Valley Lodge. We returned to the room immediately to avoid the pre-race tension that can be found as runners, crew members and race officials make last-minute preparations and adjustments before the starting gun sounded at 5:00 a.m. Me? I'm better off avoiding the mass hysteria, and besides—it's a little late now to make any last-minute adjustments that may enter into your mind. Accidentally overhearing an innocent tip, reminder, or piece of advice this late in the game is never a good thing. Stick with what got you this far, and steer clear of any too-late-in-the-game suggestions or recommendations. Staying secluded in our room at the lodge afforded us this onslaught of self-doubt and second-guessing. We had our game plan, and we were prepared to execute. We had done our homework, and we felt ready.

4:55 a.m. Saturday, Race Morning, Squaw Valley

Susan escorts Al and I to the starting line, and takes a few 'before' photographs. Later—maybe several hours, maybe a day or more—the 'after' photographs would be taken. We're hoping for the latter, as we're both aiming for running the course in 30 hours. The gun sounds promptly at 5:00 a.m., and we're on our way up the Escarpment, a tremendous 4.7 mile climb up the side of a mountain gaining over 2,250 feet in elevation.

As we crest the mountain, we find ourselves running, walking and stumbling in snow, a good two feet deep in some areas. We soon learn the art of 'butt-gliding,' as it was easier sliding down the slopes than it was trying to maintain your balance and footing. Later, my butt cheeks will remind me that butt-gliding may not have been such a good idea after all.

Al and I remain together for almost 12 miles. Al took a few spills, and the only casualty I incurred happened about eight miles into the race, as I stopped to get a rock out of my shoe by sitting on a fallen tree. I braced myself with my right hand, and quickly discovered a sharp, jagged branch puncturing my palm. It would be the only bloodshed I incurred all day, but it was painful. At least nothing bad happened to my feet. Not yet, anyway.

1:17 p.m., Robinson Flat

As I approach the 24 mile mark at Red Star Ridge, I fear that Al is having difficulty and is in danger of missing an 'absolute cutoff' (AC) soon, which means disqualification from the race. The race officials are very strict with enforcing the various AC's along the course, which allow a little extra 'cushion' for those trying to complete the course in the mandated 30 hour time limit. I make my way to Robinson Flat (mile 30) where I see Susan once again and Danielle and her husband Bill for the first time. At this point I am already exhausted: the course has been altered slightly from two years ago, and the five miles leading to Robinson Flat were a never-ending series of tortuous uphill. I remember *sprinting* to Robinson Flat in 2004 and tossing my fuel belt (which was irritating my back) to Gordon Cherr (my ill-fated pacer), as I thought I was 'running too fast' to waste any time with idle conversation. Not this year.

As I said, I was already exhausted (I would feel this way many more times) and gave my friends the 'shoot me in the head' sign. Just as I could tell their initial reaction was that my run may be coming to an end very soon, I could also see that their hopes of me finishing were rekindled after a few encouraging words from the three of them as I sat for a moment and drank some fluids while resting momentarily in a lawn chair. Susan informed me that Al had missed the cutoff at Duncan Canyon, and I felt sad, as I know how much Western States means to him.

Feeling (ever-so-slightly) refreshed, I got up from the lawn chair and resumed my journey towards Auburn. Danielle called out that she would be in Michigan Bluff to pace me. Michigan Bluff was 26 miles—and almost eight hours away. It would be dark when I met up with Danielle ... and had access to my headlamp and flashlight for the first time.

5:03 p.m., Last Chance

I had been dodging AC's for the past six aid stations, and the constant pressure was beginning to take its toll on me, both physically and worse, mentally. In fact, as I approached the Last Chance aid station at mile 43, I felt I would miss the AC and actually referred to it to another runner as my 'mercy killing.' Somehow I managed to make the AC by 12 minutes. I would live to face yet another challenge as I made my way to the checkpoint I dreaded most, Devil's Thumb, a grueling two-mile climb incorporating 37 switchbacks into a 1,600 foot climb.

As I left Last Chance, one of the volunteers offered to pour ice water on my back. I accepted, and the cold literally took my breath away. However, in the process, it gave me a renewed vigor ... a second wind ... a chance to actually *have a chance* to make it to the finish line in Auburn.

6:36 p.m., Devil's Thumb

Astonishingly, the two-mile climb up Devil's Thumb was without a doubt my finest effort of the day. I literally power-walked the entire way—up all 37 switchbacks—without so much as having to pause to catch my breath. Two years ago, I literally stopped at every butt-high rock, stump or ledge and sat to rest. It was almost incredulous to believe that I had been literally dreading this part of the course for the past seven months. I thought as I began my climb at the bottom of Devil's Thumb that this may very well be the AC I miss, thus ending my quest abruptly, having gone less than halfway towards my goal of completing the entire 100.2 miles that comprises the Western States Endurance Run.

Only eight more miles—and a brief spell of running in the dark without light—and I will meet up with Danielle. If I can hold on and make one more AC at Michigan Bluff, I can ride the wave that is Danielle's enthusiasm to the finish line.

9:13 p.m., Michigan Bluff

I made the AC with 17 minutes to spare, which isn't bad considering I just ran the last mile in the dark. I spend a little more time than normal at this aid station, as I needed to change my shirt and socks, drink a little concoction from my drop bag, and gather my lights. Bill provides invaluable assistance, while Danielle's motor is racing as she can't wait to pace me to the next checkpoint at Foresthill School, where we will meet up with Bill and Susan once again and see Al for the first time since he was removed from the race. A volunteer looks at the bottom of my feet and says the blisters on the balls of both feet look menacing. However, I don't have time to hear that now. What do you expect after running in snow, slush and streams (which were unusually high due to rapidly-melting snow in 100 degree temperatures) for over 16 hours?

11:29 p.m., Foresthill School

At Foresthill School, runners are announced as if they were royalty as they enter the checkpoint. Danielle and I are met by our three biggest fans, and I immediately ask to see a medical volunteer to see if my feet can be duct-taped. The volunteer looks at my feet and advises that I not continue. I tell him that is not an option, so he takes out a needle and lances the (many? I can't tell, because I'm not looking) blisters on both feet and tapes them up. After a couple pain-killers and a bite of cold pizza, Danielle and I are on our way for (what I've been told) the 'easy' part of the course. I wouldn't know from prior experience, as Foresthill is where I dropped out of Western States two years ago.

Everything I would be seeing now I would be seeing for the first time. That is, if you can call maneuvering through the great, big, *dark* outdoors via artificial light 'seeing.'

2006 Western States Endurance Run–with Al and Danielle at Mile 62

The Wee Hours of the Morning; Saturday turns into Sunday

Danielle and I make our way through the dark, her spirit as bright as her incandescent headlamp. We manage to dodge AC after AC—some by as little as four minutes—and it begins to wear on my psyche. For the life of me, I just can't seem to gain any significant cushion on the time allowance. Cutting it as close as I was on a course I wasn't familiar with was exhausting. Danielle tells me later that she was using her GPS wrist-watch to determine what point of each leg we were at and how fast we needed to run/walk to make it under the next AC. She would never say anything to me during the race; she would merely pick up the pace. For this—and many other things she did for me during the 12 hours she ran with me—I am forever indebted.

4:30 a.m. Sunday, Rucky Chucky River Crossing

I've heard about the mystique of this part of the race so many times that once I finish this passage, I never want to see, hear or say it again. As the river was very deep (due to the aforementioned melting snow), this year the river crossing was via boat (most years runners have to wade across the river via a guide wire), so it was virtually painless. However, jumping in and out of the boat with feet that felt like soggy sponges wasn't particularly pleasant (the balls of my feet were literally shredding apart due to the continued exposure to moisture throughout the day and night and now day again).

Bill joined us for the crossing, and once again assisted me with a fresh pair of dry socks. I notice him grimace when he sees the balls of my feet ... just before he grabs his camera to get a photograph of them.

Danielle and I have made up a little ground on the AC; in fact, we entered into the checkpoint precisely at the 30 hour cutoff, a full 15 minutes ahead of the AC.

8:06 a.m., Brown's Bar

Brown's Bar is the checkpoint I've been looking forward to the most, not only because it's 90 miles into the race, but because it is in fact sponsored by a bar. And bars have beer, and after 90 miles and 27 hours of water and numerous fluids of the sweet variety, an ice cold beer would sit quite well, thank you. Danielle and I heard loud music blaring in the woods, which was a bit ominous as it was impossible to determine if the checkpoint was right around the corner or a mile or two down the trail. As we approach the aid station, the Rolling Stones' '19th Nervous Breakdown' is playing on the stereo system. Ironically, there were almost that many (17, actually) AC's I had to deal with during the race, and each one was in fact nerve-wracking, so the song was more than appropriate.

As I suspected, there was a keg—of a fine red beer brewed locally. I don't recall the name of the beer, but I'll forever remember the taste. Interestingly, the 'bartender' asked Danielle if my stomach would handle a beer at this point in the race. Danielle answered in the affirmative without as much as a second thought. Good girl. Like I said earlier, forever indebted.

9:11 a.m., Highway 49

Bill and Susan wait at Highway 49, the next-to-last AC I have to face. As was the case with virtually every AC so far, this one was a challenge as well. A long uphill took Danielle and I to Highway 49, and just as we were about to reach the top of the hill the course took a sharp left turn and took us almost another roundabout mile to get us to the checkpoint. Once again, we made the AC, this time by a mere four minutes.

I ask Danielle to run ahead with my water bottles to have them refilled, while I proceed to the next checkpoint. I figure I don't have the luxury to wait for them to be filled as I have up until this point. Danielle agrees, and I head on to the next and final AC at No Hands Bridge, another 3.5 miles down the trail. If I make this AC in time, I am guaranteed a finish, whether I cross the finish line within the 30 hour limit or not.

I've come too far not to finish. Danielle tells me later that two runners we've been leap-frogging throughout the early morning missed the AC at Highway 49 by less than one minute. Both wept openly when they were removed from the race. I understand completely.

A couple hundred yards into this leg of the race, Susan catches up to me with my two water bottles wearing Danielle's pacer number. I find out later that Danielle had a foot injury, but didn't want to worry me with her problems, as she figured I had enough of my own. I felt bad that I couldn't sense her distress, but I admired her courage for the tough 38 miles she had endured with me—mostly in the pitch dark of a moonless night.

Although my feet were literally screaming in agony, I ran this 3.5 mile segment as hard as I possibly could. The next checkpoint was the final AC, and there was no way I was going to miss this one after dodging sixteen bullets up until this point. I remembered everything Gary Griffin taught me on the trails of Pine Mountain, and planned out my next three steps and threw caution to the wind with my trust of the stability of any rocks I may encounter. His advice proved worthy, as I made this final AC at No Hands Bridge by 20 minutes, and found myself actually five minutes ahead of the 30 hour cutoff.

There would be no more cutoffs today. I was going to finish the Western States Endurance Run. I decided to enjoy myself—cutoffs be damned.

9:59 a.m., No Hands Bridge

I'm convinced this course was laid out by the Marquis de Sade. After 97 miles of tortuous passage of repeated ups and downs over tough mountain trail and 17 absolute cutoffs, you just might expect the course to give you a break for your final three miles. Not a chance. The climb to Robie Point was—for me, anyway—practically debilitating. It was all I could do to take one small step at a time, slowly making my way up to the summit. I realized when I ran the previous section as hard as I could that I would have little, if anything left for this final seg-ment. Susan initially had high hopes of me breaking 30 hours, as she repeatedly said I only had a little over three miles to go with an hour to do them. However, I'm not sure I could have covered these last three (primarily uphill) miles in one hour if I was starting *fresh*. They were that difficult!

After reaching Robie Point, there was one more significant climb out of the trail onto the asphalt that would lead me to the finish line at Placer High School. Al and Bill had walked out on the course to join Susan and me for the final mile or so. Danielle would join us later, they said, as she was waiting outside the track, nursing her injured foot. We enjoyed ourselves, and made sure to smile at all of the residents of Auburn who were still lining the sidewalks, encouraging the remaining few runners who had managed to make that one last absolute cutoff at No Hands Bridge. I was damn proud to be—I found out later—the last of them.

Danielle met us about a half-mile from the finish line, and gave me a big hug and apologized for not being able to pace me the final few miles. I told her she had done a terrific job, and she had nothing to apologize for. In retrospect, I'm not sure I could have made it this far without her.

The five of us—Danielle, Susan, Bill, Al and I—entered the track, pausing momentarily so Bill could capture the moment on film. We proudly circled the track to the applause of the many runners, crew members, officials and Auburn locals who were on hand to pay tribute to every last one of us who had made it through the mountains.

11:16:58 a.m., Placer High School Track

For one brief moment, I'm certain time stood still. And after the anxieties, train-ing and self-doubt I experienced about this event over the past two years it well should have. Somewhere out there in the mountains I ran my 103,000[th] lifetime mile. For now, the only mile that mattered ... the only *quarter* mile that mattered ... was right here—right now—on this track in Auburn, California. The end seemed too short ... too sudden ... for what had preceded it. As Danielle, Susan and I crossed the finish line, a volunteer draped a medal around my neck, sym-bolic of officially completing the Western States Endurance Run.

Seconds later, a large television camera was planted in my face and I was sub-jected to a string of questions about the race. I'm fairly certain I answered them coherently, although I can't recall now specifically what they were. I remember telling him about butt-gliding ... where I was from ... how tough the course and the heat had been. What I didn't tell him was that, unlike many others, I had no desire to return in the future.

On this particular day I captured Moby Dick, had won the US Open and proved to be impervious to Kryptonite. There is no need to return.

Western States 2006

Checkpoints–Distance—Elapsed Time–Pace per Split

Checkpoint	Distance	Elapsed Time	Pace per Split
Lyon Ridge	10.5	3:00	17:10
Red Star Ridge	16.0	1:30	16:22
Duncan Canyon	23.8	1:54	14:37
Robinson Flat	29.7	1:53	19:09
Last Chance	43.3	3:54	17:12
Devil's Thumb	47.8	1:32	20:26
Michigan Bluff	55.7	2:42	20:30
Foresthill School	62.0	2:04	19:41
Rucky Chucky	78.0	4:01	15:04
Auburn Lakes Trail	85.2	2:25	20:08
Brown's Bar	89.9	1:21	17:14
Highway 49	93.5	1:04	17:47
Placer High School	100.2	2:07	18:58
TOTAL		**30:16:58**	**18:08**

Beauty and the Beast–Part III

Virtually moments after I crossed the finish line at Western States, I was asked the inevitable question:

Which was harder: Badwater or Western States?

I imagine some who have tackled both have had to give this question some thought, while others—like myself—can answer before the second syllable in 'Western' is spoken.

Consider:

- Badwater is 130 degrees of stifling heat. Western is a variety of dry temperatures ranging from 40 to 110 degrees (the latter incurred during a 'hot' year).

- Badwater is 134.4 miles of blazing hot asphalt through the hottest desert in the country followed by the crossing of three mountain ranges. Western is 100.2 miles of soft, mostly shaded trails through a beautiful mountain range.

- Runners in a typical Badwater field have a completion rate of less than 60 percent. Western's is usually well over 70 percent.

- Badwater's starting field is usually less than 100 runners. Western's is regularly in the mid-400's.

- Badwater has a time limit of 60 hours. Western's is 30 hours.

- Badwater has no official aid stations. Western has fully-equipped, fully stocked, and fully staffed (by some of the finest volunteers in the country) aid stations approximately every four miles along the course.

That being said, unquestionably the more difficult of the two is ... Western States.

While 'on the surface' it may appear that Western States is the easier of the two, for a road-hardened runner like me, just the opposite was true.

At Badwater you could count on the weather being consistent; that is to say (indescribably) hot. At Western, I found myself running through snow two feet deep while thinking I was overdressed in a sleeveless shirt and a pair of shorts. Later in the race, while I was swallowing dust being stirred from the trails in 100 degree heat, it felt as if I were suffocating.

At Badwater I was able to follow one of the basic tenets of my running philosophy: *no thought required.* I knew that after each step my foot would land on soft, solid (albeit hot) asphalt. At Western, each step was a surprise. Will that rock move and cause me to twist my ankle if I land directly on it? Will this patch of mud be fairly firm, or will it swallow me up to my knees? Is that wet pile of leaves going to be slippery and cause me to fall off the side of the mountain? You get the idea. Give me solid, no-thought-required asphalt any day.

At Badwater there is a 60-hour time limit; I finished with almost 23 ½ hours to spare. At Western, I missed the get-your-name-listed-in-the-results time limit of 30 hours by almost 17 minutes. If this alone is not an indicator as to which race I thought was 'easier,' nothing is.

At Badwater, I finished a surprising 6th overall and 3rd place male. At Western, I was the last runner (of slightly more than 200 finishers) to officially cross the finish line. At Badwater, I received a belt buckle—not for finishing 6th, but for finishing under 48 hours. At Western, I received a framed inspirational quote … for finishing last.

Sure, Western offered numerous aid stations as well as incredible volunteer support throughout the event. However, nothing beats having a support crew to provide me with virtually anything I needed whenever I needed it like I had at Badwater. Not having to carry my own water bottle, as was the case in Death Valley, made it that much easier to run (*no hands required,* another of the basic tenets of my running philosophy).

One thing both races had in common: I had the most incredibly proficient, supportive and encouraging crews imaginable. Paula, Gary, Eric, Josh and Al in the desert; and Danielle, Susan and Bill in the mountains. If any of you don't know how important each of you were in crossing these two finish lines, you do now.

You may be asking why this trilogy is called 'Beauty and the Beast.'

One school of thought is that the 'beauty' is the magnificent Western States trail running through the Sierra Nevada Mountains. Another is that the 'beauty' is simply my primary pacer Danielle.

Some—like myself—may refer to the treacherous Western States trail as the 'beast.' Others may consider me as the 'beast,' their reasons known only unto themselves.

Western States: A Pacer's Perspective

By Danielle Goodgion

I am very new into the Ultra running world so having the opportunity to pace Scott Ludwig in the Western States Endurance Run (WS) was not only an honor but an experience I will never forget.

I only began running Ultras this year so it was a big shock when I offered to pace Scott for the last 38 miles of WS and he accepted. Not wanting to let him down, I worked very hard to make sure I was not only physically but mentally prepared. Although I know ultra running is very mental, I didn't realize how much until the night Scott and I ran 40 miles together in the mountains.

Let the journey begin ...

Scott, Al, and Susan all left for California the Thursday before WS. Al was also running WS and Susan would be his pacer.

Because I happen to be from Truckee, the town 10 minutes from the start line of WS, my family and I planned our annual vacation with my parents and we would begin our vacation by pacing and crewing Scott and Al.

Our flight left on Friday and of course was late. We arrived into Reno after 11 p.m., gathered our luggage and drove to my parents' house to sleep for the night and drop off the kids.

Our morning began very early. We woke at 6 a.m., showered and were out the door. The first checkpoint to see Scott and Al was Robinson Flat. The plan was for him to be there by 11:16 a.m., and I did not want to miss seeing him. At this point my job was to be his cheerleader and I was taking my job very seriously. After we left my parents house, I called Susan. She informed me that they made a course change and we didn't need to be to Robinson Flat until around noon. We decided to meet in Truckee for breakfast and then we would follow each other up to Auburn where we would drop off Susan's rental car and all drive together in one vehicle.

Susan told us they both looked strong that morning and seemed very ready for this race. She did mention she was concerned about the heat though. We knew the heat was bad but we didn't realize it would be one of the hottest years in the history of the race.

So off we went. The traffic at Robinson Flat was very congested and I was very nervous we weren't going to make it. Fortunately we found a parking spot and made it just in time for the shuttle bus to take us to the location where we could meet the runners. Although once we got on the shuttle bus it took forever for us to leave because the bus driver was more interested in eating her donut than driving the bus. If you hadn't gathered, I am very impatient and the thought of missing Scott and Al made me even more impatient.

Robinson Flat

This was the first look we had at any of the runners and the time when reality sets in. It was hot and you could not only see it on all the faces of the runners but tell by the amount of runners dropping out of the race. As we sat and waited for Scott and Al, the volunteers would call out the names of people who had dropped. Every time a name was called my stomach would drop just hoping I wouldn't hear "Anyone from the Ludwig crew or Barker Crew?" Then it happened, "Barker crew, meet your runner at Foresthill." Susan and I looked at each other in disappointment. I was actually shocked! Al had spent so much time training and was so prepared. Without actually seeing him yet, of course we had all these things going through our minds. I think most of all we thought Al would be very upset and we wanted to see him. Time seemed to pass so slow, and there was little time remaining until the cut off. I still had in my mind Scott was going to make it … and then he came. OK, I would like to say he was looking awesome and ready to run the rest of the 73 mile course, but he didn't. He looked awful. He looked tired and drained. See, I must explain to you how the rest of the runners looked physically. They were built more like mountain goats; big strong legs with meat on their bodies. Scott is a road runner; he was a little more lean … and he looked BEAT! I believe he describes it as death warmed over.

At that moment, two things went through my mind. First, he is not going to make it (which was the first time I had thought this way since I knew he had made it into WS) and second, and more importantly, I wanted to take care of him. I knew he wanted to finish WS so badly and I knew he would be so disappointed if he didn't. So I did the best I could in the few minutes we had to cheer him up, get him a new pair of socks and let him know we were going to cross that finish line and accomplish his goal.

That next time we would see Scott would not be until Michigan Bluff (55.7 miles) ... if he made it that far.

Bill, Susan and I left Robinson Flat and went off to Foresthill School. We were still all shocked and not really certain what we would say to Al. We were all heart-broken for him. We waited forever at the school for Al. Susan searched every-where for him. She is a good friend and I know she just wanted to make sure he was OK. Finally we spotted him. He had the biggest smile on his face! I think we were all a bit relieved. The heat was too much for him and he didn't make the cutoff. If I remember correctly, somewhere around 25 people dropped at that check point.

Michigan Bluff

Now it was time to wait for Scott. Al was hungry so we drove back to Auburn to get pizza. I was a ball of nerves. I didn't know what to think. I am sorry to say I almost had myself convinced that Scott wasn't going to make it this time. I knew Scott was tough but was he tough enough? Everyone ate pizza except for me (a big mistake). I thought if there was a chance I was going to run, I didn't want my stomach full of pizza. I only ate salad and that wasn't nearly enough. After driving everyone crazy because I wanted to leave to make sure we made it to Scott on time, Al and Susan went back to find a hotel. Bill and I were off to Michigan Bluff. We made it there around 7 p.m. The first thing we did was go to the board which listed the runners who had dropped. NO LUDWIG!!! That was great news and I was so relieved. Since Scott was running behind at Robinson Flat, I thought he may not make it to this point until after 8 p.m. which meant I could begin pacing him there. Bill and I both prepared ourselves to run—except for one thing that I forgot at the car, my Garmin (GPS). While waiting we were able to see our good friend Prince Whatley. That was great! We also made a lot of friends at that checkpoint. One lady was waiting for her husband. She was going to share pacing him with another person. Bill and I found a spot on the trail and waited and waited and waited for Scott. We were able to see Gordy (the founder of WS); in fact it felt like we saw everyone. As it got darker we would head down the trail about a quarter mile looking for Scott. Bill and I actually began making plans for the night. At that point I was almost convinced he wasn't going to make it ... 9:16 p.m. (absolute cutoff was 9:30 p.m.) ... HERE COMES SCOTT!!!! I couldn't believe it! He actually looked much stronger than he did at Robinson Flat. We got him to the aid station and I said "Are you ready to finish this race?" I will never forget what he said; "Will you be with me from now on?" I quickly said, "Every step of the way!"

We finished getting Scott's feet taped–which looked awful at this point–and off we went. I kissed my husband (who was just wonderful the whole time) and said we would see him at Foresthill School, only about seven miles away. With all the excitement and worry of wondering if Scott was going to make it or not, I forgot to actually think about the fact that I was going to run 45 miles, not the 38 that I had expected. I had never run that far but I blew it off and thought I could do it.

The next seven miles were great! Although we had been chasing Scott the whole day, I felt fresh and excited! Scott wasn't as fresh but now I knew he could do it. In fact I remember saying to him, "Cindy was right, you'll finish this race because it just isn't you to not make it." Now remember, I had forgotten my Garmin, so I didn't have a watch to go by. All I knew was I had to keep us moving forward. Scott wasn't ready to run, so for the first part of this section we walked very fast. Then he began to feel a little better; it was cooling down and soon we were able to run for awhile.

Foresthill School

This part of the trail wasn't really that bad, probably because it was just beginning. We arrived at Foresthill School. Bill, Al and Susan were there to meet us. Bill had brought my GPS (I told you, he is wonderful). We had the volunteers re-tape Scott's feet. This time I actually got him to eat some pizza. He seemed to be in good spirits and about 11:30 p.m. we were off to finish the last 38 miles of WS.

We wouldn't see Bill again until Rucky Chucky River Crossing (78 miles). I didn't like that, but it did motivate me to know I would see him there.

As we left Foresthill School, I began to feel a pain on the top of my foot. I had never really had this pain before so I kind of just blew it off and thought "nothing a few 'Advil' can't take care of." We were able to run the first section of the course. It was flat and on the road (this made Scott very happy). This was the last part of the course we would be on that was road ... let the hills begin.

As the hours began to go by, I kept waiting for the trail to get a bit easier. I was under the impression this was the EASY part of the run. Let me tell you it didn't get any easier. We may have been going down in elevation, but the up and down climbs remained difficult.

Scott completely amazed me! It didn't take me long to realize how tough he is. In fact at one point I said to him, "I knew you were tough, but not *this* tough!" We had three checkpoints to go through before getting to Rucky Chucky where Bill would be waiting for us. Each checkpoint we made with limited time to spare. I mean five to ten minutes ahead of the absolute cutoff. Scott didn't know this until after the race, but the Garmin he dislikes so much was the one thing that kept us on track for making the cutoff times (that and Scott's iron will). When we left each checkpoint, I would find out the exact distance and the time we needed to be there. When we were coming close to the cut off time, I would speed up and Scott would follow. I knew how much pain he was in because his feet were in such terrible condition but I also knew he wanted to make it. So I would just try to motivate him as much as I could and keep him moving faster.

Most of the trail at this point was along a mountain side with a very steep drop off to the left of us. With the exception of greeting the runners that we passed or those that passed us, we didn't say much. I could just hear Scott behind me making little grunts of pain when his foot would hit a rock or he stepped too hard. We were trying very hard not to get his feet any wetter than they already were. I don't think they could have handled any more moisture. For the most part we were successful.

Rucky Chucky

It was quickly approaching 4 a.m. and we would soon be at the Rucky Chucky River crossing. I had no idea what to expect but at least I knew we were going to be able to cross in a boat. About a half mile before we reached the Rucky Chucky checkpoint we passed the lady I had met at Michigan Bluff (the one there to pace her husband). Her husband was lying on the ground claiming he was dizzy. Of course I asked if I could help, and she said no—he would be fine. All I could think of at that time is how tough Scott was and how much I wish I could take some of his pain away from him.

As we approached the Rucky Chucky River crossing I could see Bill. I was so excited to see him. Bill is always there to support me through all my races and this one was no different. Not only did he support me but he did a great job of crewing for Scott also. Another thing Scott and I had in our favor was we finally made up some time. We were actually ahead of schedule by a half hour. This was a tremendous relief to both of us.

As soon as I saw Bill and knew Scott was out of earshot, I told Bill my foot was in a lot of pain now. I knew Scott's feet were much worse than mine, but it was my job to keep Scott motivated, which meant I needed to be healthy. My foot was so swollen by this time I had to loosen my shoe laces. Every time I took a step I would stretch it forward to relieve it a bit. Bill and I decided four more Advil would help. So I took them, we crossed the River (this part I did not like), taped Scott's feet again, and off we went.

The next checkpoint we would see Bill was at Highway 49. This was about 15 miles. It was now around 5 a.m. The sun would be coming up soon. We had almost survived the dark. I knew we both would get a boost once we saw the sun. In fact, Scott told me this is the time he usually gets a second wind.

Here comes the sun … We had now remembered it was Sunday morning. We had about 20 miles to go, so at this point we were just out for 'our normal Sunday 20 mile run.' Except we were running a single track trail; not the asphalt Scott was accustomed to running on.

At this point my foot was getting very bad and I knew if I wasn't careful Scott would notice. The last thing he needed was to know I was in pain of any sort. I was also running out of energy. Remember when I said at the pizza place I had made a mistake? That mistake was not to fuel myself properly. I was paying for it now. Scott was also going through a very bad down time. I offered to sing to cheer him up, but he declined–which is probably best. The Sharky Bites he had in his pocket did help a little, though.

The trail never got any easier; we had constant ups and downs and didn't go nearly as fast as I thought we would. We continued to only make the time cut offs by minutes. All the time we had made up at Rucky Chucky we eventually lost. Scott was getting so upset and just couldn't understand why we were always so close. I knew; we simply weren't going fast enough.

Brown's Bar

Finally, we reached Brown's Bar checkpoint. In my opinion, this is the check-point that saved the race for Scott. You see, the whole time we ran together Scott only mentioned a handful of things he wished he had; Diet Coke, popsicles, and beer. I'm telling you if I could have eaten aluminum and pooped out a can of beer I would have. But as fate would have it, I didn't need to ... you see, at Brown's Bar, they had beer. They were trying to push us through that checkpoint as fast as they could. Of course, asking Scott if he needed anything, he asked for beer. They asked me if it was OK, and the look on my face was probably good enough, but I said, "YES! GIVE IT TO HIM!!"

Highway 49

That must have been great beer because Scott got his burst of energy, and we ran for a long time from this checkpoint to Highway 49. This is the spot I knew Bill would be ... this was a very important energy spurt because he only made the next checkpoint by two minutes. Being disqualified with only six miles to go would have been devastating. This was also a very important part of the race for me because my goal here was to pace Scott and this race was not about me. I knew I was not in shape to be pacing Scott anymore. My foot was hurting so badly and my energy was so low that I didn't have enough to give back to Scott. I had maxed myself out on Advil and was starting to limp when I walked. I wavered back and forth; should I have Bill pace Scott for the rest of the race? Will I be letting him down? Then we came around the corner knowing we had very little time left to make the next cutoff and we looked up only to see another mon-strous mountain to climb. I could just feel the expression on Scott's face and he was behind me. I told him "Don't look up. Just follow me." I gave it everything I had to get him to the next checkpoint and as we came down the mountain, I saw Bill and I knew I was done. All I could think was "I'm so sorry Scott, but you need more than me now." The first thing Bill said was "Do you want me to take over?" and I shook my head. Then I looked over and saw Susan. I know how badly she wanted to run with Scott. I told Bill that Susan should finish with him. He said, "Absolutely!" I ran down and handed her my pace number. My exact words to her were "He needs YOUR energy! Get him across that finish line!!" Susan gladly took the pace number and I could see she was so happy to be able to run with him.

Now comes the emotion … As I watched Scott and Susan run up the hill I knew Scott was going to make it. On the other side of me were the three people I saw not make the time cut off. The worst part was they missed the cut off by 15-20 seconds! Once they found out they didn't make it, they would first scream at the volunteer and then they would burst into tears. It was very sad and I just couldn't imagine that happening to Scott.

As Bill and I drove down the hill to the finish line, I was in a fog. I wasn't sure how to feel. I just wanted to see Scott cross that finish line. Honestly, I wanted to be the one to finish with him but I knew I had made the right decision.

Bill wanted to make sure and run from the last check point to the finish line with Scott. We were able to catch up with Al. After talking to Al for a minute, Bill and Al left for Robie Point; the last checkpoint of the race.

As I sat and waited for Scott, the time when by very slowly. I talked to a few people but nothing could keep my mind off the fact that Scott wasn't here yet. It was now past 11 a.m., the official cutoff time for the race, and now I felt like a failure. Scott didn't make it to the finish line on time. All that effort on his part and he wasn't going to finish. I was an emotional wreck. At about 11:10 a.m. or so, I saw Bill come over the hill. I ran, well, limped over to him and just started bawling. I went on and on about how I had let Scott down and kept asking if he was mad at me? He tried to calm me down and told me Scott was in a great mood. He told me he was just happy this would soon be over … and then came Scott. I walked over to him and once again started bawling. I think at first he didn't understand why I was crying and then it occurred to him. He managed to calm me down enough to tell me that he was going to be a finisher; he wouldn't get a belt buckle but he would be an official finisher. He had done it!

One of the most memorable moments at this time for me was that Bill insisted on taking a picture of me with Scott. I was adamant about him not taking that picture. But of course, he did it any way. Now, I am so thankful for that picture. I have it hanging at my desk and in my house; it will forever bring back the best of memories.

The Finish

With all of us together–Scott, Susan, Bill, Al and I–we walked the rest of the way and onto the track. At this moment time almost stopped. As we walked around the track everyone there—and I mean *everyone*—started clapping. Not only did they clap but they whistled and cheered. It was just such an honor to be part of that experience. When we crossed the finish line, a few thoughts went through my mind. The one that sticks in my head the most is that Scott my hove not been built like a mountain goat, he may not have been the fastest runner out there or the strongest physically, but there is not a doubt in my mind that he was the TOUGHEST!!!! He finished in 30 hours and 16 minutes with feet that looked like raw hamburger and never complained once. He went through checkpoint after checkpoint knowing he only made them by a matter of minutes, and he was on a single track trail with 30,000 feet of elevation change when the roads are the only thing he truly loves to run on. I don't know how he did it, but I will forever be impressed with how tough he was during that race.

Once the race was over, we were able to get Scott, Al and Susan back to their car. I hugged them all goodbye and told them to call once they got some rest.

The next morning I logged on to my E-mail and found a note from Gary Griffin. He thanked me for pacing Scott and said something very interesting that made me think. He said he wasn't sure why, but Scott's successes and accomplishments in the running world mattered a great deal to him. I realized then that they meant a great deal to me also. Going through an experience like that with a friend, especially someone you really look up to and admire, and realize that you helped make his goal a reality, is a feeling I will never forget. I am not only honored but very grateful for that experience.

2006 Western States Endurance Run–with Danielle on the home stretch

A Chronology of ALL of my TRAIL RUNS

A Finite History ('cuz there won't be any more!)

Date	Race	Distance	Time	Place of Finish
Jan 1997	Atlanta Fat Ass	31 miles	3:48:40	4th
Jan 1998	Atlanta Fat Ass	31 miles	3:49:53	5th
Jan 2000	Atlanta Fat Ass	31 miles	4:10:23	3rd
Nov 2000	JFK	50.2 miles	8:00:19	56th

Jan 2004	Atlanta Fat Ass	31 miles	4:25:54	3rd
Mar 2004	Oak Mountain	31 miles	8:50:06	68th
June 2004	Western States	100.2 miles	DNF	Completed 62 miles
Aug 2004	Hot to Trot 8 Hour Run	46.3 miles	7:55:00	4th
Jan 2005	Atlanta Fat Ass	31 miles	6:12:56	29th
Aug 2005	Hot to Trot 8 Hour Run	31 miles	5:42:00	Completed 31 miles
Jan 2006	Atlanta Fat Ass	31 miles	5:56:00	23rd
Mar 2006	Oak Mountain	31 miles	7:14:08	52nd
Jun 2006	Western States	100.2 miles	30:16:58	Dead Last
Aug 2006	Hot to Trot 8 Hour Run	43.7 miles	7:55:00	3rd

Scenes from two Western States Endurance Runs: Guess which one I finished?

CHAPTER TWELVE
RUNNING THROUGH THE PAIN

When the mind needs to overcome the matter ...

Don't kid yourself. At times, running is just like love. It hurts.

Not always, but there will be times when you will ask yourself why you are subjecting your body to the physical demands—and occasional punishment—of running.

Let me save you the trouble of finding the answer on your own, and simply tell you that running through the pain makes you a stronger person. Mentally, physically and emotionally, it makes you a stronger person.

For 25 years, I would record any pain and/or illness I was coping with in my daily running log. Once I began training for Badwater in early 2003, I discontinued this practice. After all, by that time it would have been simpler to make entries on the days I *wasn't* coping with any pain.

In this chapter:

- Injuries? Illness? Learn to Ignore Them!—A little 'mind over matter' along with a little encouragement from Dustin Hoffman is all it takes.

- Road Hazards—If you think dogs and automobiles pose the biggest threat to your running safety, think again.

- Starting with a Vengeance (but Finishing with a Whimper)—Common sense calls for a slow start and a fast finish. Unfortunately, I'm fresh out.

- The Magic Potion that is … BEER—Looking for the right fluid replacement drink for what ails ya? Look no further.

- A December to Remember—There comes a time in everyone's life when they have to admit they overextended themselves.

- A February to Forget—Remember that overextension I was talking about? Here are some of the repercussions.

- A February of Retribution—Good things come to ye who waits. One year later, I managed to make up for lost time.

- Date with a Juke Box—If running injuries were judged for creativity and originality, this one merits a '10.'

- To Sacrifice Speed—One last chance for me to prove there's still some gas left in the tank.

- Four Saturdays in October—With the exception of July 2003 (Badwater), October 2006 was the most memorable month of my running career. And quite possibly my life.

Injuries? Illness? Learn to Ignore Them!

'Mind over matter.'

I learned this well before I ever began running. A long time ago, I went to see Dustin Hoffman in 'Marathon Man.' For those of you who aren't familiar with the movie, Hoffman is a marathon runner who—through an unfortunate chain of events—is believed to have some information *(he doesn't!)* that a Nazi war criminal wants. To *get* the information, the former Nazi subjects Hoffman to an unspeakable 'dental torture' that fails to produce any results because (a) Hoffman doesn't *know* anything and (b) Hoffman is a marathon runner, and as he tells us early in the movie, he is trained to block out pain. In other words, dealing with pain is simply 'mind over matter.' I can't begin to say how many times this scene has played out in my mind over the past 28 years.

While any runner has to deal with a variety of 'inconveniences' (this will be our synonym for injuries and/or illness), those who are able to persevere in spite of them (or maybe I should say *to spite them)* tend to be better off in the long run. Believe me; I know what I'm talking about.

I've got an extensive history of inconveniences over the years. In the latter months of both 1979 and 1980 I had a problem with my right knee that just would not go away. I had it X-rayed, injected with cortisone, massaged, and covered with DMSO (a non-FDA-approved numbing agent for large domestic animals. The good news: I found out that it worked well on humans—for about 30 minutes. The bad news: I was running a marathon at the time.). Nothing worked. After running with the problem for two consecutive fall seasons, it eventually went away. It severely limited my mileage on both occasions, but it didn't break my streak; I wouldn't let it. I knew that I had to mentally block out the pain for (at least!) 24 minutes each day (enough time to allow me to run a minimum of 3 miles to keep my streak alive). Keep in mind my streak was just slightly over a year old at that time. A sign of things to come? Absolutely.

In 1982, on my initial run across the state of Georgia, I pulled up lame on the 4th day with—guess what?!—*knee problems!* Hindsight is 20-20, but alternating by running on both sides of the road probably would have alleviated this problem (and the cause of me aborting this run), as the center of the road would have been 'evened out' between my two legs, thus leveling the stress on my knees. On my second (and successful) attempt in 1992, I corrected this oversight and successfully completed the run, managing to block out the subliminal messages my knees were sending to my brain along the way.

Speaking of the run across Georgia in 1992, I had a severe pain in my left shin after completing the run. In fact, I actually had the pain on the final day of the run as I ran into Savannah. I thought it was a stress fracture. The doctor I saw two days after the run thought the same thing, but he wasn't sure. He put my left leg in an air cast from the knee down and (obviously) told me not to run. So for the next three days I (obviously) ran my requisite three miles each day after work. On the fourth day, I ran seven miles—*pain free!* Stress fracture? Probably not. A miracle recovery? Possibly, but probably not. A matter of *willing* the injury away? That's my guess.

In fact, I've learned to get through most of my inconveniences lately by willing them away/blocking them out/ignoring them until they go away/allowing my body to deal with them 'on its own terms.' I don't know exactly what is going on, but I've had a lot of success with it. I don't get sick often, but when I do the only time I feel decent is when I run. I've found that running allows me the opportunity to get some fresh air, to put my body to doing something productive/physical, and to ignore the minor aches and pains affiliated with illnesses like the flu or the common cold. Try running the next time you come down with the flu, and try this sentence out after your run:

That's the best I've felt since I came down with the flu.

My guess is that it will ring true.

At the turn of the century I had two injuries that are still with me today. I pulled my right hamstring in a 50K trail run in January 2000, and 'numbed' my right thigh in a marathon in March 2001. To this day the hamstring acts up when I run on hilly terrain or run competitively at a distance of 10K or less. In fact, in May of that year I ran a 10K and I felt my right hamstring 'pop' on my first stride in the race (this is the race that Stephanie Sudduth mentioned earlier that she won an award and I didn't. But I digress.). Each mile I ran progressively slower, as if my 'running engine' was running out of gas along the course. As for my numb right thigh, it hasn't impacted my *ability* to run, but it sure has taken a toll on my speed, as I've noticed my right foot spends a split second more time on the ground than my left during my leg turnover. That's one of the primary reasons I've turned my attention to longer distances at this point in my running career.

I'm asked all the time if I ever get injured. Obviously, the answer is 'yes.' The normal follow up question then is how I keep my streak going if I'm injured. The answer is simple: I run. Fortunately, most of my injuries are true 'inconveniences' (i.e. not of any major consequence): a pinched nerve in my left shoulder (I ran an entire marathon holding my left forearm in front of my chest—totally still—as it hurt for my left arm to 'bounce'), blisters (on virtually every square inch of both feet at one time or another), bone spurs in the balls and/or heels of my feet, toothaches (these are the worst, as my tooth will 'throb' relentlessly after I finish running; i.e. I can 'feel my pulse' in my bad tooth), and an assortment of aches and pains in a variety of areas (shoulders, back—upper and lower, thighs, neck). As I mentioned earlier, running while 'nursing' these types of injuries allows me the opportunity to turn my attention *away* from them and to something more pleasurable—*running!*

No marathoner or ultrarunner will be successful if they aren't able to run with 'inconveniences' and other aggravations. Of course, this is true for runners of any distance. Face it, folks—*running hurts!* Once you accept that fact and learn to live with it (or as the case may be, to *deal* with it), you'll be better off. Mentally as well as *physically!* Still not convinced? Try it and see. You may be surprised at how tough you truly are.

Road Hazards

(You probably never thought about ... until now)

Dogs chasing after you. Teenagers yelling obscenities at you. Ankle sprains. Blisters. Dehydration. Frostbite. Ahhh ... the joys of running.

At one time or another this (partial) listing of running hazards is sure to come your way—if they haven't already. As a runner, expect them. Knowing *when* to expect them is another story. However, helping you figure out when to expect them is not my intention. Some things you just have to experience for yourself. Angry dogs, volatile teens, physical 'breakdowns,' extreme weather—get used to them: you're a *runner,* for crying out loud.

My purpose is to point out some of the hazards of road running that you probably never thought about. Please be advised that all of these are possible. I should know, because each one is based on first-hand experience. Obviously, I *survived* each hazard, but I can assure you it's quite painful to relate these experiences to you. However, I feel obligated to provide this information so you can take the precautions necessary to stay out of harm's way. In fact, it is my privilege. Just remember—if the information in this article pays off for you down the road, *you owe me one!*

Soda Bottles

Soda bottles are usually seen tossed out of the windows of moving pickup trucks or any pre-1987 model American-made car driven by teenagers. And by 'tossed' I mean 'thrown directly at your head as the vehicle passes you while you're run-ning.' Usually the pre-toss yelling and screaming by the teenagers is a tip-off as to what will soon be coming your way; i.e. an empty RC Cola bottle.

Raccoons

Raccoons are prone to run out from behind trash dumpsters or from an area with thick foliage. More times than not the raccoon has an uncanny ability to run directly between a runner's two (moving) legs so that the runner's legs act as a giant pair of 'scissors,' thereby treating the raccoons as (figuratively) a sheet of paper about to be cut in half. Frightened? You don't know the meaning of 'frightened' (for both you *and* the raccoon) until this happens.

Wire Coat Hangers

Wire coat hangers bent into a circle (in the shape of a noose!) can really tie you up. Literally. Should you get your two feet caught in the middle of the circle, just try to take your normal three-foot stride when the 'noose' will only allow your feet to spread two feet apart from each other. You'd best start learning to break your fall with something other than your nose.

Tripping over something on your run can cause the same calamity. One time I tripped over a slight rise in the concrete (my feet stay *real* low to the ground) and managed—although I don't know how—to move my feet fast enough to literally *run under* my falling torso and run myself back into an upright position. Fear and/or panic do strange things … obviously.

Newspapers

Newspapers lying on the ground—innocently enough—can be a real problem when the ground is dry. Try turning a corner while stepping on a page or two of a newspaper lying open on the ground. Putting the 'plant' foot (for your turn) on the newspaper will cause the newspaper to slide, which will cause your plant foot to slide which will cause your body to—well—*glide* (across the asphalt). Hello, gravel burns.

A Pane of Glass

(Warning: *Pay very strict attention to the following!*) A pane of glass nearly sepa-rated me—*literally*—from the face of the earth. While running (and facing traf-fic) on the shoulder of a two-lane highway as the sun was setting, I happened to glance at the back of an approaching flatbed truck and saw the reflection of the moon in a large pane of glass (were it not for the reflection I would have never seen it) lying flat in the back. Nothing unusual about that—except for the fact that the glass protruded approximately three feet on either side of the truck. Fortunately, I managed to jump off the shoulder of the road and into the bushes as the truck passed by. Considering (a) I was within _two feet_ of the truck's path when it was going to pass by me and (b) the truck was traveling well over 50 miles per hour, had I not literally jumped off the road at that precise moment my run would have been 'cut short' that day. And by 'cut short' I mean 'severed at the waist or thereabouts.'

There you have it: five MORE things to worry about **on the run**. It sort of makes you look at that angry Pit Bull Terrier in a different light. Or the onset of frostbite. Remember, _be careful out there!_

Starting with a Vengeance

(but Finishing with a Whimper)

This is tough—damn tough—to admit, but the first step towards recovery is admission. So let me begin by being up front and telling you: I suffer from premature acceleration (PA).

I realize I'm not the only one out there with this problem, but let me be the first to have the courage to come clean in a public forum. Twenty-five years of racing the first half of virtually every 5K and 10K I entered at breakneck speed, only to hold on for dear life in the second half, is as clean an admission of my problem as any.

But my problem is worse than that. Much worse. Not only does my problem rear its ugly head in marathons, it has manifested in many of my ultras as well. Three stand out:

1995 Strolling Jim 40 Mile (actually 41.2 miles) Run

My wife and I drove the course the day before the race to get an idea what it was like. It didn't appear too difficult, at least not from behind the wheel of a Chevy Astro van. Initially I thought I stood a chance of breaking five hours, so when Cindy met me at the 15 mile mark on her bicycle I had averaged a robust 7:15 pace per (hilly!) mile. Great news, except for one thing: I had literally hit the wall.

To make matters worse, I still had a full 26.2 miles (marathon distance) left. For those of you who have hit the wall at the 20-mile mark of a standard marathon, imagine having an entire (hilly!) marathon left at that point. It was nothing less than horrific.

2000 JFK 50 Mile (actually 50.2 miles) Run

The gentleman providing the preface instructions stated that the first three miles were on an asphalt road, but once you hit the Appalachian Trail (AT) in the fourth mile you were facing 13 miles of single-lane trail, so it was best to be in the position you wanted to be in at that point. Since I wanted to be near the front (a side-effect of my chronic PA) when I hit the trail, I sprinted from the starting line. Mission accomplished. When I entered the trail, I was almost in the top 20! However, there was just one slight problem I had to contend with: I can't run trails. I hopped off the trail countless times to allow faster (trail) runners to pass, and when I left the AT, I was holding on for dear life. The next 26 miles of the course (there's that distance again!) followed a tow path along the Potomac River. Again, I was running marathon distance after (yet again) hitting the wall. Only this time, after these 26 miles, I still had eight miles left on treacherous, rolling blacktop country roads. This one took 'horrific' to the next level.

2004 Western States Endurance 100 Mile (actually 100.2 miles) Run

At the pre-race meeting, I was advised by another runner that the course was 'runnable.' My initial, sensible goal of finishing within the 30 hour time limit was now a distant memory, as I had bigger fish to fry; namely, breaking 24 hours. After all, the axiom everyone was preaching was that you add four or five hours to your fastest 100-miler on roads, and that would be a good indicator of your Western States finishing time. So adding five hours to my 100-mile best of 18:23, I figured a sub-24 was in the bag. I started off wisely by walking briskly to the top of the Escarpment (just over 4 1/2 miles into the race). Then 'sensible' and 'wise' turned into irrational and what-the-hell-are-you-thinking, as I took off like I was running the last couple of miles in a marathon. Hell, make that a 5K. Only this time, I still had over 95 miles left. By the time I reached the Last Chance checkpoint at 43 miles, my knees were in more pain than I could ever imagine. When I met up with my pacer at the Foresthill checkpoint at 62 miles, I had no other choice but to throw in the towel, seeing as my knees were holding a gun to my head.

Over time, I've learned to live and cope with my PA. Part of that is because the years have taken their toll on my body, and maybe to a lesser degree my psyche as well. 'Starting with a vengeance' has been relegated to memory status. Unfortunately, 'finishing with a whimper' is still very much alive and well.

The Magic Potion that is ... BEER

Do you ever get tired of the same old fluids that are served up by race directors with absolutely no imagination or no clue what it's like to drink Gatorade, Powerade, and water–race after race after race? Let me tell you: after a while it just gets plain *old!* As I grow older, I'm more likely to run a 50K than a 5K ... more likely to run for 24 hours than 24 minutes ... more likely, well ... to drink *BEER* than drink water while I'm running.

Sound strange? Keep reading.

I think it first dawned on me in 2003 when I was experimenting with fluids in preparation for Badwater later in the year. I had my usual lineup of fluids (I was experimenting with how *much* to drink, not *what* to drink)–water, Gatorade, Diet Coke and Diet Mountain Dew. After six hours or so, I was absolutely sickened with the thought of drinking anything sweet or anything with no flavor. Surely there was something else out there that could take the place of these fluids; something that would 'kill the sweet.' Unfortunately, I didn't make the discovery until 2004.

At an 8-hour run in August of that year, I put a couple of Coors Lights (my beer of choice) in my cooler to enjoy after the event. However, after running for about six hours, I was looking–once again–for something to kill the sweet. I saw a can of Coors Light peering through the now melting ice and right then it dawned on me: something to kill the sweet! Why not? What's the worse that could happen? Disqualification? Intoxication? Either way, it was better than the nausea that was taking over. Besides, how much harm could one little sip of beer do? None, I found out. In fact, further 'research' showed that as many as *twelve* little sips didn't hurt. In fact, I owe the successful completion of the event to my new discovery ... my new long distance magic potion–beer.

Later that year I found myself running in the 24-Hour championships in San Diego. Naturally, I had plenty of Coors Light (along with my usual lineup of fluids, which now included the mystical Red Bull as well) in my cooler. Somewhere during the wee hours of the event (around 2:00 a.m., if I recall correctly), a man whom I met at Badwater in 2003–Bill Lockton—approached me and asked me what he could do to combat his nausea. I told him of my newfound discovery and he was instantly game–anything to 'kill the sweet.' I showed him my cooler, told him to sit in my chair (the course was a one-mile loop, so runners had access to their support stations every mile), and I would catch him on my next lap to see how he was doing.

After my next lap, I found that Bill was doing just fine. In fact, Bill continued to do fine for my next lap ... and the next ... and the next. Finally on my fifth time around since Bill had popped open that first can of beer, I found my chair empty–which is how I found three cans of beer. *Empty!* Apparently, Bill had taken quite a liking to my choice of beverage.

However, after spending the next five or six laps looking for Bill on the course, I discovered that he had dropped out of the race–at exactly the point on the course where I had last seen him. My chair. Apparently, my magic potion isn't for everyone. Then again, the most I've ever consumed during the course of an event was two beers.

Until July of 2005.

At the world-famous Peachtree Road Race that year–after running it to the best of my ability for 26 years in a row–I decided that I would take it easy for a change. In fact, I called it a 'beer run.' It wasn't difficult to round up others for my 'event.' Paula, Eric, Susan, Billie Sloss (Paula's sister) and her boyfriend Bob– they all wanted to participate. We each wore our official race number as well as handmade bibs with captions such as 'will run for beer' and 'only here for the beer.' Our goal: to consume as much beer as possible–without spending a dime– during the course of the race. We all lined up in Alex Huguelet's (Paula and Eric's daughter) time group corral and took off as one—in search of the magic potion.

It only took a mile until I spotted a portable bar on the left side of the road. After zig-zagging through a dozen runners, I found my way to the side and 'bellied up' (literally) to the bar. I was surprised to find all six of my 'beermates' had found their way to the bar as well. Actually, I was more surprised we didn't knock over any other runners while we were veering off the straightaway that is Peachtree Street. The bartender offered us an entire pitcher, but since no one was willing to carry it, we each (except for Alex, Mom!) took our 16-ounce plastic cup of the golden elixir and continued with our event.

Over the next 5+ miles, we managed to find beer four more times along the course. Where? Well, not at any of the official aid stations along the course, but from the coolers of fans watching the race and doing what most people do at 7:45 a.m. on the 4th of July if they're not running: drinking beer. I noticed our pace for 'beer miles' was approximately 9:15 per mile, while our pace for non-beer miles was around 8:20. After 60 ounces (granted, I did drink a lot of foam–all that running really shakes up a beer), I was surprised to discover that (a) the pain in my legs that I had experienced for the last four months was gone and (b) I crossed the finish line in under 55 minutes (55 minutes is the unofficial time to beat to earn a T-shirt … according to legend, anyway).

While I didn't set any personal bests at Peachtree, I did manage to catch a buzz well before 8:00 a.m. After a typical Peachtree (where I run hard), that doesn't usually occur until about 8:20. So, I guess I did set a personal best after all.

However, this personal best lasted for a total of two months. At the Labor Day 5K in Macon, I managed to beat my previous best by a good 15 minutes, as the race started at 7:15 a.m., I finished at 7:34 a.m. and the beer started flowing immediately afterwards. Good times. And Paula, Billie, Bob and Al were all there to share in them.

Whether it is during or immediately after a race, you can't go wrong with an ice cold beer.

I would be remiss if I didn't mention one last discovery I've made in this discussion of the finer points of running and beer.

After running the 100-Mile Championships in Ohio in September of 2005 (during the competition I was sipping on a Coors Light throughout the wee hours of the morning–in fact, Susan and I were caught by an official of the event and asked 'is that a *beer* you're drinking?' I guess my reply of 'Absolutely' caught him off guard, as we were allowed to finish the race). However, I digress.

After the race, we (Susan, Al, Gary Griffin and his wife Peg–who served as our one-woman support crew) went back to the hotel for a shower and a nap. Later in the evening we went to dinner, where I drank two large Coors Lights on draft. Quickly (I was pretty dehydrated). When we returned to the hotel, I discovered I still had two Coors Lights left in the cooler. Better yet, Peg (a self-proclaimed beer snob) had three bottles of her Labatt's Blue left. So, faced with the dilemma of if getting to be late in the day, an early wake up call scheduled for the next morning, and the possibility of wasting five perfectly good beers, what did Peg and I decide to do? Drink the beer! Once they were gone (45 minutes later), Peg suggested I buy some more.

This is where my latest discovery comes into play. I've discovered that (a) if you run for an extraordinarily long amount of time and (b) become dehydrated while doing so, you can (c) drink as much beer as possible (i.e. without drowning yourself) and not become inebriated. Hard to believe?

Be in San Diego on November 12th for the 24-Hour championship. I'll prove it to you.

A December to Remember

Since I was going to turn 50 in December 2004, I wanted the month to be memorable. I think I was successful. In fact, not only will *I* remember it; I took some of my closest friends along for the ride as well.

I'll start with a duplication of my running log entries (indicating my daily mileage), and then we'll go from there:

Week	Sun	Mon	Tues	Wed	Thurs	Fri	Sat
1				10	10	10	23
2	20	8	8	7	6	50	31
3	20	10	10	10	10	10	21
4	20	10	10	10	13	21	22
5	26	18	10	10	10	31	

First Week–Nothing to Write Home About

An uneventful week. That is until Saturday, when Kelly pushed (pulled?) me 23 miles at an I-don't-really-want-to-run-this-fast eight minutes per mile pace. The weather was cold all week, so all the runs were pleasant. That is, if you don't include Saturday.

Second Week–A Fifty-Fifty Fiftieth

I turned 50 on Friday, so I wanted to do something special—like running my age in miles (since I had done the same when I turned 40 and 45). I tapered during the week, and then at midnight Thursday Susan and John Saunders met me at the Riley Field track to 'celebrate' my birthday. During the wee hours of the morning we were joined by Kelly (3 miles), Al (5), Paula (6), and Prince (18). John stopped at 31 miles and Susan—bless her heart—stayed with me for the entire 200 quarter-mile laps (which took just over nine hours to complete).

I took a short nap (one hour, maybe) Friday and then Kelly and I headed to Tallahassee to run a 50K on Saturday. We stayed with Gordon Cherr and his wife Sherry Friday night, and Gordon escorted us to Wakulla Springs where the ultra was being held. Kelly ran a great race and won it for a second time. Fred Johnson and Kelly ran together for a while (I had no desire to stay with their sub-8 minute pace), and when Fred fell back late in the race I made a valiant effort to catch him, only to have him clip me by four seconds at the finish line. After a quick shower at the Cherr residence, Kelly and I returned to Peachtree City (thank goodness Kelly drove—I managed to get in a 13-minute nap on the ride home).

Third Week–Time to Rest

Sunday I ran 20 miles with Al, Susan and Eric. Eric almost talked me into running another six miles so I could do a 50-miler, 50K and marathon over three consecutive days. I, however, was satisfied with my '50-50' on Friday and Saturday. After all, I *am* 50 now—gotta slow down some. Saturday was an easy 21-miler with Susan (10 miles), Al (14), and Jerry Shoemaker (6), who was on cloud nine after qualifying for the Boston Marathon the week before—after ten years of trying!

Fourth Week–I'm Blaming This on Eric

Sunday I ran 20 miles with Al and Susan. Paula and Eric ran the first three miles with us, and suggested we all do 25 miles on December 25th. Naturally, I was all for it (especially now that my two sons don't make any effort to get up early on Christmas morning; I knew I had more than enough time to run 25 miles, take a shower, eat breakfast, and *then* wake them up). However, Eric had second thoughts and suggested we run '26 on the 26th' instead. Again, I was all for it.

Seeing as I had a four day weekend, I ran 21 miles on Friday with Paula (8), Al (10), and Susan (21), 22 miles on Saturday (Christmas) with Paula (10), Eric (10), Al (20), and Susan (22). During Saturday's run, we finalized our plans for '26 on the 26th.'

Fifth Week–Going Out with a Bang

I had been thinking about the days of the month and what I'd been running—50 miles on my 50th birthday, a 50K the next day, 26 miles on the 26th—and thought how appropriate it would be to end the month (and the year) with yet another 50K by running 31 miles on—you guessed it—the 31st. During our 26 miles on December 26th (actually, Paula did 12, Eric bailed out at 15, Al did 23, and Susan did all 26 with me), Eric mentioned that I should run 31 miles on the 31st. If the thought hadn't already crossed my mind earlier, I would have blown the idea off. However, since someone else said it after I had thought about doing it, I knew it was fate that I would do it. So I made plans, and lined up 'the usual suspects.'

At 6:30 a.m. on December 31st, we decided to run the six 5.2 miles loops that make up the Peachtree City 50K. Al and Paula ran the first loop with me, Kelly the second and third (Jerry joined us as well for these two loops, still ecstatic about his Boston qualifier), Eric and Prince the third and fourth, and John (bless him) all six (although he skipped the half-mile out-and-back the last four loops, so his total was only 29 miles). Where was Susan? In Ohio with her family for the holidays. But she did catch a flight back to Atlanta on January 1st, so she and I could join Darksiders Gary Griffin and George Palmer in Mobile, Alabama for the First Light Marathon on January 2nd. Happy new year to us!

A February to Forget

Whoever thinks that February is the shortest month is wrong. Dead wrong.

Maybe it was payback for my memorable December. Or maybe—just maybe—it is simply a sign to slow down.

Whatever the case, I'm glad it's over. Once you read this, I trust you'll understand why.

I'll start by sharing my running log entries for February of 2005:

Sunday	Mon-day	Tues-day	Wednes-day	Thurs-day	Fri-day	Satur-day
		9	9	11	9	26.2
11	11.5	9	9	9.5	9	12
26.2	12	11.5	9.5	11.5	9	31
23.5	9	14.5	8	8.5	8.5	13
13	9					

Truth be known, January wasn't so memorable, either

I guess I would be remiss if I didn't mention my January performances first (and
they say *February* is an ugly month):

- First Light Marathon (Mobile, AL) on January 2–a 3:54 on a right leg
  that was working at about 70 percent of its normal strength. About every
  two miles I experienced a shocking sensation that ran throughout my
  entire leg and almost caused me to collapse several times.

- Fat Ass 50K (Marietta, GA) on January 8–a 6:12 on a right leg that was
  working at about 50 percent of its normal strength. About every mile I
  experienced the same shocking sensation. Now I have an idea of the sensation a dog feels like when they run up against an electric fence.

- Museum of Aviation Marathon (Warner Robins, GA) on January 15–a
  3:54 on a right leg that was working at about 30 percent of its normal
  strength. My leg felt like it was literally 'dangling' in its hip socket. Not
  only that, my left leg took a beating since it was handling more of the load
  than the right leg.

- Callaway Gardens Marathon (Pine Mountain, GA) on January 30–a 3:52
  on a right leg that was working at about 20 percent of its normal strength.
  About every half-mile I experienced the same shocking sensation. Besides

that, it also felt like I had a metal stake being driven deeper into my right heel with every step.

You'd think I would have had an inclination as to how long (and slow) February was going to be, but not me … the eternal optimist. I just knew my recovery was right around the corner, and I wasn't going to slow down until I found the cure.

The Ugly Truth: Sub-four no more

I started February by running slow and easy, hoping I'd 'recover' in time to run a solid Tybee Island Marathon on February 5. Race morning, I knew I was still hurting, and ran the first 20 miles with Eric. Paula joined me for the final six miles, and by that time my right leg was hurting so bad and I was running so slow that I'm quite sure Paula didn't even work up a sweat … even after finishing a hard half-marathon less than an hour before. My time? Another 3:54 (like a broken record!). The next morning I ran what may have been (up until that point, anyway) the most painful 11 miles of my life.

Undaunted (in my dictionary, 'undaunted' is a synonym for 'oblivious'), I ran the next week slow and easy, hoping I'd 'recover' in time to run a decent Mercedes Marathon on February 13. Race morning, I knew I was *still* hurting, and Susan and I decided to start the race at the back of pack. *Literally* at the back of the pack; even behind the 'balloon lady,' a tiny gray-haired lady who the announcer referenced earlier by saying that runners falling behind her would be asked to leave the course. Then it struck me: *I may not be able to keep up with the balloon lady!* Honestly, I wasn't even sure I would be able to run a step; in fact, Susan and I optimistically anticipated a 5 ½ hour finish. After running the first six miles at a ten-minute per mile pace, we somehow managed to pick up our pace during the race and actually ran a negative split, finishing in what may have been the finest 4:19 in the history of marathoning. Coincidentally, it was the first time I failed to break four hours in a marathon. Ironically, I was happy with it!

The Uglier Truth: It's Getting Worse

Oblivious, I ran the next week slow and easy, hoping I'd 'recover' in time to run a decent Silver Comet 50K on February 19. Race morning, I knew I was still hurting, and fortunately for me, I showed up late for the start of the race (it started in Rockmart, Georgia, which I thought was just outside of Atlanta; I didn't realize it was almost *all the way to Alabama!).* I had planned on running 50K with Prince, who would then turn around and run the next 50K alone (he was going to run the 100K option). He wanted to run a nine-minute pace for the first half of *his* race, and I thought I might be able to do that. Like I said, fortunately for me, I showed up late for the start of the race.

Susan, who was working the finish line, had some time to kill before she had to work. Since the race had officially started 20 minutes earlier, we decided to run out nine miles (the course was 15 ½ miles out and 15 ½ miles back), turn around and come back so Susan could report for duty, and I would go back out on the course, catch Prince and run to the finish line with him. Did I say 'run' out nine miles? I meant 'hobble,' in my case. By the time I caught Prince with five miles to go, I was in pain reminiscent of the pain I felt the day after the Tybee Marathon. Once we crossed the finish line, I still had two more miles to run to get my full—albeit improvised—50K. Prince (wisely) called it quits after 50K. Hell, I must be contagious on top of everything else.

The next morning (Sunday), I walked 3 ½ miles to meet up with Paula, Susan, Eric and Al for our regular Sunday morning run. Almost five hours later, my 23 ½ mile walk/run was over. Remember the day-after-Tybee pain? Well, that was small potatoes compared to the pain I felt the *next* morning (Monday), when I ran and (mostly) walked nine slooow and painful miles. I made an appointment to see my family doctor the next day.

If I mention 'doctor,' you know it's bad

Tuesday was another slooow-but-not-as-painful nine miles. I saw my doctor that afternoon, and he took an X-ray of my right leg and saw a small 'bump' on the shin. He wasn't sure what it was, but said that the bone breaking and piercing through my skin during a run was a definite possibility. Seeing as my doctor knows my running history, he asked if I would 'cut back' (as opposed to 'stop altogether', advice he gave me the first time he saw me) for a while to let it heal … whatever 'it' is.

When I got home that night, I put my 'mind over matter' philosophy to the ultimate test. I just *knew* I could run a pain-free 5 ½ miles. Boy, was I wrong. I *walked* a very painful 5 ½ miles (once I get a distance in my head, I stick with it!). I called Andy Velazco—ultrarunner, friend, and *orthopedic surgeon*—and asked if I could see him the next day.

After walking a gentle eight miles Wednesday morning, I took my X-ray to Andy. He said the 'bump' was most likely an old stress fracture with a lot of scar tissue formed over it, and told me it was nothing to worry about. He also I suggested I walk my daily minimum (which is three miles, although the *Streak Registry* says one mile is enough to sustain a streak) for a while. He said he recovered from a running injury once by biking for a month. Personally, I'd rather knit than bike. So 'walk' it is.

Walking takes (freakin') forever

I decided to walk (although I incorporated enough 'slogging'–a slow jog–to maintain the streak) exclusively for the next ten days, which meant I would run again on Saturday, March 5. I learned a lot during those ten days:

- While your body temperature raises 20 degrees when you run, it does no such thing when you walk. I literally froze the first week because I was dressing as if I was going to be running; I would have been better off walking in my pajamas.

- Running in the rain feels sensational. Walking in the rain just sucks. Next time I walk in the rain I'm taking an umbrella.

- When the temperature is 22 degrees, it is almost perfect running weather. Conversely, when the temperature is 22 degrees, it is almost *deadly* walking weather.

- A decent walking pace for me is 15 minutes per mile. It takes a long time to *walk* just a *portion* of what I ordinarily *run* each day. I spent a long time on the roads and trails during those ten days—about 20 hours (one full day!) to walk (and slog) a mere 96 miles. Did I say 96 miles? I meant *thirty*, Andy!

The Test

Saturday, March 5. 7:00 a.m. I am dressed to run, and anxious to see if my 'rest' paid off. I haven't been this nervous since I ran the Boston Marathon for the first time. For that matter, I wasn't this nervous at the starting line of the Badwater Ultramarathon. Hell, I wasn't even *this* nervous the last time I had blood drawn (if you knew about my fear of needles you'd understand). I walk the first mile to be cautious, and then make my valiant attempt to run. A mere four steps later I realize the rest didn't help; I am still hurt. Around five miles the pain subsided. Perhaps my leg was going numb. Perhaps I am just accustomed to the pain. Perhaps my thoughts of 'mind over matter' were working. But I do know one thing: I am hurt; *seriously* hurt.

I'm pretty sure I was utilizing 'mind over matter' to the max, and managed to eek out 13 miles. As I write these words a mere six hours later, I am considering my options for the immediate future:

- See another doctor, perhaps a neurologist. Maybe a chiropractor (*are they doctors?*).
- Try another 'recovery through walking.'
- Shut up and run.

Whatever I choose to do, I hope something breaks. Figuratively, not literally.

A February of Retribution

'Payback is Hell'

It seems like a lifetime ago—perhaps in a different life altogether—that I wasn't sure I would ever run again. Truth be known, it was exactly twelve months ago, or as I referred to it at the time, my 'February to Forget.'

February 2005—28 days of misery, pain and suffering. The (still) undiagnosed pain in my right leg—a pain that would appear in different spots (knee, ankle, calf) in different forms (one day it would feel like a shin splint, the next day a stress fracture, then the next day a pulled muscle) in different intensities (irritating, aggravating, *unbearable*)—resulted in performances I'd just as soon pretend never happened. My first marathon over four hours ... my slowest 50K ever ... a ten-day experiment of primarily walking—*walking!*—in an effort to repair the damage.

Eventually, after fifteen treatments over a period of two months by a chiropractor, the pain(s) subsided. Perhaps my eventual recovery was the result of his treatments and adjustments, or perhaps it was a simply a matter of time healing all wounds. Most likely, it was a combination of both. Either way, running again was a welcome relief—both literally and figuratively.

The horrid memory of February 2005 is now officially that—a memory. Payback is hell. Literally and figuratively.

The Road to Hell actually began in January of 2006. It was then that I decided on running marathons on four consecutive weekends to run myself back into some semblance of running fitness, beginning with the Callaway Gardens Marathon on January 29. While a 3:29 was not one of my bests, it was a step in the right direction. An age group victory, albeit against limited competition, was encouraging as well. Plus, it was 23 minutes faster than my time at Callaway last year.

The next weekend, a 3:24 at Tybee Island (February 4) was satisfying, although I did struggle a bit at the end. Still, it was 30 minutes faster than my time from last year.

Next was the Mercedes Marathon in Birmingham, Alabama (February 12). A 3:26 on a hilly course in frigid temperatures and windy conditions wasn't bad, especially considering how I struggled to a 4:19 last year. A third place age group finish in a competitive field was a positive sign, considering that for the third week in a row I was running what I considered to be 'comfortably fast'—at this point in my running career, I just don't see the point in 'gutting out' races anymore.

The fourth marathon was in the city of my alma mater, the University of Florida. *Gainesville!* It just so happens that I ran my very first marathon, almost 27 years ago, in this very same place in the now-defunct Florida Relays Marathon. Now, 123 marathons later, I'm back in Gainesville to run the Inaugural Five Points of Life Marathon (February 19). My 3:18 placed me third in my age group in yet another competitive field, and my finishing time was (a) my fastest marathon in three years and (b) 26 minutes faster than my first marathon 27 years ago. Considering I was still running what I considered to be 'comfortably fast,' I was extremely pleased with my efforts over the past four weeks.

It may seem odd, but over the past four weekends it seems I (re)learned how to run the marathon. Each successive week the splits for the two halves of each marathon were getting closer and closer, indicating that I was (re)learning how to pace myself. Each successive week I was putting more focus into running aggressively (competitively) as opposed to defensively (trying to survive). And each successive week, I felt a little bit better once I crossed the finish line.

The best was yet to come. The next weekend I entered the Silver Comet Ultra Run (50K) in Rockmart, Georgia (February 25). Originally I had intended to use the race as a cool down after my four 'comfortably fast' marathons over the past month. Prior to the race I was so relaxed sitting in my car—listening to the rain fall—that I almost fell asleep. Once the race began, I found the weather to be *my kind of running weather*—cold and rainy. I decided I would, for the fifth week in a row, run 'comfortably fast.' However, a combination of the cooperative weather, a wonderful new pair of running shoes (New Balance 901's, if you're interested), and the sudden realization that 'comfortably fast' was making me 'relatively competitive' made me up the ante, so to speak. 'Comfortably fast' quite honestly almost became 'gutting it out.' At the halfway point, my 1:56 indicated that I could possibly break four hours—something I hadn't done in a 50K in over seven years.

At this point in my life, I was convinced there were two running benchmarks I would never reach again: a sub-three hour marathon and a sub-four hour 50K. Suddenly, the latter was a reality. Around the 35K mark, *almost* (gutting it out) became *absolutely*. I was now on a mission. To say my desire to break four hours was 'aggressive' is an understatement. For whatever reason, at approximately three hours into the race, running this race in under four hours now became the single most important thing I could ever hope to do in the twilight of my running career.

I hit the marathon mark in 3:19—just seconds slower than my time in Gainesville six days ago. My pace remained even for the last five miles, and I managed to hold on for a 3:56:59! As I crossed the finish line, I'm pretty sure I didn't tip anyone off as to how I was feeling emotionally. Physically? That's a different story. It was ridiculously apparent that I was cold; soaking wet and quite literally beat to a pulp. It was obvious I had gutted it out, something I thought I would never do again.

Now, how was I feeling emotionally? Absolutely *ecstatic!*

Epilogue. Twelve months after my dreaded 'February to Forget' of 2005, I'm feeling positive and confident about my running again. I am back and gaining my confidence back for the 'home stretch' of my competitive running career.

Date with a Juke Box

As fate would have it, Al Barker and I were selected for a second time (the first time was in 2004) in the 2006 Western States lottery. Al and I entered via the 'buddy system,' which meant we were both either going to get in the race or *not* get in the race. All or nothing. One for all and all for one.

Just prior to the lottery, the Race Director announced that since there were so many applicants for the 2006 edition of the race, there was only a 37 percent chance of being selected in the lottery. I looked at that as me having a 63 percent chance of *not* being selected which—given my affinity for trails—would be just fine with me. Imagine my shock when Al and I were selected as participants in the 100-mile horror through the Sierra Nevadas. Unbelievable—Al and I were now a miraculous two-for-two at being selected in the Western States lottery via the buddy system (our 2004 acceptance into the race and subsequent failure on the trails has been well-documented in the pages of this book). Maybe this will be our year. Second time's a charm, as they say (or at least as *I* say since there most certainly won't be a *third* time).

Now I had to focus my attention on getting ready. Since I don't live near any trails to speak of, I'm fairly limited in my training regimen to adequately prepare for a trail run. Therefore, I focused my immediate attention on specific races of marathon distance or longer leading up to our trip out west: Museum of Aviation Marathon (1/14), Atlanta Fat Ass 50K (1/15), Callaway Gardens Marathon (1/29), Tybee Island Marathon (2/4), Mercedes Marathon (2/12), Five Points of Life Marathon (2/29), Silver Comet Trail 50K (2/25), Shamrock Marathon (3/18), Oak Mountain 50K (3/25), and Strolling Jim 40-Mile Run in early May. Ten events of 26.2 miles or longer leading up to the 'big one' in June.

The one question I keep getting asked: 'How come you didn't run Huntsville's (Alabama) Mountain Mist 50K' (a noted trail run on January 28)? Well, it's because I had a date with a juke box. Let me explain.

At my warehouse, I put together a 101-day weight loss contest (which began on January 3). Since I am the 'man in charge,' I consider it my duty to lead by example, which meant that I felt obligated to win the contest (the winner is determined by the largest percent of body weight lost at the final weigh-in on April 14). Not only did I feel obligated to win, I took the liberty of guaran-damn-teeing all of my employees that I would win. Since I was about to begin a fairly strict diet—which dramatically limited my calorie intake—and was still running 85 miles a week, I felt fairly comfortable doing so.

After the first four weeks, I found myself in second place—a couple of ounces out of first place. Since the contest was shaping up as a battle of attrition, I felt confident of my position. After all, I was a runner—the only one of the 25 contestants that was.

However, my problem is that I don't always consume enough calories to run the distances my training regimen for Western States called for.

I'll be honest: I didn't run Mountain Mist because (a) I understand the course is very technical and difficult, (b) I literally hate technical and difficult trails, and (c) hell, I even hate the flat and easy trails. Besides, I figure the Atlanta Fat Ass in January followed by the Oak Mountain 50K in March will be ample trail running to get me ready for Western. Come June, whatever I lack in trail expertise I'll make up for in blood, sweat and tears (hopefully not in that order). I also didn't run Mountain Mist because I was going to run the Callaway Gardens Marathon that very same weekend.

Susan, Jeff Olive and I made the trip to Callaway Gardens in a driving rainstorm at 5:45 a.m. that Sunday morning. The first half of the marathon was run in a virtual downpour. Fortunately, the second half found the skies clearing up and the temperature staying cool enough to keep the runners comfortable. However, there was a problem with the aid stations—someone had stolen the Gatorade the night before the race. Therefore the only fluid at the aid stations was water. Water—as in 'zero calories.' I was honestly counting on the calories in the Gatorade to get me through the race, as I knew I might be heading for a major calorie deficit without it. Fortunately, I was fine. Unfortunately, I was only fine for the first 18 miles. For the last eight miles of the race, it felt like my legs were literally *eating* themselves (forgive me, but that's the best way I can describe it). I hung on to finish in a modest 3:29 (which was incredibly good enough for sixth place overall).

After the race, the three of us decided to eat at the Pine Mountain Waffle House for a late breakfast. I ordered a waffle and a diet Coke, but midway through the waffle my vision blurred, then came back, only to blur again to the point that I literally couldn't see. Once my vision returned, I told Susan and Jeff I was dizzy (which I was) and that I was going to sleep in the car until they were ready to leave.

A moment later, I woke up with Susan kneeling beside me asking me if I was OK. I told her that I was, and asked her what that loud noise was (it sounded like a waiter had dropped a stack of plastic dishes). She explained that it was me—bouncing off of the juke box.

Apparently after I had excused myself from the table, I took a couple of steps only to literally pass out on my feet, fall face first into the juke box (luckily I hit my chin—not my teeth), landed on my knees and fell flat on my back. Fortunately, we were in a Waffle House so this maneuver wasn't too uncommon to the staff. However, it managed to alarm Susan and Jeff, who seemed genuinely concerned for my safety and well-being.

I slept for most of the 75-minute drive home, and spent the rest of the day 'in recovery' (drinking and eating whatever I could force down). I thought back to the other two times I've passed out after a run: in May of 1979 after completing the Brunswick Marathon in 90-degree heat, and in July of 2003 after finishing the Badwater Ultramarathon and waking up during the night to visit the bathroom. On those two occasions at least I had a substantial reason for passing out—unlike this time, when a simple diet brought me to my knees.

To Sacrifice Speed

In mid-2002, when I set my sights on completing the 2003 Badwater Ultramarathon, I knew that by converting my training program entirely to ultramarathoning, I would be sacrificing not only a great bit of what little free time I had, but any semblance of *speed* I had as well. Today, almost three years after reaching Badwater's finish line at the portals of Mount Whitney and realizing I was right on both counts, I have to ask myself: Was it worth it?

I had two wakeup calls recently. The first was when I looked back over my last 27 marathons (dating back to October 2002) and noticed that I had written in my running log that I had 'paced' another runner(s) in 24 of them. The reference to 'pacing' wasn't like the days of yore (in the 90's) when I was pacing fellow runners to Boston Marathon qualifying times in the 3:05-3:30 range. Theses were more like long training runs with paces ranging from eight to nine minutes per mile; it just so happens that one (or more) of my training partners ran the marathon with me.

The second wakeup call was when a fellow runner who had just qualified for Boston (without my pacing experience) asked me if I was going to run Boston with her in 2006. I told her (a) I didn't think I had a qualifying time and (b) I wasn't even sure what my qualifying time was. Given my love of the Boston Marathon, you would have thought I was kidding in point (b). I wasn't. I did look it up, however, and found that I needed a 3:35 or better to qualify. As for point (a), I actually did have a qualifier (Atlanta, November 2004), but that is irrelevant to this story.

Following these two wakeup calls, I decided that I would run marathons on four consecutive weekends (beginning with Callaway Gardens Marathon on January 29) with a goal of qualifying for Boston in all of them. A secondary goal was to break 3:30 each time, and a third goal was to run a faster time each successive week.

I realize that ten years ago, being unable to qualify for Boston never crossed my mind. It was automatic; so much that I took for granted. At that time, I'm fairly sure I could have run qualifiers on four consecutive *days*. But as the saying goes, 'that was then, and this is now,' And in a world of 'what have you done for me lately,' it was certainly time to see what–if anything–I had left.

Callaway Garden Marathon, January 29. I ran a cautious 3:29, so I met my first two goals (qualifying first and breaking 3:30 second). Finishing sixth overall and winning my age group was a pleasant surprise.

Flashback–Callaway Gardens Marathon, 1999. I paced Nancy Stewart to a 3:10, which qualified her for Boston for the first time, even though in the last three miles of the race, Nancy had to walk occasionally for a total of about seven or eight minutes.

Three months later Nancy was a member of the women's team champion Atlanta Track Club at the 1999 Boston Marathon.

Tybee Island Marathon, February 4. I ran a fairly even pace towards a finishing time of 3:24, achieving all three of my goals (qualifying, breaking 3:30, faster than previous week).

Flashback, Tybee Island Marathon, 1999. I ran my only sub-three hour Tybee in 2:59, winning the men's masters championship.

Flashback, Tybee Island Marathon, 2002. I ran a 3:08, drove back to Peachtree City after the race, and then drove to Callaway Gardens the next morning to run another marathon. I met future Badwater crew member–and good friend–Gary Griffin around the four-mile mark at Callaway, and we ran together the last 22 miles, finishing in 3:22.

Mercedes Marathon, February 12. I ran a solid pace in extremely cold, windy conditions on a hilly course (forcing me to walk for almost a minute around the 20-mile mark) and finished in 3:26. I met my first two goals, although I failed to lower my time from the previous week.

Flashback, Vulcan Marathon (the forerunner of the Mercedes), 1994. My (then 9-year old son Josh) paced me on his bicycle. I ran a comfortable 3:08, and had to push Josh up two hills towards the end of the race–a total of about 1 ½ miles. To this day, it remains my fondest marathon memory, and was the very first time I won an award in a marathon. Correction: it was the very first time we *won an award in a marathon.*

Flashback, Vulcan Marathon, 1999. I ran a 3:05, and successfully defended the men's masters' championship I had won in 1998.

Five Points of Life Marathon, February 19. I ran the best of the four marathons in my favorite city on earth–Gainesville, Florida–finishing in 3:18. Despite finishing 20th overall, I was relegated to a third-place finish in my (apparently pretty competitive) age group. I met all three goals, and was pleased to run my fastest time of the four marathons in front of 'the home crowd' in Gainesville.

Flashback, Florida Relays Marathon, 1979. I ran my first marathon in Gainesville, Florida. My graduate school professor and mentor, Tom Saine, met me at the 18-mile mark to pace me to the finish. When we met, my pace was just under eight minutes per mile. I held on to 'run' the last eight miles at just under 10 minutes per mile, finishing in 3:44. Considering I had only been racing for four months, I was satisfied with the time.

In summary, I realized my conversion to training strictly for marathons and ultramarathons would have its consequences, primarily the sacrifice of what little speed I had left. I also realize there are other factors at work which support my conversion to the 'long, slow stuff:'

- My age (now 51), which has caused me to realize the theorem that runners lose one percent of their speed per year after age 40 may be an understatement.

- 27+ years of running every day, which has taken its toll on my body–especially the 'human shock absorbers' non-runners refer to as 'knees.'

- 101,000+ lifetime miles, which has not only taken its toll on my body, but in the sacrifice of countless hours of sleep. Sweet, precious sleep. (I live by the old adage; I'll sleep when I'm dead).

You may ask if I have any regrets.

The week after the Five Points of Life Marathon, I ran the Silver Comet Ultra Run 50K and finished 4th overall in a time of 3:57–my fastest 50K in over seven years and a Georgia state age group record.

Referring back to the very first paragraph–which asked 'was it worth it?'

I wouldn't have it any other way.

Four Saturdays in October
Tales of Blood, Sweat, and Tears ... and More Blood

October may just be my favorite month of the year. It offers weather any red-blooded runner would die for, nature is busy working its magic, marathon season is right around the corner, and every Saturday offers a plethora of my (2nd) favorite pastime, college football.

What could be better?

Contents

Homecoming

My wife and I were fortunate to get our hands on two tickets to the Florida Gators' homecoming football game against the LSU Tigers, so we headed off to Gainesville the first weekend in October. For me, going to Gainesville is always a homecoming in a sense, as up until the time in my life that I enrolled at the University of Florida, the longest I had ever lived in any one place was three years. As my dad was an officer in the U. S. Navy, he was transferred–from Virginia, to Holland, to Rhode Island, to Hawaii, to Florida–every three years during my childhood. So when I completed my Master's at UF in 1978, it signified the longest I had ever lived in one place in my life (4 ½ years).

The weekend's festivities were terrific; Gator Growl (the world's largest student-produced pep rally) on Friday night and a great win over LSU on Saturday afternoon followed by an evening of food, drink and more football (on television).

Of course, another of my favorite things to do in Gainesville is run. It's always refreshing to run the routes I used to run daily–Lord, has it been almost 30 years?–in the late 70's. When I'm in Gainesville, I always incorporate what was–at that time–my 'long run' route of 5.4 miles into my run, a loop which essentially takes me around the perimeter of the campus. Running in Gainesville is always refreshing, to the point that I can almost imagine being a student in college all over again.

This year I made it a point to run by several places that were significant in my development as a runner:

- **Murphree Hall**–My very first dorm (room 549, no air conditioning, community bathroom). It also served as the start and finish line of my very first streak (not of the consecutive-days-running variety, either) in the fall of 1973. I mention this because even though I was not a runner at this point in my life, I did run very fast for the five or six minutes of this particular 'streak.'

- **Percy Beard Track**–In the spring of 1974 I took a freshman physical education course. We were required to do a 12-minute run that was to be graded. I ran (by my count) 6 ½ laps, although I was somehow credited with 7 ½ laps which earned me an 'A' for the activity. It was my first experience having my laps miscounted. (Later in life I would have my laps miscounted, but it always occurred when the count was in triple digits).

- **Phi Kappa Tau Fraternity House**–In the fall of 1976, one of my fraternity brothers was in the hallway and I noticed he was soaking wet and wearing shorts and sneakers. He told me he had just finished running six miles. I couldn't believe that I actually knew someone who could run that far.

- **Arts and Sciences Building**–in the fall of 1977, I met the two college professors in the Speech Department who would eventually inspire me to run–Tom Saine and Doug Bock. They spoke of a huge race in Atlanta called the Peachtree Road Race that had over 7,000 runners that they someday–somehow hoped to run. I couldn't believe that there was a race with that many participants.

- **Maguire Village**–Cindy and I lived in off-campus married housing during graduate school, and it was here that I began running in the summer of 1978 and started my streak (not of the no-clothes-on-while-running variety, either) on November 30 of that year.

- **Leonardo's Pizza**–I ran my first official race that started and ended at our favorite place to eat. I ran the five mile 'Leonardo Loop' in a resounding 36:32. I thought I was hot stuff, seeing as I ran almost a seven minute pace for five consecutive miles.

- **University of Florida Library**–I met up with the members of the Florida Track Club one Wednesday evening in early 1979 for a quick three mile group run. The other members enjoyed their quick three mile group run. Me? I enjoyed my not-so-quick three mile *solo* run.

- **Percy Beard Track**–The same track where I made an 'A' in Phys Ed was also where I ran my first sub-six minute mile–a robust 5:57. It also served as the start and finish line of my first run of over 13 miles in March 1979, the Florida Relays Marathon. One of my graduate advisors, Tom Saine, met me at the 18-mile mark and accompanied me to the finish. To this day, it is the only marathon finish line my original running mentor has crossed.

Like I said earlier, one of my favorite things to do in Gainesville is run. There's nothing like it–I consider it the running capital of the east (Eugene, Oregon is often referred to as the running capital of the west). Frank Shorter, Marty Liquori, Barry Brown, and Keith Brantley … all have their running roots in Gainesville.

Saturday morning of homecoming weekend I stopped in the middle of my run at Percy Field track to run a lap for old time's sake. It had been almost four years since I ran on a track with speed as my primary objective, so I knew I was in for a rude awakening. Although I was battling a severe case of sciatica from the five hour drive the previous day, I gave it my all for one lap around the track. Once I caught my breath, I was shocked to see my time–one minute and thirty eight seconds. The reason for my shock: my best marathon performance equated to a pace slightly over one minute *thirty-six seconds* … and that was for the equivalent of *105 consecutive la*ps around a track. How could this be? Had I sacrificed that much of my speed in the quest for endurance?

The next morning out on my run, I felt myself drawn to the track once again. I lined up on the starting line and decided–come hell or high water–I was going to run a full mile as fast as I possibly could. I started my chronograph and I was off. The first lap hurt every bit as much as the single lap the day before, but I stuck with the plan of running a full mile. I put more effort into those four laps than I've put into almost anything I've run in the past four years. When I reached the finish line, I stopped the chronograph but opted not to look as it this time; I wasn't sure I could handle any more disappointment

I ran back to the hotel and after a quick shower, Cindy and I headed north to Atlanta. As always, I felt a little sad leaving the city that gave birth to my running career ... a city that was my first real home before we settled in Atlanta.

Postscript

Five weeks later I ran a marathon in North Georgia. It was the first time since our trip to Gainesville that I had reason to wear my chronograph. As I got ready to set it to time my race, I noticed the three digits still displayed on the face:

5:57

Happy Homecoming!

Oh, Deer

It's pre-dawn on yet another cool—almost cold, brisk Saturday morning in October. I'm running with Meghan, a nursing student who asked me to run 20 miles with her in preparation for her first official marathon Thanksgiving morning in Atlanta. We are 12 miles into our run when I notice a fawn lying motionless next to the curb of the road. As we approach it, I fear the worst—its young life has been ended by a two-ton hunk of metal moving 50 MPH. I grimace as we approach what I thought was a lifeless form of one of nature's most magnificent creatures.

Suddenly I am startled; at first by Meghan's sudden shriek, and immediately afterwards by the sight of the fawn rapidly clawing at the ground with its two front legs—its hind legs rendered useless from the impact—helplessly dragging itself away from the road ... away from these menacing humans. After a few seconds the fawn is lying at the base of a street light, frantically panting and gasping as this recent exertion—coupled with the impact of the aforementioned metal—has take its toll on its young, fragile body.

Meghan and I proceed, at first not knowing how we could provide any assistance and then picking up our pace so that we could contact someone who could. We found a Waffle House, where I asked to use the telephone and immediately dialed 911. I provided the necessary information and asked—no, *pleaded*—that someone tend to the fawn as soon as possible. Once I was assured that it would be done, I thanked the waitress for the use of the phone and Meghan and I continued our run, hoping for the best and fearing the worst.

A couple hours after we completed our run, I drove to the spot where I had last seen the deer. There was no trace of it. In my mind a rescue unit had arrived at the scene, calmed the animal, and delivered it to an animal emergency room that was treating its extensive injuries and was in the process of nursing it back to health. Susan Lance–who was a veterinarian in a former life–told me what in all probability had happened to the deer. In my mind, *my* version is the one I chose to believe.

I thing about that morning now and then. I think about the cool, brisk morning–the type of morning when it's not unusual to see a dozen or so deer rambling in and out of the trees. I think about the spot in the road where I noticed the fawn, and the vivid memories and emotions it will stir every time I run past it. I think about what the fawn must have been thinking as it lie there–motionless, helpless, cold and afraid–on the cold, black asphalt. I think about the fawn's mother, and how helpless she must have felt not being able to come to her child's rescue. I think about what ultimately happened to the young creature; *my* version, thank you.

Perhaps I was thinking about all those things exactly one week later as I approached that same spot in the road ...

To be continued ...

A Most Spectacular Fall

It was 5:45 a.m. on a cool, crisp Saturday morning. The trees–illuminated by the moon–bore the brightest array of oranges, reds and yellows that I'd seen in many years. The deer, as is usually the case this time of year, were in abundance, as they floated across the road–usually in 'threes'–right in front of me. I was four miles into my run, and looking ahead to the final nine. It was exhilarating. It was, if I may say so myself, a most spectacular fall.

I never saw it coming. I'd run on this particular road well over 3,000 times since we moved to Peachtree City in 1990. But on this beautiful autumn morning, I tripped over an object imbedded in the freshly-paved asphalt and landed with both arms outstretched (picture Pete Rose as he sides headfirst into second base) and landed flat on my chest. The impact was so sudden and so, well, powerful, that it took me a while to get back on my feet. I laid there on the road, analyzing

in my mind the injuries I had just sustained. Once I stood up, I hobbled over to
the nearest streetlight and saw that I had torn a hole in the palm of my glove on
my right hand. Fortunately, I found no traces of blood on my hands. My right
hip, however, was another story. Initially I found a bit of blood, and when I got
home (after running the final nine miles of course) I found a large hematoma on
my hip (that was literally the size of an egg) centered in the middle of a large
bruise that measured ten inches from one side to the other. I then rolled up my
sleeve, as I knew my right elbow had absorbed quite a blow, and my right sleeve
was saturated with blood. My wife suggested I needed stitches, but I told her I'd
never had stitches in my life and I wasn't about to start now—especially not for an
advanced case of road rash.

Thinking back to that particular fall, it was so impressive I believe the Russian
judge would have given it a solid '9.'

Throughout my running career I've been fortunate to stay on my feet—at least
most of the time. In fact, when I fell on 10/21/06, it brought my lifetime 'falls
while running' total to 7 ½. How do I know my total falls were 7 ½? Believe me,
I realize any fall/injury/illness (well, maybe not illness) jeopardizes my running
streak, so I pay particular attention to where my feet land while I run. That's one
of the (many!) reasons I don't like running on trails. That being said, here's a history of those 7 ½ falls:

- Rex, Georgia (Fall #1)–I got two feet caught in the middle of a wire coat
hanger lying on the side of the road, which took me to the ground in the
same fashion a lasso brings down a steer at a rodeo.

- Stockbridge, Georgia (Fall #2)–While making a 90 degree turn, I placed
one foot on a couple open pages of a newspaper lying on the ground. The
top sheet 'slid' off the sheets beneath it and my foot went right along with
the top sheet.

- Fayetteville, Georgia (Fall #3)–When a friend of mine noticed that I was
running the same 11 or 13 mile route every weekday morning (at any
point in the run, I could tell her exactly what time it was—without benefit
of a watch or chronograph), she suggested that I mix it up a little. The
very next day, I ran through a church parking lot and failed to notice a
speed bump (which was painted black and placed in the middle of a black
asphalt parking lot) that was a good two inches higher than the distance

between my foot and the ground. The next day I was back to my familiar 11 mile route (and still am to this day).

- Sierra Nevada Mountain Range, California (Fall #4)–At the bottom of one of the canyons somewhere around the 50 mile mark of the Western States Endurance Run, I found myself at a standstill (I was tired, sore and almost dehydrated). I backed out of the way of a runner who wanted to pass me, and my feet slid on some wet leaves and I fell backwards, striking my head on a rock. Twelve miles later, I dropped out of the race.

- Oak Mountain, Birmingham, Alabama (Falls # 5 & 6)–In the latter stages of the Oak Mountain 50 K Run, I got a little 'bold' during a couple flat sections of the course and didn't focus on my impending footing as well as I should have. Naturally, I paid the price for it. Twice.

- Sierra Nevada Mountain Range, California (Fall #6 ½)–In the early stages of the Western States, I caught my foot on a fallen tree that I tried to hurdle. I fell forward but managed to break my fall by putting my hand out and grabbing another fallen tree. Although I never technically fell (to the ground, anyway), I did pierce the palm of my hand on the sharp branch protruding out of the tree.

- Peachtree City, Georgia (Fall #7 ½)–You know the story on this one. By far, the most painful and physically damaging of them all.

How do they stack up against one another? Let's look at the chart below (using the 10 point scale with 10 being 'outstanding'):

Fall Number	Creativity	Execution	Body Damage	Total Points
1	9	9	2	20
2	8	7	6	21
3	2	4	5	11
4	10	7	2	19
5	1	7	2	10
6	1	5	3	9
6 ½	7	6	8	21

7 ½	3	9	9	21

If nothing else, this chart gives me something to aspire to: a perfect score of 30.

Down This Road Before

It's 9:00 a.m. on a cool, breezy, Saturday morning in October. Not too bad considering where I'm running–Ponte Vedra Beach, Florida. I'm 16 miles into my planned 20 mile run, but it's starting to get even cooler, an ocean breeze is picking up and I'm feeling terrific. I've still got over five hours before we head to Jacksonville for the Florida-Georgia football game. I've just decided to add four miles onto my route since I've got so much time and everything seems to be clicking on all cylinders.

The first 16 miles took me on a route which was like a second homecoming for me this month (the first being three weeks ago when I returned to my alma mater, the University of Florida, for its homecoming game against Louisiana State University)–a return to the area where I attended and graduated from Duncan U. Fletcher Senior High School. My wife Cindy and I started dating during our senior year, and we've been together ever since.

Several miles into my run and I'm passing what used to be the Royal Palms movie theater. In its day, it was a true multiplex–it had two screens. Cindy and I had our first date there (following a two course dinner–three, if you include the drink at Burger King) on January 6, 1973–we saw a horror double feature starring Vincent Price.

A couple miles later, I pass the tiny Presbyterian Church in Atlantic Beach where we were married on June 18, 1977. I remember it as if it were yesterday–there was a heavy rainstorm right before the ceremony and the power went out, causing us to have an impromptu candlelight wedding service. Between the (literal) heat of the moment caused by wearing a tuxedo in a church in Florida in the summer without air conditioning as well as the (figurative) heat of the moment caused by the anxiety of saying 'I do,' I was (literally and figuratively) drenched.

The miles–and the memories–continue to come and go virtually without either exertion or effort. I'm in a zone–my entire body feels better than it has in ten years, and my mind is picturing memories made from over three decades ago as if they happened three days ago. Hell, three hours ago. Maybe this is what it's like to experience a 'runner's high.'

I run by my old high school, and see the field–now littered with portable classrooms that are still trailers to me–where I ran a 600-yard time trial as a junior and was only beaten by two boys in my class, both members of the cross-country team. (At the time, they were known as 'dorks.' After all, this wasn't the west coast, where it was 'cool' to run ... remember Steve Prefontaine?)

I run by the Dunkin' Doughnuts on Beach Boulevard, where Cindy's father used to buy two dozen doughnuts–at 99 cents a dozen!–every Sunday for us to enjoy. He always made sure to get vanilla cream-filled and vanilla frosted (two of each) for me.

I run by Jacksonville Beach Golf Course where I played most of my high school golf matches. I remember how far I used to hit a golf ball when I was a little, shall we say *beefier* than I am today. Remember, at that time I ate (at least) four doughnuts a week and, other than the aforementioned 600 yards, had never done anything physically which would officially qualify as a 'run.'

I run by the building that Rose's Department Store used to occupy, where I held my first part-time job so that I could afford to take Cindy to horror movies every Friday. I'll never understand why she wanted me to quit; I guess she didn't want my grades to suffer.

I run by Beach Bowl, the bowling alley where I spent more time than I care to remember knocking down pins. Pins that were in the same formation ... time after time after time. Speaking of time, what a waste of it ...

I run by Mickler's Point where Cindy and I used to go to ... er, to get away by ourselves so we could get some serious studying done.

Back to the present. As I said, I'm 16 miles into my run and trying to decide which route to take to add on another four miles. I'm enjoying the weather, floating along effortlessly, and my mind is bouncing around between the past (our high school years at the beach) and the present (the football game this afternoon). Unfortunately, I'm not thinking about the future, the 'future' in this case being my next step.

Before I know it, I'm falling forward–quickly–after tripping over a slight imperfection in the sidewalk, and I can't allow my right hip, still housing a slight hematoma, to strike the ground unprotected. I place my right hand on my hip, and when I strike the asphalt my hip doesn't feel a thing.

My face, however, is a different story. While my right hand (which happened to experience a particularly grisly case of 'road rash') was busy padding the impact of the sidewalk on my right hip, my face was totally unprotected.

The good news: my face broke my fall.

The bad news: my fall broke my face.

My chin absorbed quite an impact. When I got back on my feet, I noticed a small pool of blood where my chin had been a few seconds before. I placed my left hand on my chin, and before I know it my hand is saturated. In blood. Mine.

I place my thumb at the 'point of impact,' and am able to stick it up to the first knuckle underneath–and inside–my jaw. I look down and see that my white shirt is now brandishing streaks of crimson. I run–as fast as I can–until I find a parked car so that I can look in the rear view mirror to see the damage. When I do, I notice a large 'flap' of skin hanging beneath my chin, dripping–almost spouting blood. The front of my white shirt is now a sheet of crimson. I decide to get back home (in this case 'home' being the house of Cindy's brother Don and his wife Diane, who are putting us up for the weekend) as fast as I can. That is to say before I literally bleed to death.

The quickest route home is another two miles, so I figure at the 'panic pace' I'm running, I'll be there in 13 minutes. I'm wrong; it was less than 12. I yell for Don to come out to the driveway once I get to his house. After he … and later Cindy … do what they can to make me presentable, Cindy and I are off to the 24-hour walk-in medical clinic so that I can receive medical attention. I just know that my streak of almost 52 years without a stitch is about to end. Two hours … and probably two pints of blood … later, I'm being sutured by a young female doctor who is quite impressed with the 'depth' of my injury. Thirteen stitches later–the first ones I've gotten in my life–I am free to go. I have doctor's orders not to cheer at the football game this afternoon, as she fears I might tear the sutures loose.

(This reminds me of all the times I've had to visit my personal physician, and the many times he advised me not to run until I was healed/well again. To this day, he believes I follow his advice ... bless his heart).

I try to figure out why I fell–on two consecutive Saturdays–on the drive back to Don and Diane's. I fell both times by catching my right foot on an unexpected rise in the asphalt of less than two inches. I think about my recent bouts with sciatica in my right leg ... and the hamstring soreness I've had ever since Western States five months ago ... and the problems I had extending my right leg over the last ten miles of the Berlin Marathon four weeks ago. Then it comes to me: I'm not lifting my right leg as high as I'm accustomed to. Then I wonder if it's a symptom of old(er) age ... or overtraining (or *under*-training, for that matter) ... or am I truly 'injured?' Whatever ... I'm just sorry the impromptu medical procedure took as long as it did (almost three hours), as I wanted to get another two miles so I would have at least an even 20 miles for the day.

All is not lost, however. At least I have another entry for my *Chart of Falls:*

Fall Number	Creativity	Execution	Body Damage	Total Points
1	9	9	2	20
2	8	7	6	21
3	2	4	5	11
4	10	7	2	19
5	1	7	2	10
6	1	5	3	9
6 ½	7	6	8	21
7 ½	3	9	9	21
8 ½	4	8	10	22

At 22 points, a new standard has been established. That's the least I would expect from my latest fall.

Slowly but surely, I'm turning running into a contact sport.

CHAPTER THIRTEEN
RUNNING THROUGH THE
DATA
Numbers, Numbers, Numbers

Numbers play a significant role in the life of any runner: mileage, pace, weight, pulse, finishing times, splits, lung capacity, body fat percentage, starting times, race dates, etc., etc., etc. Virtually every goal, target or objective you set for yourself as a runner will be expressed in numbers. The results of your training and racing will, in most cases, be expressed in numbers.

I have always been a numbers person; I trust many of you have already made that assumption by now. That being said, the simple fact that this portion of the book has been contained in one chapter shows a lot of restraint on my part.

This chapter explores how numbers factor into my life as a runner, and perhaps how you can use them to factor into yours as well.

In this chapter:

- It Happens Every January 1st—Need to have a game plan to stick to your New Year's Resolutions? Make them public. In print.

- It Happens Every December 31st—Time to get out the scorecard to see how I did.

- Those Restful Holidays—Looking for something to do on those rare days when you don't have to go to work? Run. A lot.

- A Decade on the Darkside—Once I began running with Al Barker, my running went to another level.

- Two Months and a 'Lap around Earth'—The sixty busiest days of my life. Of course, I managed to do my fair share of running.

- The Long Road to 100,000 Miles—100,000 lifetime miles is the second milestone I managed to reach in my running career.

- The Longest Week—What would you get if you ran the seven biggest days of your life in succession?

- Premeditated Moments of Spontaneity—Well, they seemed like good ideas at the time.

- (Averaging almost) 13 for 13—After 13 years, it's time to stop the madness.

The next two articles appeared in the newsletter of the running club I belonged to at that time. Seeing as most of my New Year's Resolutions in the past never made it through the spring season, I decided to put myself on the line by making them public.

It Happens Every January 1st

Every January 1st it happens. No, not another Southern-style serving of black-eye peas for good luck. Well, actually, that *does* happen. And no, not yet another major-league hangover as a result of saying sayonara the night before to the previous 365 days. Well, actually *that* happens, too. What I'm referring to is the inevitable establishment of the upcoming year's (soon-to-be-forgotten) *New Year's Resolutions!*

Obviously, every January 1st I fall into this trap, and without fail, by the onset of spring they are all a distant memory. But this year—1993—things will be different. Why? Three reasons:

- I plan on achieving all of them.

- I am making them public via this article.

- I intend on following up on them in an article approximately one year from today for everyone to see.

That being said, allow me to share my resolutions for 1993:

Lift Weights Twice a Week

I've made this resolution every year since I started running in 1978. So far, I'm 0-for-14. But this year the Ludwig family finally got the weight system dear old dad wanted from Santa Claus. The very same weight system I have always sworn would allow me to actually *keep* this perennial resolution. No more bench-pressing the 75-pound barbell in the garage. From now on, I'm going first class.

Cut Annual Mileage by 20 percent

The last 10 years, my annual mileage has averaged 3,050 miles. Logging 200 miles a month will allow me to achieve this goal (12 X 200 = 2,400). Of course, cutting my distance by 20 percent may have a reciprocal effect on my weight (a 20 percent gain?). And, with the added weight from my increased muscle tissue from my increased weight workouts, I may have a difficult time achieving this one.

Set a Personal Best in a Race of any Distance

Thirty additional pounds (an estimate based on the anticipated results of my last resolution) to my 5'10" frame may make this one difficult. Additionally, I have slowed down in my race times over the past five years. To achieve this resolution, track workouts are implied. Over the years, I have managed to do as many track workouts as weight-lifting workouts. Maybe I can find a 'first-ever' race of a distance of—let's say, 13.5 kilometers or so. This would guarantee a 'personal best' in a race of *any* distance.

Limit Beer Consumption to 288 Ounces

The equivalent of 24 12-ounce beers, or one full case. I make this resolution for two reasons:

I have managed to avoid hangovers for the past six years and have no intention of *ever* having another one.

I hate wasting calories on liquids (everything else I drink has either zero calories or one calorie: diet sodas, coffee, water. A light beer contains 96 calories, by the way).

This should be my second-easiest resolution to keep, the easiest being the next one, which is:

Keep the Streak Going

As January 1st of 1993 arrives, the streak (consecutive days of running) will be 14 years and 33 days. As far as I know, my 'competition,' Ron Hill of England, still has his streak intact (his being 13 years longer than mine), but he remains 11 years older than me. So technically, I *could* eventually catch him

There you have it: my resolutions for 1993. An item of interest regarding the last one: many times I have made the resolution to take a day off from running, thus ending the streak. To date, I have (obviously) always failed to keep that resolution. Maybe this year the streak will come to an end. Wait a minute: I said this year will be different. These resolutions are in black and white, have been made public, and will be followed up on a year from now. I've got to keep them this time.

But then again, there's no one holding a gun to my head.

It Happens Every December 31st

About a year ago I set five New Year's resolutions for myself in black and white in these very pages. Now, 365 days later, it is time to see how I did. Seeing as I'm an ex-teacher (from waaaaaaay back), I will grade myself by allowing a maximum of 20 points for each of the five resolutions for a possible total of 100. Here goes:

Lift Weights Twice a Week

As there are 52 weeks in a year, my goal was 104 weightlifting sessions, right? Well, not exactly. The resolution was phrased as 'twice a week.' Initially, my total of 112 sessions would appear to have met my obligation, but when I examine each week individually, I see that I truly lifted 'twice a week' 39 times. That's 75 percent of the 52 weeks, so 75 percent of the 20 points results in a score of 15. I'm giving myself two bonus points since I lifted more than 104 times (I'm only doing this because I hate lifting weights almost as much as I hate running on a track).

Net Score: 17 points

Cut Annual Mileage by 20 percent

A 20 percent reduction in my last 10-year average of 3,050 miles per year indicates my goal was 2,440 miles. My total of 2,822 is a 7.5 percent reduction, so I only met 37.5 percent of my goal. 37.5 percent of 20 is 7.5 points; however, a great deal of my 'overage' is attributed to (a) my youngest son Josh wanting me to run several miles with him in the afternoon on occasion (I do *my* running in the morning), and (b) running 20+ miles the last eight Sundays of the year with my new training partners, two real mileage monsters (but they know I love it). Since (a) and (b) were uncontrollable and in no way my fault, I'm giving myself five bonus points for being 'forced' into this additional mileage.

Net Score: 12.5 points

Set a Personal Best in a Race of Any Distance

I had my sights set on a 25K in October (a distance I hadn't raced in seven years); however, an unscheduled business trip (of which I go on maybe once every three years) fell on that same weekend and I had to travel to Dallas. I missed the race, but I ran my fastest (and only) training run ever in the Lone Star State. I did, however, pace Josh in several 5K races during the year and he managed to lower his PR *four times*! For no other reason than I feel like it, I'm taking a little credit and giving myself five points.

Net Score: 5 points

Limit Beer Consumption to 288 Ounces

288 ounces equates to 24 12-ounce beers. I'm here to tell you this resolution was a tough one, but I made it! Don't believe me? I have documentation for every single one. I had beers at a Super Bowl party (drinking beer was required), a basketball postseason victory dinner (I was the coach and I deserved it), the first day I mowed the lawn (hot!), while serving as marshal at an LPGA tournament ('look, lady, I think it's out of bounds, and if I think it's out of bounds, by God, it's out

of bounds'), after a Grand Prix race (I would have only had one beer, but *some-how* an extra 'free' pitcher wound up on my table, and I hated to see it go to waste), the day I finished my backyard project that I had started last summer, the day I finished painting my fence (which, coincidentally, I also started last summer), after my Peachtree Road Race practice run and after the race itself (more required beer drinking), during a Van Halen concert (I had 3 beers @ $3.50 each; $5.00 if you wanted them cold), at my 20th high school reunion (not required, but strongly encouraged), on Labor Day (I labored), in Dallas on the aforementioned business (*honest!*) trip (after all it was Lone Star Beer), and at a fellow runner's birthday party (still even more required drinking). Total beers consumed for the year–21! Not only did I meet this goal, *I exceeded it by three beers!* Therefore, I am giving myself three bonus points!

Net Score: 23 points

Keep the Streak Going

The streak lives.

Net Score: 20 points

Note: In the January 1994 issue of *Runner's World* (that I just happened to read on Christmas Day), I discovered the ever-elusive streak of England's Ron Hill was over after 29 years. As my streak is now in its 16th year, it's going to be harder than ever for me to end it. I gave myself an early Christmas present for the year 2008: *a day off!*

Let's tally up the scores of these five resolutions. 17+12.5+5+23+20 = **77.5 points.** When I was grading (back in my teaching days), this would equate to a C+. All things considered, not half bad. What lies ahead next year? That's for me to know and for you to find out (I haven't said that in years; in fact, I think I resolved to quit saying it back in the 6th grade).

Those Restful Holidays

Holidays are the rewards for working 40+ hours a week, 52 weeks a year, over and over and over again. A time for rest and relaxation, right? *Wrong!* Holidays are a time for *running more* than one's ordinary workweek allows, what with all that free time and all, not to mention the additional calories that will be consumed. The following chart shows the mileage I grinded out on the more familiar national holidays; out of sheer curiosity I included my *birthday* mileage as well.

My analysis follows:

Holiday Mileage

Year	New Years	Memo-rial	July 4th	Labor Day	Thanks-giving	Christ-mas	Birth-day	Total	Aver-age
1979	10.3	6.2	6.2	4.3	2	2.5	4.1	**35.6**	**5.1**
1980	3	6	6.2	11	4.8	4	4	**39**	**5.6**
1981	10	7	7.9	11	26.2	7.1	7.1	**76.3**	**10.9**
1982	15.2	9	8.8	6.2	26.2	7.1	3	**75.5**	**10.8**
1983	9	10.5	9	10.3	26.2	7.1	8	**80.1**	**11.4**
1984	8.8	8.7	10	9.5	26.2	9	9.3	**81.5**	**11.6**
1985	9.4	10.2	9.3	8.5	26.2	10.8	9	**83.4**	**11.9**
1986	12.3	10.2	9.6	12	26.2	10	10	**90.3**	**12.9**
1987	11.8	8.5	8.2	8.2	26.2	8.5	6.7	**78.1**	**11**
1988	9.3	8	6.2	8.7	26.2	8.5	8.9	**75.8**	**10.8**
1989	10	9	6.2	8.2	26.2	9	8	**63.5**	**9.1**
1990	9	11	8.2	7	13.1	8	8	**64.3**	**9.2**
1991	8	5.5	7.2	8	13.1	8	7	**69.9**	**10**
1992	7	8.5	7.2	8.3	26.2	7	6	**70.2**	**10**
1993	9.3	6.5	6.2	7	26.2	7.5	6.5	**69.2**	**9.9**
1994	7	11.1	14.2	16.7	26.2	12	40	**127.2**	**18.2**
1995	35	10	11.9	8.2	26.2	15	21.5	**127.9**	**18.3**
1996	9.2	11	7.7	10	26.2	10	10.1	**85.2**	**12.2**
1997	8.7	14.1	8.2	13	26.2	14.5	12.5	**97.2**	**13.9**
1998	11	19.5	12	14	28.7	20	11.5	**116.7**	**16.7**
1999	10	17	8.7	8.1	26.2	11	46.5	**127.5**	**18.2**
2000	11.2	14	11.2	11.2	26.2	12	21.5	**107.3**	**15.3**
2001	15.1	14	11.7	9.2	26.2	15.1	10	**101.3**	**14.5**
2002	12	11	10.2	12	26.2	20	10	**101.4**	**14.5**
2003	20	8	11.2	10	35	17	8	**109.2**	**15.6**

2004	20	15	11.5	11.5	26.2	22	50	156.2	22.3
2005	7	23	11.2	9.1	26.2	13.6	31	121.1	17.3
2006	11.5	31	11.2	13.5	26.2	12.5	7	112.9	16.1
Totals	320.1	323.5	257.3	274.7	673.1	298.8	385.2	2543.8	13.0
Average	11.4	11.6	9.2	9.8	24.0	10.7	13.8	13.0	

New Year's Day

Each year I make a resolution to cut back on my mileage. Most years I fail, some more miserably than others. 'Double digit' days (10 or more miles) on January 1st usually set the 'trend' for the remainder of the year *(high mileage!)*. The last three *single* digit mileage days (1996, 1997 and 2005) were my last *sincere* attempts to cut back. Both failed—miserably. The 35 miles in 1995 was to celebrate a fellow runner's 35th birthday (since they moved into a new age group!). Races of interest of this day were all variations of the Atlanta Track Club's 'Resolution Run:' 5, 10 or 15 kilometers. Fortunately, the races always start around noon, so if you need to get rid of any New Year's Eve 'cobwebs,' you have a little more time to recover than you would a race with an early morning start.

Memorial Day

A day usually reserved for working in the yard (summer's just around the corner!). I've run races of one mile, 5K and 10K. In 1997 I set my one mile P.R., so the additional mileage you see on the chart was part of my 'celebratory run' afterwards. And yes, I intentionally *didn't* mention what I ran the mile in (but it's *still* my P.R.). In 2006 Susan Lance and I began a new Memorial Day tradition by running what we call the 'Tri-County 50K,' a run that starts in Fayette County, passes through Spalding and Coweta, and ends up back in Fayette County.

July 4th

The Peachtree Road Race—28 year's worth! What other race (or holiday) allows you to be well into a beer buzz by 9:00 a.m. while half the field hasn't even crossed the *starting* line yet? Any mileage over 6.2 was my warm up (the post-race beer usually prevents me from doing any warm *downs*).

Labor Day

One of my favorite events is the Labor Day Race (whether it is the 5K or 10K) in Macon (a curse upon the Cobb Classic for infringing on this sacred day with its overblown—and overrated—production). Most years I run after the race—if I ran well, it was part of my aforementioned celebratory runs; if I ran poorly, it was my 'punishment' run. As Macon's starting and finishing lines are not in the same spot, oftentimes I will run to the start either before or after the race (depending on where I left the vehicle). In 1994, Al Barker and I ran back to the start to pick up the vehicle (why the high mileage, you may be asking? Well, we got 'lost' several times. Why? We did if after drinking the better part of a case of beer (historical footnote: 1994 was the last year Macon served bottled beer. In 1995 kegs were introduced, and each year the beer truck seems to leave earlier and earlier. Of course, this could all be my imagination).

Thanksgiving

The Atlanta Marathon, the easiest marathon logistically for me to run, is one of my favorites. I'm able to park right next to the start/finish line (which is also close to the porta-johns as well as the post-race refreshments) and there is no awards ceremony to wait around for (awards are mailed to all winners). I've been a part of it since it made its 'downtown debut' in 1981 (although I had weak moments in 1989 and 1990 and opted for the half marathon). The past several years it's been held on the 1996 Olympic marathon course. In 2003, Prince Whatley did an 8.8 mile warm-up so our total mileage would commemorate his 35th birthday.

Christmas

What better present to give myself than a long run? I really enjoy getting up early Christmas morning and getting my run and shower in before anyone else in the house wakes up (actually, I enjoy that almost *every* day). When Justin and Josh were little, this meant 7:00 a.m. Now that the boys are older, I have enough time to run those two Atlanta Marathons I skipped in 1989 and 1990 before they wake up.

Birthday

Not a holiday, but another day to give myself the gift of a long run. I've run my age in miles when I turned 40 (my birthday is December 10, 1054), when I turned 45 (note: I ran a little longer than 45 miles as I forgot to factor in the 1 ½ miles I ran with my dog Magic), and when I turned 50 in 2004 (50 miles—200 laps on a track!). I've also accompanied two other runners when they turned 35 and 40, respectively. I'm considering converting to *kilometers* when I turn 55 in 2009.

Summary

My most prolific holiday? Thanksgiving with a 24.0 mile average, thanks to 24 Atlanta Marathons. My 'rest' holiday? The 4th of July with a 9.2 mile average, thanks to 28 straight Peachtree's (10K) and the early-morning beer fest afterwards. Also, over the past 28 years, I noticed I've raced on virtually half the holidays. It's interesting (to me, anyway) that my average holiday run is 13 miles. My average daily mileage over the past 28 years is slightly over 10.2 miles, so my holiday runs are (on the average) 27 percent longer than my average run. Don't ask me what I do on my vacation days—you don't want to know.

A Decade on the Darkside

High mileage has been the norm for me for the past ten years. It all began when Al Barker, Valerie Reynolds and I started running 20+ miles every Sunday so that we would be in year-round marathon shape 'just in case a marathon broke out.' Over the next decade, marathons (and runs much longer than a marathon) did in fact break out. A lot. Actually, a *whole* lot.

In my younger days (well, maybe not necessarily *younger* days, but before my legs had over 90,000 miles on them), I had some semblance of speed. In fact, I had a pretty good stretch of eight years (1994–2001) where my 5K and 10K times were fairly respectable. However, in 2001—once I set my sights on completing Badwater in 2003—my focus was on running long … running slow … and running even longer … and slower. In July of 2003, Badwater became a reality. My speed, however, had become a distant memory.

The chart below tracks my 'decade on the Darkside.' From left to right, the chart includes for each 'Darkside' year my total mileage, average miles per day, number of days with 10+ miles, my best 10K performance, my best 5K performance, total number of races, total number of marathons, the total number of ultramarathons, the total miles in actual races, the average distance of all races, the highest mileage month, and the lowest mileage month.

Year	Total Miles	Avg per Day	10+ Days	10K Best	5K Best	Total Races	Total Mara.	Total Ultras	Racing Miles	Avg Race	High Month	Low Month
1994	4649	12.74	260	36:14	17:48	30	6	0	265	8.8	501	267
1995	4744	13.00	307	36:45	17:24	33	7	1	351	10.6	450	302
1996	4404	12.03	256	36:56	17:45	38	6	0	327	8.6	407	293
1997	4628	12.68	284	38:00	18:14	30	7	1	324	10.8	434	324
1998	5402	14.80	335	37:12	17:55	30	10	3	468	15.6	538	364
1999	4630	12.69	313	36:52	17:46	26	8	0	296	11.4	425	352
2000	4644	12.69	287	37:55	18:04	29	9	2	394	13.6	424	349
2001	4777	13.09	315	37:38	18:02	24	9	1	337	14.0	449	341
2002	4586	12.56	289	38:13	18:45	22	9	2	449	20.4	409	324
2003	5037	13.80	284	39:47	19:40	22	9	6	673	30.6	473	374
Total	47501	13.01	2930	36:14	17:24	284	80	16	3884	13.7	538	267

While the total mileage remained consistent from year to year, a noticeable decline in my 5K and 10K speed is apparent. Once I began training for Badwater in the summer of 2001, my focus was more on running long than running fast. Obviously (just look at my 5K and 10K 'bests' in 2002 and 2003). These slower times are best explained (actually, maybe 'justified' is a better word) in the column showing the average distance of all races: 20.4 miles in 2002 and 30.6 miles (indicating my 'average' race was an ultra) in 2003. As I stated earlier, the emphasis was more on (long, slow) distance than speed.

I've been wondering how I would recognize when my 'fast' days would officially be a memory. To do that, I've devised the following formula:

When you can't run a 10K at the same pace you ran your marathon PR, your racing career is over.

My marathon PR that I ran what seems like a lifetime ago reflects a pace of 6:26 per mile. Holding that pace for a 10K translates to a time of 39:58. Now looking at my best 10K in 2003—39:47—shows that I have just about run out of speed. It appears the time is right to focus on what I've always done best: run long and if that doesn't work, run even longer.

This makes sense. I figure I have a better shot at breaking 18 hours for a 100-miler than I do at breaking 18 minutes for a 5K. I have serious doubts I will ever see another sub-three hour marathon. Trying to run four-hour 50K's has replaced attempting to run a four minute mile.

Thinking back to the early years of running on the Darkside, I remember running marathons in just over three hours and thinking of them as nothing more than a tempo run. Today, I can't envision running a 3:00 marathon in absolute top condition (although I'm not sure what that means anymore).

This year I'm going to stick to the resolution I've made for the last ten years: cut back on my mileage. I've developed a plan to reduce my annual mileage by 10+ percent. On Mondays, Wednesdays and Fridays I am limited to 'single digits' (i.e. less than 10 miles); on Tuesdays and Thursdays I am allowed anywhere in the range of 10–13 miles; and on weekends, I can run whatever I like. One thing I won't give up is my weekly 20-miler (ordinarily reserved for Sundays). After all, you just never know when a marathon—*or more*—might break out!

These days I find I'm really enjoying the longer distances. It's probably a good thing, as the memories of 18 minute 5K's, 37 minute 10K's and three-hour marathons seem more remote with each run.

I've given in to the fact that I will never run as fast as I did a short time ago. Actually, 'short' is a misleading adjective. It may have been a short time ago with respect to *time*. However, *distance* is another story.

Besides, I realize now that I can attribute the end of my racing career to a disease I've acquired—anal glaucoma. What is anal glaucoma? Essentially, it means that I just don't see my ass ever running fast again.

Two Months and a 'Lap Around the Earth'

The sixty-day period between September 10 and November 8, 2004 was exhausting. Eight out-of-town trips, 24,798 miles (about the length of the equator) of traveling (which required 82 hours of sitting in an airplane or a car), and 836 miles of running. I went through so many time zone changes (not to mention the one hour 'fall back' on October 31), I'm still not sure my body has adjusted.

Friday, September 10–Saturday, September 11

Destination: Gainesville, Florida to attend the University of Florida's opening football game (614 miles via car).

Memorable Run: a 10 mile run in White Springs at 7:00 a.m. Saturday morning. Hot, humid, and numerous encounters with dogs.

Memorable Events: A one hour delay during the football game due to 'electricity' in the air followed by a trip to JC Penney after the game ... to buy some dry clothes (after sitting in a driving rain for the entire second half).

Monday, September 20–Saturday, September 25

Destination: Stuttgart, Germany for a business trip with Porsche (9,346 via airplane).

Memorable runs: An 11 mile run to see King Ludwig's castle in Ludwigsburg on Tuesday (followed by a nine hour flight), and a 20 mile run through the countryside in Asperg on Friday.

Memorable Event: Sitting in the front row at a rock concert in a German night club the night before the flight back to Atlanta, then running 10 miles on two hours sleep in a driving rainstorm the next morning.

Saturday, September 25–Wednesday, September 29

Destination: Portland, Maine for a business workshop with a one-day stop in Virginia Beach to visit my parents (2,050 miles via airplane).

Memorable Runs: A 10 mile run Sunday at 5:30 a.m. in Virginia Beach, and a 21 mile run on Wednesday in Portland, Maine.

Memorable Event: Catching lobsters on a lobster boat (and then not being able to eat them for dinner that night–it's tough to eat something you saw alive earlier in the day).

Thursday, September 30–Tuesday, October 5

Destination: Salt Lake City, Utah to run in the St George Marathon and take a short vacation at the Sundance Resort in Provo (3,168 miles via plane)

Memorable Runs: The St George Marathon, where I paced Paula–who was in excruciating pain due to the neuroma in her foot the entire race, although she never complained.

Memorable Event: Getting my wife Cindy to take her first trip to this event (it was my sixth time at St George) with me.

Saturday, October 16

Destination: Birmingham, Alabama to participate in Porsche's employee 'Track Day' (276 miles via car).

Memorable Run: A 12 ½ mile run at 6:00 a.m. in Peachtree City before driving to Birmingham. I wanted to get there early enough to attend a product seminar–against the wishes of my oldest son, Justin, who was going with me–since 'one lucky winner' from those attending the boring-as-hell seminar would receive a BOSE home entertainment system ('you'll never win, Dad').

Memorable Event: getting a test ride in the Carrera GT, and hitting a top speed of 145 MPH–achieved in a ¾ mile straightaway.

Monday, October 18—Wednesday, October 18

Destination: Ontario, California to visit a Porsche facility (3,798 miles via airplane).

Memorable Run: A 10 mile run Wednesday morning in a driving rainstorm on streets and sidewalks that were not designed to handle the conditions (imagine running in an ankle-deep puddle … for 10 miles).

Memorable Event: Being caught in a two-hour traffic jam to make the three mile trip to the hotel on the first day–as there was a potential 'jumper' on a bridge over I-15 (note: he didn't).

Monday, October 25—Wednesday, October 27

Destination: Detroit, Michigan to attend a convention (1,198 miles via airplane).

Memorable Run: Running nine of my 14 miles on Tuesday on a treadmill (prior to that I had a total of eight lifetime miles on a treadmill).

Memorable Events: Experiencing shin problems after running on a treadmill, and learning that the University of Florida had fired its football coach, Ron Zook.

Friday, October 29–Sunday, October 31

Destination: Jacksonville, Florida to attend the Florida-Georgia football game (574 miles via car).

Memorable Run: Running in the Pumpkin Run 5K through Evergreen Cemetery in Jacksonville on Sunday (where Cindy's Grandparents are buried).

Memorable Events: Watching the Georgia band spell 'Georgia' with the 'R' after the second 'G' at halftime, and showing up for the 7:00 a.m. race (as it was advertised in the newspaper) at 6:30 a.m. only to learn that the race was actually starting at 8:00 a.m. (I spent the extra time doing a nine-mile warm-up through the cemetery).

Thursday, November 4–Monday, November 8

Destination: San Diego, California to compete in the 24 Hour National Championship (3,774 miles via plane).

Memorable Run: 24 hours Saturday and Sunday around a one-mile loop on the San Diego coast.

Memorable Events: Running with Susan Lance for approximately 17 hours. She was absolutely phenomenal in her first run (a) over eight hours long and (b) over 41 miles long–she covered 107 miles and competed the entire 24 hours. She finished in 5th place, ahead of many 'favorites' including two-time Badwater Champion, Pam Reed.

Aftermath

I'm exhausted, but the Peachtree City 50K is this weekend, and as Race Director …

After the Aftermath

The Peachtree City 50K is now history, and it went extremely well (although there were a few extraordinary circumstances to contend with–a runner who tripped, fell and had to be taken by ambulance to the emergency room–a runner bitten by a dog–a large tree falling less than an hour before the start of the race directly across the path of the course).

However, the time to rest will have to wait for another day. After all, right now I have to hook up my new BOSE home entertainment system.

The Long Road to 100,000 MILES

When I crossed the finish line of the 2005 Atlanta Marathon on Thanksgiving Day shortly before noon, it signified an achievement I had focused on for over ten years—my 100,000[th] lifetime mile. From the time I began my streak on November 30, 1978 until the day when I ran my 50,000[th] mile in the spring of 1995 (having averaged 8.3 miles per day up until that point), I didn't realize *how* focused I was until I did the math and determined I averaged 12.9 miles per day for my second 50,000 miles.

2005 Atlanta Marathon–Celebrating 100,000 miles with Paula

Having made the same New Year's Resolution every year since the early '80's, maybe now is the time to make it and actually manage to *keep* it: cut back on the miles. At this point I have no short or long term running goals, with the exception of one day owning the longest consecutive-days running streak in the world. In the short term, there's not much I can do about it except to keep on plugging. In the long term, I've just got to stay healthy, focused and motivated to keep doing what's become a normal part of my daily routine—at this point no different than waking up or brushing my teeth. Sure, I have the occasional day when I'd prefer *not* to run. But those days are few and far between—about once every six months or so. However, no matter how I feel when I *begin* my run, once I'm out there, it's hard to quit. I've found the saying 'the first step is the hardest' is one of the absolute truths in the world (of running).

Looking back over my training logs, I determined which days I hit the 'stepping stones' (10,000 miles, 20,000 miles, etc.) along the way:

Stepping Stone (Mileage)	Year (Julian day of the year)	# days to run latest 10,000 miles	Average miles per day during this period	Anything of Significance?
10,000	1983 (39)	1531	6.5	No
20,000	1986 (104)	1161	8.6	No
30,000	1989 (147)	1139	8.8	No
40,000	1992 (260)	1208	8.3	No
50,000	1995 (117)	953	10.5	No
60,000	1997 (194)	808	12.4	No
70,000	1999 (190)	726	13.8	No
80,000	2001 (170)	711	14.1	No
90,000	2003 (204)	764	13.1	Yes (1)
100,000	2005 (328)	855	11.7	Yes (2)

1.   *I hit 90,000 miles somewhere during the second day of the Badwater Ultramarathon. Where? I'm not sure, but it was somewhere in the desert.*

2. *I hit 100,000 miles (exactly) as I crossed the finish line of the Atlanta Marathon. It would have been Magic's 14th birthday.*

Time will tell when (more likely, *if*) I will hit 200,000 miles. One thing I do know is that when I ran the Friday after Thanksgiving, I was over halfway there.

The Longest Week

Did you ever wonder how far you would have run if you took the farthest you've ever run on seven individual days and added up the miles? Probably not.

Did I? Given my propensity to play around with numbers, I'm sure you already know the answer to that question.

But I took it a step further. I made a game of it.

The game is called *'The Longest Week.'* You play by taking the longest runs you've ever completed that began on seven different days. Some runs may be less than 24 hours in duration, while some may be longer. However, the total *time* spent running these seven events cannot exceed 168 hours (the equivalent of an entire week). Add the total miles. Highest total mileage wins.

Here's how I did:

Year	*Event*	*Duration of Run*	*Miles*
1988	Atlanta Track Club 24 Hour Run	19:31:10	101
2002	USATF 24 Hour Run	24:00:00	129
2003	Badwater Ultramarathon	36:32:46	134.4
2003	USATF 100 Mile Run	18:23:18	100
2004	San Diego 1 Day Run	24:00:00	111.4

2005	USATF 100 Mile Run	21:32:34	100
2005	San Diego 1 Day Run	24:00:00	114.4
TOTAL	**Seven Events/Seven Days**	**167:59:48**	**790.2**

How would this measure up against some of the better ultra runners in the United States? I'm sure the truly talented 24-Hour runners in the country—Roy Pirrung and Kevin Setnes immediately come to mind—would probably total somewhere in the neighborhood of 1,100 miles if they played *'The Longest Week.'*

Then there is always Yiannis Kouros, arguably the finest ultra runner on the planet. In 2006 Kouros—the man who lapped me about 30 times on the 1.091 mile lap used at Olander Park for the 2002 USATF 24 Hour Run I included in my total above—recently ran a world-record 644 miles in only *six* days. Six *consecutive* days.

Guess he's playing his own game ... *'The Longest DAY.'*

Premeditated Moments of Spontaneity

I've been prone to Premeditated Moments of Spontaneity (PMS) my entire life ... those things you decide to do that initially seem like a good idea when they first run through your mind. But then in retrospect—once you get to actually analyzing them and (heaven help you) actually *doing* them—you've got to ask yourself what the hell you were thinking in the first place.

For example, I decided to play organized football for the first time when I was 13 years old-and weighed 137 pounds–to impress a girl. Since the league weight limit was 135, I spent hours in the sauna before each game sweating off the extra pounds so I could play just one series of downs (in a 56-0 blowout) all season long. The girl, by the way, fell for our starting halfback after our second game.

Or when I decided that the best way to impress a girl during my senior year of high school as by shooting spitballs into the back of her head during a varsity basketball game. That girl, by the way, ended up marrying me.

The point is I don't always think things entirely through before I choose to do them. Some wind up having a happy ending (Cindy), while others–like I said earlier–make me ask myself what the hell was I thinking. Obviously, as running plays a rather prominent part in my life, I've had more than my share of PMS in that arena.

Running with the Florida Track Club in 1978

After being a runner for all of a month, I thought I was ready to run with the big dogs. Roughly a quarter mile into a three-mile group run, I realized the field was distinctly divided into two groups, them and me.

The 1979 Brunswick Marathon

My first marathon ever, the 1979 Florida Relays Marathon, was my first time to say 'never again' after a marathon. Two months later–in a moment of impulsiveness–I drove to Brunswick, Georgia to run in my second marathon, which offered the following: 41 runners, 31 finishers (I was 29th), two volunteers, one aid station (at the turnaround) and 90 sweltering degrees of heat and humidity. To cap it off, if offered my first up-close-and-personal experience with exhaustion and blacking out. Appropriately, this was the last time the race was held.

1982 Georgia Crossing–Attempt #1

The ultimate in 'sounding like a good idea at the time.' After being motivated by another runner who ran the length of the state of Georgia fro north to south, I wanted to be the first to run the state from west to east (Columbus to Savannah). After completing 159 of the 280 mile route in four days, I cried 'uncle;' or should I say my knees did? I didn't realize how much damage running on the gradual slop of only one side of the road (facing traffic) for that long would do on my knees. The hobbling I did for the next month afterwards was a constant–and considerable reminder.

The 1988 24-Hour Endurance Run

The event, the National Championship, was one I thought would be right up my alley. Since it was in my home town of Atlanta, Georgia, how could I not participate? My 101 miles met my pre-race objective of 100 miles, but it could have been better had it not rained throughout the evening. Cindy took two of the three pairs of running shoes I was alternating to a local Laundromat to dry them. The good news is they were returned to me dry as bone. The bad news is the shoes were a bit smaller than they were when I wore them earlier in the evening. A couple of days later, black toenails were in vogue.

The 1990 New York City Marathon

For the first ten years of my running career, the New York City Marathon was a dream of mine. When I finally found my place on the starting line on the Verrazano Narrows Bridge in 1990 in my first–and what will be my only—26.2 mile jaunt through New York, I was totally intrigued by the crowd of 1,000,000 spectators lining the course. In fact, I was so inspired, I slapped hands with so many of the fans during the first hour of the race that my right arm was sore for days afterwards. As for it being my 'only' New York City Marathon, I wasn't particularly thrilled being treated like cattle as we were moved from one corral to another prior to the start of the race.

The 1991 Georgia Long Distance Relay

When I was asked to be part of an eight-runner ream for this event, my mind must have focused on the fact that it consisted of running 120 miles on the desolate roads of North Georgia. My mind must have blocked out the part about it being (a) a relay and (b) running through the mountains. I say that because (a) relays have no place in my running world and (b) I hate running up and down mountains. However, never being one to say 'no' after I've committed to something by saying 'yes,' I participated in the relay which called for me to run three legs of approximately five miles each. As I didn't want my legs to get stiff between well-*legs*, I decided to run one with each of my seven teammates. At least I got 50 miles out of my weekend in the mountains–my two days of hell. Did I say 'hell?' That was simply short for Helen, Georgia, the site of the event.

1992 Georgia Crossing—Attempt #2

I made two mistakes when I first tried this ten years earlier: (1) the aforementioned problem with running on one side of the road, and (2) not getting rid of the detailed maps and course description (hotels, convenience stores, fast food establishments) after calling it quits. That left me with no choice but to try it again. Fortunately, this time the run proved to be a success. Unfortunately, I discovered that running with (alleged) shin splints afterwards while wearing air casts on my legs is very uncomfortable.

Running on Vacation

Vacation from work never means a vacation from running. In fact, chances are you'll find me running more miles than usual on vacation than when I'm taking care of my normal work and family commitments. After all, chances are good I'm *eating* more. From a PMS perspective, two vacations stand out. (1) On a group ski trip to Sarajevo, Yugoslavia, my only route for running took me dawn and back up the mountain on which we were staying. My first trip down, I was stopped by Yugoslavian soldiers stations as the base of the mountain who thought I was a spy. (2) On a cruise on the S.S. Norway, I found myself adrift as sea for over 24 hours at a time. To keep the streak alive, I had to run on the 'jogging deck' which was, if I remember correctly, 98 lengths to the mile. I wore out a pair of shoes making over 4,000 U-Turns that week …

Weekday Running

For well over two decades, during the week I have *finished* my daily run (normally 8-12 miles) by 6:00 a.m. Obviously, that means an early bedtime (9:30 p.m.) and an even earlier alarm (between 2:30 and 3:30 a.m.), which pretty much puts me in a totally different time zone than my family and friends. The pros? It's never too hot, there is virtually no traffic to contend with, and starting each day with a run just makes me feel good all day long. The cons? Getting out of a warm bed on a really cold and/or rainy day, having to jump-start your day with two strong cups of coffee, and, of course, the aforementioned early bedtime. Regardless, it is now habit, and my personal slogan is:

At 4:00 a.m. the roads are all mine!

(Any and all) Trail Ultras

As I've run 14 trail ultras, chalk up another 14 cases of PMS to my resume. I simply have no business on trails. Why do I say that? Here's what happened at a 50K trail run on Kennesaw Mountain, conducted under the auspices of nationally-ranked trail runner Janice Anderson:

- As I have stated (many times) before, I hate trails.
- I don't personally know of any trails.
- The race was held on the trails of Kennesaw Mountain (did I mention I hate mountains, also?).

- I've never run on Kennesaw Mountain.

- Janice's pre-race directions were simply 'run the 7.75 mile loop four times.'

- I didn't know the 7.75 mile loop.

- Janice added that the 7.75 mile loop was marked in chalk, and that you can't get lost if you follow the arrows.

- It rained precisely as the race began at 8:00 a.m.

- All the chalk immediately washed away.

- I was forced to follow Janice–who is part mountain goat–on the 7.75 mile loop.

- I stayed with her for 30 miles, at which point Janice began sprinting to the finish.

- Not wanting to get lost on that final mile–and yes, I realize I had already run this particular mile three times–I sprinted after her.

- I pulled a hamstring in the process of sprinting after her.

- If I failed to mention it earlier, I hate trails.

Oddly enough, I finished in third place.

2005 Debbie Reynolds 20-Miler

As Al, Susan and I were planning on running in the 24-Hour Championship in San Diego, we thought it would be a good idea to do a long run during the night as part of our preparation. We chose to do it after we attended a concert by Debbie Reynolds at the Peachtree City Amphitheater. So after Ms. Reynolds finished 'rocking the house,' the three of us laced up our running shoes around midnight and headed out to the local track. Eighty laps and 200 minutes later, we called it a night. Literally.

Considering all three of us exceeded 100 miles at the event in California, we considered the preparatory run as a critical element of our respective successes. To this day, Al, at the time 60 years young, is the only runner I personally know who has both run a sub-five minute mile in his younger days and run over 100 miles in 24 hours at age 60. That's quite an accomplishment! (From a personal standpoint, I like to think of myself as the only runner who has completed Badwater and made a hole-in-one playing golf).

2003 Badwater Ultra Marathon

The ultimate case of PMS. The instant I watched the documentary "Running on the Sun," chronicling the 1999 edition of the event, I knew that one day I would find myself traversing Death Valley and crossing that finish line on Mount Whitney. I *knew* it! Premeditated and spontaneous? Absolutely!

Beginning a Consecutive-Days Running Streak

To say my consecutive-days running streak is a result of PMS isn't far from the truth. It just so happens that back in the day when my streak hit 50, 100 and 200 days I would wonder when it would come to an end. In the back of my mind, I couldn't see any reason for it to end, other than the simple fact that I didn't want it to turn into an obsession.

Now that I dodged the 'obsession' bullet and the streak has become my habit, my daily run is no longer related to PMS. It is now simply the way it is. I've been fortunate for the last 28 years not to have any major injuries or illnesses that were significant enough for me to end the streak. Actually, if they *were* significant enough, a small injection of PMS is all it would take to keep the streak alive.

That being said, you may question whether or not there is an end in sight.

Not on your life.

(Averaging almost) 13 for 13

When I first became a runner, I was—in my estimation—pretty conservative with my daily mileage. In fact, over the first 15 years of my running career (1979—1993), I averaged a mere 7.9 miles per day. I was pretty much a 5 and 10K kind of guy, sprinkling in a couple of marathons a year. Occasionally I would even stretch myself and run an ultra.

Back then, it was cool to run fast times. It was cool to wear fancy running shoes and clothing. It was cool to let everyone know that you were, in fact, a runner. It was cool letting others see you doing what so few can honestly say they enjoy doing—*running!*

But that was then ... before I knew better. Before I realized there was more to running than just being 'cool.' Before I crossed over ... to the Darkside.

The past 13 years (1994—2006) have made me realize that I have become a purist of the sport. I no longer aspire or desire to run fast times; getting to the finish line is all that matters. I no longer care about fancy running shoes and clothing; if my feet don't hurt, and I stay warm in the winter and cool in the summer, I'm content. I will not tell you that I'm a runner (if you don't already know) or tell you *about* my running (unless you ask me directly); but then again, I've always been that way (if your audience is not sincerely interested, then believe me— there is nothing more boring to talk to them about than running). On most days, you will never see me running (unless you're one of the two or three other runners I see in the morning well before the sun comes up).

I run because I enjoy it. It makes me feel good. It makes me think more clearly. It's the perfect way for me to jump start my day. After 28 years, I can't imagine my life without it.

However, after averaging almost 13 miles per day for these past 13 years, I believe it's time for me to drop it down a notch.

For the past 13 years, I have become a victim of the numbers game. If I needed to run an extra two or three miles at the end of a week to reach 100, 110 or 120 weekly miles, I found myself doing just that. The same could be said to finish off a 400, 450 or 500 mile month, or a 4700 or 4800 mile year. Many years I would set annual mileage goals, and 'load up' on the front end of the year to ensure I would reach the goal, only to find myself in overdrive at the back end of the year and exceed the goal by two or three hundred miles.

But it didn't end there. If a fellow runner were to suggest running an unusual distance of, let's say 31 miles on the 31st day of a given month, the power of suggestion replaced my power of reason and I would do it. Or if the group run for Sunday was planned to be 23 miles, and everyone in the group opted for a shorter distance because we ran a taxing workout or race the day before, my mind would be set on 23 miles so I would run the distance without their companionship.

However, as 2006 drew to a close, I think I may have finally conquered the beast that is the numbers game. During the first week of November I totaled my mileage and determined that if I averaged 14.28 miles a day for the remainder of the year, my average for these last 13 years would be an even 13.0 miles per day. That didn't seem too difficult; after all, I averaged 14.8 miles a day for the entire year in 1998. However, I made every effort not to fall prey to the numbers game, so I didn't add up my mileage for the next eight weeks. Subconsciously, I could sense how far I was falling off the pace that would lead me to the magic '13.0 average.' Consciously, I was not going to add up the miles until after midnight on the last day of the year, when 2006 turned into 2007 and all bets were off.

I stuck to my guns, and sensed that I needed to run somewhere in the vicinity of 90 miles or more on December 31, 2006 to attain a 13-year total of 61,724 miles, which would have made my daily average an even 13.0 miles. I ran 24 miles that day, satisfied that I was no longer a victim of the numbers game.

On January 1, 2007, I added up my mileage and calculated my 13-year average to be 12.991 miles per day. Lucky for me I didn't add up the mileage 24 hours earlier, as I would have discovered that I only needed another 40.8 miles—a distance that I most likely would have ran—on December 31 to bring the average up to an even 13.0.

But for the sake of argument, I'm rounding 12.991 up to 13.0. The beast is dead.

For now, anyway.

Year	Total Miles	Avg per Day	10+ Days	10K Best	5K Best	Total Races	Total Mara.	Total Ultras	Racing Miles	Avg Race	High Month	Low Month
2004	4758	13.00	256	40:49	20:58	19	6	8	571	30.0	485	328
2005	4638	12.71	279	43:41	19:35	21	9	7	633	30.1	435	342
2006	4787	13.12	291	48:23	19:55	20	9	7	587	29.3	448	343
13 Year Total	61684	12.99	3756	36:14	17:24	344	104	38	5675	16.5	538	267

Note: This chart is a continuation of the one found in 'A Decade on the Darkside.'

Chapter Fourteen
Running through the Finish Line
Why Stop Now?

Now that two of my three milestone goals have been achieved (100 marathons and 100,000 miles, but I'm still several hundred short of reaching 1,000 races), what lies ahead?

Before I look past today, I'd like to reflect on a few things from these past 28 years ... Things I've learned about running. Beliefs I've developed about running. Things I've accomplished in running. Things I want to pass on to you, the reader, so you can learn from my successes, my failures, and most of all my experiences. Things that I firmly believe will help you promote and develop our sport in the years ahead.

At the end of this chapter, I'll let you know my plans for the immediate future. Who knows—you may be a part of it!

In this chapter:

- Addiction, Obsession or Passion?—It took years of analysis to determine the boundaries of my affection for the sport.

- Running's Theory of Relativity—If there's one thing I've learned in 28 years of running, it's to keep my mouth shut.

- Keeping It All in Perspective—Like I said before, if there's one thing …

- How Far is 'Far'?—A college fraternity brother of mine once ran six miles without stopping. I couldn't believe it.

- These are a Few of My Favorite Things—Running movies, running books, running coaches (on second thought, scratch that last one)

- Rewards for a Runner—Running to lose weight is just the beginning.

- Strange, but Absolutely True—Insights from inside on the mystery and mystique of running.

- The (Ill)logic of a Runner—Strong passion = Irrational thinking.

- Please—Not ANOTHER T-shirt!—If you ever considered being a Race Director, please read carefully. If you're already a Race Director, here's what your customers are thinking.

- These Things Really Bug Me—Pet peeves … all related to running.

- The Ten Commandments of Running—Feel free to have them etched into a slab of marble.

- Christmas Gift Ideas for the Runner—When you're tired of giving the runner in your life socks.

- Proud Moments—Individual accomplishments that have meant the most to me in my running career.

- Lifetime Achievement—Some things take a lifetime to achieve, but believe me: they're well worth the wait.

- In Summary …—A chronology of my life as a runner.

- A Running Resume

- Where Do I Go from Here?—Believe me, I'd like to 'retire to the couch,' but I just don't have it in me. Yet.

- Epilogue—Sharing a bond with the reader.

- Acknowledgements—I couldn't have done it alone. Any of it.

Addiction, Obsession or Passion?

I've been accused of being addicted as well as obsessed with running. *Am I?*

To answer that question, a little research is in order.

- An *addiction* implies doing something habitually or excessively.
- An *obsession* is a persistent, disturbing preoccupation with an idea or feeling.
- A *passion* is the object of one's affection or enthusiasm.

That being said, let's see how each one stacks up on its own merits.

My running is not necessarily a habit, but simply a part of my daily routine, no different than brushing my teeth or washing my hair. I do it every day–without fail and without question. The thought of not doing it never crosses my mind. To me, a habit is something you do uncontrollably, like grinding your teeth or biting your fingernails. *Excessive?* Although I do tend to overdo my running at times (in terms of mileage), running every day is–for me–not excessive. Most people don't think twice about brushing their teeth twice or more a day; to me, the same applies to running.

Is my running an *addiction?* Doubtful.

I begin every day with run. After that, do I think about it *compulsively* throughout the day? No(t usually). Am I *preoccupied* with thinking about running throughout the day? No(t usually). Are my thoughts about running *disturbing?* No(t really, unless you count Badwater).

Is my running an *obsession?* Unlikely.

Running has always been a source of enthusiasm for me. I'm often asked if there are ever days I don't really want to run. I answer honestly; about once every six months I wake up without the desire to go outside and pound the pavement. Thankfully these days are few and far between. However, most days I find myself ending a run much sooner that I wish I had to. After 28 years, the enthusiasm is still there. So is my *affection* for the sport. I can't imagine my life without it.

Is my running a *passion*? By now, you should be able to draw your own conclusion.

Running's Theory of Relativity

Over the years I've become very familiar with two universal truths in the sport of running:

1. Runners like to talk about their accomplishments.

2. No matter how impressive you believe your accomplishments are, there is always someone one step ahead of you.

In most cases, when a runner (for lack of a better word) boasts of their accomplishments, another runner one step ahead of you is usually within earshot. Lord knows running is humbling enough already; it doesn't make any sense to put yourself in this type of predicament!

One of the basic tenets of running is that you DO NOT discuss your running unless you are asked a direct question about it (i.e. 'How many marathons have you run?'). If you simply answer the question with the facts, it isn't boasting and therefore you will not subject you to any embarrassment if there is a runner 'one step ahead' of you within earshot–like in the following example:

Joe is in the locker room after running his 22nd marathon. We know this because he is not bashful about telling everyone within earshot this is so. A runner from one corner, obviously tired of hearing Joe boast about his 22nd yells out that it was his 45th, then a runner from another corner shouts out that it was his 67th, and then yet another calls out that he just ran his 84th, As fate would have it, Norm Frank was in the locker room. Who is Norm Frank? Only the man with the most marathons in the world!

If memory serves, this particular marathon put Norm Frank's marathon total somewhere in the high 600's. This exchange actually happened following the 1999 Chickamauga marathon. What really impressed me was that Norm, who heard every word spoken in the locker room, said nothing. Not a single word. Norm Frank … as humble as the sport is humbling.

Now remember, if you asked a direct question about your running accomplishments, reporting the facts will not subject you to an embarrassing moment. There is absolutely nothing embarrassing when, after someone asks your best marathon time, you reply '3:02', and a runner nearby says his best is a 2:53 (of course that runner just put himself in the 'Joe Territory,' as there may be someone within earshot with a faster time than his who may want to chime in). Your best course of action is simply to turn to this runner and say something like 'that's terrific' or inquire where he ran that time. Of course, asking 'who asked you' is also acceptable …

Here's another I was involved in this past spring:

My wife and I were timing the running events at my son's high school track meet one afternoon. Another husband and wife team (both runners) was also timing, as was one other gentleman. The other gentleman (who had a son on the track team) was talking to this other couple about how poor his son's running form was. He went on to say that his son got his form from his 'old man' (HIM!), and went on to say (with his chest out) how, although his form was poor, it got him through 20 years of running and carried him through a marathon (as in 'a'–SIN-GULAR!–marathon). He added that training for the marathon was the 'hardest month of work he had ever done.' Obviously, he was quite impressed with himself.

I had my back to them the entire time, as I was timing a runner. Then the wife said to this gentleman that if he wanted to know about marathons, he should talk to me (of course, I acted oblivious to the entire exchange). She then asked how many I had run or had I lost count. Naturally, I turned around and asked 'how many WHAT?' When she said 'marathons,' I said '90.' (I HATED that it was such a round number, as it almost sounded like a lie) I WANTED to add that I would run my 91st that coming Saturday, my 92nd the FOLLOWING Saturday, and my 93rd next month at Boston. But I didn't. Remember, only answer the direct question, which was 'how many marathons?'

The gentleman said nothing. Not one word. Norm would have been proud of me.

Keeping It All in Perspective

The Much-Anticipated Sequel to 'Running's Theory of RELATIVITY'

'No matter how impressive you believe your accomplishments are, there is always someone one step ahead of you.' Apparently the runner I met at the airport on the Sunday before the 2003 Boston Marathon didn't believe this adage. He should have.

I arrived at the gate for my flight to Boston about 90 minutes early, well ahead of Paula and Al who were on the same flight. Another runner (wearing his Chickamauga Battlefield Marathon shirt) sat across from me and asked if I was by chance 'going to Massachusetts.' At this point he would have been better served to keep quiet. However, as I didn't appear to be *much* of a runner– wearing a short-sleeved button down plaid shirt, khaki shorts, and white tennis shoes–he must have felt 'safe' to proceed with his inquisition and/or ill-fated attempt to impress me.

Following is the exchange he and I shared. In parenthesis and italics, I have added what I could have said and/or added, but that would have added insult to injury. I only added it to reinforce Running's Theory of Relativity. We'll pick up the conversation after I replied 'yes' to his 'going to Massachusetts' icebreaker:

Anonymous Runner: So, are you all set to run the 'big 26' (miles) tomorrow?

Scott: Yes. *(Actually I'm running the course twice tomorrow; from finish line to Hopkinton and then the marathon at noon. So actually I'm ready for the 'big 52.')*

AR: This will make 39 marathons for me. (slight pause, as I didn't respond) How many will this be for you?

S: As a matter of fact, tomorrow will be my 100th marathon. *(Actually, it would be more than that, but I've been on a two year countdown to make this Boston my 100th marathon, so I've had to skip several marathons the last two years that I ordinarily would have run.)*

AR: This will be my 6th Boston, though. (another pause) How about you?

S: My 10th. (*The last six of which have been in a row.*)

AR: I just moved here a year ago from Las Vegas. I've done a lot of marathons out west. One of my favorites is the St. George Marathon. All downhill!

S: Actually, it's got a significant uphill around eight miles.

AR: So you've run it?

S: Four times. (*I matched my PR there as a matter of fact*) My friend, Al, who will be here shortly, has run it 10 times. We're both running it this year.

AR: The Las Vegas Marathon is a good one. Ever heard of it?

S: I ran it in 1994. Al ran it also. (*Personally, I hate that marathon. Boring course, too much exposure to automobile fumes, unimaginative course layout. I wouldn't recommend it to anyone!*)

AR: I'll bet you never heard of the Top of Utah Marathon.

S: Al ran that one. Another downhill marathon.

AR: There are a lot of marathons out west. There doesn't seem to be as many out here.

S: Actually, there are six in the state of Georgia alone. That's six you can do every year without ever having to 'leave home.'

AR: You can't do them all, because two of them are on the same weekend.

S: But they're on different days: Tybee Island on Saturday and Callaway Gardens on Sunday.

AR: Like someone would actually do that …

S: I've done it every year but this one. I had to skip Callaway to allow Boston to be #100. (*And believe me, all my friends made me feel like such a weenie!*)

AR: I just ran a marathon three weeks ago. In Macon.

S: Al and I ran it, too.

AR: I also ran one in Warner Robins in January. In fact, I placed in my age group, because the overall master's winner was pulled from my age group which allowed me to receive an award.

S: That was me. (*Actually, Kelly and I ran the race together as a training run. We were just shooting for a sub 3:20. Kelly was the 3rd place female and I was male master's champion—not bad for a training run.*)

At this point Al and Paula showed up at the gate. After a round of introductions, Paula, Al and I engaged in small talk. Notice, I didn't include 'Anonymous Runner'–he was pretty quiet after our exchange. Finally.

How Far is 'Far'?

'Far' is a relative term. Although it means basically the same thing ('a considerable distance') to everyone, what defines 'a considerable distance' varies from one person to another. In this case, one *runner* to another.

As I approach the 28-year mark of my running career, I've gone through an evolution of 'far' as it applies to me personally.

The first time I ever ran any kind of prolonged distance was in June of 1978. I was in graduate school at the University of Florida, and several of my classmates and I accompanied two of our professors (both runners) to an educational seminar (translation: beer bust) in Atlanta. One of the professors asked me to run with him in Piedmont Park. He wanted to run six miles (six repeats of a one-mile loop). I ran the first mile, then realized I needed to rest. I joined him every other loop for a grand total of three miles. My first exposure to *distance! (What's really odd about my first three miles was that my _arms_ were sore the next day—they weren't used to the movement associated with running. My legs, however, were fine.)*

Later that summer I—more or less—became a runner. At first, I'd run two miles around the married housing complex where Cindy and I lived. I eventually started running 'long' on Sundays: a run around the entire perimeter of the University of Florida! That's right, 5-point-4 miles! Without stopping! In fact, one day in the fall of 1978 I ran 13 miles—to win a bet from this same professor! *(Unfortunately, I spent the next two days never very far from a bathroom—my stomach was torn to shreds!)*

After buying our first house in Atlanta in 1980, I started running *really* long every Sunday: 10 miles! Again, *without stopping!* I distinctly remember how much I enjoyed watching the New York Marathon (when they still televised the entire event live) on that special Sunday in the fall, feeling very content that I had already completed *my* long run. After all, 10 miles is pretty far! What's another 16.2?

In the mid-1980's I began running every Sunday with my first real training partner, Ed Rush. Ed was slightly older, slightly taller, and slightly heavier than I was (15 years, 7 inches, and 100 pounds, respectively), but he (and I) really enjoyed our long run—all 16.2 miles of it. Ed and I regularly ran the Atlanta Marathon and the Jacksonville Marathon (when it was still held in January) for several years. We both felt we were accomplished distance runners, having run 16.2 miles almost every Sunday and all. Without stopping.

After moving to Peachtree City in 1990, I ran without a training partner for several years. Eventually I began running every Sunday morning with Bill McBride and Bob Trombly, both who were a decade older than me and both incredibly fast. Every Sunday would turn into a battle between the two of them, with me caught in the middle. It was common to run our 15+ mile course at a 6:40 pace, which for that distance was almost my *race pace!*

In the fall of 1993, I began running on Sundays with Al Barker and Valerie Reynolds (and a revolving-door group of several others). The regular Sunday route for this group was 13 miles, but Valerie and I quickly altered the route to make it 17 miles. Before long the Sunday run evolved to 18, then 19, and finally 20 miles. 13 years later, Al and I are still devoted to our 'Sunday 20.' Occasionally, however, there are slight deviations from 20 miles. For instance:

- Running a person's age (one mile for every year) when they celebrate a birthday moving them to another age group. For example, when Valerie turned 35; when Jerry Shoemaker turned 40; when I turned 40, 45, and

50 (O.K., so my training partners 'teamed up' for these last two and ran it 'relay-style').

- When longer runs (23 miles, 26 miles, 30 miles) are done leading up to a marathon someone wants to do well in.

Today, it's harder for me to grasp what constitutes 'far.' Yes, 129 miles at the 24-Hour Championships in September of 2002 was certainly 'far.' Badwater's 135 miles was most definitely 'far.' But to others, these distances pale in comparison to *their* definitions of 'far:'

- There is an annual 3,000+ mile race across America. I'd consider that far.

- There are annual 2 day, 3 day, 4 day, 5 day and 6 day runs. You're sure to go far over that amount of time.

- There is a 3,000 mile race in the Northeast that—get this—is run around a city block. The city block is only a little over ½ mile around.

- Supposedly, someone has 'run around the world' (however that's done?!). However it was done, though—that, my friends, is *FAR!*

The bottom line is this: 'far' is nothing more than a perception. If *you* think a distance is 'far,' then is most certainly *is*.

These are a Few of my Favorite Things

After 28 years of research, experimentation, trial-and-error, and word-of-mouth I have compiled a list of my favorites in the world of running. Feel free to use any of it you consider pertinent to your needs or goals.

Movies

'Running' starring Michael Douglas as a marathoner competing in the Montreal Olympics. Hokey? A little. Inspirational? Certainly. Entertaining and motivating? Absolutely!

'Pre', one of the two films on the life of Oregon runner Steve Prefontaine (the other was 'Without Limits') whose life was cut tragically short in an automobile accident.

'Running on the Sun,' the documentary about the 1999 Badwater Ultramarathon that paved the way to my own participation in the event in 2003. Little did

I know that I would one day be 'trading paces' with two of the stars of the film, Pam Reed and Adam Bookspan.

'*On the Edge,*' perhaps the only fictional movie about running starring a real, live ultrarunner–actor Bruce Dern.

'*The Games,*' starring Ryan O'Neal. It's the story of runners from four different countries who ultimately cross paths at the Olympic Marathon. If I'm not mistaken, it was based on a screenplay written by Erich Segal ('Love Story'). Another one you'll have a hard time finding.

'*The Jericho Mile*' featuring Peter Strauss running a really quick mile … inside prison walls to the beat of the Rolling Stones' 'Sympathy for the Devil.' Inspirational as hell!

'*Running on the Sun Redux,*' the documentary chronicling the trials and tribulations of my five-person crew and me at the 2003 Badwater Ultramarathon. Good luck finding a copy on Amazon.com.

Books

Jim Fixx's **Complete Book of Running**. I read it once during graduate school and I became fascinated with running. I still am today.

Running through my Mind. It most likely would never have been written had I not read Jim Fixx's book.

Magazines

Ultrarunning. Incredible runners, incredible accomplishments, fascinating reading. Of course, there are parts of it you need to read with a medical dictionary by your side.

absolutely true … Tales from the DARKSIDE. Of course, I may be a little biased. Similar to what you'll find in *Ultrarunning,* but you most definitely won't need the medical dictionary. A bulls#$* detector may come in handy, however.

Sports Drink

Gatorade. I graduated from the University of Florida. What did you expect me to say?

Running Shoes

Note: Shoe models change every year.
These two pairs, however, will forever remain my favorites.

Adidas Adios. I ran some of my fastest (and most comfortable) marathons in these shoes.

New Balance 828. Great for high mileage. I ran the 2002 24-Hour Endurance Run and 2003 Badwater in these shoes (I rotated three pairs during each event). Very comfortable and easy on the feet.

Running Sandals

Nike Straprunner. Great for the downhills during extreme ultradistance runs (100 miles plus). Not recommended for running on trails (rocks, etc. get between the bottom of your feet and the sandals) or for long distances (limited shock absorption).

Races (Road)

Boston Marathon (April). You didn't need to ask, did you? It remains the runner's 'Holy Grail.' Almost forgot: the people of Boston treat each marathoner like an absolute Running God. No, I'm not exaggerating (April).

St. George (Utah) **Marathon**. It offers great weather, a downhill course (if you're a three-hour marathoner, and you should expect to finish seven or eight minutes faster than normal.) (October)

Steamtown (Scranton, PA) **Marathon**. Scenic, fast course with great hospitality. It has the charm and ambiance of the Boston Marathon (but on a much smaller scale). (October)

The two premier events in Atlanta, Georgia: **The Peachtree Road Race 10K** (4th of July), the largest 10K in the United States with a starting field of 55,000 runners and the **Atlanta Marathon** (Thanksgiving Day), the perfect way to make room for a big turkey dinner later in the day.

Races (Trail)

My favorite trail run? Any that doesn't have me in the field. In my universe, 'favorite trail run' is an oxymoron.

Coach

Me. Who knows me better than *me?*

Finally, I would be remiss if I didn't include **several things I can do without:**

Movies–any comedy based on running (There was a TV movie a long time ago staring Bob Newhart, one of my all-time favorite comedians. Was it funny? Absolutely not.).

Books–pretty much any book ever written about running tends to be somewhat … shall we say *redundant?*

Magazines–pretty much every magazine about running tends to be somewhat … shall we say *identical?* Interested in reading about twelve different ways to run a faster 5K? Sign up for a one-year subscriptions to *Runner's Planet**

*Actually, for a novice runner, a subscription for one year may be a good investment. However, after receiving twelve monthly issues, the information gets somewhat repetitive.

Sports Drink–since all sports drinks are virtually the same, all I ask is that Race Directors don't serve up one that tastes like swill.

Races (road)–any race that treats a runner as if they are (a) a number, not a person; (b) cattle; or (c) wealthy enough to pay ridiculously expensive entry fees. Hello, New York City Marathon. Hello, Bay to Breakers.

Races (trail)–every last one of them.

Coaches–every last one of them.

Rewards for a Runner

For the most part, running gets a bum rap. How many times have you heard someone say 'If running is so much fun, how is it you never see a runner smiling? The point is, running is quite an enjoyable and rewarding activity. However, even I—the most devoted runner I know—have at times wondered why I continue to put in the miles day after day.

If you too have wondered the very same thing, sit back and relax: I'm going to remind you why. Here are some of the rewards running offers:

- *The solitude and peace of mind you encounter while running, something that you quite possibly never have the opportunity to enjoy in your otherwise hectic, something-to-do-every-minute world.*

- *The joy of completing an invigorating training run on a hot summer day, followed by an ice-cold drink and that oh-so-good feeling on your parched throat. Bonus! Run some water from your garden hose over your legs after your run (but remove your shoes first).*

- *The shedding of unwanted, unsightly, unsolicited, unwelcome and unnecessary inches from your physique that is a natural byproduct of a sound running program.*

- *The ecstasy of crossing the finish line after running a strong race.*

- *The unworldly comfort you feel running the first few weeks in a new pair of running shoes that seem to mold to every nuance of your feet.*

- *Setting a P.R., or winning an award in your age group at a road race.*

- *Carbo-loading before a marathon (whether or not it really aids your performance).*

- *The thrill of finishing a marathon, whether it be a good performance or not. In the marathon, finishing is both the ultimate goal and the ultimate challenge.*

- *Finally getting 'elbow room' in a road race with a large field of runners (i.e. Peachtree).*

- *Finishing a long run on a cold winter day and relaxing in front of a roaring fire afterwards—while enjoying your favorite 'adult beverage' (hot cocoa for the children).*

- *Seeing the smile of joy on your child's face as they finish their first race (parents only).*

- *Being outside to share the wonders of nature that non-runners may miss: the brilliant sunrise on a cool spring morning, a family of deer as they search for food, the gradual change in the color of the leaves with the arrival of fall ... every run offers a new experience.*

- *The physiological, psychological, and emotional benefits one derives from being a runner.*

Need more? Didn't think so ...

<u>Strange ... but absolutely True</u>

I've found many things to be true in running that have absolutely no bearing on sanity, logic and practicality. Here are a few:

- As much as I hate to admit it, in any race of marathon distance or less I feel a need to outrun other competitors, primarily those I believe are in my age group. In races of distances greater than a marathon, I am the most supportive, helpful, encouraging person to other runners that I can be.

- Any type of fluid that is considered to be a source of electrolytes, glucose, energy, etc. may as well be classified as a placebo. If they do indeed enhance performance, I have yet to notice. For me, a cup of water is fine, thank you.

- In the midst of a race, hearing the theme song from 'Rocky' has a positive impact on my performance. Conversely, hearing the theme song from 'Chariots of Fire' makes me feel like I'm running in slow motion (and on really bad days, through quicksand).

- I realize I will never run races much faster if I don't do speed work. Note the operative word 'if.' Don't blame me if my muscles twitch at the wrong speed.

- If I was blindfolded and ran in a $50 pair of running shoes and then in a $150 pair, I would not be able to tell the difference.

- On a cold day, if my hands and throat stay warm, my whole body stays warm. Also, I enjoy running in tights on really cold days (less than 10 degrees) because they look neat, although in all honesty I don't think it ever gets cold enough for me to really need them.

- Ideal day for me to run: 20 degrees, overcast, dry, no wind.

- There is a certain temperature—usually in late winter or early spring—that causes perspiration to run directly in my eyes while I'm running. When this occurs, they burn like hell. I think it's somewhere around 60 degrees, but I usually don't remember this until my eyes are on fire.

- Given the choice of several distance options at a road race, I opt for the longer distance (i.e. a marathon over a half marathon). I must have slow twitch muscles in my brain, too (or is it fast twitch? Whatever.).

- In 95 percent of the races I've run competitively, I finished one place 'out of the money.' For example, if awards are given to the first two finishers in an age group, I'll finish third. Once I ran a 5K race and finished 4th overall. Awards were given three deep in each age group. Would you believe the first three overall finishers were all in my age group? Naturally, I went home empty-handed.

- I run faster in cold weather. I'm sure there's a formula to determine the temperatures effect on me (i.e. 10 percent faster/more endurance when it's 30 degrees as opposed to 80 degrees), but I have not yet attempted to figure it out. I think maybe cold weather makes my slow twitch muscles slow down (or is it my fast twitch muscles speed up? Whatever.).

The (Ill)Logic of a Runner

Early to bed, early to rise. An easy, relaxed five mile run before a healthy, balanced breakfast. A calm eight hour shift on the job. Home by 5:30 for a nutritious dinner. Maybe a short bicycle ride afterwards, followed by a warm, refreshing shower. Finally, in bed by 10:00 for a sound eight hours of sleep. Your overall impression of the sensible, healthy lifestyle of the average runner, right?

WRONG!!! If the runner described above exists, I have yet to meet them. The lifestyle of the runner in the first paragraph exists only in the minds of those who don't qualify as 'runners.' Joggers maybe, but most definitely not *runners*. Although the aforementioned perception is nice, it is far from the truth. Non-runners may believe that all runners are logical, sensible people with an intelligent approach to a healthy, wholesome lifestyle. If they were accurate, then

I would be the farthest thing from a runner. My approach to running is most definitely *not* logical or sensible, and absolutely the farthest thing from intelligent. However, it's worked for me.

Here is a sampling of some of my idiosyncrasies as a runner. You may find a few that we have in common, but don't count on it:

Before I laced up my first pair of running shoes, I may have had this same perception of runners. It didn't take long to figure out the error of my ways. Consider the following:

- Paying $15, $20 and sometimes $30 to run a race anywhere from 5K to 26.2 miles for the privilege of wearing yet another $2.50 T-shirt glorifying the race you just paid a king's ransom to run. Not to mention you already own dozens of T-shirts from *other* races you've run, enough to wear a different one each day for an entire year?

- Driving 50, 75, sometimes even several *hundred* miles to run a race of 6.2 miles. One would think that after a one-way drive of two or more hours, the completion of the race would take a little longer than 40 minutes. One would be wrong.

- Always stating your training regimen in 'miles,' while most of the races you complete are calculated in 'kilometers.'

- Running everyday regardless of how bad your feel physically (flu, aching joints, etc.) because you are able to block out the pain while you actually *run*, although the minute you stop running the pain returns and intensifies.

- Vowing during the last six miles of every marathon you ever run (excluding Boston, which passes by quicker than a good night's sleep) that this will be your absolute *last* marathon, then making plans a mere three days later for your *next* one.

- Dreaming of eating an entire half-gallon of vanilla ice cream as a reward for a 20-mile run, and never having the appetite for it after completing the run.

- Running every day for 28 years in temperatures that have ranged a total of ONE HUNDRED AND EIGHTY DEGREES (the highest being 133 and the lowest—minus 57 after factoring in the wind chill)!

- Vowing every year to reduce your annual mileage, while actually *increasing* it most years?

- Doing your weekday run every morning at 4:30 a.m. (or earlier) for over 20 years, and every day swearing you will cut your run short when you wake up and *never* doing so.

- Running a second time on any given day when you eat an extra snack during the course of the day (i.e. three extra miles for a piece of birthday cake at the office).

- Deep down inside, knowing the reason you have not reduced your annual mileage is because you know in your heart that the 24-hour endurance rune will one day become an Olympic event and you want to be ready.

- Taking a week's vacation to run across the state of Georgia, only to fall short on the 4th day after 159 miles (121 miles short).

- Spending $80 on a pair of running shoes doesn't bother you, but FIFTY-FIVE DOLLARS for a pair of DRESS SHOES? Ridiculous!

- Given the choice, you'd rather *fly* 500 miles to a race than drive 50 miles.

- You recover quicker from a 25-mile training run than you do from a shopping at the mall or climbing four flights of stairs.

Not exactly the characteristics of a logical, sensible person. But most definitely the characteristics of a runner.

Believe me, I should know.

Please–Not ANOTHER T-Shirt!

Having run a race or two in my life, I feel qualified to offer the following suggestions to improve the state of road racing. Race Directors, please take note:

- Change the distance of the marathon to 20 miles (or, at least put on 20-mile races). Eliminating that nasty final 10K would increase the number of participants and make hitting the wall nothing more than a bad memory. Just think: the time it would require to complete the event would be about an hour less ... for both the runner *and* the race director!

- Develop a universal barcode system for race numbers. One number for each runner for (any and) every race. For example, I would be issued a universal race number 121054 (my birthday!), with a corresponding bar code on the race bib. Once my entry fee for a particular race was paid, my race number would be 'activated' for that race. Following the race, the number would be 'deactivated.' It would be the runner's responsibility to maintain their number from race to race or pay for a replacement bib when needed. Think of all the trees that have been earmarked for future race numbers that would be saved!

- Using the new scan bar and barcode readers, races could have digital readouts at specific points along the race course that upon approach, would display each individual runner's overall position, age group position, current pace, and projected finishing time.

- Replace 'age groups' by 'stride length groups.' Personally, I believe I would fare better against everyone with a 40 inch stride than I would runners of age 40.

- Ensure that all aid station volunteers *know what they are doing*! I've gone through one station too many in desperate need of a drink only to find (a) volunteers standing behind the aid tables, requiring the runner to practically stop to get their fluid, (b) volunteers who, unwilling to get wet, not fully extending their arm holding the fluid causing the runner to miss the drink, (c) volunteers dousing runners with cups of water (and even sports drinks), whether or not the runner wants to be doused, (d) volunteers being caught empty-handed (without a drink) as the runner passes by, and (e) volunteers who, being empty-handed, cut from one side of the course to the other side (where the fluids are) to get more fluids, causing the oncoming runners to have to 'dodge' them.

- Hand-in-hand with the above, I believe all runners should point to the volunteer they wish to get their fluid from as they approach the aid station. I've used this method for the past several years, and with the exception of (a), (b) and (d) above, it works almost every time. Try it at your next race (providing, of course, that there *are* aid stations at the race). Which reminds me:

- Races must fulfill their obligations/commitments with respect to the (ever-increasing) entry fees being charged. For example, a 10K with a $25 entry fee should offer:

  1. A well-organized packet pick-up, start, finish and awards ceremony.

2. A nice, safe course with an adequate number of course monitors, aid stations and traffic control.

3. An efficient awards ceremony, with presentable awards for an appropriate number of runners (based on the size of the field).

4. Ample post race refreshments.

5. Friendly volunteers and race officials who treat the runners with respect.

6. A race director who realizes the success of the race *depends* on the runners.

7. An attractive, unique memento of the race for all runners (more on this later).

8. Accurate and readily available race results following the event.

• How about a universal starting time for all races, so those runners who race frequently don't have to adjust their timetable from one race to the next (i.e. an 8:00 a.m. start one week followed by a 9:00 a.m. followed by a 7:30 a.m., etc.)? Why not settle on *one time* for all races? 7:00 a.m. works for me.

• Runners 'pacing' a fellow runner are acceptable, as long as they don't line up at the starting line, pass through the finish chute, or interfere with other runners along the course.

• Do not incorporate a relay into the race. If you want to conduct a relay race, make it a separate event. There is nothing more frustrating or–OK, I'll admit it, *discouraging*–than running an event–let's say a marathon–and having a runner (who is competing in the relay) come flying by you every five miles (or whatever distance each leg of the relay calls for).

• Develop a method of differentiating runners in different age groups. It would be nice to know who your competition is. Personally, I am the worlds' worst at judging age. At my age, I mistake men from ages 30 to 60 for being in my age group. My good friend Al, who is now in his early 60's, just targets the 'wrinkled necks.' That being said, may I recommend different bib colors to distinguish age groups … or a different color ribbon that runners could pin to their backs … you get the idea. ANYTHING that would differentiate age groups.

- Race directors should consider automatic disqualifications for runners breaking the basic tenets of road race etiquette, such as (a) slower runners lining up at or near the front of the race, (b) runners making sudden, abrupt 'lane changes' that may affect another's performance, or (c) runners wearing the T-shirt for the race in which they are participating *during* the race (one of my all time pet peeves).

Actually, item (c) would not even be a consideration if race directors would get creative and not make the race t-shirt the traditional memento for their respective races. Me personally? I'd prefer a six-pack—gotta' replace those carbohydrates!

Note: The idea for a universal barcode system mentioned earlier was an idea I had in the early 1990's. In fact, a slightly different version of this article appeared in a running club newsletter, and included this idea. I wanted to mention this in case the person who invented today's 'chip timing' used at most major road races used my idea to spawn his. If so, I thought he or she may want to forward me an appropriate 'consulting fee.'

These Things Really Bug Me

In layman's terms, these would be known as pet peeves. Applying them to running, I'm not sure what you'd call them, but they certainly get under my skin. Perhaps they get under yours as well.

- The inability (or maybe it's just my inability) to run a 'negative split' race (running the second half of the race faster than the first). As my favorite distance is the marathon, this is the ideal strategy; if only I could do it. In hundreds of races at many distances I've carried out this strategy exactly once, a 10K with the first 5K being all *uphill* and the final 5K all *downhill*. Pretty much a built-in negative split (although I did my best to screw it up, being a poor downhill runner and all–I always feel like I'm running 'with my parking brake on' for fear of falling forward face first).

- Drivers failing to use their turn signals, both when I'm driving and running. I detest stopping during a training run to allow a car to pass by, only to have the car turn–without signaling–off the street I want to cross before it gets to me.

- Seeing (more and more) adolescent runners lining up at the front of a road race. There's nothing more difficult (or irritating) than having to 'hurdle' over an 11-year-old runner who runs the first ¼ mile in 70 seconds and the remainder of a 10K in 70 minutes. This is not only dangerous, both to the child and the other runners, but it makes you wonder who is allowing the child to do this? Or, worse yet, *encouraging* them to do this?

- Running hard for the first mile of a major road race (Peachtree, for example) and passing an overweight, obviously out-of-shape 'runner' who, for some unknown reason, has actually managed to get his overweight, obviously out-of-shape 'body' to that point in the race at that time. How the 'runner' got there is a mystery; all I know is that it sure is discouraging to weave through a sea of fellow runners to make some headway in a major race ('weaving,' by the way, forces you to run farther than the stated distance of the race) only to find yourself running side-by-side with a (singular) 'mass of humanity.'

- When running the last mile of a marathon, hearing an onlooker shout 'only one mile to go' and using that inspiration to begin picking up the pace for a couple minutes and then hearing the *exact same thing* a half mile later. And sometimes yet *again* another 100 yards or so later. At that point in a marathon, one would be better served to hear the onlookers 'boo' than to receive bad information about how much distance remains.

- Running next to a 'heavy breather' during a race. When this happens (i.e. the runner sounds as if they are about to have a coronary any moment), I always think I should be feeling *equally* bad since we're running the same pace. Then I have an attack of hypochondria and my race time and my body begins to suffer. Usually, when a 'breather' pulls up beside me in a race, I either pick up the pace or let the breather pass, depending of course on *my* breathing at the moment.

- Not having the option of paying a lesser entry fee for a road race if I choose not to receive a T-shirt.

- Acquaintances of mine who invariably ask after every race I run (particularly Peachtree) if I 'won.' It doesn't matter if I ran a P.R. or placed in my age group; they want to know if *I won*!

- Needing both of my shoe laces tied before a race with the exact same amount of tension. I'm convinced that if they are not identical in pressure it will affect my performance as well as the future well being of my feet. Usually prior to racing I will tie and re-tie my shoelaces at least once for every mile of the race. Once I ran a 50-mile race at Stone Mountain that began at 7:30 a.m. I started tying my shoes at 3:15 that morning.

- Never being able to keep the two New Year's resolutions I make without fail: to cut down on my mileage and to lift weights regularly.

- Running socks that advertise themselves as being 'blister-free.' As long as a foot and a sock are two separate entities: (a) the two have the very real possibility of moving independently of one another; (b) if the two movements are not 'in synch,' friction results; and therefore (c) blisters may occur. Unless a runner has ¼ inch of nylon surgically attached to their feet, there will not be such a thing as 'blister-free socks.'

- A flyer for a road race that describes the severity of the hills on the course in terms of elevation gain or loss. Reading about a race with a '250 foot elevation drop' tells me that it is downhill–*period!* I don't have a clue how much downhill it implies. (Note: if the course is a loop course–starting and ending at the same place–I know there is no net gain or loss in elevation. Remember: what goes up must go down ... and vice versa).

- Finishing 4th in my age group in a race that gives awards three deep. Then realizing my finishing time was quick enough to win not only the age group immediately older than mine but also the age group immediately *younger* than mine as well.

- Going on a training run where all the miles are marked. I find that if I (or my training partners) wear a chronograph, the training run inevitably becomes a 'race.' I'm more inclined to run wherever I want on a training run and measure my distance via elapsed time on my watch.

- Getting an incorrect mile split in a race. Once I ran a 5K where my 2nd mile was called as a '5:14.' Figuring I was about to collapse (as I intended on running a 5:45 pace), I coasted a bit on my 3rd mile, which ended up being a 6:30 (I wasn't coasting *that* much). I should have figured at the two-mile split that it was incorrect; however, as my P.R. *in the mile* is only a 5:10. I've considered running races without wearing a chronograph. But

I think that wearing one inevitably helps me out with my overall pacing, particularly in a longer race.

• Being beaten in a race by a runner wearing a shirt with a collar OR shorts with pockets OR socks other than white in color OR headphones OR pushing a baby stroller. *Especially* if they're pushing a baby stroller.

• Runners who allow other *faster* runners to wear their numbers in a race in order to establish a qualifying time for the *slower* runner for a future race (i.e. Peachtree, Boston).

• This one has bugged me for a long time: In 1977 Jim Fixx published *The Complete Book of Running*. One brief year later, he published *Jim Fixx's Second Book of Running*. First of all, how much ink does one need to talk about putting one foot in front of the other over and over again, and second (and I know it's been bugging each of you as well)–*if the first book was complete, why did we need a SECOND book?*

• People who use 'I don't have enough time' as an excuse for not running. *Make time, people!*

• Inaugural marathons that, backed by large corporate sponsors, charge outrageously high entry fees in their first year of existence before they've established any credibility. (Note to Disney and Country Music Marathons–don't wait up for me).

• Running training guides and manuals. Everyone is different, so there can't possibly be one way for everyone to achieve the same results with their running. Experimentation and experience, those are the *true* 'training manuals.'

• Running coaches. Remember: experiment, experience, but most definitely do *not* throw money away on a running coach. Buy another copy of this book for that friend of yours who has wanted to give running a try instead.

• (Obvious) non-runners wearing expensive running shoes as fashion statements.

• Organizations that–in an effort to make a quick buck–put on a race but in reality have no business doing so.

• Runners who want to be writers. Is there a subject on the planet any *duller* to write about than running?

The TEN COMMANDMENTS of RUNNING

This may sound unbelievable—in fact, I'm having a hard time believing it myself—but I think I've stumbled across the Ten Commandments of Running. That's right, written by the Almighty Strider Above.

Laugh if you want, but last Sunday after a particularly exhausting 23 mile run I found an old sheepskin scroll in the hollowed-out trunk of a dead oak tree. What was I doing by a dead oak tree? I thought I might be able to revive it with a little 'water.'

Anyway, back to the scroll: it contains 10 entries, each pertaining to my favorite form of cardiovascular conditioning—running. I'm certain they're commandments. What else *could* they be?

Never being the selfish type, I'll share them with you—if you promise not to laugh. Remember, *HE'S* watching.

1. **Thou shalt not falsify one's ability to cover great distances on foot in a short amount of time.**

    Comment: Running is the most humbling sport. 'Fib' on your Peachtree 10K application about your expected finish time and you'll be (a) blown away by others in your group, (b) highly embarrassed, (c) exceedingly humbled, (d) eating a large dose of crow, or (e) all of the above. My guess would be (e).

2. **Thou shalt not discuss the athletic endeavor known as 'running' at social gatherings ad nauseam.**

    Comment: Especially if you are the only runner there. It's the easiest way known to man to alienate people (particularly non-runners).

3. **Thou shalt not consider thyself physically superior to fellow man due to the fact that one does indeed incorporate running into his or her own life.**

    Comment: Sometimes this one can be tough but remember a runner's definition of being in 'good shape' is another person's description of 'walking death.'

4. **Thou shalt not covet they fellow runner's stride.**

   Comment: This one is particularly tough on us short runners with (naturally) short legs and therefore (quite obviously) a short stride.

5. **Thou shalt not run to the extent that replenishing one's lungs with air from the heaven above becomes trying.**

   Comment: I believe the Big Guy is referring to oxygen debt, or 'sucking wind.'

6. **Thou shalt not develop a physical or psychological dependency or addiction to running.**

   Comment: If only I'd found the scroll a few years ago …

7. **Thou shalt not spend more of one's wages on running shoes than one spends on food shelter and clothing.**

   Comment: This commandment alone proves these were written long ago, possibly as far back as when running shoes were under $95 a pair.

8. **Thou shalt not run in shoes crafted for anything other than running.**

   Comment: Doesn't this one contradict 7?

9. **Thou shalt not believe in running euphoria.**

   Comment: I believe HE means 'runner's high,' where runners find themselves in a state that causes them to hallucinate and believe all sorts of implausible concepts and desires to be a possibility if not a reality. Pure nonsense, if you ask me. And finally, the last commandment:

10. **Thou shalt persevere through these five words; 'There is no finish line.'**

    Comment: Nike has apparently been around for a looooooong time.

There you have it. Words to run by, words to live by, words to die by. As for me, I'm going out for a run: after all, there is no finish line.

Christmas Gift Ideas for the Runner

(Who pretty much has everything ever made for a runner)

There are only so many gloves, reflective vests, logbooks, ear warmers and chronographs a runner can use. If you're really stuck on what to get the runner in your life for Christmas, consider the following two *(really inexpensive!)* ideas.

It's a fact that most runners are collectors. T-shirts from races they've run. Trophies and plaques they've received for race performances. Race patches, race posters, race 'finish line' photos—all collectibles.

Me? I collect races and miles. These are simple to 'collect,' as I simply write them down in my runner's log (well, not really that 'simple,' as I have all my *races* cross-referenced chronologically as well as by distance and all my *miles* by week, month and year—with calculations showing average miles run per day, week, month, etc.).

But races and miles are intangible things. I also have my fair share of:

- Race t-shirts (most of which have been given to friends, family, coworkers—many of whom have told me to *stop* as they have enough).
- Trophies (banished to the garage)
- Plaques (banished to a box beneath the bed)
- Finish line photos (hanging—*framed*—in the garage on my 'Wall of Fame' near the 'trophy case')
- Patches (safely stored on a shelf in the office, neat and out of sight)
- Posters (banished to the garage to keep the trophies and photos company)

I'll be fair and tell you my wife graciously allows my precious Boston Marathon prints to hang in our bedroom and master bathroom. Fortunately, 'Boston blue' matches the color scheme of the room.

Two things I make an *effort* to collect, however, are **running pins** and **marathon medals**. Here's where my Christmas gift idea comes in. Most runners really don't have anywhere to display their pins (they most likely end up in a jewelry box or drawer) and are destined to hang their medals by their ribbons on a hook or nail somewhere (like in a garage). However, if you would like to give the runner in your life a nice and *visible* means of displaying his or her pins and medals, try these two ideas:

Running Pins

Have a piece of colored corkboard framed, allowing about half an inch from the corkboard to the glass. A pattern of how you want the pins arranged can be diagrammed on the *back* of the corkboard, and each time a new pin is added simply make a hole from the back (courtesy of the diagram) and then take the pin and guide it through the hold from the *front* of the corkboard. Dip the pin in silicone first, which will prevent the pin from 'spinning.'

Marathon Medals

Select a room where you believe a medal display would be an attractive addition. Now pick a spot on the wall in that room where you think the medals should be on display. Purchase some 1 inch X 3 inch wood (make sure the pieces are flat and solid). Determine how long your piece(s) of wood should be. After cutting the wood to the appropriate length(s), paint or stain the wood to 'match' the room (whether it is the molding, the trim around the doors/windows, the walls, etc.). Mount the wood to the walls, and screw in small metal hooks (gold, silver, bronze) an appropriate distance apart along the wood on which to hang (*without* the ribbons) the medals (it's best to add one metal hook at a time, as all medals are not the same size). Once finished, if the display is within reach of a young child, be careful—they're prone to 'spin' the medals as they think the whole thing is a toy.

Sage Advice

Some of you may have been looking for running advice in these pages, and by now I'm guessing you're a little disappointed. However, I'd like to leave you with 15 pearls of wisdom I've managed to pick up over the years. Just don't expect to read the generic advice (do speed work, rest, drink, etc.) you're likely to find in virtually every 'training book' ever written. It always amazes me how the simple, basic advice these books offer is somehow stretched into 200 pages or more.

So, speaking from pure experience, here goes:

1. When it comes to running a marathon, don't put all your eggs in one basket. Face it, some days you're just not going to have your 'A' game. It's one thing to gut out a 5 or 10K when you're not at your best; a marathon is a different story. So on those days that you're not at your best, just take it easy and enjoy the ride, and remember that 'tomorrow is another day.'

2. Be very wary of running inaugural races, particularly marathons. I've been to many that—for a variety of reasons—weren't around to celebrate their 'second annual' event. It's best to select races that have proven themselves; let someone else be the guinea pig for anything that promotes itself as an 'inaugural event.' Later, you can hear all about it.

3. Remember, when you're running outside, after one mile the temperature will feel 20 degrees higher than it actually is. Dress—and run—accordingly.

4. Find running shoes that are comfortable and work for you, and then look for them when they become year-end closeouts or discontinued models. Then, buy as many pairs as your budget allows. As for those who would tell you that running shoes have a 'shelf life' and it's not wise to stock up on shoes—hogwash.

5. On a training run, you should be able to hold a conversation and smile. If you can't do both, you're overdoing it.

6. When it comes to running a marathon or longer, there is absolutely no training substitute for mileage. None.

7. However, training runs on hills is a viable substitute for speed work.

8. If you have trouble finding time to get in your daily run, do it first thing. If you hate getting out of bed earlier than normal, never underestimate the power of caffeine.

9. In races of marathon distance or less, nine out of ten runners tend to be competitive, and they are out to do anything in their power to beat you. In races longer than a marathon, nine out of ten runners tend to value camaraderie, and they are out to do anything in their power to make sure both of you make it to the finish line.

10. In marathons, the 'wall' you may hit will be physiological. In ultras, the 'wall' you hit (and you will hit it!) will be psychological.

11. You will get the best running advice from ultramarathon veterans.

12. If you are capable of running a marathon, you are capable of completing an ultra.

13. In ultras of 50 miles or longer, once you've had your fill of electrolyte replacement drinks, water, and soda, try beer. It's 'anti-sweet' flavor will hit the spot, and alleviate some of the nausea. (Note: Milk is a viable substitute as well)

14. Good running books, movies and magazines are a great motivator.

15. Never take your ability to run for granted. Never.

Proud Moments

Running every day for 28 years almost guarantees you the opportunity to achieve things that you can be proud of for years to come. I've been fortunate to have several such achievements that—when I look back on—make me realize I've had a running career that I can be proud of. Of course, I haven't lost my enthusiasm for the sport just yet, and I hope to have several more 'proud moments' in the years ahead. But at this point in my running career, I consider these to be the running achievements of which I am most proud:

Completing the Badwater Ultramarathon in 2003

As I stated on my application for this event, finishing would be the 'crown jewel' in my running career. Running in Badwater, having minimal difficulties, being supported by a phenomenal crew, breaking 40 hours, and finishing in 6th place— it doesn't get much better than that.

Running in the Boston Marathon in 1987

You never forget your first ... Boston. I still remember how choked up I was when I ran my *qualifying* marathon in Jacksonville, Florida in January of 1987. Words can't describe the feeling I had when I crossed the finish line for the first time on Boylston Street (and setting a P.R. was *even more* icing on the cake).

Running Across Georgia in 1992

'Something I always wanted to do,' and even more so after my initial failure in 1982. As far as I know, I am the first runner to do it and to date, the *only* runner to do it.

24-Hour Run in 2002

As my friend Gary Griffin told me prior to the event, 'make a name for yourself' at Olander (site of the event). A 4th place USATF ranking and a National Master's Championship did just that. If I've ever been in a 'zone' while running, it was during my 24 hours in Ohio.

50K Wins

Winning the 1995 Atlanta Fat Ass 50K (Stone Mountain) and the 1998 Tallahassee 50K (Wakulla Springs) were two of the real highlights of my running career. Never being particularly fast, wins have been few and far between.

High Mileage in 1998

5,402 miles is a record that will stand in my personal record book for eternity. I am particularly proud of the 2,967 miles I ran the last six months of the year—accomplished by running 277 times in 184 days.

The 2002 Peachtree City 50K

Coordinating the first ultramarathon in Peachtree City was, quite honestly, 'something *else* I always wanted to do.' Having the 2003 edition of the race selected to host the First USATF Georgia Association Ultramarathon Championship adds one more layer of 'icing on the cake.'

Marathon P.R. in 1988

A 2:48:41 at Jacksonville, Florida, where the weather was so cold, wet, and windy that my thoughts during the run were of *survival* rather than of pace or strategy—well, you can imagine my surprise when I crossed the finish line and saw the aforementioned time flashing on the digital clock. Aside from seeing the first four numbers of my PR on the digital clock of the finish line at the St. George Marathon in 1994 (2:48:45), I doubt I'll ever see them again.

10K P.R. in 1994

Running a 36:14 at the age of 39 was not only a surprise, it served as the stepping stone for me to compete on the Atlanta Track Club Men's Masters Competitive Team.

15 Sub-3 Hour Marathons

As I get older and wonder 'where did all my speed go,' I appreciate how difficult it is for an ordinary runner like me to break the three hour barrier in the marathon. If there are ever any laurels I will catch myself resting on, it will be these.

Completing the Western States Endurance Run in 2006

After a failed attempt at completing this race in 2004, crossing the finish line in Auburn, California after 100 *trail* miles through the mountains of the Sierra Nevadas was the farthest thing from my mind that I ever envisioned me doing.

Lifetime Achievement

As I've always considered endurance (and not speed) to be the strongest part of my running, it would make sense that there are several achievements that I am proud of that took—in most cases—my running 'lifetime' to accomplish.

The Streak

Since November 30, 1978, I've run every day. I still consider running a privilege and something I will never take for granted. The thought of ending the streak no longer crosses my mind, and I have absolutely no intention of doing so. After all, if I took a day off from running today and started another streak tomorrow, it would take me until I'm 80 years old to catch up to where my streak now stands. That would make it highly unlikely that I could ever achieve the longest recorded running streak in history *(read into this sentence what you want)*.

100 Marathons

The marathon is my absolute favorite distance. Whether I'm racing, pacing a fellow runner, or using it as a training run, there is no feeling in running quite like the one you get when you cross the finish line in a marathon. None.

100,000+ Miles

This statistic—more than any other—represents the dedication and love I have for the sport. I am proud to say that I've done the equivalent of 'running the equator' four times.

This Book

I've wanted to write a book about running as far back as I can remember. I made a note in my running journal in 1979 about an idea I had for the title: *Footsteps*. That may be the *only* thing about the book that's changed in 28 years. Many of the articles in this book were written during various stages of my running career.

Josh's Running

My youngest son Josh has terrific potential as a runner. He set P.R.'s at the age of 11 that many adult runners only dream about, such as 40:47 for 10K and 18:10 for 5K. As a high school reshman he ran a 5:10 mile. Although he never beat me 'head-to-head,' I had the good sense to stay away from him in the shorter distances once he turned 15. I'm really glad Josh was part of my terrific Badwater crew.

11 Boston Marathons/24 Atlanta Marathons

My two favorite marathons. I regret not running Boston between 1987 and 1994, as well as opting for the Atlanta *half*-marathon in 1989 and 1990 (otherwise, I would have run 26 consecutive Atlanta Marathons). I expect these two races will be on my annual running calendar for many years to come.

The Formation of the DARKSIDE

Although the fall of 1993 marked the 'early days' of the DARKSIDE, it wasn't until December of 2001 that the DARKSIDE Running Club was officially formed. With an ever-growing membership (which includes some truly outstanding runners), I expect great things in the years to come. Our quarterly newsletter—in my opinion—is already the finest running periodical of its type. Not only does the DARKSIDE have outstanding *runners*, it has outstanding *writers* as well.

Marathon Pacing

At this point in my running career, there is nothing I enjoy more than pacing a fellow runner in a marathon. Unless that would be pacing a fellow runner to a *Boston-qualifying time* in a marathon. There was a time when I could comfortably pace someone as quick as three hours (of course, depending on which marathon was selected). Now I would say that 'comfortable' pace is closer to 3:20 (again, depending on which marathon was selected). Regardless, if I believe I'm able (to successfully pace someone), I'm always glad to do it.

28 Consecutive Peachtree Road Races

I've begun every 4th of July since 1979 the same way: run a hot, hilly and humid 10K down the middle of Peachtree Street in Atlanta, and top it off with a 'cold one' afterwards. While I no longer focus on short, fast races, I am proud to say that I finished in the 'Peachtree Top 1,000' the first eleven years the award was given.

My Overall Health

Without decent health, the streak wouldn't exist. 100 marathons would be a dream, not a reality. 100,000 miles would merely be the odometer reading in my car. My health, like my running, is one other thing I will never take for granted. I've been (moderately) injured and/or ill over the last 28 years, and I remember much too vividly how I wished I was able to run longer than I actually did during those times. Fortunately, those times have been few and far between.

In Summary ...

It's difficult to condense 28 years of running into a few pages. Difficult, maybe, but not impossible. Perhaps as you peruse it, you'll run across something that will have you running out the door ... or running around in circles ... or running through the wall ... or simply running around the block. If so, then I would consider this book a success.

1979

I set seven goals my first full year of running, and achieved six of them. They were:

1. To run in and finish a marathon (accomplished three times: March, May and November).

2. To run 1,800 miles (totaled 2,154).

3. To run a 40:30 in a 10K (39:38 in Griffin, GA)

4. To run a 5:45 mile (5:37)

5. To run everyday for the entire year (accomplished).

6. To do 30,000 sit-ups (32,700)

7. To finish the year weighing 145 pounds (I ended up at 146)

I think I would have made the 7th goal had I not been reduced to low mileage in December, the result of sore knees due to reaching goals 1, 2 and 5. While reviewing my journal, I noticed that for the first four months of my running career, I ran in tennis shoes before breaking down and buying a $5 pair of running closeout shoes (at the original Athletic Attic in Gainesville, Florida!) which, when I ran in them for the first time felt like 'running on air,' according to my journal.

1980

My lowest annual mileage for the 28 years–1,787–as the knee continued to cause me pain. In fact, on January 4th I considered ending my streak before changing my mind and running at 10:00 p.m. in a snowstorm in Birdsboro, Pennsylvania. The entry in my journal stated 'my knee felt better,' but thinking back, I'm sure it was merely numb from the cold. I managed to run 27 races, setting P.R's in seven distances. Not bad considering the pain I was in.

1981

Another heavy year of racing; 26 races and nine P.R.s. I ran my first of 24 (so far) Atlanta Marathons on Thanksgiving Day. Little did I know at the time that this marathon would be my greatest foe in the years to come as it presented a challenge I simply cannot seem to overcome: breaking the three hour barrier in the Atlanta Marathon. Years later, I have found that no matter how hard I train or how much I rest, whatever shape I'm in or how well I run the race, I simply cannot break three hours in Atlanta.

1982

My first ultramarathon: The Stone Mountain 50 miler. I managed to run a 7:28:25, good enough for a sixth place finish. I also made my initial attempt at running across the state of Georgia (from Columbus to Savannah along Highway 280). From October 30th through November 2, I managed to cover 159 miles (that's the good news!). However, the course was 280 miles (that's the bad news). On the fourth day, I was reduced to (at best) a moderate drag. I threw in the towel, vowing never to try this again (and stuck by this vow for 10 years). The remainder of the year, my knees gave me problems, mainly because I ran every single mile on Highway 280 facing traffic, causing my left leg to reach farther than my right to strike the pavement. I'm sure my body is still out of alignment because of it. On November 16, my life changed forever; our first son Justin was born.

1983

Not a memorable year, as I got into L.S.D.: 'Long Slow Distance'. It paid off too, as I ran 26 races with moderate success. I noticed this was the last year I noted every new pair of running shoes in my journal. I'm glad I stopped, or I'd be calculating how much money I've spent on running shoes in my lifetime. Ouch.

1984

My first 3,000 mile year (actually 3,074), and my first encounters with the effects of adequate hydration during a marathon. In January, I ran the Jacksonville (Florida) Marathon in 3:00:22, and in November I ran the Atlanta Marathon in 3:01:36. In Jacksonville, just before the race I loaded up on two large glasses of water that led me to a tree ('this is Nature calling') for a full minute around the 10-mile mark of the race. In Atlanta, 32 ounces of Gatorade one hour before the race resulted in two very costly pit stops along the course—costly in the sense that I had to stray *way* off the barren course so I didn't make a public display of my pending emergencies. This problem plagues me to this day, although the 'public display' aspect no longer crosses my mind.

1985

On November 9, I ran my best-ever 10K race: 36:17. Naturally, my first reaction was that the course was short (what an optimist!), but I later found out the course was certified. On October 21, our second son, Josh, was born.

1986

The first year I did any real serious speed work. 'Ninety minutes of misery' every Wednesday night at the local elementary school track paid off, as I ran 34 races and set eight personal records (PR's) including a 2:53:29 marathon–*without a pit stop!*–in Jacksonville. I set PR's in three other categories as well:

- Total Miles–3,812
- Total Sit-ups–48,450

- Total number of days with 10 or more miles–259

As you may have gathered, running drew a little nearer to an obsession this year. I thought that (a) if there was daylight and (b) I wasn't at work, then (c) I should be running.

1987

A 2nd consecutive sub-3 hour marathon in Jacksonville (2:56:31) qualified me for the Boston Marathon for the first time. Then at Boston on April 20, I ran a 2:53:18 in a race *that went-by-so-fast-that-it-seemed-like-30-minutes*. As icing on the cake, the time was a PR as well. This was the first major high point of my running career, and I will never forget the choked-up feeling of pride I experienced when I crossed the finish line and had the Boston Marathon medal placed around my neck. This is truly the Olympics for the everyday runner. I even have a videotape of the race (ESPN covered it that year) and I have my '15 seconds of fame' (actually, the cameras were focusing on the runner who used to wear bull horns–he was known as 'Cowman') as I was approaching the five-mile mark. OK, so I should say as *Cowman* was approaching the five-mile mark. But I was running right next to him.

1988

I was still on a roll, as I managed to lower my PR in the marathon to 2:48:41 in Jacksonville. The weather was perfect for me: 38 degrees with a slight drizzle. After I finished, I could have sworn I had frostbite in 21 major areas of my body. I was pale as a ghost, my teeth chattered for what seemed like a full hour, and my body was literally chilled to the bone. In September I ran in a 24-hour endurance run, and managed to cover 101 miles (and change), finishing 27th and becoming a nationally-ranked ultramarathoner in the process. I got my ranking as the race served as the TAC Championships, and everyone in it was ranked. Anyway, 27th in the entire country ain't bad–now only if it were an Olympic event.

1989

The only out-of-the-ordinary event this year was a midnight five-mile race in Pigeon Forge, Tennessee. Let me be the first to tell you–if you don't *train* at midnight, you have no business *racing* at midnight!

1990

I ran my first—and last—Bay-to-Breakers in San Francisco. Ditto the New York City Marathon (a 3:12:55 in 74 degree heat). In both races, the officials were ill-prepared to handle the incredibly large numbers of runners, and could learn a lesson or two from the organizers of the Peachtree. One strange thing I remember (there were many but this one sticks out–no pun intended) was a group of naked runners protesting something via graffiti written in mud on their bodies, but I couldn't tell you which of the two races I saw them in.

1991

I eliminated a bad habit this year–*sit-ups*! Eleven years and 360,050 sit-ups later (yes, I counted them all), I decided that all the things I heard about sit-ups being 'bad' for your back were true. The highlight of the year: a 3:00:20 Atlanta Marathon (the closest I have ever been to breaking the three-hour barrier there)! I have to admit I was in super marathon condition for this one, but my old nemesis won again (yes, there was a 30-second pit stop–like always–in the midst of the race).

1992

I ran in only 10 races this year, and three of those were to pace my youngest son Josh in 5K events. To tell you the truth, I got more pleasure from those three races than I did in the 600+ that I have run (well, maybe excluding Boston) in my running career. I ran the Atlanta Marathon in 3:05:21 on the Olympic course, realizing in the process that if the course is not changed again (which is done frequently), I will never break three hours in Atlanta. The new course is a killer, and the hills and the heat proved to be really tough on the Olympic marathoners in 1996. Also, I realized a major goal I failed at in my initial attempt 10 years earlier; I ran the 280 mile trek from Columbus to Savannah in a little over six days.

1993

The first year I set goals for myself since my initial year of running back in 1979. They have changed slightly since then, with one exception: to run every day for the entire year. I feel grateful for the run of good health I've experienced over the last 15 years, particularly when I felt that I was starting to slow down due to all the wear and tear on my legs. I figured the pounding was beginning to take its toll on my body as well as my mind. However, I regained my motivation to run early in the year, and managed to regain some of the speed and conditioning I hadn't experienced in 10 years. Finally, in the fall, I began running (long!) every Sunday with Al Barker and Valerie Reynolds, laying the foundation for the creation of the Darkside Running Club.

1994

A man in Pennsylvania who is compiling a list of all 'streak' runners in the United States has me recorded as having the 9th longest active streak in the country. As I got closer to becoming a Masters runner (I turned 40 on December 10th), I managed a P.R. for 10K at the Piedmont Classic in March, running a surprising 36:14. A P.R. at this distance was particularly unexpected as this year marked the beginning of my high mileage years. Beginning in 1994, I ran over 4,000 miles for 13 consecutive years. This year my total was 4,649 miles, including my first 500+ mile month (August–501 miles). I also returned to Boston, seven years after my debut there (counting this one, I will run 10 out of the next 11 years). I also ran a(nother) surprising race at the St. George Marathon in October–2:48:45, missing my all-time P.R. by only four seconds. I began a tradition by running 40 miles to celebrate my 40th birthday.

1995

The first time I averaged 13 miles a day for an entire year. On top of that, I won my very first race of the year–the Atlanta Fat Ass 50K on January 8, covering the 31 miles in 3:48:23. Al Barker and I traveled out west for the Las Vegas marathon in February, and after the race I was closer to death than I've ever been before (90 degree weather isn't conducive to marathoning!). I ran a respectable Boston Marathon (2:59:36), finishing in 1,015[th] place. My mileage odometer hit 50,000 mark on April 27th. Two Atlanta Track Club teammates and I won the Men's Masters Team Championship at the Marine Corps Marathon in the fall (my contribution was a 3:02:26).

1996

I ran 38 races, the most I've ever run in a calendar year. I ran a P.R. at the Atlanta Mile (5:10) at age 41. I ran another solid Boston 2:59:57); however, even though I was only 21 seconds slower than last year, I finished 1,230 positions farther back in the field (I was 2,245[th] overall). As it was the 100th anniversary of the Boston Marathon, the field was expanded to 36,000+ runners. Even though the size of the field was triple the norm, the Boston Athletic Association did an excellent job preparing for the event. If only we didn't have to sit on the bus in Hopkinton for an hour before we were able to exit (these were school buses–with no restroom facilities. Fortunately, there was a wooded area nearby). I ran my fastest

Peachtree ever–36:56 (349th place). It's amazing what a cool morning (63 degrees at the start) will do for you in the summertime. Al, Val and I also went to Columbia, South Carolina to watch the Women's Olympic Marathon Trials. We were honored to meet Joan Benoit and a host of other world-class runners after the race.

1997

I won a 5K for the first (and to date, *only*) time in Andrews, North Carolina. After the crowds at Boston last year, I decided to skip the race this year. Mistake. I missed running on Patriot's Day in Massachusetts terribly. In July I ran a 3:18:51 at the Grandfather Mountain Marathon in Boone, North Carolina. The rule of thumb for this race up the mountain is to 'add 20 minutes to your marathon time.' That being the case, I was proud of my time, especially considering it won me a Master's title. I ran the Chicago Marathon for the very first time (2:57:38) and the inaugural Silicon Valley Marathon in San Jose, California. Miler Steve Scott fired the stating pistol for the latter.

1998

My highest mileage ever–5,402 (including 2,967 the last six months of the year). During the year, I ran 10 marathons (my highest total in one year) and a monthly mileage high in December (538). In September I participated in National Run-to-Work Day, leaving the house at 2:00 a.m. so I could run the 28 miles to JCPenney, take a shower, and be at my desk by 6:30 a.m. For the first time, I ran back-to-back marathons (Chickamauga, where I paced Thomas Jones* to a Boston-qualifying 3:29 on Saturday, and Vulcan, where I won the Master's title with a 3:02 on Sunday). I ran the Steamtown Marathon in Scranton, Pennsylvania (2:37:39), an incredibly underrated event. In December I won the Tallahassee 50K, running a P.R. of 3:44:58. It may have been the high mileage I ran during the last six months of the year, but I felt wonderful the entire 31 miles! I honestly believed I could have run five or six more miles at the pace I ran the race.

*After Thomas and I crossed the finish line, two paramedics rushed Thomas into an ambulance and sped off to the hospital. Apparently he had become dehydrated during the race. I didn't even get to congratulate him on qualifying for Boston.

1999

I won the Master's title at the Tybee Island Marathon in 2:59:48. Unfortunately, on the race application for this event in 2000 listed me as defending Master's champion (and included my time as well). Naturally, this 'winning time' attracted lots of faster runners. In 2000 I didn't even place in the top three in my age group! I ran my best cumulative time for back-to-back marathons (6:19:05 at Tybee Island and Callaway Gardens). My son Josh made the trip to Boston with me, and I was proud that I ran a good race (2:58:53, 722th place) with him in the crowd along Boylston Street. During the summer I was 1/100th of the Atlanta Track Club Men's Masters team that set a WORLD RECORD for the 100 x 1 Mile Relay (my mile was 5:22; the team average for the event was 5:23, so I did my part). I ran well at the St. George Marathon (2:53:15) and won the Master's title again at the Vulcan Marathon (3:05:07). Finally, to celebrate my 45th birthday, I ran 46 miles (I meant to do 45 miles, but I miscalculated). Many of my running partners joined me throughout the day to run with me.

2000

I ran the Tybee Island and Callaway Garden marathons back-to-back again, in a composite time of 6:21:05. Considering I was still recovering from pulling my hamstring at the Atlanta Fat Ass 50K at Kennesaw Mountain in January (Damn mountains! Damn trails! Damn mountain trails!), that wasn't too shabby. I went to Columbia, South Carolina to see the Women's Olympic Marathon Trials. Once again, our group had the opportunity to speak with Ms Benoit. I ran the Tour-de-Pain in Jacksonville, Florida in August, consisting of three events: a four mile run Friday evening, a one mile run Saturday morning and a 5K run Saturday night. Despite my hamstring problem, I won my age group. In November, to commemorate my friend Normer Adams' 50th birthday, I accompanied him to Maryland to run in the JFK 50 Mile Run. As 13 miles of the course was on the Appalachian Trail (Damn mountain trails!), I wasn't too happy with my finish (note the operative word: 'finish').

2001

I ran a good Shamrock Marathon in Virginia Beach in March (3:00:59), but in the process pulled a muscle in my right thigh/groin area which 'numbed' my right thigh. To this day, the area remains numb (and yes, I let a couple doctors see it—and no, they didn't have a clue how to fix it). I've lost a little speed the last couple years in the turnover in my right leg (that's my story and I'm stickin' to it). I ran in the inaugural Baltimore Marathon (and in all probability my last one–too hilly!) and won the Master's title at the Tallahassee 50K (3:57:31). I ran the latter with Kelly, who won the Women's title (finishing one second ahead of me). In December the DARKSIDE Running Club was (officially) formed.

2002

The first issue of *absolutely true.... Tales from the DARKSIDE* was published! I ran in three inaugural marathons: Mercedes (Birmingham, Alabama), Cherry Blossom (Macon, Georgia), and Bay-Bridge (Chesapeake, Virginia). I ran a solid 129 miles at the USATF 24-Hour Championship in Ohio in September, finishing in 4th place overall and 1st place in Master's (I ended the year ranked 5th in the country in this event). In November, the 1st Peachtree City 50K was hosted by the DARKSIDE Running Club. An impressive six runners broke the coveted four-hour mark (I finished 7th, missing the four-hour mark by 12 seconds).

2003

I started the year on a positive note: winning the Master's Championship at the Museum of Aviation Marathon–just by simply pacing my friend Kelly! On the 4th of July, I completed my 25th consecutive Peachtree Road Race (only to keep the streak going!). I did a 'double' at the Boston Marathon (running the course from finish-to-start and start-to-finish). This year's Boston, incidentally, was my 100th lifetime marathon. I completed five ultra runs (my adventure at Boston being the first) in seven weeks in preparation for Badwater. Speaking of Badwater, my lifetime mileage hit 90,000 somewhere along the route from Death Valley to Mount Whitney. I completed—albeit reluctantly–in the USATF 100-Mile Championship in Ohio (figuring after Badwater, how tough could it be?). The Peachtree City 50K, hosted by the DARKSIDE Running Club, served as the first-ever USATF Georgia Ultra Marathon Championship. I made an appearance on the cover of the October 2003 issue of *Ultrarunning*, as I was shown running directly behind eventual winner Pam Reed at Badwater.

2004

In the March 2004 issue of *Atlanta Sports and Fitness Magazine*, I was selected as Georgia's 2003 Ultrarunner of the Year, due in no small part to my performance at Badwater. I ran a 40:49 10K, qualifying me for Time Group 1 at Peachtree for maybe the last time in my running career. However, after my first official DNF at a race–the Western States Endurance Run–it was all I could do to hobble the 6.2 miles of Peachtree a couple weeks later. I managed to squeeze out 111.4 miles at the 24 Hour Championship in San Diego to finish in 12th place. The Peachtree City 50K, in only its third year of existence, served as the USATF National 50K Road Championship. To celebrate my 50th birthday, I ran 50 miles on a track in Peachtree City, followed by a 50K in Tallahassee the very next day.

2005

An excruciating and mysterious pain in my right leg caused me great difficulty the first six months of the year. I exceeded the four-hour mark in a marathon for the first time in my life–twice. At the 100 Mile Championship at Olander Park, Ohio I finished a respectable 18th, and two months later matched that place of finish in the 24-Hour Championship in San Diego by running 114 miles. At the Atlanta Marathon, I reached the lifetime 100,000 mile mark when I crossed the finish line.

2006

Starting off the year on a positive note, I ran marathons on four consecutive weekends and managed to run a Boston-qualifying time in each of them, followed by a Georgia state age group record in a 50K the week after them. Pam Reed's autobiography was published, and if you look closely (i.e. with a magnifying glass or better yet, a microscope), you can see me directly behind Pam in the photograph of the start of Badwater. I finished off my (hopefully) last of 13 consecutive years of high mileage, averaging 12.99 miles per day for that window of time. On April 16th, I ran for my 10,000[th] consecutive day. My running streak and consecutive Peachtree Road Races both hit the 28 year mark, and the United States Running Streak Association now officially lists me as having the 36th longest active streak in the country. I've actually 'dropped' 27 spots in the last 12 years. I won the Master's title at the 50 Mile Run in Tallahassee to celebrate my birthday. The year comes to an end with me nursing too many injuries and ailments to list, and vowing to cut back on my mileage in 2007 in a concerted effort to rest and recover.

Oh yeah, I almost forgot: I finished the Western States Endurance Run, officially bringing my career as a trail runner to an end. Ironically, I was the last official finisher.

A Running Resume

Total Lifetime Mileage–105,495

Average Miles per Day during each month

- January–9.88
- February–9.97
- March–10.06
- April–9.60
- May–10.27
- June–10.00
- July–10.11
- August–10.59
- September–10.68
- October–10.53
- November–10.58
- December–10.45
- Average per day–10.22

- Total Lifetime Races—676

- 10K–241 (1st–48:53 in 1978; Fastest–36:14 in 1994)

- Marathon–128 (1st–3:44:11 in 1979; Fastest–2:48:41 in 1988)

- 5K–122 (1st–21:07 in 1979; Fastest–17:12 in 1988)

- Ultras–40 (1st–50 miles in 7:28:25 in 1982; Fastest–50K in 3:44:58 in 1998)

- 8K–38 (1st—36:32 in 1978; Fastest–29:27 in 1987)

- 15K–24 (1st–1:09:55 in 1979; Fastest–56:23 in 1986)

- 10 Miles–15 (1st–1:15:12 in 1979; Fastest–1:01:50 in 1997)

- Half Marathon–12 (1st–1:31:45 in 1980; Fastest–1:22:33 in 1986)

- Other assorted distances–56

Races Completed 10 or more times

- Peachtree Road Race–28 (1st–42:03 in 1979; Fastest–36:56 in 1996)

- Atlanta Marathon–24 (1st–3:13:00 in 1981; Fastest–3:00:20 in 1991)

- Chattahoochee 10K (formerly Piedmont Classic)–14 (1st–37:36 in 1983; Fastest–36:14 in 1994)

- Charles Harris 10K–12 (1st–37:46 in 1985; Fastest–36:45 in 1995)

- Boston Marathon–11 (1st and Fastest–2:53:23 in 1987)

- Tybee Island Marathon–10 (1st–3:03:53 in 1997; Fastest–2:59:48 in 1999)

Overall Wins

- Glenwood Hills (Ellenwood, GA) 4 Mile Run–1982

- Atlanta (GA) Fat Ass 50K—1995

- Andrews (NC) Race for Life 5K–1997

- Tallahassee Ultra 50K–1998

Masters Wins

- Super Chill (Cherokee, NC) 10 Mile Run–1997

- Grandfather Mountain (Boone, NC) Marathon–1997

- Museum of Aviation (Warner Robins, GA) Marathon–1998, 2003

- Vulcan (Birmingham, AL) Marathon–1998, 1999

- Tybee Island (GA) Marathon–1999

- Tallahassee (FL) Ultra 50K–2001, 2005

- Tallahassee (FL) Ultra 50 Mile Run–2003, 2006

Memorable Moments

- USATF National 24 Hour Endurance Run Masters Champion–2002

- Badwater Ultramarathon (6th place overall, 3rd place male)–2003

- Georgia Ultrarunner of the Year—2003

- Georgia State Age Group (50-54) Record for Road 50K–2006

- Western States Endurance Run Finish (Dead Last)—2006

Where Do I Go From Here?

Many years ago I set three distinct running goals for myself:

- Run 100 marathons.

- Run 1,000 races.

- Run 100,000 miles.

Now that two of the three have been achieved (through the end of 2006, I have run 676 races (and for the record, 128 marathons and 105,495 miles), I realize the third and final goal will take time and will require patience. Lots of it, which is the critical element to being successful at the ultra distances I've grown fond of at this point in my running life.

One goal that has 'evolved' is that I would one day like to hold the longest running streak in the country. Of course, there are 35 other runners (that we know of) who have something to say about that, as they all currently have longer active streaks than mine. Again, patience will be required.

Here's a unique goal that ran through my mind the other day: to run 100 marathons in the state of Georgia (through 2006, I have a total of 60), and perhaps—should I reach 100—to make it a 'double' by doing it at Atlanta and having it be my 200th overall marathon as well.

Here's another: to start my own '50 States Club' for runners who complete 100 miles or more in specific states. If I were to start the club today, I would have 14 states … and one foreign country (Germany).

Of course, there's at least one more trip to Boston in my future. Cindy promised to go once we became empty nesters, and Josh pledged at the outset of this book that he would one day make the trip from Hopkinton to Boylston Street … and I certainly want to be there for that.

One more: to write a book about the superheroes I've grown to know throughout my running lifetime. They're amazing individuals, and each one has their own unique story to tell. Maybe one day they'll allow me to be the one to tell it.

EPILOGUE

I hope you've enjoyed reading this book as much as I've enjoyed writing it. It was truly a labor of love, and represents the best 28 years of my life.

Like I said, I don't know what lies ahead for me in the world of running, but like Al Barker asks:

Isn't that the beauty of it?

I do know that as long as I have the physical ability (as well as a conscious say in the matter) my streak will continue. I know I will continue to encourage others to accomplish things in their running they never dreamed possible–mainly because they *are* possible! I know I will continue to write about running, although I'm not sure what direction I'll head next. I know running will remain the greatest sport on the planet, and I know I will do everything I can to promote it as such.

More than anything else, I know I still love to run. That, my friends, is one thing I know will never change.

In time, I'm sure our paths will cross—if not physically, then most certainly spiritually. After all, we share a common bond–a passion for the greatest sport on the planet.

Until then, gotta run …

Acknowledgements

Boy, where do I begin?

I would be remiss if I didn't thank **my graduate school professors and original running mentors, Thomas Jefferson Saine III and Douglas Bock**. Without their inspiration and motivation, I would have never laced up a pair of running shoes.

I can't put into words how much **my close running friends–Al Barker, Paula May, Eric Huguelet, Susan Lance, Kelly Murzynsky, Gary Griffin, Danielle Goodgion, Prince Whatley, Stephanie Sudduth, Gordon Cherr, Fred Johnson, Valerie Reynolds, and Ed Rush** have meant to me—in my personal life as well as my running career. I am honored you were willing to share your stories with me in these pages. I know the readers will find inspiration in your words, just as I have through the miles and years of our friendship.

My parents, Gloria and Bip, for their support in my running, even though they still believe I am going to hurt myself running each and every day, particularly on the longer runs. They always taught me to do my best, and I want them to know I've given running everything I've got. I know deep down inside they are both proud of what I've done, both in my personal life and my running career. Thanks for pointing me in the right direction.

My two sons, Justin and Josh, who have two entirely different perspectives of my running. Justin, the passionate one, isn't really into sports, and is equally impressed/unimpressed whether I've run 10 miles or 100 miles. Josh, who has *lived* the sport, knows what it takes out of you, and it always makes me smile when I overhear him telling his friends about his 'dad's running.'

I want to thank all the many **race directors, race volunteers, and avid runners** who have touched—and in many cases impacted—my life. Without you all, running wouldn't be the great sport that it is today and continue to be into the future. I've tried my best to show my appreciation through the years, and if there was ever any doubt how much you've all meant to me, I hope that by now it has been erased.

My very best (non-running) friends, Bruce Cowart and Stan Patterson. They have helped me complete the part of my life that isn't related to running, which–believe me–is no small order.

My best pal Magic, who I think about and miss every single day.

My two buddies Maui and Mollie—who are always by the front door to greet me after a run. Yes, I realize your priorities are actually 'first treat, then greet,' but you always give me something to look forward to at the end of my run.

My wife Cindy, who has urged me to cut back on my running for the better part of the past 28 years. I can't count how many times I wasn't feeling 100 percent and she encouraged me to 'run the minimum—three miles.' She realizes it's hopeless, but she continues to do it just the same. I also know she does it because she loves me; that's why I don't mind hearing her say it.

My friend Stephanie Robinson, who helped me compile over 28 years of work and material and put it in one place—between the covers of this book.

Finally, I owe so much to **the sport of running**. It changed me in so many ways–physically, mentally, emotionally and spiritually. It's afforded me the opportunity to meet some of the finest people in the world. And for the past 28 years it's allowed me to do something each and every day that some people never have the opportunity to do:

CROSS THE FINISH LINE.

978-0-595-46523-
0-595-46523-4

Printed in the United States
115774LV00003B/34/A